BUILDING A NEW ROME

BUILDING A NEW ROME

The Imperial Colony of Pisidian Antioch
(25 BC–AD 700)

Edited by Elaine K. Gazda and Diana Y. Ng
in collaboration with Ünal Demirer

Kelsey Museum Publication 5
Ann Arbor, Michigan 2011

Published by
Kelsey Museum of Archaeology
The University of Michigan
434 South State Street
Ann Arbor, MI 48109-1390
USA

ISBN 978-0-9741873-4-1

Front cover:
"Envisioning Antioch," a collage combining artifacts brought to Ann Arbor from Pisidian Antioch in 1927, the drawings of Frederick Woodbridge from the 1927 Michigan expedition, and digital images from the 2004 expedition. Digital artist: J. Matthew Harrington

Back cover:
Digital reconstruction of Pisidian Antioch. Digital model: J. Matthew Harrington

This book is available direct from
The David Brown Book Company
PO Box 511, Oakville, CT 06779, USA
(Telephone 860-945-9329; Fax 860-945-9468)

and

Park End Place, Oxford OX1 1HN, United Kingdom
(Telephone 01865-241249 Fax 01865-794449)
www.oxbowbooks.com

To the memory of Francis W. Kelsey and other staff members of the 1924 Michigan expedition to Pisidian Antioch, who, through their pioneering modern archaeological work at the site, inspired these reinterpretive essays.

The 1924 Michigan expedition staff (left to right): Easton Kelsey, Frederick J. Woodbridge, Francis W. Kelsey, David M. Robinson, George R. Swain, Enoch E. Peterson, Feizy Bey, Horace Colby, and Haidar Bey (the government inspector). Photo: G. R. Swain, Kelsey Museum Archives neg. no. 7.1664b.

Contents

Illustrations

Foreword

Since the summer of 2004 when I first met the authors of this book in Yalvaç, I have been eagerly looking forward to this publication. I had long admired the work that the University of Michigan carried out at Pisidian Antioch in 1924, and I was delighted to learn that archaeologists from Michigan were once again taking an interest in the site. As director of the Yalvaç Museum I did not have an opportunity to examine in person the wonderful archive of photographs from the 1924 excavations at the Kelsey Museum in Ann Arbor, but the photographs in the reports I read filled me with nostalgia; they conveyed the romance of digging during the time of transition between the Ottoman Empire and the young Republic of Turkey.

As often happened to ancient sites in Turkey, natives of the region pulled out many of the stones and reused them in houses and official buildings. Fortunately at Antioch, this practice stopped in the 1960s when Yalvaç acquired a proper museum for housing the antiquities of Antioch. For those stones that did not enter the museum, I am happy that they were not burned in a lime kiln, as so often happened in post-classical times. Instead, the Turks who removed them from the site gave them new life in the walls of their houses and mosques.

The authors of this book have done a wonderful and useful study of our site of Pisidian Antioch. I believe that most people have never understood what an important site it is, and this book will reveal, enlighten, and complete many things that regrettably had to be abandoned by the Michigan team at the close of the 1924 season. The remains of this once monumental city were largely left unpublished, and they were reburied over the years. Without doing excavation, the authors have collected and assessed the archival data and recently acquired knowledge of the site, including that from my own excavations of the theater, and have put it into an accessible form. Along with the virtual reality model of the site, this book will give Antioch the visibility that it deserves in the scholarly world and beyond.

Ünal Demirer
Archaeologist, Miletos Museum
Director, Yalvaç Museum (2002–2004)

Preface and Acknowledgments

In my dual role at the University of Michigan as a curator at the Kelsey Museum of Archaeology and professor of classical art and archaeology in the Department of the History of Art, I have long pursued a program of research focused on archaeological material and works of ancient art in the Kelsey Museum's collections, as well as on the museum's archives of past Michigan archaeological field projects. My intention is to help maintain the currency of those collections and projects by integrating the museum's resources into the teaching programs of the university and by producing exhibitions and accompanying publications that involve the work of students. In the process students gain a platform for creative rethinking of the materials and the issues that arise from them. *Building a New Rome: The Imperial Colony of Pisidian Antioch (25 BC–AD 700)* is the result of such a project, which draws heavily from the University of Michigan's archive of documents, photographs, drawings, and related archaeological materials from Michigan's expedition to Pisidian Antioch in 1924. This project builds upon the university's initial investment in Pisidian Antioch—Michigan's first excavation of a classical site—by reassessing the results of that project in light of more recent research at Antioch and at other cities of the Roman Empire, particularly those in Asia Minor.

Research on this book began in the context of a graduate seminar on the Roman cities of Asia Minor in 2004 in which Pisidian Antioch served as the principal case study. At first the seminar's work focused on the excavation records, artifacts, and publications related to Michigan's 1924 expedition, and from the start we intended to prepare a small exhibition and publication. At the urging of the participants, however, the project, including this book, expanded into something larger and far more ambitious than they or I had initially imagined. During the course of the seminar it became increasingly apparent that our understanding of the site and the excavated structures would be immeasurably improved by studying the remains in person and by seeing comparable Roman cities and their architectural monuments. Thanks to a generous grant for International Experiential Learning for Graduate Students and Professional School Students awarded to us by the International Institute of the University of Michigan, supplemented by funds from the Department of Classical Studies, the Department of the History of Art, the Interdepartmental Program in Classical Art and Archaeology (IPCAA), the Kelsey Museum of Archaeology, and the Horace H. Rackham School of Graduate Studies, we set out for Turkey in late July of 2004 on a ten-day study trip.

At Pisidian Antioch, we were graciously received by Ünal Demirer, who was then the director of the museum in Yalvaç where the majority of finds from the site are housed. Mr. Demirer, who was also in charge of the archaeological site, not only introduced us personally to the site and the recent work that he and others had done there but also permitted us to study the ruins and related finds in the museum and to photograph them for our research. On-site discussions with Mr. Demirer sharpened our sense of where fruitful work could be done. Mr. Demirer generously shared his observations on the theater, where he had recently excavated, and many of the results of his excavation inform the chapter on the theater, which he coauthored with Hima Mallampati. Without his collaboration and ongoing encouragement this book would not have been possible.

Our field trip in 2004 was followed by a second seminar in 2005 in preparation for the exhibition. By that time the Kelsey Museum had launched a project to expand its gallery space by adding a new wing, and it soon became apparent that we needed to identify an off-site exhibition space for the Antioch show. We were fortunate to engage the gallery in the Duderstadt Center, which is also home to the university's Digital Media Commons. Our project expanded again when we met with members of the staff of the Digital Media Commons and learned of possibilities presented by new visualization technologies and the availability of experts and facilities at the University of Michigan. With the enthusiastic encouragement of Dr. Klaus-Peter Beier, then director of the UM3D Lab in the Digital Media Commons, we set about to design a collaborative project that resulted in a virtual reality model of the city and the nearby sanctuary of Mên Askaênos as well as tangible models of most of the excavated buildings. Because the archaeological site had been extensively robbed of architectural stones following Michigan's season at Antioch, this technology became an essential tool in facilitating our attempts to envision the ancient buildings as they might have appeared in antiquity.

For this part of our project the students participated in two workshops on 3-D modeling offered by the UM3D Lab in the spring of 2005, in which they learned the essentials of making a model of the monuments they were studying, and three of the students went on to participate in an engineering class taught by Dr. Beier. The 3-D project is described in detail in the chapter by J. Matthew Harrington, who took the lead in building the virtual reality model of the city. We are grateful to Dr. Beier and to staff members of the UM3D Lab, Lars Schumann, Scott Hamm, and Eric Maslowski, who assisted in developing a fly-through virtual model and adapted it for projection both in the exhibition gallery and in the CAVE (Cave Automatic Virtual Environment). Brett Lyons printed the tangible models of the buildings on the Lab's 3-D printer. Our work with Dr. Beier and his team of assistants was funded by a generous grant for Interdisciplinary Collaborative Projects in the Humanities, Summer Grant Program, awarded by the Institute for the Humanities and the Horace H. Rackham School of Graduate Studies at the University of Michigan, a grant that also funded many of the exhibition's physical components and assisted with the cost of producing this publication. We owe warm thanks to Professor Daniel Herwitz, director of the Institute for the Humanities, for his energetic support of and ongoing interest in this project.

In 2005 we contacted Professor John W. Humphrey of the University of Calgary, who in 2001, together with Dr. Mehmet Taşlıalan, Demirer's predecessor as director of the museum in Yalvaç, had undertaken to make an updated map of the archaeological site by measuring and plotting recently excavated parts of the city. We are grateful to Professor Humphrey for sending us his unpublished map and allowing us to incorporate it into our exhibition and publication. We also contacted Professor Roger Bagnall, then of Columbia University, who in 2001 had commissioned two Russian scientists, Tatiana Smekalova and Sergei Smekalov of St. Petersburg, to make a selective magnetometric survey of the site, the results of which they generously shared with us. Likewise, E. J. Owens of University of Wales in Swansea shared the results of his research on the water system of Antioch, much of which had not yet been published. Adrian Ossi then incorporated all of the recently generated information into a new site plan, which became the base map for our 3-D reconstruction of the site.

Logistical as well as financial assistance for the exhibition and this book was provided by the Kelsey Museum of Archaeology. We owe our thanks to Professor Sharon Herbert, director of the Kelsey Museum, for her support of the project and to Professor Margaret Root for her help at the organizational stage of the exhibition. We also gratefully acknowledge the assistance of museum staff members: Scott Meier, exhibitions coordinator; Sebastian Encina, coordinator of collections; Robin Meador-Woodruff, then registrar; Suzanne Davis, conservator; Todd Gerring, public programs officer; Margaret Lourie, editor; Lorene Sterner, graphic artist; Helen Baker, administrator; Jackie Monk, office assistant; Sandra Malveaux, secretary; and Alexander Zwinak, facilities manager. At the Digital Media Commons and Duderstadt Center Gallery we received invaluable advice and assistance from Glenda Radine, public relations manager; Kathi Reister, gallery coordinator; and Tom Bray, managing producer, media resources.

The authors and I are grateful to the following scholars for their helpful criticisms of various chapters: Beate Dignas (chapter 8), David Potter (chapters 4 and 8), Rossitza B. R. Schroeder (chapter 6), Brenda Longfellow (parts of chapter 2), and Robert Chenault (chapters 4 and 6). John Cherry and Jeremy Rutter commented on a Bronze Age sherd found at Antioch in 1924. Marc Waelkens offered astute comments on our project during his visit to Ann Arbor in 2006 for the opening of the exhibition. Thomas Drew-Bear called our attention to his recent work on the *Res Gestae*, and Hadrien Bru directed us to his recent research on the question of the origins of Antioch's Italian colonists. Early in the course of our research Benjamin Rubin and Adrian Ossi organized photographs and archival materials for the project, and Özgen Felek translated a number of Turkish articles; Lynley McAlpine and Helen Giordani provided late-stage research and editorial assistance; and James McIntosh offered editorial critiques of the manuscripts. In 2008 Diana Ng joined me as coeditor, and Adrian Ossi prepared many of the plans illustrated in the chapters.

In the course of preparing the appendix on archival resources for Michigan's 1924 expedition, we were helped by a number of people. Stephen Mitchell and Maurice Byrne gave us permission to reproduce much of the material they include in appendix 2 of S. Mitchell and M. Waelkens, *Pisidian Antioch* (1998). Aileen Ajootian of the Department of Classical Studies and the staff in the Archives and Special Collections of the J. D. Williams Library at the University of Mississippi provided information and access to the Papers of David M. Robinson. Likewise, the staff of the Avery Architectural and Fine Arts Library at Columbia University, especially Janet Parks and Jason Escalante, assisted with the Frederick J. Woodbridge Records and Papers. Any errors of fact or interpretation are the responsibility of the authors and editors of this volume.

I owe a special debt of gratitude to all the young scholars whose work appears in this book who, despite the long delay in the publication, owing to my preoccupation with the construction and installation of the William E. Upjohn Exhibit Wing of the Kelsey Museum, stayed with the project and continued to revise their essays as new information became available. In the meantime, some of them have produced dissertations related to their work on Pisidian Antioch and, in doing so, deepened their own understanding, and that of all the participants, of the city's place within the larger sociopolitical terrain of Roman Asia Minor and the Roman Empire as a whole. As always, I have relied on the ongoing moral and intellectual support of my husband, James McIntosh. He, along with our daughter Karina McIntosh, accompanied our group to Turkey in 2004, and he has followed this project with informed interest. His insatiable curiosity about all things historical is a constant source of inspiration.

Elaine K. Gazda
Curator of Hellenistic and Roman Antiquities,
Kelsey Museum of Archaeology and
Professor of Classical Art and Archaeology,
Department of the History of Art

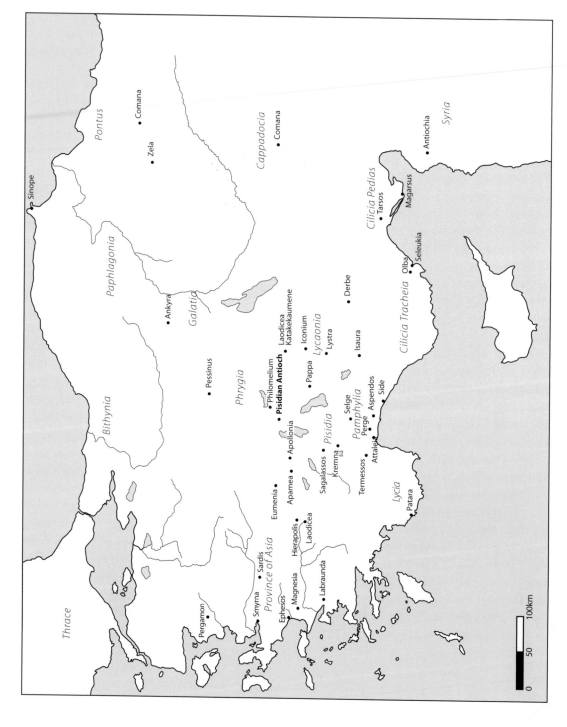

Fig. 1.1. Map of Roman Asia Minor. Drawing: L. Sterner. After Mitchell and Waelkens 1998, fig. 1.

1 Introduction:
The Project and Its Scholarly Context

Elaine K. Gazda and Diana Y. Ng[1]

Situated on the southern slopes of the Sultan Mountains in the rugged region of west-central Anatolia near the modern city of Yalvaç, Pisidian Antioch had a complex history informed by a variety of cultural groups. The city was founded initially in the 3rd century BC by the Hellenistic kings of the Seleucid dynasty, with Greek settlers from Magnesia on the Meander (fig. 1.1), and was ruled for two and a half centuries by Seleucid, Attalid, and Galatian kings. It was refounded as a Roman colony by the emperor Augustus when, around 25 BC, he annexed the territory of Galatia to the Roman Empire and settled veterans of the Roman army at Antioch. Prior to the arrival of the Romans, the sanctuary of Mên Askaênos on the nearby promontory of Kara Kuyu had brought the city renown. The Roman imperial colony grew in prestige among its peers as home to a center of the imperial cult, and in late imperial times, it garnered further prestige when it became the capital of the province of Pisidia and the seat of a Christian bishopric.

The Augustan colony of Antioch, characterized by Barbara Levick as "a little Rome," had Roman governmental forms and neighborhoods named for places in the capital city.[2] Located along a strategic overland artery between Syria and the west coast of Asia Minor, it played a major role in Rome's colonial project in central Anatolia. The Augustan colony not only served Rome's military and economic needs but also presented a striking example, from the Roman perspective, of the benefits that Roman civilization provided to local populations. Yet, despite Antioch's prominence in antiquity, the city has attracted relatively little archaeological exploration in comparison with cities of Asia Minor such as, among others, Ephesos, Aphrodisias, Pergamon, Perge, Side, Sagalassos, Hierapolis, and Sardis.[3] Pisidian Antioch has thus remained on the fringes of exciting recent developments in research on the Greek East in the Roman era.

Two principal ancient literary sources inform us about Antioch. Strabo, in book 12 of his *Geography* written in the late 1st century BC or the early 1st century AD, notes the famous sanctuary of Mên Askaênos in the vicinity of Antioch, and the book of Acts in the New Testament chronicles the missionary journeys of St. Paul and his companion Barnabus, implying in the view of many scholars that Antioch was one of the first cities they visited in Asia Minor.[4] Numerous inscriptions provide further ancient testimony of the city, its inhabitants, and its institutions. Nonetheless, following the demise of Pisidian Antioch, probably as a result of an Arab invasion in the early 8th century AD, little was recorded of the city until the 19th century, when in 1833 Lord F. V. J. Arundell visited and identified the once-famed site and produced a map of its visible ruins (see fig. 2.1).

[1] In this essay Elaine Gazda is responsible for the first three sections and Diana Ng for the fourth and fifth sections.

[2] Levick 1967, 78; see also Rubin, chap. 2, this volume.

[3] We normally adopt the Greek spelling for place names except where conventional usage dictates the Latin version.

[4] St. Paul's letter to the Galatians (4:8–20) is also considered by many scholars to be a good contemporary source.

The Archaeological Exploration and Analysis of the Site

The story of Antioch's modern discovery and exploration is told in considerable detail by Mitchell and Waelkens in chapter 2 of their book, *Pisidian Antioch* (1998). Although the city had been identified by Arundell and studied by him and others in the 19th century, the first excavations were not undertaken until 1912, by Sir William Ramsay of Edinburgh, Scotland. Ramsay's team focused initially on the sanctuary of the local deity, Mên Askaênos, but in 1913 and 1914 they turned to the city of Antioch itself and dug there at the complex that would later be identified as the imperial cult sanctuary, as well as at the Byzantine church (later called the central church), the northern city gate (now the nymphaeum), along the proscenium of the theater, and in an adjacent cistern.

With the outbreak of the First World War excavations ceased, to be taken up again in 1924 under the terms of a project developed by Francis W. Kelsey of the University of Michigan in cooperation with Ramsay, who held the excavation permit. Michigan's team was directed in the field by David M. Robinson, then of Johns Hopkins University. When they arrived in Turkey in the spring of 1924, tension between Ramsay and Robinson arose almost immediately. Their differing priorities and archaeological methodologies hampered the expedition, and Ramsay left the site in midseason. While work proceeded productively thereafter, further difficulties arose in relation to the transfer of Ramsay's permit to Michigan. Ultimately Kelsey decided that the team should publish the important findings of the 1924 season before returning to excavate again in the spring of 1927. Meanwhile, Kelsey turned his attention to Karanis in Egypt and Carthage in Tunisia, where he started new excavation projects, and to Pompeii, where he had begun working on a large book. After Kelsey died unexpectedly in May of 1927, Michigan's return to Antioch never materialized. It was not until the present project began in 2004 that archaeologists from the University of Michigan again took an interest in the archaeology of the city.

Many of the records of the 1924 season at Antioch are stored at the University of Michigan, and they eventually became part of the archives of the Kelsey Museum of Archaeology and the Bentley Historical Library. Those archives contain the daily journal of excavations, correspondence, offprints of publications, approximately 1,800 photographs, 85 squeezes of inscriptions, 46 artifacts, and field notebooks, sketches, architectural drawings, and plans made by the excavation architect, Frederick J. Woodbridge, and his assistant, Horace Colby. Many of Woodbridge's drawings and field notebooks remained in his possession and, following his death in Rome, were deposited by his widow at the American Academy in Rome, where Woodbridge had done further work on several drawings as late as the 1970s. In 2005 the American Academy agreed to transfer the drawings to the Kelsey Museum in order to reunite two important components of the excavations records. Another set of archives are among Robinson's papers in the Archives and Special Collections of the J. D. Williams Library at the University of Mississippi, and some artifacts from Antioch, including three fragments of the *Res Gestae* of Augustus, are displayed in that university's museum. Further documents are among Woodbridge's records and papers at the Avery Architectural and Fine Arts Library of Columbia University. Checklists of the Antioch-related contents of these archives appear in the appendix of this book. In addition, an extensive collection of digital images of Pisidian Antioch and the sanctuary on Kara Kuyu, taken by the authors of this book during a study trip to Antioch in 2004, is maintained in the Kelsey Museum.

The remains of the Roman city that were excavated or reexcavated in 1924 include the elaborate city gate (the Arch of Hadrian and Sabina), the imperial cult sanctuary and the adjacent Tiberia Platea, the central church, and the basilica, now called the Church of St. Paul, and parts of two main streets. The team also noted, but did not excavate, the theater and the north nymphaeum, which Ramsay's team had referred to as the northern city gate (see chapter 2). The sanctuary dedicated to the Anatolian deity

Mên Askaênos, located a few kilometers from the city, did not figure in the 1924 project, although on three or four occasions members of the expedition visited the sanctuary site. On one of these excursions they took photographs of votive inscriptions and sketched a plan of the sanctuary.[5]

The work of the Michigan team was only partially published, and it was not until the 1950s and 1960s that significant scholarly attention was again devoted to Pisidian Antioch. In her book of 1967, *Roman Colonies in Southeast Asia Minor*, Barbara Levick used epigraphic and literary evidence to shed light on the ethnic mixture of the settlers of the colony, the interaction between the established Greek inhabitants and the new Latin/Italian colonists, and the function of Pisidian Antioch as an outpost on the frontier of the Roman Empire. Levick's research, however, did not include excavation. In 1979 the Turkish archaeologist Mehmet Taşlıalan became director of the Yalvaç Museum, and during his long tenure numerous excavations and other studies were undertaken, often in collaboration with foreign teams.[6] In 1982 and 1983, Stephen Mitchell and Marc Waelkens conducted a detailed field survey of the visible remains of the city and the sanctuary of Mên Askaênos, later published in their book, *Pisidian Antioch* (1998). In the 1990s Thomas Drew-Bear identified new inscriptions during survey research in the region of Antioch. In 2001 two other projects were carried out. John W. Humphrey's team from the University of Calgary produced a new site plan of the city, and Roger Bagnall, then of Columbia University, commissioned a magnetometry survey of selected parts of the site, which was conducted by Tatiana Smekalova and Sergei Smekalov of St. Petersburg.[7] The research of all these scholars, along with the records of the Michigan expedition of 1924, provided essential foundations for our own work. Also essential were the proceedings of the first international conference on Pisidian Antioch held at Yalvaç in 1997, which brought together forty scholars who work on a wide range of materials and topics related to the site. The proceedings, edited by Thomas Drew-Bear, Mehmet Taşlıalan, and Christine M. Thomas, appeared in 2002.[8]

In 2002 Ünal Demirer became director of the Yalvaç Museum and in that year published a helpful guide to the site. Demirer undertook excavations in the theater and at the city gate, and he consolidated the floor mosaic in situ in the Church of St. Paul. Some of the results are published here for the first time (chapters 4 and 6).[9] During Demirer's directorship Vincenzo Ruggieri of the Pontifical Oriental Institute obtained an excavation permit, but poor health prevented him from undertaking work in the field. He did, however, publish articles on Byzantine sculptures from Antioch and the vicinity.[10] Demirer's successor as director of the Yalvaç Museum, Ali Harmankaya, did further

[5] These visits are noted in the Journal of Excavations. See Raff, chap. 7, n. 22, in this volume. The plan (see fig. 7.3) was sketched by Woodbridge based on an earlier one drawn by E. R. Stoever, who had worked with Ramsay.

[6] Taşlıalan's excavation reports appeared regularly in the proceedings of work conducted by Turkish museums. See Taşlıalan 1993; 1994; 1995; 1997; 1998; 2000; 2001; 2002; Taşlıalan et al. 2003. For a brief reference to Taşlıalan's work at the sanctuary of Mên, see his foreword to Drew-Bear, Taşlıalan, and Thomas 2002. Taşlıalan also published two guides to the site in 1990 and 1991.

[7] Mitchell and Waelkens (1998) also includes a chapter on the aqueduct by J. Burdy, M. Taşlıalan, and themselves and another by J. Öztürk and S. Mitchell on the three churches of Antioch that were then known. Humphrey's project

remains unpublished, but he graciously allowed us to work with his site plan. The magnetometry survey was published by Taşlıalan et al. 2003.

[8] Drew-Bear, Taşlıalan, and Thomas 2002. The papers are usefully organized under the following subheadings: the Early Christian Period, Epigraphy, Archaeology, Numismatics, and related topics that lie outside Antioch proper. This publication was anticipated by a "declerations book" (*sic*) of the conference papers published in 2000 in İsmit. We owe thanks to Ünal Demirer for providing us with a copy of this earlier publication.

[9] Demirer 2002; Bru and Demirer 2006.

[10] Ruggieri 2004; 2005; 2006.

excavating in the imperial cult sanctuary and also uncovered a basilica that was identified by the magnetometry survey of 2001. Currently, Mehmet Özhanlı and Fikret Özcan of Süleyman Demirel Üniversitesi in Isparta are undertaking fieldwork at Antioch and, as of 2009, have collaborated with the Austrian Archaeological Institute, Ephesos Excavation, under the direction of Sabine Ladstätter on a new topographical survey of the site.[11]

The Scope of This Book and Intentions of the Authors

The present book does not purport to be a definitive publication of the Michigan 1924 expedition. Rather, drawing heavily upon the expedition archives housed at the University of Michigan and the publications that have centered primarily on the architecture of the site since Arundell's time, we attempt here to present fresh perspectives on Pisidian Antioch and the sanctuary of Mên Askaênos by offering tentative reconstructions of the excavated monuments and situating them in their multifaceted social context. The architectural reconstructions proposed by the authors take advantage of 3-D virtual reality technology, a flexible medium that allows one to represent buildings, albeit provisionally, as complete structures in their urban and suburban environments and to revise the model with relative ease when new information becomes available. This effort necessitated close study of the records for each architectural component and supplying missing information on analogy with better-preserved counterparts elsewhere. The making of a 3-D model thus enhanced our research on the excavated structures and introduced new questions and observations concerning the form, decoration, and chronology of the monuments. Although this model shows monuments from the early Roman through the late antique period as if they existed simultaneously, it can be modified to show how the city developed over time.

Regarding individual structures, our 3-D model of the city presents for the first time plausible, if simplified, reconstructions of the theater, the Hadrianic arch (city gate) and adjacent cascade, the baths, nymphaeum, monumental aqueduct, and two of the churches, along with the complete imperial cult sanctuary and the adjoining Tiberia Platea. Not since the architect for the 1924 expedition, Frederick J. Woodbridge, made careful reconstruction drawings of parts of this sanctuary and the city gate has the architecture of those structures been so compellingly visualized. The partial reconstruction of the sanctuary of Mên is, likewise, the first attempt to envision the sanctuary in three dimensions, as a functional space. Whether viewing a fly-over of the entire 3-D model in its landscape setting or navigating through the city and sanctuary on a large-scale screen or in a CAVE (Cave Automatic Virtual Environment), viewers can now more vividly imagine the experience of ancient residents and visitors to Pisidian Antioch and approach a better understanding of their lived environment. This model reminds one that Pisidian Antioch was not merely a collection of monumental buildings and inscriptions. It was a community, with a vibrant mix of people who walked through city gates, worshipped at sanctuaries and churches, were entertained in the theater, and thronged the streets, patronizing shops and refreshing themselves at public fountains and the baths. A DVD of the 3-D movie of the site is included in this book.

Beyond offering reconstructions of the excavated buildings, the city, and the sanctuary of Mên Askaênos, the authors evaluate these monuments in relation to the social and political imperatives of Pisidian Antioch's hybrid culture—one that overlaid a Roman imperial colony on a Hellenistic Greek city in an Anatolian region long inhabited by Phrygians and Pisidians. In doing so, they

[11] See Harmankaya and Gümüş 2006; Özhanlı 2009b. In 2010 the Austrian team engaged in a study of the city wall and of the pottery from the ongoing excavations. We are grateful to Mag. Helmut Schwaiger and Dr. Alexander Sokolicek of the Austrian Archaeological Institute for sharing this information with us.

attempt to set Pisidian Antioch into the broader context of scholarship on Rome's colonial project in the Eastern empire.

Recent Research Directions on Roman Asia Minor and Colonies

Recent years have seen an impressive amount of scholarly literature dealing with questions of ethnicity, cultural interactions, colonialism, and elite patronage in the colonies and cities of the Roman Empire.[12] Regarding the question of ethnicity at Pisidian Antioch, Barbara Levick's important prosopographical work in her 1967 book addresses the issue of the origins of the colonists, but it does not consider in as much depth the ethnic composition of the population prior to the refoundation of Pisidian Antioch by the Romans.[13] Levick's analysis of textual and epigraphic evidence reflects her understanding that by the time the Roman colony was established by Augustus in the 1st century BC, Pisidian Antioch "was a fully developed Greek *polis*."[14] Levick's view of the Roman colonization of Pisidian Antioch—in which a Greek city was superseded by "a little Rome on the border of Phrygia and Pisidia"[15] before gradually being assimilated back into the dominant Greek cultural identity of the region[16]—sets up a bipolar framework for the understanding of Roman imperialism in the East, with a slow pendulum swinging between the Greek and Roman poles.

Recent scholarship on colonies and imperialism, however, presents a picture that is rather more nuanced, recognizing greater complexities in identity and its negotiation—in cultural, religious, and political terms—across the Roman Empire, from Britain and Gaul to Italy to the East.[17] Susan Alcock (2005) uses Pisidian Antioch as a case study to describe the Roman colonial project in the East as one that involved cultural identities that extend beyond the Roman and the Greek to enfold the Italian, the Phrygian, and the Anatolian.

Scholars of Asia Minor have continued to raise and probe questions concerning ethnicity, communal identity, and Anatolian culture. For example, the recent collection *L'Asie Mineure dans l'Antiquité: échanges, populations et territoires: regards actuels sur une péninsule* (Bru, Kirbihler, and Lebreton 2009) includes a number of essays that explore the religious traditions, cultural identity, and ethnic makeup of different regions in Asia Minor, including Pisidia. Our volume demonstrates that similar issues can be examined with subtlety and insight while focusing on the evidence supplied by monumental urban and extraurban sanctuary architecture. In particular the authors of the present volume examine the impact of the Roman settlers at Antioch and their working relationship with

---

[12] See recent volumes such as Howgego, Heuchert, and Burnett 2005; Stein 2005; Bradley and Wilson 2006; Scott and Webster 2003; Revell 2009—which engage with Roman colonies and imperialism across the empire, from Asia Minor to Gaul and Britain. Also see Bru, Kirbihler, and Lebreton 2009.

[13] Bru 2009 complicates the notion that the Italian colonists who settled at Antioch came directly from Italy. He argues that they came from Hispania Baetica, where Italian veterans had settled colonies in the 2nd century BC. He is the first to take issue with the conventional view that Pisidian Antioch was colonized by Italians from the Roman heartland, and this line of reasoning provides an avenue for further research into the ethnic composition of Pisidian Antioch and into what exactly it meant to be a "Roman" settler in Anatolia. Doni 2009 discusses the ethnicity of the Pisidians, clarifying our understanding of not only the

people but also the region and its history from the Bronze Age to the Hellenistic.

[14] Levick 1967, 72.

[15] Levick 1967, 78.

[16] Or as Levick (1967, 130) puts it, "the culture of the Italian settlers became attenuated and lost itself, so that eventually the colonies were almost indistinguishable from other towns in the region," a process that Levick strongly links to the decreasing use of Latin in the colonies. In Antioch, official use of Latin continues healthily into the late 3rd century, but private usage of Greek on dedications and funerary inscriptions dominates as early as the late 1st century AD (136).

[17] See n. 12 above.

the Greek-speaking *incolae*, as well as the accommodation of Pisidian, Phrygian, Greek, Roman, and Christian identities over the long history of the colony.

The Chapters in Scholarly Context

Prior to the arrival of the Augustan colonists at Antioch, Roman *negotiatores*, businessmen living in Asian cities in the Hellenistic period, blended for the most part into the preexisting social and political structures of the cities in which they lived.[18] When a city was refounded as a colony, however, the new settlers did not just join a community; rather, they brought and imposed their own ways of doing things on a preexisting society. Ossi and Harrington's chapter 2, on the layout of the city and its water supply, respectively, suggests how this process of transformation took place in physical terms. In offering a chronological account of the architectural development of the Roman settlement, they speculate about how Roman architectural elements were incorporated into the fabric of the earlier, now no longer extant, Hellenistic city. Structures such as the monumental aqueduct that was built at the refoundation of the colony and the imposing 2nd-century bath complex represent the continuing importation into Pisidia of not only Roman architecture and engineering but also of Roman social customs. In a similar vein, the imperial cult sanctuary, carved out of bedrock in the early days of the colony to create a precinct for the worship of Augustus, has long been thought to best exemplify the visible projection of Roman physical, cultural, and political authority over Antioch.[19] Yet Rubin's treatment of this emblematic sanctuary in chapter 3 demonstrates that the architectural form of the precinct itself was not entirely unfamiliar to the local, non-Roman population. Rubin argues that members of the Greek-speaking elite actively cooperated in the planning and construction of the sanctuary and that their participation alongside the Roman colonists fostered cohesion among the different segments of Antiochene society. From this social cohesion emerged a new identity for Pisidian Antioch as a loyal imperial colony that nonetheless embraced Anatolian and Hellenistic architectural and religio-political traditions.

This new blended identity, binding colonists and *incolae* under the leadership of the Roman emperor, was reinforced beyond the boundaries of the imperial cult sanctuary—in the theater and in the city streets and beyond the city to the sanctuary of Mên Askaênos. In chapter 4, Mallampati and Demirer argue that the orientation of the theater along an east-west axis parallel to that of the imperial cult sanctuary and iconographic similarities between the sculptural decoration of the theater and that of the temple of Augustus strongly suggest that there was an intended visual correspondence between the two structures. The authors argue, in addition, that from the Augustan to the late antique/early Byzantine period the theater at Antioch was an important venue where the local population could display its loyalty to the emperor and thus to the empire. The connection between the theater and the imperial cult would have been strengthened in the 4th century AD when the theater, like others in Roman Asia Minor, was modified to accommodate crowd-pleasing performances in honor of the emperor, such as animal games, gladiatorial combats, and water shows organized and paid for by officials of the imperial cult. In staging the festivities and games that tied the city more closely to the emperor and his cult, Pisidian Antioch engaged in a mode of communication that was prevalent in

---

[18] Yet there were tensions. The most notable instance of hostility was the massacre of Roman citizens at Ephesos, Pergamon, and throughout Asia Minor in 88 BC by supporters of Mithradates, who were subsequently dealt harsh punishment by Sulla, reported by Appian in *Mithridatic Wars*, 4.22–23. See also Mitchell 1993, 1:29–30; Levick 1967, 69.

[19] For example, Alcock 2005, 316: "The entire complex—from its architectural prototypes, to the *Res Gestae*, to the symbolism of victory and of the Golden Age typical of Augustan propaganda—seems extraordinarily 'central' in its inspirations and aspirations."

the eastern part of the Roman empire, where theatrical spectacle, political allegiance, ruler worship, and civic identity had long been intertwined.[20]

One of the major concerns of the cities of Asia Minor in the 2nd and 3rd centuries was the promotion of their civic identities in order to impress the emperor and attract official privileges and honors for its leading citizens as well as benefits for the general populace. In the 2nd century, Asian cities looked to their mythical histories and foundation legends to construct identities that linked them to their Hellenic pasts and to venerable heroes of the Greek mainland, the region that enjoyed the greatest cultural prestige in the empire.[21] At Antioch in the 2nd century the nostalgic desire for a foundation story expressed itself in non-Hellenic terms. Here the celebrated story centered on the refounding of the colony by Augustus and the cultural link thus forged to Rome. This assertion of Antioch's Roman self-image is most clearly embodied in the triple-arched Hadrianic city gate dedicated in AD 129, most likely in anticipation of the emperor's visit to the city. Although other arches were erected around the same time in Perge and Attaleia, in chapter 5 Ossi portrays the arched gateway at Antioch as unique in its emulation of, and calculated dialogue with, the triple-arched propylon of the city's own Augustan imperial cult sanctuary. He argues that the form and iconography of this city gate reiterated and reinforced Antioch's special status as a Roman imperial colony and, further, that the appropriated Augustan symbolism was intended to appeal directly to the emperor Hadrian, who publicly promoted his own personal affinity for Augustus.[22]

Antioch's identity as a Roman community, glorified by the Hadrianic city gate, is complicated by the apparent revival in the 2nd century of the cult of Mên Askaênos centered at the extramural sanctuary nearby. This Anatolian god was particularly revered in Phrygia and Pisidia, and though evidence of Mên's cult is found in many places in Asia Minor, the sanctuary near Pisidian Antioch is the only cult center of this deity whose architectural remains have been identified.[23] Two chapters in this volume focus on evidence for the appearance of the sanctuary and on the role of the cult in promoting community among the diverse ethnic elements of Antioch's population in the 2nd and 3rd centuries of the empire. In chapter 7, Raff presents a provisional reconstruction of the sanctuary's architecture by comparing the plans of the individual buildings to those of similar structures found in Greek sanctuaries in Asia Minor and on mainland Greece. The architectural similarities suggest parallels to Greek cultic practice, but in some of the buildings in the sanctuary of Mên at Antioch Raff also notes an element of local taste. The theory of Mitchell and Waelkens, which holds that the temple of Mên was built in the 2nd century BC under the patronage of the Attalids of Pergamon, finds support in the strong resemblance of the sanctuary's layout to that of Greek sanctuaries elsewhere. However, Raff is in accord with Khatchadourian's view that the temple of Mên was probably rebuilt in the mid-2nd century under the Antonines on the plan of the older Hellenistic temple. In her complementary study of the social and political significance of the worship of Mên at Antioch in the Roman imperial period (chapter 8) Khatchadourian sheds light on the sanctuary as a site where different segments of

---

[20] See Price 1984; Burrell 2004; Ng 2007.

[21] See Ng 2007; Price 2005, 115–123; Newby 2003; Scheer 1993; Boatwright 2000.

[22] Bru 2009, 263 notes the dedication of this arch to Hadrian and wonders whether its significance was enhanced by the fact that the original colonists hailed from Hadrian's homeland of Iberia.

[23] Labarre (2009) argues for the primarily regional worship of the cult of Mên in Anatolia, and in particular in Phrygia and Pisidia, and distinguishes it from other Asiatic cults that were widely exported throughout the empire, such as those of Mithras or the Magna Mater. He disagrees with Lane's argument (see n. 23) that the Romans promoted their ties to the region through the Mên cult and the sanctuary at Pisidian Antioch.

the Antiochene population gathered for a common purpose. Khatchadourian argues that the god's appeal to Phrygians, Pisidians, Greeks, and Romans, attested by dedicatory inscriptions, was a unifying element for the community. Her examination indicates that the sanctuary of Mên Askaênos, as a site for interaction among Antioch's various ethnic groups, was a distinctive, local counterpart to the Roman imperial cult sanctuary that, in the Augustan period especially, sought self-consciously to bring together the diverse peoples of Antioch in the new colonial project. The strong Phrygian and Pisidian associations of the cult do not, however, mean that it was not a participant in Roman imperialism. Following E. Lane, who proposed that the Roman colonists may have understood the epithet Askaênos as a reference to Ascanius, the son of Aeneas of Troy,[24] Khatchadourian sees the possible exploitation by the imperial administration of this mythological connection between Rome and the deity as a means of reaffirming Rome's longstanding connection to the region. The resurgence of the cult of Mên makes clear that there was always more to the population of colonial Antioch than just Greeks and Romans, and that the Anatolian culture and traditions that had been overlooked for a long time in modern scholarship were very much in the mind of the Romans who ruled the region. Indeed, it appears Roman-ness itself was seen as malleable and subject to manipulation so as to serve the needs of the emperor.

Elite participation in civic politics and patronage has long been a major concern of scholarship on the provinces of the Roman Empire. The role of local notables as mediators between their home communities and the Roman imperial authorities, the tensions and obligations that underlie the dealings between these parties, and the physical manifestations of these relationships in the form of public monuments and benefactions are still being explored in the most recent scholarly literature.[25] Almost all of the monuments discussed in this volume—the imperial sanctuary, the theater, the Hadrianic arch, the Church of St. Paul, and the sanctuary of Mên Askaênos—required gifts of local benefactors or imperial officials, and all provided highly visible sites for elite dedications and display. As a result, the importance of Antiochene notables as patrons and mediators between the different populations of the city, between the city and the emperor, and later between the city and the official Christian hierarchy is a thread that weaves throughout the chapters of this book. The authors all argue, in one way or another, that elite Antiochenes helped to plan and implement the city's building projects and that they did so in ways that ensured the broadest appeal to and comprehension by the city's multicultural population.

The imperial cult sanctuary was rendered accessible to the population by its local backer through its blended architecture and dedicatory inscription;[26] the theater hosted all sectors of the population at elaborate spectacles; the Hadrianic arch was donated by a local patron with an eye to impressing the emperor Hadrian with Antioch's unique colonial history; and the sanctuary of Mên provided yet another venue for elite self-promotion in an atmosphere of cultural and religious unity amid diversity. Beginning in the 4th century, church buildings paid for by wealthy Christian Antiochenes helped to transform the city—which by then was also the seat of a bishopric—both physically and spiritually, as described by Herring-Harrington in chapter 6 on the churches of Antioch. Civic benefactors gradually shifted their attention away from structures associated with polytheism, such

[24] Lane 1975b; 1976.

[25] See Veyne 1990 and Gauthier 1985. For more recent work, see Longfellow 2010; Zuiderhoek 2009; Bekker-Nielsen 2008; Eilers 2003. The authors of numerous essays in Howgego, Heuchert, and Burnett 2005 emphasize the control of

images and coins by the elite and the conflation of elite and civic identities that results; Woolf 1998 examines the role of the elites in communities in Gaul.

[26] See Rubin's essay, chap. 3, this volume.

as the theater, to Christian churches, but, although the newly sanctioned religion provided fresh motivation and venues for public generosity, the practice of elite euergetism seems to have carried over smoothly from the earlier imperial period.

In chapter 9, Harrington documents and describes the process of building the extensive 3-D model of the site and explains how the cityscape was quite literally given depth and fullness. In addition, he advocates that such models be regarded as scholarly arguments in their own right.

Covering a wide range of evidence and themes, this book serves, then, as a survey of and guide to archaeological work at the site. More importantly, it enlarges our knowledge of the social history of Pisidian Antioch in the Roman and early Christian periods. Beyond that, in asking questions of the unique data set presented at Pisidian Antioch that are being asked now of Asia Minor as a whole, and indeed of all parts of the Roman Empire, it situates Antioch more fully in relation to the ongoing debates over Anatolian archaeology and history and aspires thereby to contribute more broadly to our understanding of life in the provinces of the Roman Empire.

2 Pisidian Antioch: The Urban Infrastructure and Its Development

Adrian J. Ossi and J. Matthew Harrington

The urban infrastructure of a city, including the layout of its streets, the placement of major public buildings within that layout, and installations for the provision of water to the inhabitants of the city, provides the backbone for ancient civic life. At least by the mid-2nd century AD, certain architectural amenities were expected by city dwellers throughout the Roman Empire. Pausanias, the Greek geographer and traveler, in fact writes disparagingly of one settlement that lacks them: "From Chaeroneia it is twenty stades to Panopeus, a city of the Phocians, if one can give the name of city to those who possess no government offices, no gymnasium, no theatre, no market-place, no water descending to a fountain . . ."[1] At the time of the founding of the Roman colony of Antioch around 25 BC, if not before, the city began to acquire just such amenities, often at the expense of its leading citizens, who garnered prestige through their acts of civic generosity.

This chapter summarizes our current understanding of the chronological development of Antioch's urban infrastructure from its earliest foundation in the Hellenistic period to its eventual destruction in the 8th century AD.[2] The first section reviews previous research on the city's urban layout and presents an updated plan of the city that is based on the latest scholarship available in 2005.[3] The second section discusses the internal development of the city by highlighting four historical periods: Hellenistic, early Roman imperial, mid- to late imperial, and late antique/early Byzantine. The third section discusses the extramural elements of the hydraulic infrastructure, specifically two aqueducts that brought water to the city from springs in the surrounding mountains. This overview provides essential context for the studies of individual structures that are presented in the following chapters and also highlights potential directions for future research at Pisidian Antioch.

The City Plan

Two plans of the visible remains of Pisidian Antioch were produced prior to the Michigan excavations in 1924. The first, drafted by F. V. J. Arundell when he identified the city for the first time, was published in 1834 (fig. 2.1).[4] Although some of Arundell's identifications, such as the Arch of Hadrian and Sabina as a temple of Bacchus, were incorrect,[5] his plan generally corresponds with the remains visible today. The relative positions of the buildings on the second plan, published by G. Weber in

[1] Pausanias, *Description of Greece* 10.4.1, Loeb trans.

[2] This chapter is a collaboration between Adrian J. Ossi, who studied the urban layout, and J. Matthew Harrington, who researched the hydraulic systems.

[3] The various sources of information compiled into the new plan and the scholars who provided that information to us

are discussed below.

[4] Arundell 1834, second plate following p. 358; Mitchell and Waelkens 1998, 21 fig. 3.

[5] Arundell 1834, 268. Arundell's identification was based on the presence of a block decorated with a thyrsus, a pinecone-tipped staff used in the worship of Bacchus.

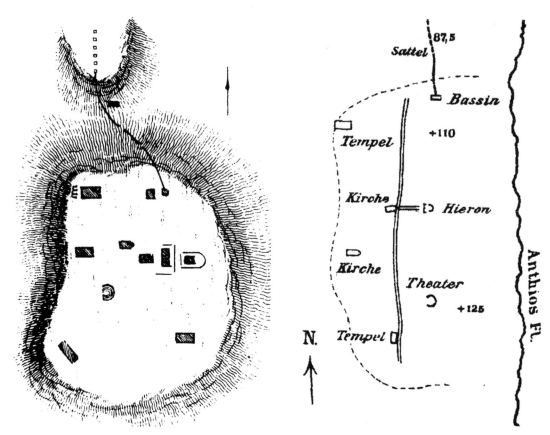

Fig. 2.1. Sketch plan of Antioch published in 1834. After C. Burton in Arundell 1834, second plate following p. 358.

Fig. 2.2. Sketch plan of Antioch published in 1904. After Weber 1904, pl. 3.

1904 (fig. 2.2),[6] are less accurate than those on Arundell's plan. Weber's plan also includes a hypothetical north-south street that does not correspond to either of the large streets that were subsequently uncovered.

In 1924, the first accurately measured plan of the city was drawn by Frederick J. Woodbridge, the architect assigned to excavations conducted by the University of Michigan (fig. 2.3).[7] Woodbridge's plan shows the structures that were excavated that season: the temple of Augustus, the so-called Platea Augusti, the Tiberia Platea, two churches, and the city gate (now identified as the Arch of Hadrian and Sabina). The Michigan team also used test trenches to identify the location of the city's main north-south street,[8] whose position is roughly indicated on the plan as white space between the topographical lines. The main east-west street, which was not excavated but was able to be located among the visible remains, is indicated in this way as well. The plan also shows several structures that were easily identifiable without excavation, including the theater in the center of the city, the nymphaeum at the north edge of town (incorrectly identified in photo captions as a city gate in 1924), a rough outline of the fortification wall, and the track of the monumental aqueduct outside the city.

---

[6] Weber 1904, pl. 3; Mitchell and Waelkens 1998, fig. 4.

[7] Robinson 1926a, fig. 2. See also Ossi 2005/2006.

[8] Journal of Excavations, entries for June 16 and 30. Mitchell and Waelkens speculate that the name Augusta Platea may have applied to another public space in the city. See p. 18, n. 34 below.

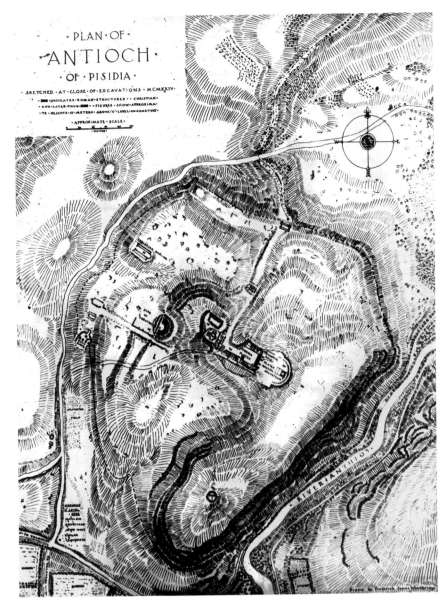

Fig. 2.3. Photograph of the measured plan of Antioch produced by Frederick J. Woodbridge during the University of Michigan excavations in 1924. Photo: G. R. Swain, Kelsey Museum Archives neg. no. 4.4273.

Following the 1924 excavation season, the site lay unstudied for many years. In 1962 M. Ballance produced a new plan of the site,[9] but this plan was never published.[10] In 1998, Stephen Mitchell and Marc Waelkens published an updated plan.[11] Their plan (see fig. 4.2) includes data from a site survey they conducted in 1982–1983, as well as some information from excavations conducted by Mehmet Taşlıalan, then director of the Yalvaç Museum, beginning in 1991.[12] Excavations at Pisidian

[9] French et al. 1963, 4.

[10] According to Mitchell and Waelkens 1998, 32.

[11] Mitchell and Waelkens 1998, fig. 18.

[12] E.g., Taşlıalan's reconstructed plan of the theater (Taşlıalan 1998, plans 1–2) and the intersections of side streets with the *decumanus maximus* (Taşlıalan 1995, plan 2).

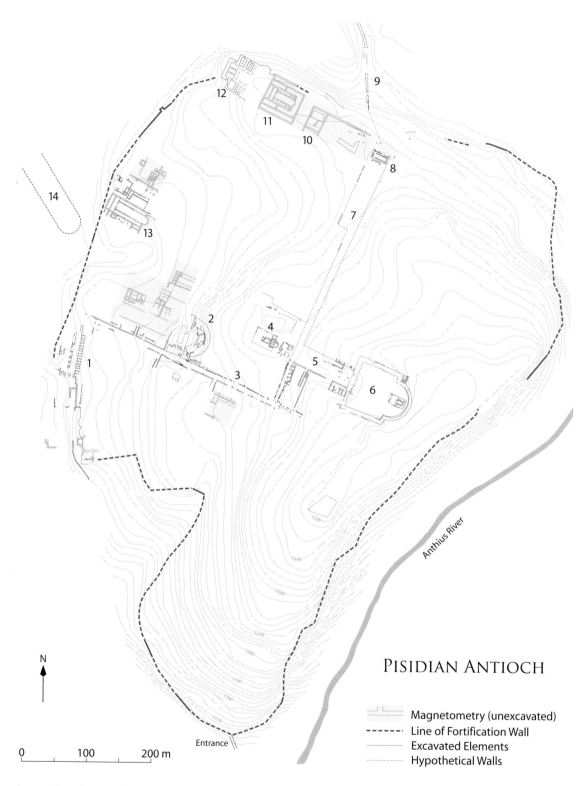

N

0   100   200 m

Entrance

PISIDIAN ANTIOCH

Magnetometry (unexcavated)
Line of Fortification Wall
Excavated Elements
Hypothetical Walls

Fig. 2.4. Plan of Pisidian Antioch. (1) entrance platea and Arch of Hadrian and Sabina, (2) theater, (3) *decumanus maximus*, (4) central church, (5) Tiberia Platea, (6) imperial cult sanctuary, (7) *cardo maximus*, (8) nymphaeum, (9) monumental aqueduct siphon, (10) possible cistern, (11) palaestra/north church, (12) bath building, (13) "Church of St. Paul," (14) approximate location of stadium. Combined drawing by A. J. Ossi.

Antioch continued in the 1990s and 2000s under the auspices of the Yalvaç Museum. In 2005 the newly identified north church was uncovered; and in 2008 a segment of a north-south street located southeast of the theater was excavated,[13] and in 2009 "a topographical survey in the city measuring the recently excavated structures" was performed jointly by Süleyman Demirel Üniversitesi in Isparta and the Austrian Archaeological Institute.[14]

Here we present a new plan that includes the most up-to-date information available in 2005 (fig. 2.4). It is primarily based on a previously unpublished plan produced in 2001 by a team led by J. W. Humphrey of the University of Calgary in cooperation with M. Taşlıalan.[15] Humphrey's plan, which he generously shared with us, includes greater detail of the streets and other structures revealed in Taşlıalan's excavations than had previously been available. To Humphrey's plan we have added the results of a magnetometry survey commissioned by Roger Bagnall, then of Columbia University. This survey was conducted in 2001 by T. Smekalova and S. Semakalov with the cooperation of M. Taşlıalan.[16] We have also inserted plans showing the actual state of the temple of Augustus and the bath building, based on recent published research.[17] Finally, we have included a revised hypothetical plan of the theater based on Ünal Demirer's excavations (see Mallampati and Demirer, chapter 4, this volume) and the approximate outline of the city's extramural stadium, located using published photographs and Google satellite imagery.[18] A discussion of the chronological development of the urban layout of Pisidian Antioch follows.

Chronological Development of the Urban Layout and Intramural Hydraulic Systems

The foundation of a city is only the beginning of a long process of development, which can include spurts of new construction, periods of decline, and episodes of renewal. Modifications to the fabric of a city can directly affect the social, civic, and cultural life of its residents by altering the pattern of use of particular public spaces. We present four schematic phase plans that show the development of Antioch's city center from its archaeologically murky beginnings in the Hellenistic period, through its refoundation as a colony in the early Roman period and its development during the course of the imperial period, to its conversion into a Christian capital in late antiquity and early Byzantine times.

Hellenistic Period (300–25 BC) (fig. 2.5). As its name implies, Antioch was founded in the Hellenistic period by a ruler of the Seleucid dynasty, possibly Antiochus I or II, who reigned in the first half of the 3rd century BC.[19] Few positively identifiable Hellenistic-era remains have been found at the site,[20] but scholars generally agree that the Roman colony probably occupies the same

[13] Harmankaya and Gümüş 2006; Özhanlı 2009a.

[14] H. Schwaiger, personal communication, July 2010.

[15] Originally drawn by I. Cowell and K. Hainsworth in 1982–1983 and updated by B. Wolf and M. Nikolic in 2001.

[16] Using variations in the magnetic signatures of different types of soil and stone, this technique electronically gathers information about structures buried beneath the soil without excavation. The results were partially published in Taşlıalan et al. 2003, and the full results were graciously supplied to the Kelsey Museum by R. Bagnall, T. Smekalova, and S. Smekalov. Our provisional plan of the north church is based on the magnetometry survey, not on the excavation of the building that has since taken place.

[17] We have replaced the reconstructed plan of the temple of Augustus on Humphrey's plan with an actual-state plan (after Mitchell and Waelkens 1998, fig. 21). Only an outline of the bath building was included on Humphrey's plan, so we have inserted a plan of its substructures that was published by Taşlıalan (1993, plan 4).

[18] The stadium is mentioned by Taşlıalan (1991, 33), Mitchell and Waelkens (1998, 91), and Demirer (2002, 103, with photo).

[19] Mitchell and Waelkens 1998, 5–6.

[20] One stretch of wall that is aligned with the street grid, located just south of the Tiberia Platea, has been stylistically dated to the Hellenistic period (Mitchell and Waelkens 1998, 99).

Fig. 2.5. Schematic hypothetical plan of the Hellenistic elements of Antioch's layout. Drawing: A. J. Ossi.

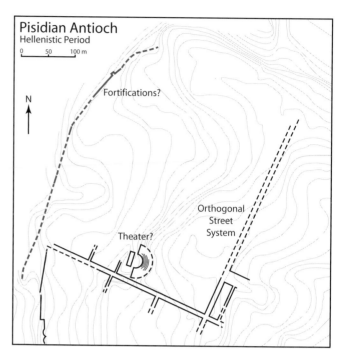

site as the Hellenistic city. If this is the case, the orthogonal grid of streets may be the most visible aspect of the Hellenistic city to have survived. The Seleucids typically laid out their cities, such as Hierapolis in Phrygia and Antioch-on-the-Orontes in Syria, on an orthogonal grid.[21] Although the limited amount of excavation that has occurred at Pisidian Antioch does not fully elucidate the city's layout, the exposed remains confirm that Antioch had an orthogonal street system oriented about 30° east of true north. All of the streets and major buildings, except the street that provided access to the city at the western edge of the site,[22] conform to this orientation, and the results of the magnetometry survey suggest the same alignment for unexcavated buildings in the areas surveyed.[23] South of the Tiberia Platea in the center of the city, the streets on all four sides of one city block have been uncovered. According to Mitchell and Waelkens, the dimensions of this block, 28 × 56 m, are similar to those of several other Seleucid foundations.[24]

Beyond the street system, traces of Antioch's Hellenistic form are few. Many Hellenistic cities were fortified, and it is possible that Antioch was as well, but the excavated portions of the city wall appear to have been built in the Roman period or later.[25] The theater may originally have been built in the Hellenistic period because the detached stage building is not typical of Roman-era theaters, as noted by M. Taşlıalan.[26] The current state of excavation and research at the theater, however, has revealed no direct evidence of Hellenistic construction (see Mallampati and Demirer, chapter 4, this volume). Other remains found outside the city wall, including a stadium, an aqueduct, and a sanctuary of Mên, might have originated in the Hellenistic period. Taşlıalan suggests based on limited excavation that

[21] Hierapolis: D'Andria 2001, 99–100. Antioch-on-the-Orontes: Pollitt 1986, 277.

[22] The entry street might have been built out of alignment in order to provide easier access into the city by following the natural topography of the hill. See Ossi, chap. 5, this volume, for further discussion of this area.

[23] Taşlıalan et al. 2003.

[24] Mitchell and Waelkens 1998, 99.

[25] Mitchell and Waelkens 1998, 94.

[26] Taşlıalan 1998, 325 and 333–335.

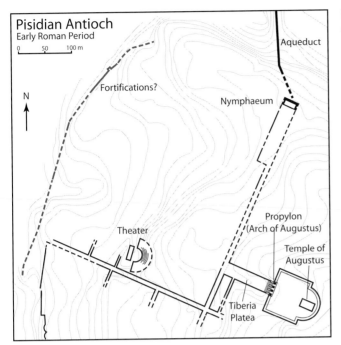

Fig. 2.6. Schematic plan of the early Roman elements of Antioch's layout. Drawing: A. J. Ossi.

the stadium located outside the western wall of the city may originally have been built in the Hellenistic period.[27] Near a spring in the mountains Owens has identified several terracotta pipes that might belong to a Hellenistic aqueduct, the details of which will be discussed later in this chapter.[28] The most significant feature of Antioch that may have survived from the Hellenistic period is the sanctuary of Mên Askaênos, located atop a mountain 3 km from the city. Although absolute dating evidence is lacking, the temple of Mên follows a plan that compares closely with Hellenistic temples at Priene and Teus, leading Mitchell and Waelkens to assign a date in the 2nd century BC to the temple of Mên (see also Raff and Khatchadourian, chapters 7 and 8, this volume).[29] Further excavation will be necessary to clarify the earliest phase of Antioch's urban layout.

Early Roman Imperial Period (25 BC–AD 100) (fig. 2.6). Surviving monuments dating to the early Roman period provide our first firm chronological evidence that the orthogonal street system as we know it was in use. The two main streets, identified by scholars with the traditional Latin terms of *decumanus maximus* for the main east-west street and *cardo maximus* for the main north-south street,[30] meet at right angles in the south-central area of the site. In traditional Hellenistic and Roman grid plans, the streets are spaced at regular intervals, but Taşlıalan's excavations have uncovered evidence of side streets intersecting the *decumanus maximus* at irregular intervals.[31] Some of these

[27] Taşlıalan 1991, 33, cited by Mitchell and Waelkens 1998, 110.

[28] Owens and Taşlıalan 2008, 303; 2009, 308.

[29] Mitchell and Waelkens 1998, 63–68. Both Raff and Khatchadourian in this volume (chaps. 7 and 8) believe that many of the remains at the sanctuary of Mên date from an extensive renovation during the reign of Antoninus Pius in the 2nd century AD. Ossi, chap. 5, this volume, suggests

that the 2nd-century revival of the cult of Mên may have begun in the reign of Hadrian after the emperor visited the city in AD 129.

[30] Note that we have no evidence of the ancient use of these terms in Antioch.

[31] Taşlıalan 1995, plan 2; Mitchell and Waelkens 1998, 99.

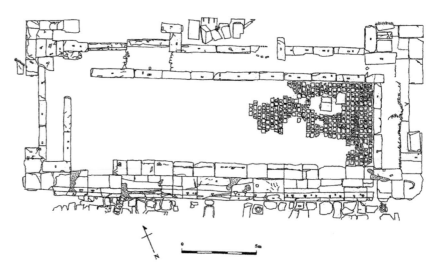

irregularities might be due to the presence of the theater on the north side of the *decumanus maximus* because street grids were sometimes altered to make room for large public buildings. In other cities such as Aphrodisias, residential quarters conformed most strictly to the grid scheme, but no such areas have yet been excavated in Antioch.[32] Further excavation, or perhaps a more comprehensive magnetometry survey, would be necessary to understand Antioch's grid system more fully.

Antioch's streets are typically 10 m or less in width, but in several key locations streets spread out to form plazas 20 m or more in width. Scholars use the term "platea" to identify such plazas in Antioch, based on ancient inscriptions that use the term.[33] Two such plazas are closely associated with early Roman monuments that probably date to the reign of Augustus. One platea, at the north end of the *cardo maximus*, ran up to the steps of a monumental fountain house, or nymphaeum, and the width of the platea is nearly identical to the width of the nymphaeum (see fig. 2.4). To the current authors, this relationship suggests that the platea and the nymphaeum may have been designed and built at the same time. The platea has not been excavated, but exposed coping stones that define the western edge of the street show that the plaza extended south from the nymphaeum for over 100 m before narrowing to the width of a normal street. Mitchell and Waelkens suggest that this plaza may have been called the Augusta Platea, a name that survives on a Roman honorific inscription.[34] Because this platea has not been excavated, we must refer to the nymphaeum in order to date the complex. E. J. Owens has studied the remains of the nymphaeum and dates its original construction to the Augustan period.[35] The nymphaeum (fig. 2.7) had a U-shaped plan, with one draw basin on each of the three sides, and was probably covered by a simple protective roof.[36] A water storage tower was built against the back wall of the nymphaeum, shielded from view by the fountain's façade.[37] Outside the city, the remains of a long monumental aqueduct, which will be discussed further later in this chapter, lead directly to the back of this nymphaeum. As the provider of a key resource for the inhabitants of the city, the nymphaeum

[32] A geophysical survey revealed the grid layout of Aphrodisias (Ratté 2001, 119 and fig. 5-2); the geophysical survey undertaken at Antioch was of a more limited nature (Taşlıalan et al. 2003).

[33] Mitchell and Waelkens 1998, 101, 219–221; Spanu 2002.

[34] Mitchell and Waelkens 1998, 220–221. The inscription was

found in the village of Hisarardı, located just northeast of the site of Antioch. See also Rubin, chap. 3, pp. 44–45, n. 48.

[35] Owens and Taşlıalan 2008, 306–307.

[36] Owens and Taşlıalan 2008, 304–305.

[37] Owens and Taşlıalan 2008, 303.

Fig. 2.8 (above). View of the base of a fountain in situ in the Tiberia Platea. This fountain is one of four that originally stood at the foot of the steps. Photo: D. M. Robinson, Kelsey Museum Archives neg. no. KR043.08.

Fig. 2. 9 (right). Circular inscribed block that credits Baebius Asiaticus with paving the streets of the city, located in front of the steps in the Tiberia Platea. Photo: G. R. Swain, Kelsey Museum Archives neg. no. 7.1472.

would have been a locus of social activity, and, as Mitchell and Waelkens have pointed out, the associated platea may have been one of the important civic and commercial centers in the early days of the colony.[38]

The second Augustan-era platea was one of the first monuments excavated at Pisidian Antioch, at the beginning of the Michigan team's expedition in 1924.[39] Called the Tiberia Platea after an inscription found during excavation, the plaza leads eastward from the *cardo maximus* and connects the main street with the city's primary urban sanctuary (see Rubin, chapter 3, this volume). The platea, ca. 21 m wide, had shops lining part of its length, and at the east it terminated in a monumental flight of steps that led up to a triple-bayed arch. This arch, dedicated to Augustus in 2/1 BC, acted as the ornamental propylon to the sanctuary. Four small fountains (fig. 2.8), which were probably fed by the monumental aqueduct mentioned above, stood at the foot of the steps and could have provided water for commercial activities in the Tiberia Platea and perhaps for ritual activities in the sanctuary. An inscription set into the pavement near the steps credits a rich Roman citizen, Baebius Asiaticus, with paving some of the city streets and records the total length of streets paved at 3,000 Roman feet (fig. 2.9). Mitchell and Waelkens calculate the combined length of the *decumanus maximus*, the *cardo maximus*, and the Tiberia Platea, 2,900 modern feet, as roughly equal to the length paved by Baebius Asiaticus.[40] While the inscription does not include the usual Roman dating formulae, it is possible that Baebius's street paving was part of the original construction of the platea at the end of the 1st century BC.[41]

---

[38] Mitchell and Waelkens 1998, 101.

[39] Robinson 1924a, 437; Journal of Excavations, entries for May 10–June 15. See also Rubin, chap. 3, n. 27, who dates the paving late Augustan or early Tiberian.

[40] Mitchell and Waelkens 1998, 221. Ca. 880 m.

[41] Mitchell and Waelkens 1998, 221; Demirer 2002, 72.

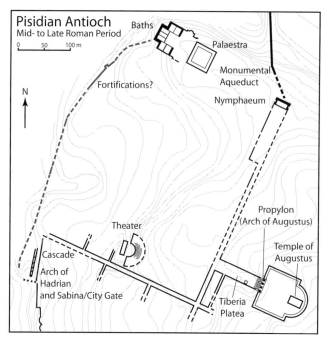
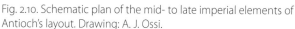

Fig. 2.10. Schematic plan of the mid- to late imperial elements of Antioch's layout. Drawing: A. J. Ossi.

Fig. 2.11. View of the cascade at the entrance platea, with the semicircular fountain in the foreground (2004). Photo: A. J. Ossi (CG 118).

Two other elements of urban infrastructure may have been constructed in the years shortly after the city's refoundation as a Roman colony. The first of these is the theater, the earliest archaeologically attested phase of which dates to the Augustan period (see Mallampati and Demirer, chapter 4, this volume). The second is the city wall. If a wall was not already in place during the Hellenistic era, one may well have been built in the early Roman period, given the colony's function in protecting Roman interests in the region. Portions of the wall, such as the bastion located south of the Arch of Hadrian and Sabina, are built of large ashlar blocks and may date to this period, but Mitchell and Waelkens emphasize that because of extensive rebuilding no part of the wall can be securely dated prior to the late antique period.[42]

Mid- to Late Imperial Period (AD 100–300) (fig. 2.10). By the 2nd century AD, a high point in the political and economic development of Roman Asia Minor, the urban layout of Antioch had been fixed, and building activity focused on developing and expanding the existing urban infrastructure. For example, during the reign of Hadrian a new platea was added to the street system by refashioning the street that led into the city on the western edge of town.[43] The street was widened, and a row of shops was built on each side. Fifteen shops are visible on the east side of the street, and the fragmentary remains of two or three are visible on the west side. This location must have become a hub of commercial activity, for, as shown on the city plan, it contains the highest concentration of shops yet uncovered in the city. The Tiberia Platea was home to several shops,[44] but they did not run

[42] Mitchell and Waelkens 1998, 94.

[43] See Ossi, chap. 5, this volume, for further discussion of

this platea and fig. 5.3.

[44] See Rubin, chap. 3, this volume.

Fig. 2.12. Current view of the exterior wall of the bath building, composed of massive ashlar blocks (2004). Photo: E. K. Gazda (BB 21).

its entire length, and only two other isolated groups of shops—four near the theater, five near the intersection of the two main streets—are identifiable on the city plan (see fig. 2.4). The new platea was entered at the south through Antioch's second triple-bayed honorific arch (see Ossi, chapter 5, this volume). A long water channel was built running down the middle of the street (fig. 2.11), fed either by the monumental aqueduct that was already in existence or by an aqueduct composed of terracotta pipes that may have been built at this time.

This terracotta aqueduct, the remains of which will be discussed further below, may have been part of a major refurbishment and expansion of the city's hydraulic system in the middle of the 2nd century AD. The primary purpose of the terracotta aqueduct may have been to supply the massive bath complex that today dominates the northwest corner of the site (fig. 2.12). Although only the substructures of the bath building are preserved,[45] the structure is similar in plan to the enormous bath complexes constructed in other cities around this time.[46] The bath building itself may have been flanked by a palaestra, or exercise yard, to the east.[47] East of the possible palaestra, the magnetometry survey revealed a subsurface structure that has been identified as a large cistern.[48] According to E. J. Owens, the terracotta aqueduct may have fed this cistern, which in turn could have supplied water for the baths and the cascade at the city's entrance platea.[49] The relative chronology of all of the relevant features—the terracotta aqueduct, the bath building, the cistern, and the cascade—is not certain, but the evidence suggests a extensive expansion of the city's hydraulic system in the 2nd century AD, and parallels in other cities in Asia Minor make the hypothesis plausible.[50]

Other parts of the city were also further developed in the 2nd century AD. For example, the nymphaeum at the northern end of the *cardo maximus* was refurbished around this time.[51] The open

[45] Taşlıalan 1993, 263–267.

[46] See Nielsen 1990 and Yegül 1992 for discussions of bath buildings and bath-gymnasium complexes in the Greek and Roman periods.

[47] Mitchell and Waelkens 1998, 199.

[48] Taşlıalan et al. 2003, 278.

[49] Owens and Taşlıalan 2009, 312.

[50] E.g., at Aphrodisias, where during the reign of Hadrian a new aqueduct, bath complex, and monumental pool were constructed (Ratté 2002, 22–23; Reynolds 2000, 5–10 and 16–20). For discussion and illustration of numerous major bath-gymnasium complexes built throughout Asia Minor in the 2nd century, see Yegül 1992, 250–313.

[51] Owens and Taşlıalan 2008, 307–309.

Fig. 2.13. Digital reconstruction of the second phase of the nymphaeum at the north end of the *cardo maximus*, with the monumental aqueduct visible in the background at left. Digital model: J. M. Harrington.

space between the three original draw basins was closed off and transformed into a large collecting basin, and a long narrow draw basin was installed along the front of the whole monument. At this time the roof was probably removed, the back walls raised, and the façade articulated with a series of columns and niches for the display of statues (fig. 2.13). Numerous other cities, including Ephesos, Perge, and Sagalassos, have nymphaea of this type.[52] The Tiberia Platea was also further developed; toward the end of the 2nd century, a small round building (see fig. 3.24) that probably housed a commemorative statue was built along the south edge of the platea.[53] In the context of Antioch's intramural development in the 2nd century AD, it is also worth recalling that the extramural sanctuary of Mên Askaênos experienced a revival in the middle of the century (see Raff and Khatchadourian, chapters 7 and 8, this volume).

Late Antique/Early Byzantine Period (AD 300–713) (fig. 2.14). In late antiquity, both alteration and continuity can be found in Antioch's urban layout and infrastructure. The most significant change came with the construction of three Christian churches inside the city (see Herring-Harrington, chapter 6, this volume). A small church was built near the *cardo maximus*, opposite the entrance to the Tiberia Platea and aligned with the central axis of the imperial cult sanctuary. Another church, which was revealed in the magnetometry survey and has since been excavated,[54] replaced the palaestra to the east of the bath building. The largest of the three churches, the so-called Church of St. Paul, was built along the western edge of the city wall, in an area that contains no known imperial public structures. In some other cities in Asia Minor, such as Aphrodisias and Sagalassos, major churches were created by altering and repurposing a pagan temple, but this sort of cultic reuse does not seem to have occurred at Antioch.[55] Even when a fourth church was built to replace the sanctuary of Mên Askaênos high up on the mountain of Kara Kuyu, the Christian cult building occupied a fresh site on the road approaching the sanctuary. The location of these newly built cult centers, then, would have shifted the focus of religious ritual away from preexisting polytheist temples and probably altered the patterns of use of the associated urban spaces. Notably, all three of the churches in the city conform

[52] See Dorl-Klingenschmid 2001 for a comprehensive survey of nymphaea in Asia Minor. For a more detailed examination of the patronage of nymphaea in the Roman period, see Longfellow 2010.

[53] Mitchell and Waelkens 1998, 154–157.

[54] For the magnetometry survey, see Taşlıalan et al. 2003. The

church was excavated in 2006, and in 2009 a new study of its remains was undertaken by Süleyman Demirel Üniversitesi in Isparta and the Austrian Archaeological Institute (H. Schwaiger, personal communication, July 2010).

[55] Aphrodisias: Cormack 1990, 75–88. Sagalassos: Waelkens 1993a, 49 and figs. 69 and 71.

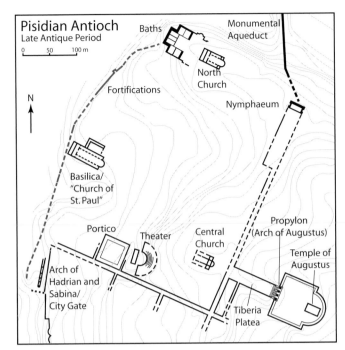

Fig. 2.14. Schematic plan of the late antique elements of Antioch's layout. Drawing: A. J. Ossi.

to the grid plan that had guided the organization of the city since, presumably, its Hellenistic foundation, and so the main streets continued to be in use throughout late antiquity. The surfaces of the streets themselves reveal their long lifespan. Blocks of various stone types with surfaces worked in different ways can be seen lying side by side in the preserved pavement. This variety may be evidence of numerous repairs over the years.

The city's fortification wall must have been repaired, or entirely rebuilt, at some point in late antiquity.[56] The portions excavated by Taşlıalan along the western, southwestern, and southeastern edges of the city show a variety of construction techniques and, in some places, a high proportion of reused masonry, including blocks with decorative moldings and inscriptions.[57] These details match the description given in 1861 by Léon de Laborde, the earliest traveler to describe the fortifications.[58] The reused stones built into the wall suggest a late date of construction for these stretches of wall, when some buildings in the city had fallen out of use, perhaps due to earthquake damage or neglect, and could be dismantled for building materials. Elsewhere in the city entire buildings were repurposed. The triple-bayed arch near the entrance to the city, which was merely an ornamental gateway as originally constructed, was converted into a closeable city gate (see Ossi, chapter 5, this volume), and the bath house, whose massive bulk dominated the northwest corner of the hill, may have become a fortified bastion.[59] A new survey of the city's fortifications, performed in 2010 and sponsored by Süleyman Demirel Üniversitesi in Isparta and the Austrian Archaeological Institute, may provide greater detail concerning the building phases of the city wall.[60]

[56] Mitchell and Waelkens 1998, 94.

[57] Taşlıalan 2001, figs. 1–2, 7 (molded blocks), figs. 3a–f, 4 (inscribed blocks).

[58] De Laborde 1861, 113–114; quoted in Mitchell and Waelkens 1998, 23. De Laborde had visited Antioch in 1826.

[59] Mitchell and Waelkens 1998, 95.

[60] H. Schwaiger, personal communication, July 2010; and A. Sokolicek, personal communication, February 2011.

Fig. 2.15. View of the monumental aqueduct in 1924. Photo: G. R. Swain, Kelsey Museum Archives neg. no. 7.1362.

Other late antique repairs to the urban infrastructure are visible, in both the archaeological and epigraphic records. For example, an inscription records that in the early 4th century AD the theater was refurbished and possibly expanded westward to include a courtyard and perhaps porticoes (see Mallampati and Demirer, chapter 4, this volume). This inscription was carved on the curved face of an arch that spanned the *decumanus maximus* near the south entrance to the theater. Elsewhere in the city, the nymphaeum, which had already undergone one renovation in the 2nd century AD, was transformed into a more functional water distribution center, or *castellum aquae*, by the addition of two pipelines to the front corners of the structure that carried water to other parts of the city.[61] Burdy and Taşlıalan have noted that at least one of the piers of the monumental aqueduct was rebuilt after it had collapsed,[62] and two preserved inscriptions that probably date to the late antique period mention repairs and refurbishments to the city's hydraulic infrastructure.[63] The changes to the nymphaeum and the repairs to the monumental aqueduct may have been part of these refurbishments.

Extramural Hydraulic Infrastructure: Antioch's Two Aqueducts

The most complex and extensive component of Antioch's urban infrastructure was its hydraulic system. Several components of the system have already been mentioned in the preceding discussion: two aqueducts, three public fountain installations, a cascade, a large cistern, and a massive bath building. The most visible element of the hydraulic system, an aqueduct bridge with fourteen arches still standing today (fig. 2.15), is perhaps Antioch's most frequently illustrated monument, and it has become an emblem of the modern municipality of Yalvaç.[64] The visibility of this monumental aqueduct has made it one of the most thoroughly studied structures associated with the city. The standing remains were illustrated as early as 1834 by F. V. J. Arundell (fig. 2.16),[65] and in 1904 G. Weber surveyed and published the visible remains for a distance of 1.2 km from the city.[66] In 1924

[61] Owens and Taşlıalan 2008, 309–311.

[62] Burdy and Taşlıalan 2002, 327 and pl. 14.

[63] Mitchell and Waelkens 1998, 227–228; Owens and Taşlıalan 2008, 311.

[64] A stylized image of the aqueduct is a major component of the city's logo (http://www.yalvac.bel.tr).

[65] Arundell 1834.

[66] Weber 1904.

Fig. 2.16. View of Antioch and its aqueduct as seen by Arundell in 1833. After L. Haghe in Arundell 1834, plate following p. 270.

the Michigan team followed the remains of the aqueduct to its source ca. 11 km from the city and discovered a series of tunnels and bridges in the mountains ca. 4–5 km from the city. Although they took numerous photographs and made drawings of several architectural details of the aqueduct, the members of the Michigan team did not publish these findings.[67] More recently, a survey performed by J. Burdy and M. Taşlıalan has provided detailed information about the monumental aqueduct.[68] Since then E. J. Owens has studied the evidence of how the water supply was used within the city,[69] and he has recently identified a second aqueduct that brought water from a different source.[70] In order to distinguish between the two aqueducts in this essay, we refer to the more visible and well known of the two as the "monumental aqueduct" and the one recently identified by Owens as the "terracotta aqueduct," based on the type of conduit employed.

Monumental Aqueduct. The most completely preserved remains of the hydraulic system belong to the first known and most visible of the city's two aqueducts. The bold architectural form that dominates the landscape (fig. 2.15) and has become an icon of the city was only a small part of the whole. The greater part of the system was composed of a well-built underground channel, or *specus*, which began at a source spring roughly 11 km northeast of the city. In this vicinity Burdy and Taşlıalan have identified three springs as potential sources, and the most likely candidate is located at an altitude of

[67] Some of the Michigan team's results were subsequently published by Mitchell and Waelkens (1998, 175–191). The photographs and drawings are housed in the Kelsey Museum of Archaeology.

[68] Burdy and Taşlıalan 1997; 2002.

[69] Owens 2002; Owens and Taşlıalan 2008.

[70] Owens and Taşlıalan 2009.

Fig. 2.17. View looking into the *specus*, or channel, of the monumental aqueduct where it tunnels into a mountain. Photo: G. R. Swain, Kelsey Museum Archives neg. no. 7.1482.

Fig. 2.18. A half-buried aqueduct bridge in the mountains. Photo: G. R. Swain, Kelsey Museum Archives neg. no. 7.1355.

ca. 1,465 m above sea level.[71] With its terminus within the city lying at ca. 1,178 m above sea level, the aqueduct drops a total of ca. 287 m along its length. More than half of this drop, however, occurs in the first 2 km nearest the source,[72] so that the great majority of the system has a gentle slope of 2 m/km.[73] Scholars surmise that the steep drop of the higher section must have been navigated by a series of artificial cascades, but no evidence of such installations has yet been discovered.[74]

In the gently sloping central portion that navigates through the mountains, archaeologists have surveyed three sections of the underground channel and three bridges that carried the channel over ravines. The surveyed sections of the underground channel are built in the typical Roman manner, whereby an oversized tunnel is carved through the bedrock, and the walls, floor, and vaulted ceiling of the channel are built of masonry within (fig. 2.17). In several sections surveyed by Burdy, the masonry walls and floor of the channel were covered in waterproof cement,[75] while the Michigan team photographed and drew another section where no such cement covering was evident.[76] The interior dimensions of the channel are typically around 0.7–0.8 m in width and 1.3 m in height, but

[71] Burdy and Taşlıalan 2002, 324; Mitchell and Waelkens 1998, 177.

[72] Mitchell and Waelkens 1998, 193 fig. 37.

[73] Mitchell and Waelkens 1998, 193.

[74] Mitchell and Waelkens 1998, 193.

[75] Burdy and Taşlıalan 2002, 325.

[76] Mitchell and Waelkens 1998, 178 and pl. 117.

Fig. 2.19. The remains of a long aqueduct bridge in the mountains. The aqueduct would have continued across the ravine at the same level as the top of the standing arch at left. Photo: G. R. Swain, Kelsey Museum Archives neg. no. 5.0133.

these dimensions vary from section to section.[77] The floors of the different sections of channel were constructed in different ways, perhaps depending on the slope of the aqueduct at each point. The section studied by the Michigan team had flat tiles or stones forming a V-shaped channel in the floor.[78] Two different sections surveyed by Burdy had flat floors, in one case composed of cement, in the other formed by broad terracotta tiles laid into a cement bedding.[79] The terracotta tiles in this last section, which is particularly steep and makes two sharp turns, may have protected the floor of the channel from erosion by fast-moving water. Where the channel emerged from the ground closest to the city, the foundations of the channel were deeper and stronger than elsewhere, and the channel was covered by thick limestone slabs rather than masonry vaulting.[80] Burdy located three sets of manholes that gave access to the tunnel.[81] These manholes are all similar in construction, square in plan (ca. 0.76–0.78 m per side), with footholes going down the wall for ease of access and with a large limestone slab as a cover.[82] The manholes were probably used both during the construction of the aqueduct and for maintenance and repairs during its period of use.

Optimal functioning of an aqueduct required an even slope; consequently, the channel would cross valleys or other irregularities in the terrain on elevated bridges. Three such bridges have been identified in the upper reaches of Antioch's monumental aqueduct, all built of well-worked limestone blocks joined with dovetail clamps. The first two bridges are about 5 km from the city and stand about 100 m apart from each other. The first bridge, which today is about two-thirds buried (fig. 2.18), comprised three arches with a total span of 30 m, a maximum height of perhaps 5 m, and width of 2.05 m.[83] The second bridge, which is largely destroyed except for one standing arch (fig. 2.19), spanned

[77] Mitchell and Waelkens 1998, fig. 33; Burdy and Taşlıalan 2002, pl. 6.

[78] Mitchell and Waelkens 1998, 178.

[79] Burdy and Taşlıalan 2002, 325.

[80] Mitchell and Waelkens 1998, 180.

[81] Burdy and Taşlıalan 2002, 325.

[82] Mitchell and Waelkens 1998, 180.

[83] Mitchell and Waelkens 1998, 180.

Fig. 2.20. Small aqueduct bridge in the mountains. Photo:
G. R. Swain, Kelsey Museum Archives neg. no. KS286.08.

50 m on five arches, with a maximum height of about 11 m and a width of 2.2 m.[84] The third bridge,
almost fully preserved at a distance of about 3.5 km from the city (fig. 2.20), contained a single arch
and was 15 m long, 5 m high, and 2.1 m wide.[85]

The portion of the aqueduct closest to the city contained two major structural elements (fig.
2.21): the monumental arcade mentioned above (fig. 2.15), which is the fourth and longest bridge in
the system, and a pressurized siphon that crossed the final valley just outside the city wall (fig. 2.22).
Starting just over 1 km from the city, the long bridge spans a dip in the terrain for a distance of about
275 m.[86] The tallest arches in the span are ca. 7.5 m in height, and the width of this bridge, 2.1 m, is
similar to the width of the three bridges in the mountains.[87] The long bridge contained 44 arches that
seem to have been built in two sections, identifiable by their different measurements. On average,
each of the first 21 arches spanned 4.0 m by means of 11 voussoirs (the wedge-shaped blocks that
make up an arch), while arches 23–44 used 15 voussoirs to span 4.6 m each.[88] Arch 22, where these
two groups meet, employed 13 voussoirs. The bridge also makes two shallow turns to the left as it
approached the city, near piers 13–14 and piers 20–23. Several of the piers are trapezoidal in plan to
accommodate these turns.[89]

About 800 m from the city wall, the long bridge terminated in a large tank (fig. 2.21). This tank is
the first element of an inverted siphon, which uses pressure generated by gravity to force water to flow
through an enclosed pipeline over a dip in the terrain. For crossing deep valleys, an inverted siphon
is an alternative to an aqueduct bridge that would require the construction of very tall piers.[90] In an
inverted siphon, water collected in the header tank feeds into a pipeline, and, as long as the outlet

[84] Mitchell and Waelkens 1998, 181.

[85] Burdy and Taşlıalan 2002, 325.

[86] Burdy and Taşlıalan 2002, 326.

[87] Mitchell and Waelkens 1998, 185.

[88] Mitchell and Waelkens 1998, 185.

[89] Burdy and Taşlıalan 2002, 327; Mitchell and Waelkens
1998, 185.

[90] Tall aqueduct bridges can still be seen throughout the
Mediterranean region; examples include the aqueduct at
Segovia in Spain and the Pont du Gard outside of Nîmes
in France.

Fig. 2.21. Digital reconstruction of the monumental aqueduct as it approached the city. At center is the collecting basin for the siphon, which runs between the basin and the city wall in the distance. Digital model: J. M. Harrington.

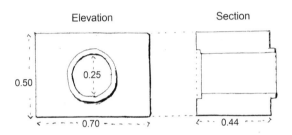

Fig. 2.22. Drawing of a siphon block from Antioch. After Weber 1904, fig. 8.

of the tube is at a lower level than its source tank, pressure forces the water to flow down one side of the valley and up the other side. At Antioch, such a system was used to cross the 33 m–deep valley that bordered the northern edge of the city. The pipeline was composed of large stone blocks with a cylindrical opening passing though the length of the block (fig. 2.22).[91] Each block had a protruding collar that encircled the hole on one side and a recessed area surrounding the hole on the opposite side. This allowed each block to interlock with the next to ensure a tight seal. These pipeline blocks were supported on a built foundation, the remains of which can be seen crossing the valley floor north of the site (fig. 2.23). Among these remains, Burdy has identified two low bridges that raised the siphon above the deepest parts of the valley floor.[92] This reduced the amount of pressure in the system and decreased the chances of a failure.

After climbing the hill and entering the city, the pipeline of the siphon emptied into the water tower that was hidden behind the monumental nymphaeum (see fig. 2.7), as mentioned above. From here water could be distributed to any part of the city that was below the level of the water in the tower. This includes the vast majority of the area within the city walls. Owens has noted that the aqueduct bridges are wide enough (2.1 m) to have carried two siphon tubes, and he has identified two types of siphon blocks with pipelines of different dimensions.[93] It is possible that the second pipeline could have been diverted to another as yet undiscovered water distribution tower elsewhere in the city.

[91] Mitchell and Waelkens 1998, pl. 128.

[92] Mitchell and Waelkens 1998, fig. 34b; Burdy and Taşlıalan 2002, 328.

[93] Owens 2002, 338–339.

Fig. 2.23. View of the remains of the siphon in 1924. Photo: G. R. Swain, Kelsey Museum Archives neg. no. 7.1138.

Terracotta Aqueduct. The monumental aqueduct is the most highly visible component of Antioch's extraurban hydraulic system, but recent research has shown that it was not the only source of flowing water for the city. Owens describes a series of remains that he identifies as a second aqueduct, which in contrast to its ostentatious cousin was composed of a simple terracotta pipeline that snaked its way across the landscape.[94] The remains of this terracotta aqueduct include a collecting tank at the source spring, fragments of pipelines located at various points between the spring and the site of Antioch, a header tank on a ridge opposite the city, and possibly a large cistern just inside the city wall. The source spring is ca. 15 km northwest of the city, and the remains of the collecting tank measure 9.70 × 4.15 m.[95] Owens identified four different types of terracotta pipes both in the vicinity of the collection tank and in the fields between the spring and the site, as well as several sections of trenches and walls that would have carried pipelines.[96] The differently sized pipes, he suggests, could be evidence of the exploitation of the same spring as a water source at different times. This exploitation may have begun as early as the Hellenistic period, given the similarity between some of the pipes and those from the Hellenistic aqueduct in Pergamon.[97] Owens has identified a collecting tank on a ridge opposite the bath building and terracotta pipes in the saddle between this ridge and the city that are similar

[94] Owens and Taşlıalan 2009, 307–312.

[95] Owens and Taşlıalan 2009, 307.

[96] Owens and Taşlıalan 2009, 308.

[97] Owens and Taşlıalan 2009, 308.

to those from a siphon in nearby Kremna, another Roman colony.[98] This terracotta siphon is to be distinguished from the stone siphon of the monumental aqueduct, discussed above. As mentioned above, the magnetometry survey conducted in 2001 revealed a 14 × 12 m subsurface structure on the northern edge of the hill, which the surveyors suggest may have been a cistern (see fig. 2.4).[99] Owens suggests that if this unexcavated structure proves to be a cistern, it may have been the destination of the terracotta aqueduct and the primary water storage tank for the baths.[100] It should be noted that these conclusions are preliminary, and much more fieldwork will be required to unravel the various phases of the terracotta aqueduct and, indeed, Antioch's entire hydraulic system.

Future Directions and Conclusion

The preceding discussion has emphasized what we are able to deduce about the urban infrastructure of Pisidian Antioch based on the current state of research, but it is worthwhile to point out some rather glaring holes in our knowledge. First, thus far we have very little physical evidence of the city's civic infrastructure—no dedicated agora or market, no *bouleuterion* or council house, no civic basilica or law courts. It is possible that some civic activities, such as legal proceedings or meetings of the city council, took place in some of the urban spaces known to us, such as the Tiberia Platea or the plaza inside the imperial cult sanctuary. It is more likely, however, that a civic agora remains to be discovered. Pausanias leads us to expect as much, and many cities of Asia Minor in the Roman period were so equipped.[101] Second, the exploration of domestic structures in Antioch has been extremely limited.[102] The majority of the area within the walls of virtually any city was taken up by housing, and the life of these structures can tell us much about the history of the community. Both of these matters—the location of the civic buildings and the layout of domestic areas—could be investigated initially by means of an expanded magnetometry survey. The discovery of Antioch's north church by means of this non-invasive technique demonstrates its potential. Third, there is much to be learned about the city's hydraulic systems, especially concerning the terracotta aqueduct. A new survey of the remains of both aqueducts using modern digital tools such as Geographic Information Systems (GIS) could enhance our understanding of these important structures. As fieldwork proceeds under the auspices of Süleyman Demirel University (directed by Mehmet Özhanlı and Fikret Özcan)[103] and the Austrian Archaeological Institute (directed by Sabine Ladstätter), many questions regarding the urban infrastructure and chronology of the site will no doubt be addressed.

Future directions aside, the preceding discussion provides a snapshot of Antioch's urban development in four distinct periods. The authors of the following chapters discuss certain individual structures within (and outside of) the urban fabric, and while reading these chapters it is important to keep in mind the overall arc of the city's development. A Hellenistic city, probably planned with an orthogonal grid of streets, was refounded and extensively redeveloped in the Augustan period. The hydraulic delivery system and a major urban sanctuary were constructed, each in association with

---

[98] Owens and Taşlıalan 2009, 308–312.

[99] Taşlıalan et al. 2003, 278.

[100] Owens and Taşlıalan 2009, 312.

[101] See Parrish 2001 for a survey of the typical urban amenities found in the cities of Asia Minor, with numerous examples.

[102] The Michigan team excavated several rooms along the *cardo maximus* that they identified as Byzantine houses (Journal of Excavations, entries for June 16–19), but no architectural drawings of these remains seem to have been produced. The head of a statue of Augustus was found in one of these rooms.

[103] See Özhanlı 2009a; 2009b.

a platea that could act as a multifunctional public space. In the high imperial period, the hydraulic system seems to have been expanded with a new aqueduct, a refurbished nymphaeum, and a massive new bath building that itself would have been a major part of daily life in the city. At the southwest entrance to the city, a new platea, punctuated by an honorific arch and an artificial cascade of water, was added to the urban layout. In the late antique period, the construction of new centers of religious worship may have changed patterns of use in various public spaces. Most significantly, the largest and grandest church was located not in the historical city center but at the western edge of town, close to the city wall. Ritual activity at this church must have drastically altered the use of the surrounding space, perhaps to the detriment of the public spaces in the center of the city. But in many places in the city there is clear evidence of the maintenance and refurbishment of ancient structures, which indicates a continuity of use in those parts of the urban fabric. To a Hellenistic Antiochene, late antique Pisidian Antioch would largely have seemed like a foreign city, but in certain places, such as the continually refurbished theater, he might have felt right at home.

3 Ruler Cult and Colonial Identity: The Imperial Sanctuary at Pisidian Antioch

Benjamin Rubin[1]

During the late 1st century BC, the city of Pisidian Antioch underwent a profound socio-cultural transformation. After nearly 250 years as a semiautonomous Greek polis under the Seleucid, Attalid, and Galatian kings, Antioch was officially annexed by the Roman Empire in 25 BC. As part of his campaign to pacify the recalcitrant region of Pisidia, the emperor Augustus dispatched a colony of Roman veterans from Legions V and VII to settle at Antioch.[2] These veterans were charged with the responsibility not only of guarding the strategic plain of lower Phrygia but also of spreading Roman culture and institutions to the "barbaric" mountain tribes of northern Pisidia.

The precise number of veterans that Augustus dispatched to Antioch is difficult to determine. Based on statistics provided by Strabo for other Augustan colonies, B. Levick estimates the number at around 3,000.[3] From the names attested on tombstones and other public monuments, it appears that the majority of the colonists hailed from towns in Etruria, Campania, and northern Italy, where they were recruited by Julius Caesar to fight in the civil wars.[4] They may also potentially have been recruited in Baetica, as H. Bru has recently argued.[5] Most of the colonists came from poor, non-aristocratic families, but when they arrived in Antioch, they established themselves as the new political elite, dissolving the preexisting social institutions of the former Greek polis. As was common in many Roman colonial situations, the incoming veterans allowed the indigenous Graeco-Phrygian population to live on in the colony, but only as *incolae*, or "resident foreigners," stripped of all citizenship rights they once possessed.[6] Only the very richest and

[1] A version of this chapter first appeared in Rubin 2008. The current text has been revised and updated to reflect scholarship published since then. I am grateful to Elaine Gazda and Diana Ng for their help in the editorial process. I would also like to thank Margaret Cool Root, Janet Richards, Carla Sinopoli, Marc Waelkens, Christopher Ratté, and Raymond Van Dam for reading and critiquing earlier drafts of this chapter.

[2] Ramsay 1916, 89–96; Levick 1967a, 58–62; Mitchell 1976, esp. 302–308.

[3] This is only a rough estimate. It is possible that the number could have reached as many as 5,000 to 6,000. See Levick 1967a, 95–96.

[4] On the ethnic origins of the colonists, see Levick 1967a, 56–67; Mitchell 1976, 302–308; Syme 1995, 234; Mitchell and Waelkens 1998, 9.

[5] See Bru 2009, esp. 264–269.

[6] The ethnic composition of Antioch's *incolae* is difficult to determine given a paucity of evidence, as is the size of the preexisting population. Several Neo-Phrygian inscriptions found in the territory of Antioch attest that Phrygian continued to be spoken alongside Greek and Latin (Brixhe and Drew-Bear 1978). Whether Phrygian was the primary language spoken at Antioch, however, remains unclear. Interestingly, there are also a large number of grave inscriptions written in Pisidian that come from the region just south of Antioch around Hoyran Gölü, a large lake situated between Phrygia and Pisidia (Brixhe and Gibson 1982). In order to supply and house the labor force necessary to build the monuments of the Augustan colony (i.e., the theater, bath house, water system, and imperial cult sanctuary), Antioch must have already had a significant preexisting local population prior to the arrival of the Roman colonists. Such an ambitious building program would have involved hundreds of both skilled and unskilled workers (i.e., architects, masons, quarrymen, brickmakers, carpenters, cart drivers, etc.), many of whom were undoubtedly former residents of

most powerful members of Antioch's indigenous Graeco-Phrygian elite were granted *civitas* status in the initial refoundation of the colony in 25 BC.[7] This small but highly influential group of indigenous Graeco-Phrygian elites played an important role in the colonial administration by acting as cultural liaisons between the Roman colonists and the local population at large. Over the course of the 1st century AD, the reconfiguration of Antioch's civil society became increasingly reflected in the city's built landscape. The old institutions of the former Greek polis disappeared as the Roman colonists transformed Antioch into what Levick has described as "a little Rome on the border of Phrygia and Pisidia."[8] At the heart of this new Rome, the Roman colonists worked together with their partners in the Graeco-Phrygian elite to construct a lavish sanctuary complex dedicated to the emperor Augustus. It is my contention that the collaboration between the Roman colonists and the Graeco-Phrygian elites took place during the initial design and planning phase of the imperial sanctuary. The physical construction of the sanctuary was undertaken by a team of local workmen, either from Antioch itself or some other nearby city, such as Sagalassos or Magnesia-on-the-Meander. Greek masons' marks discovered on the cornice blocks from the imperial temple apparently demonstrate that the masons were trained in Asia Minor.[9]

The imperial sanctuary featured a Corinthian prostyle temple ornately decorated with sculptures and reliefs celebrating the bounties of the Pax Augusta. This temple stood at the rear of a wide colonnaded plaza entered through a monumental propylon at the west end. Built in the form of a Roman triumphal arch, the propylon was adorned with sculptures commemorating the victories of Augustus on land and sea, as well as a Latin copy of the *Res Gestae*. This elaborate program of text and images made a compelling visual statement designed to articulate the legitimacy of Roman colonial rule at Antioch by emphasizing both the futility of resistance and the benefits of cooperation to the local population.

The communal rituals performed within the imperial sanctuary further reinforced the legitimacy of Roman colonial rule. On special holidays, such as the emperor's birthday, the people of Antioch gathered together to offer prayers and sacrifices on behalf of Augustus. The rituals associated with the imperial cult were relatively standardized throughout Asia Minor.[10] They included gladiatorial games, animal sacrifices, and public unveilings of the emperor's portrait known as the "imperial mysteries."[11] Since Antioch was located in the newly annexed province of Galatia, it seems likely that the entire population also had to swear a loyalty oath to Augustus and the imperial family.[12] By taking

the Hellenistic city. Based on modern population statistics, Mitchell estimates that at least 50,000 people lived in the city of Antioch and its surrounding *chora* during the Roman period. This would place the ratio of locals to colonists at around 15:1—assuming that some of the Roman colonists brought their families with them. See the discussion in Mitchell and Waelkens 1998, 3–10; Levick 1967a, 68–76.

[7] The number of indigenous Antiochenes on the citizenship rolls gradually rose over the course of the 1st century AD due to manumission, intermarriage, and citizenship grants to military veterans. See Levick 1967a, 75–76; Yegül 2000, 134.

[8] Levick 1967a, 78.

[9] See Robinson 1924a, 442. Mitchell and Waelkens's contention (1998, 115) that the masons' marks are written in Latin seems to be in error. I inspected the original squeezes in the archives

of the Kelsey Museum of Archaeology, and several sets of the masons' marks include characters that do not appear in the Latin alphabet, such as Δ and Θ.

[10] Price 1984, esp. 188–191 and 207–220.

[11] A priest known as a *heirophantes* or *sebastophantes* performed the unveiling of the emperor's portrait. See Pleket 1965; Bowersock 1982, 172–174; Price 1984, 190–191; Burrell 2004, 152. At Antioch, the priests of the imperial cult may have also performed some sort of ritual recitation of the *Res Gestae* since only a small proportion of the population could read Latin (Rubin 2008, 31).

[12] In 3 BC, "all the people" of Paphlagonia swore an oath to "Caesar Augustus and to his children and descendants." This oath was found recorded on a plaque in the city of Neapolis, formerly Phazimon. For discussion of this oath, commonly

part in these rituals, the people of Antioch recreated the ideal social hierarchy envisioned within the sculptural program of the imperial sanctuary. Every segment of Antioch's diverse population came together to give thanks for the blessings of Augustan rule. The communal nature of the imperial cult at Antioch engendered a shared sense of participation in the Roman project of empire building that served as the fundamental ideological basis for the structure of Antiochene society from the 1st century BC until the rise of Christianity in the 4th century AD.

We owe most of our knowledge about the Augustan imperial sanctuary to the excavations undertaken by W. M. Ramsay and D. M. Robinson and funded by the University of Michigan in 1924.[13] Over a period of just four months (May 1–August 11), the excavators succeeded in clearing almost the entire sanctuary. Stone robbers had carried off much of the original architecture, but enough survived for the excavators to prepare a conjectural reconstruction of the sanctuary with the help of architect F. J. Woodbridge. Over the years, scholars have come to accept most of Woodbridge's proposed restorations, but several key elements of the sanctuary's design and function still remain highly controversial. Perhaps the most controversial topic is the dedication of the imperial temple itself. Without the benefit of a dedicatory inscription, Robinson argued on iconographic grounds that the temple was dedicated to Augustus and the Anatolian god Mên Askaênos.[14] Few scholars, however, now accept the validity of this identification.[15]

In this chapter, I attempt to resolve some of the controversial issues surrounding the reconstruction and dedication of the imperial sanctuary. Based on a new inscription found in the Tiberia Platea, I argue that the imperial temple was not dedicated to Augustus or Mên but rather to Jupiter Optimus Maximus, Augustus, and the Genius of the Colony. If correct, this new dedicatory formula has profound implications for our understanding of how and why the imperial sanctuary was built and by whom. The three gods named in the inscription are clearly Roman in origin, but the tripartite structure of the dedication itself conforms to a local epigraphic formula popular in the Greek cities of Asia Minor. This usage strongly suggests that members of the local Greek-speaking elite from the former Hellenistic colony directly participated in the design, construction, and final dedication of the imperial temple. Such an interpretation runs counter to the prevailing model, which treats the imperial sanctuary as a monument built exclusively by and for the Roman colonists.[16] I argue instead that the construction of the imperial sanctuary was, in fact, a collaborative effort between the Roman colonists and local Graeco-Phrygian elites designed to unite Antioch's disparate colonial population into a single, unified and easily governable whole.

Reconstructing the Imperial Sanctuary

The architect F. J. Woodbridge produced the first reconstructions of the Augustan imperial sanctuary in 1924. Using all the available information from the excavations, he drafted a series of ground plans and elevation drawings depicting the sanctuary's central temple and propylon (figs. 3.1–2).[17]

known as the Gangra oath, see Lewis and Reinhold 1951, 634–635; Price 1984, 79; Mitchell 1993, 102. See also the oath "*pro salute Augusti*" found in Baetica, Spain (González 1988).

[13] W. M. Ramsay carried out a preliminary excavation of the imperial temple in 1913 and clandestinely in 1914. His excavations were halted by the outbreak of World War I and never fully published. In fact, the fullest account of the excavation appears in a three-page report prepared by T. Callander for F. W. Kelsey.

[14] Robinson 1926a, 12 and 18.

[15] The dedication of the temple is discussed at length below.

[16] This interpretative model is most fervently championed by S. Mitchell. See Mitchell 1993, 104; Mitchell and Waelkens 1998, 167. See also Magie 1950, 1:460, 2:1320; Levick 1968, 52; Burrell 2004, 170.

[17] The first frontal elevations of the temple and propylon

Fig. 3.1. Woodbridge's reconstruction drawing of the
Augusteum from 1924. Kelsey Museum Archives
AAR-2446.

Fig. 3.2. Woodbridge's reconstruction of the propylon (Arch of Augustus) from 1924. Kelsey Museum Archives AAR-2447.

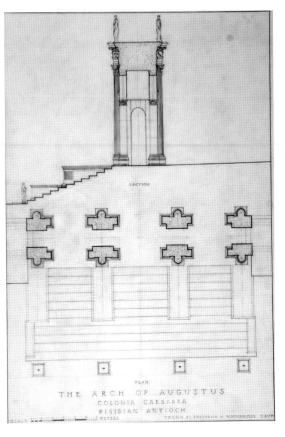

Fig. 3.3. Woodbridge's reconstruction drawing of the
Augusteum from 1971. Kelsey Museum Archives AAR-2385.

Fig. 3.4. Woodbridge's profile drawing of the propylon
from 1971. Kelsey Museum Archives AAR-2434.

These beautiful ink drawings and pencil sketches remain to this day the basis for all subsequent
reconstruction drawings. Nevertheless, over the past eighty years, other scholars have suggested
some substantial modifications. Even Woodbridge himself had second thoughts. In 1971 he prepared
a second series of renderings consistent with his revised vision of the imperial sanctuary. Among
these drawings was a new frontal elevation of the temple with a roof added to the rear portico, as
well as a profile view and revised frontal elevation of the propylon (figs. 3.3–5). These new drawings
add much to our understanding of the Augustan imperial sanctuary's overall architectural design
and figure prominently in my discussion below.[18]

During the 1980s and 1990s, a new generation of archaeologists and art historians began to take
interest in the Augustan imperial sanctuary. In 1983 K. Tuchelt became the first scholar to publish
a plan of the temple since the appearance of Woodbridge's initial drawings in 1926.[19] Mitchell and
Waelkens's architectural survey of the sanctuary area, carried out between 1982 and 1983, tends to
support the original reconstructions of the sanctuary proposed by Woodbridge and Robinson. They
disagree on only minor points, such as the number of columns in the *pronaos* of the temple and the
location of the *Res Gestae* on the propylon.[20]

appeared in Robinson 1926a, along with a detailed ground
plan of the site.

[18] For further discussion of these drawings, see Ossi
2005/2006; Ossi and Rubin 2007.

[19] Tuchelt 1983, esp. 503–506.

[20] See Mitchell and Waelkens 1998, 136 and 146.

Fig. 3.5 Woodbridge's reconstruction of the propylon (Arch of Augustus) from 1971. Kelsey Museum Archives AAR-2386.

The most recent attempt to reconstruct the architecture of the imperial sanctuary was under-taken by M. Taşlıalan, the former director of the Yalvaç Museum. Taşlıalan conducted a campaign to clean and conserve the long-neglected remains of the Augustan imperial sanctuary. Over the course of his work, Taşlıalan uncovered new details that had been missed in Ramsay and Robinson's large-scale clearing operations. For example, while cleaning the remains of the western portico, Taşlıalan discovered three rooms adjoining the propylon, which he suggests were offices for the use of cult personnel.[21] This is an important discovery, not only from the standpoint of accurate architectural reconstruction but also because it opens up a new debate concerning the role of the porticoes in the functionality of the sanctuary at large.

Based on the work of Woodbridge, Mitchell, Waelkens, and Taşlıalan, it is now possible to reconstruct the overall design and function of the Augustan imperial sanctuary. From its inception, the sanctuary consisted of three interrelated architectural elements: the temple, the colonnaded plaza, and the monumental propylon. Built high on the city's eastern acropolis, the sanctuary commanded a panoramic view over the surrounding landscape (see fig. 2.4).[22] The temple complex was approached from the *cardo maximus* through a wide colonnaded street known as the Tiberia Platea (fig. 3.6).[23]

[21] Taşlıalan 1993, 267.

[22] The so-called acropolis or southern acropolis is a large hill located ca. 300 m south of the imperial cult sanctuary. Today, the only visible remains on the southern acropolis belong to a late Roman fortification. It is unclear how the

space functioned earlier in the city's history. The southern acropolis is called the "acropolis" simply because it is the highest point in the city. See Mitchell and Waelkens 1998, 95.

[23] The name Tiberia Platea comes from a Latin grain edict discovered by Robinson near the base of the propylon

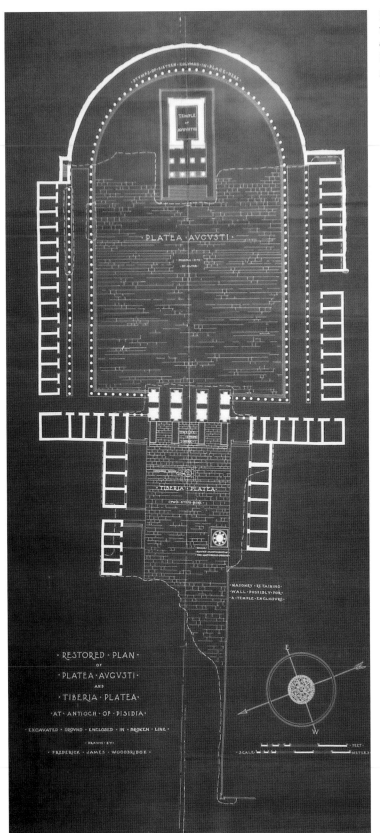

Fig. 3.6. Restored plan of the Augustan imperial cult sanctuary from 1924. Kelsey Museum Archives AAR-2444.

Fig. 3.7. Turkish workmen pose in the Tiberia Platea near the base of the propylon staircase in 1924.
Photo: Kelsey Museum Archives neg. no. 7.1116.

Although not technically part of the sacred precinct, this street effectively served as a forecourt to the imperial sanctuary.

The Tiberia Platea

In 1924 Ramsay and Robinson cleared the entire Tiberia Platea. From their photographs and descriptions, it is clear that they found the platea more or less as it was prior to the destruction of Antioch in the early 8th century AD (fig. 3.7).[24] According to Woodbridge's field notes, the Tiberia Platea measured approximately 85 m long and 22.9 m wide.[25] The entire surface of the street was paved with white limestone pavers, similar to the ashlars used in the walls of the temple and the propylon. A massive inscription found in situ near the steps of the propylon records that a certain T. Baebius Asiaticus paved the Tiberia Platea in fulfillment of his duties as municipal aedile (fig. 3.8).[26] It is not

staircase in 1924 (Robinson 1924b). The inscription was found in secondary use, which has caused many scholars to question whether it actually refers to the street where it was found. Nevertheless, most scholars continue to use the term out of convenience. For a discussion of the problems associated with the name, see Mitchell and Waelkens 1998, 219–220; Spanu 2002.

[24] According to the 9th-century historian Theophanes the Confessor, the Arab armies of Abbas sacked Antioch in AD 713 and enslaved all the citizens. This event clearly marked the end of Antioch's status as a major urban settlement. See

Ramsay 1924, 175; Demirer 2002, 37.

[25] Woodbridge's top plan of the Tiberia Platea should be trusted over H. Stierlin's plan, which erroneously depicts the Tiberia Platea as a walled, colonnaded square (ca. 65 m × 65 m) with three small entrances on the north, south, and west sides. See Stierlin 1986, 175. Stierlin's erroneous plan is also reproduced in Ortaç 2002, 178.

[26] In fact, Baebius actually takes credit for paving "III (*milia*) *pedum*" of road. Undoubtedly, this "three thousand feet" of road includes the Tiberia Platea, but what other areas of

Fig. 3.8. The inscription of T. Baebius Asiaticus.
Photo: Kelsey Museum Archives neg. no. 7.1121.

known when exactly Baebius held the aedileship, but most scholars date both his career and the pavement of the Tiberia Platea to the early 1st century AD.[27]

The Tiberia Platea must have fulfilled many of the same functions traditionally associated with a Greek agora or a Roman forum. The main street of the Tiberia Platea apparently acted as a public square, where the citizens of Antioch could socialize in the shadow of the imperial sanctuary. The numerous dice games and "two or three Latin crosses" found by Ramsay and Robinson scratched into the pavement testify to the long-term popularity of the square as a place for gaming and relaxation.[28] During their excavations in 1924, Ramsay and Robinson also found over a dozen shops, bars, and restaurants lining the north and south sides of the platea. The small finds recovered from these business establishments suggest that the area experienced an extended period of use stretching from the 1st century AD well into Byzantine times.[29]

The Augustan Propylon

At the western end of the Tiberia Platea stood a magnificent triple-arched propylon, which served as the main entrance to the Augustan imperial sanctuary (figs. 3.4–6).[30] The second triple-bayed

---

the city Baebius paved remains a subject of debate. Mitchell argues that Baebius must have paved the *cardo*, the *decumanus*, and the Tiberia Platea since altogether their lengths add up to about 2,973 feet. While this is one possible scenario, it seems rather too convenient that the only three excavated streets just happen to be those paved by Baebius. Robinson 1926b, 235; Mitchell and Waelkens 1998, 221.

[27] Either in the later reign of the emperor Augustus or in that of Tiberius. Mitchell and Waelkens 1998, 221.

[28] Robinson 1924a, 441.

[29] In the Journal of Excavations, Robinson records a number of Byzantine and early Romans coins, as well as copious amounts of "iridescent" glassware, pottery, oil lamps, and small bronze artifacts ranging in date from about the 1st to

8th century AD. Although Robinson kept rather poor notes concerning small artifacts, it is still possible to check his initial observations by consulting photographs in the Kelsey Museum Archives. See, for instance, Kelsey photo nos. 7.1198 (glass fragments) and 7.1194 (bronze items). The discovery of a silver drachma of Alexander the Great and a "Ptolemaic coin with an eagle" suggests that the Tiberia Platea may have served as an agora or shopping area even before the foundation of the Augustan colony. See the entry for May 18 in Robinson's Journal of Excavations. For further discussion of the Tiberia Platea, see the note at the end of this chapter.

[30] Woodbridge reconstructs the propylon as ca. 10 m tall or 12 m with the attic sculptures. Taşlıalan's reconstruction is slightly shorter, ca. 9 m tall or 11 m with attic sculptures (Taşlıalan 1994, 264–265). Woodbridge's reconstruction is better proportioned and should be preferred over Taşlıalan's.

arch built in Asia Minor, the Augustan propylon was modeled directly on the design of honorific arches in Rome and the Western empire.[31] An inscription emblazoned in bronze letters across the architrave announced that the propylon was dedicated to the emperor Augustus in 2 BC, the year in which he received the title *pater patriae*, "Father of the Country."[32] In 1924 Woodbridge proposed the first conjectural reconstruction of the propylon's structural layout and sculptural display, which is still accepted by most scholars today (see fig. 3.2).[33] According to Woodbridge's reconstruction, the propylon consisted of three archways and stood atop a twelve-step staircase linking the Tiberia Platea with the sacred precinct above. Both the interior and exterior faces of the propylon were adorned with relief sculptures that celebrated the victories of Augustus on land and sea. Along the attic ran a frieze of weapons and trophies, as well as a depiction of Augustus's conception sign, the capricorn (fig. 3.9). While not a symbol of victory in itself, this capricorn was probably intended to signify that Augustus's rise to power was preordained in the stars.[34] The arch spandrels on both the interior and exterior of the propylon were decorated with reliefs depicting victories, winged *genii*, and captive barbarians (figs. 3.10–12), further reinforcing the triumphal theme.[35]

A. Ossi has argued that designers of the Augustan propylon intentionally used multivalent imagery in order to appeal to Antioch's diverse multicultural population.[36] This theory is strongly supported by reliefs, such as the depiction of the local god, Mên Askaênos (fig. 3.13).[37] Mên appears in the attic frieze of the propylon dressed as a youthful warrior wearing a horned helmet and a sword scabbard slung across his chest.[38] The iconography of this figure reinforces the martial theme of the Augustan arch. Moreover, its presence also creates a symbolic link between Augustus and the city's traditional tutelary deity, Mên Askaênos.[39] Such a connection was undoubtedly orchestrated to make Roman rule seem more palatable to Antioch's resident *incolae*.

On the attic of the propylon were a series of statues, each around 2 m tall, which depicted the goddess Victoria, Augustus, and other members of the imperial family.[40] The statues have survived in only fragmentary form, so it is difficult to propose a reliable reconstruction of the overall program. Nevertheless, one statue deserves particular mention. In 1924 Robinson found the lower half of a draped male figure with remnants of a barbarian captive kneeling at his feet (fig. 3.14).[41] The mutilated condition

[31] The first triple-bayed arch built in Asia Minor was the Agora Gate at Ephesos dedicated by Mazaeus and Mithridates in 4/3 BC. Alzinger 1974, 9–16.

[32] Mitchell and Waelkens 1998, 147.

[33] See Robinson 1926a, 21.

[34] The capricorn is one of the many symbols commonly associated with Augustus, particularly on gems and intaglios. Perhaps the most famous example occurs in the *Gemma Augustea*, where the mythical beast is depicted superimposed over the sun or star, which hovers above Augustus's head. For the importance of astrology in Augustan ideology, see Barton 1995; Zanker 1988, 84 and 231; Ossi 2009, 73.

[35] For further discussion of the identification and meaning of the spandrel figures, see Rose 2005, 55; Rubin 2008, 39–42; Ossi 2009, 76–84.

[36] Ossi 2009, esp. 76–87.

[37] K. Tuchelt discovered the frieze block depicting Mên in the Konya Museum. It has since been returned to Yalvaç. See Tuchelt 1983, 519; Rubin 2008, 71; Ossi 2009, 85–87.

[38] For further discussion of the iconography of Mên, see Ossi 2009, 85–86.

[39] Ossi 2009, 87.

[40] In addition to the sculptures published by Robinson, there is also a badly broken female head from the Tiberia Platea, which may belong to the propylon group. The right rear portion of the head survives, showing a smooth neck and bound up hair (H. 0.25, W. 0.19, D. 0.18). See the May 13 entry in the Journal of Excavations and Kelsey photograph no. KR009.06. For other sculptures, see Robinson 1926a, 41–45; 1926c; 1928.

[41] Robinson 1926a, 42.

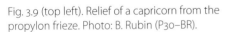

Fig. 3.12 (middle right).
Spandrel relief depicting a
nude captive.
Photo: B. Rubin.

Fig. 3.13 (bottom left). Relief
depicting Mên Askaênos
from the attic of the
propylon (2006).
Photo: B. Rubin.

Fig. 3.14 (bottom right).
Emperor with captive from
the attic of the propylon.
Photo: Kelsey Museum
Archives neg. no. 7.1434.

Fig. 3.9 (top left). Relief of a capricorn from the
propylon frieze. Photo: B. Rubin (P30–BR).

Fig. 3.10 (top right). Spandrel relief of Victory.
Photo: Kelsey Museum Archives neg. no.
7.1139.

Fig. 3.11 (middle left). Spandrel reliefs
depicting winged *genii*. Photo: B. Rubin
(P43–BR).

of the statue prevents certain identification, but the statue may well depict Augustus or some other male member of the imperial family.[42] By the reign of Augustus, images of this type were relatively common in the Western empire but rare in the East.[43] If the statue at Antioch indeed depicts an emperor, it would be one of the earliest known manifestations of the emperor-with-captive motif in the monumental art of Asia Minor.[44] Such a dramatic presentation of the emperor on the attic of the propylon sent a clear message to Antioch's resident *incolae*: Roman rule is inevitable and resistance futile.

This message was reiterated by the Latin copy of the *Res Gestae*, which was inscribed at eye level on the propylon.[45] The inscription's fragmentary condition makes it difficult to reconstruct its original placement on the propylon.[46] Woodbridge and Robinson propose the most plausible reconstruction of the *Res Gestae* inscribed on four monumental pedestals built into the propylon's staircase (see fig. 3.5).[47] Mounted on the staircase of the propylon, the *Res Gestae* would have been clearly visible to all those who entered the imperial sanctuary.

The Colonnaded Plaza

The propylon opened eastward onto a wide colonnaded plaza, commonly known today as the Augusta Platea (figs. 3.6 and 3.15).[48] The Antiochenes carved this entire plaza—an area of over 6,000 m²—from

[42] Graeco-Roman gods are rarely represented with bound captives at their feet. The main exceptions to this rule are Victory and Roma, who are often portrayed in a similar manner to the emperor. See, for instance, the reliefs from the Sebasteion at Aphrodisias (Smith 1987, pl. iv; Rose 2005, 27). There are also a few instances of other gods depicted with captives at their feet, such as the reliefs of Athena and Ares on the loggia of the *bouleuterion* at Sagalassos (Waelkens 1993, 37).

[43] As early as the 70s BC, coins in Italy began to depict Roman governors standing over personifications of conquered provinces. See Kuttner 1995, 76–79.

[44] Given Antioch's proximity to Aphrodisias, it is worth considering whether this statue may have served as a model for images like the famous relief of Nero grasping a captive Armenia at the Sebasteion. See Smith 1987, 117.

[45] The *Res Gestae* (literally, "The Things Accomplished") is an autobiographical text composed by the emperor Augustus prior to his death in AD 14, which details his many accomplishments, including his settlement of the Pisidian colonies (*Res Gestae* 28.1). According to the document's preface, the *Res Gestae* was originally intended to appear on two bronze columns in front of Augustus's mausoleum, but the only three surviving copies of the inscription come from imperial cult monuments in Ankara, Pisidian Antioch, and Pisidian Apollonia. See Brunt and Moore 1967, 2; Guven 1998, 32–37; Rubin 2008, 117–135; Cooley 2009, 6–18.

[46] In 1913 and 1924 Ramsay and Robinson unearthed hundreds of small fragments of the *Res Gestae*, which had been smashed and scattered throughout the Tiberia Platea (Rob-

inson 1926e, 2; Ramsay 1926, 108–113). Hammer and chisel marks on the existing fragments suggest that the *Res Gestae* was intentionally destroyed sometime in late antiquity. Robinson argues that Christian iconoclasts smashed the *Res Gestae* in the 4th or 5th century AD (Robinson 1926b, 2). However, it is also possible that the Arabs destroyed the inscription during the invasion of AD 713.

[47] See Robinson 1926b, 23. It is unclear why Tuchelt and Taşlıalan chose to reconstruct the propylon without pedestals (Tuchelt 1983, 503; Taşlıalan 1995, 256, 264–265). The pedestals—or "profile bases," as Robinson calls them—appear in multiple photographs from the 1924 excavations now housed in the Kelsey Museum Archives (e.g., KR041.11, KR042.01). Ramsay and von Premerstein argue that the *Res Gestae* was carved on the interior of the propylon's central arch bays. This theory has since been accepted by a number of other scholars. See Ramsay and von Premerstein 1927, 13–16; Mitchell and Waelkens 1998, 146; Roehmer 1997, 69; Taşlıalan 1994, 251–253; Tuchelt 1983, 514. However, this reconstruction is only possible if the propylon had monolithic piers wide enough to display the entire *Res Gestae*, which is far from certain. Woodbridge and Robinson reconstruct the propylon with a small transverse passageway running north-south bisecting the piers (see fig. 3.4). The existence of this passageway is attested by several architectural fragments, including an arched block, which could have come only from the roof of the passageway. The Agora Gate at Ephesos also features a similar transverse passageway. See Alzinger 1974, 9–16; Ortaç 2002, 175–177. Ossi (2009) believes that the archaeological evidence for the Augustan propylon at Antioch is inconclusive regarding the precise location of the *Res Gestae*.

[48] While scholars often refer to the plaza as the Augusta

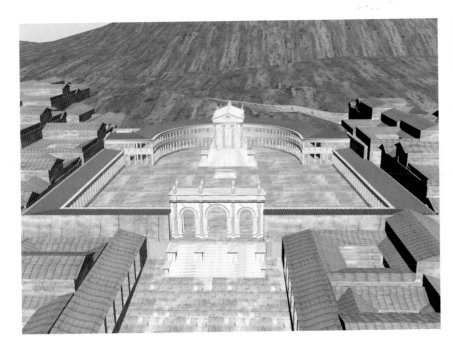

Fig. 3.15. Digital reconstruction of the Augustan imperial cult sanctuary; aerial view of the propylon, the Augusta Platea, and the imperial temple. Digital model: J. M. Harrington.

the living rock of the eastern acropolis. At the front of the plaza was a rectangular courtyard, ca. 83 m × 66 m, designed to house the rituals and sacrifices of the Roman imperial cult. The courtyard was paved with white limestone pavers and enclosed on three sides (north, south, and west) by a single-storied Doric portico, ca. 4 m tall and 6 m deep.[49] Along the rear wall of the western portico was a series of small rooms that faced eastward onto the Augusta Platea.[50] The precise function of these rooms is unknown; however, it seems likely that they were used as some combination of workshops, storerooms, and offices for high-ranking cult personnel.

The imperial temple stood at the rear of the plaza, at the center of a two-story semicircular portico. The rear wall of the hemicycle still stands to a height of ca. 6.4 m.[51] The porticoes that enclosed the Augusta Platea served a variety of architectural functions. On festival days, crowds of worshippers

Platea, it is unlikely that the plaza was ever known by that name in antiquity. The title Augusta Platea derives from a decontextualized honorific inscription from Hisarardı, which Ramsay (1916, 106) erroneously linked to the imperial plaza. See Ossi and Harrington, chap. 2, n. 34 for an alternative interpretation.

[49] Taşlıalan 1995, 254.

[50] In 1924 the Michigan team discovered the remains of a single room attached to the western portico. According to Woodbridge's plan, this room was located approximately 3 m from the northernmost propylon pier (see fig. 3.6). The Michigan team also excavated the foundation of a partial room (i.e., a single interior wall) 3 m south of the propylon. Taşlıalan later excavated an additional three rooms north of the propylon. These rooms are clearly illustrated in Taşlıalan's preliminary plan of the sanctuary but strangely do not ap-

pear in his final plan, which was published only a year later (Taşlıalan 1993, 272; 1994, 254). Taşlıalan identifies all of the rooms along the western portico as offices for cult personnel (Taşlıalan 1993, 267). Although possible, it seems unlikely that such a large block of rooms in a multifunctional space such as the Augusta Platea would only have a single use. These rooms may have also functioned as archives for storing public documents or perhaps even as ritual dining rooms. On the use of imperial cult temples as document archives, see Fayer 1976, 110–111; Burrell 2004, 19.

[51] The rear wall of the hemicycle has traditionally been represented as a true semicircle. This is not the case, however. The wall is, in fact, a polygon with ten irregularly shaped facets, which is clearly illustrated in the plan commissioned by J. Humphrey. Undoubtedly, these facets are the result of the rock-cutting technique employed by the craftsmen who carved the hemicycle.

would have gathered in the porticoes while they waited to take part in processions and animal sacrifices on behalf of the Roman emperor. The porticoes provided these worshippers with shade from the sun and shelter from inclement weather conditions.[52] During annual festivals of the Roman imperial cult, throngs of pilgrims poured into Antioch from the surrounding countryside, many of whom had no place to stay but the imperial sanctuary itself.[53] By providing these pilgrims with free temporary lodging, the porticoes along the Augusta Platea ensured that even the poorest members of Antiochene society had access to the rituals and sacrifices of the Roman imperial cult. The political significance of this access should not be underestimated. Without the tacit acceptance of local villagers, the Roman colonists who settled at Antioch faced the constant threat of a popular uprising. Making it possible for local villagers to participate in the Roman imperial cult inspired a sense of camaraderie, which helped alleviate tension that may have developed between the town and countryside.

In addition, the wealthiest members of Antiochene society used the porticoes around the Augusta Platea as a conspicuous location in which to erect honorific statues of the Roman emperor and his family. In 1924, the excavators found dozens of fragments of imperial portrait statues scattered throughout the Augusta Platea.[54] These statues probably stood in several locations inside the imperial sanctuary, including the courtyard and porticoes of the Augusta Platea,[55] as well as the cella of the imperial temple itself.[56] We can add to this group the head of the emperor Marcus Aurelius discovered by Taşlıalan among the ruins of the western portico in 1991 (fig. 3.16).[57] The discovery of this head is significant because it suggests that the Antiochenes continued to update the sculptural program of the imperial sanctuary well into the late 2nd century AD. By erecting imperial portrait statues in the Augusta Platea, powerful members of Antioch's urban elite publicly affirmed their loyalty to the Roman emperor while simultaneously advertising their own personal wealth and resources to

[52] Providing shelter to pilgrims was the most basic function of all *stoas* in Greek sanctuaries. See Coulton 1976, 9–12.

[53] As an assize center, Antioch served as the administrative capital of a large territory, first in the province of Galatia and later in the province of Pisidia. During annual festivals of the imperial cult, people from the surrounding territory were lured by the promise of free food and entertainment. The majority of these pilgrims were poor farmers, who lacked the resources to pay for proper lodging. See Price 1984, 83–86 and 101–114; Mitchell 1993, 102.

[54] For a discussion of the sculpture from the imperial sanctuary, see Robinson 1926a, 41–45 and 69. The excavators also found numerous fragments, which they did not publish—most notably, the leg of a colossal male figure, probably an emperor. See the "Sculpture Inventory" in Robinson's excavation journal. Ramsay's sculptural finds from 1913 were inventoried by Callander, with the latest correction done in 1925, in a list now in the Bentley Historical Library. Robinson published a single photograph showing the sculptural fragment that he deemed most interesting from the 1913 campaign (Robinson 1926a, 68, fig. 127). The photo depicts a hodgepodge of portrait and other heads along with architectural fragments recovered from three separate locations: the Augusteum, the sanctuary of Mên, and an "exploratory" trench dug near the proscenium of the theater. Many of

the heads seem to depict members of the Julio-Claudian dynasty, which suggests that they may have come from the Augusteum, but there is no way to know for certain.

[55] It was common practice throughout the Roman world to erect large statuary groups in the forecourts of imperial cult temples. See, for example, the temples at Apollonia (*MAMA* 4:48–50), Sagalassos (Talloen and Waelkens 2005, 236), and Lepcis Magna (Rose 1997, 184–185). The hemicycles of the Forum of Augustus in Rome are also known to have housed sculpture galleries, which contained statues depicting the illustrious ancestors of the emperor Augustus (Zanker 1968, 14 ff.). It is tempting to reconstruct a similar gallery in the hemicycle of the imperial sanctuary at Antioch.

[56] After Augustus's death in AD 14, it seems likely that the Antiochenes began to add new statues to the cella of the imperial temple in order to reflect contemporary political developments in Rome. This phenomenon is well attested at a number of Augustea across the Roman Empire, including those at Bubon (İnan 1993; Rose 1997, 171), Cestros (Højte 2005, 342), Eretria (Schmid 2001, 123–134), Lucus Feroniae (Moretti 1985; Rose 1997, 93), and Narona (Marin 2001, 97–112; Marin and Vickers 2004, 70–166).

[57] Taşlıalan 1993, 268, fig. 21.

Fig. 3.16. Portrait head of Marcus Aurelius found in the Augusta Platea (2006). Photo: B. Rubin.

their fellow Antiochenes. It was particularly important to add new statues to the imperial sanctuary upon the ascension of each new emperor. Otherwise, the Antiochenes risked offending the incoming emperor and losing the lucrative monetary and social benefits of imperial patronage.

From a visual perspective, the porticoes along the Augusta Platea served as a dramatic architectural frame for viewing the imperial temple. As Mitchell and Waelkens have observed, the semicircular arrangement of columns along the rear wall of the plaza generated an impressive "optical effect" that made the whole sanctuary appear larger than it really was.[58] Moreover, the linear progression of columns along the outer edge of the sanctuary directed the viewer's eyes toward a central focal point at the back of the temple's cella—an effect that seems designed to draw attention to the colossal cult statue or statues housed within.

By the late 1st century BC, colonnaded *temenos* enclosures of this kind had become a regular part of sanctuaries across the Roman Empire. Nevertheless, scholars have persistently tried to trace the design of the imperial sanctuary back to a specific Greek or Roman precedent. For example, Mitchell and Waelkens have argued that the axial plan of the imperial sanctuary directly recalls the design of the Forum of Augustus in Rome.[59] While there are indeed close parallels between these two monuments, it is misleading to imply that axial planning was somehow a distinctive feature of Roman architecture. A number of Hellenistic sanctuaries in Asia Minor also incorporated axially aligned *temenos* enclosures similar to the one at Antioch—most notably the Sanctuary of Artemis at Magnesia-on-the-Meander, Antioch's mother city.[60] The only architectural element of the imperial sanctuary that could be described as "Roman" is the semicircular portico behind the temple.

[58] Mitchell and Waelkens 1998, 164.

[59] They also cite the forum in Nîmes, which housed the Maison Carée, as another close parallel. See Mitchell and Waelkens 1998, 160. I would add the Forum Iulium to the list of potential Roman architectural precedents for the layout of the Augustan imperial sanctuary. Not only did the Forum Iulium have an axial plan, but it also had side rooms built into the surrounding porticoes, much like the imperial sanctuary at Antioch. For a reconstructed plan of the Forum Iulium, see Ulrich 1993, 52.

[60] Hoepfner 1990, 18–20; Bingöl 1998, 23. Close comparanda can also be found at Kos, Teos, Pergamon, Priene, Assos, and, of course, at Antioch itself at the extramural sanctuary of Mên. See Pollitt 1986, 232–233; Uz 1990, 52; Bohtz 1981, 3; Bayhan 2005, 27–28; Bacon, Clark, and Koldewey 1902, 75–108. In Anatolia, temples with accompanying colonnades even predate the classical and Hellenistic periods. See, for instance, the Phrygian temple of Cybele at Midas City, which dates somewhere between the 8th and 6th century BC (Berndt 2002, 8–14). For the development of the Greek *stoa* in the Hellenistic period more generally, see Lehmann 1954; Coulton 1976, 168–183.

Fig. 3.17. Foundation of the Augusteum and the surrounding semicircular portico (2005). Photo: B. Rubin.

As Tuchelt has pointed out, semicircular porticoes first began to appear in Roman Italy during the late 2nd century BC, after which they soon became a standard element in the Roman architectural repertoire.[61] Notably, the semicircular portico in the imperial sanctuary at Antioch is the first of its kind ever built in Asia Minor.[62] This fact strongly suggests that Roman architects participated in the design and construction of the imperial sanctuary. However, it is difficult to know whether the local Graeco-Phrygian population would have recognized the origin or novelty of the semicircular portico, especially since it was so close in form and concept to the rectilinear porticoes that commonly appeared in Hellenistic sanctuaries throughout Asia Minor.

The Imperial Cult Temple

The temple is by far the best studied of all the monuments in the imperial sanctuary. Ramsay and Robinson excavated the temple over the course of three field seasons between 1913 and 1924. During their excavations, they recovered enough of the temple's original architecture to propose a reliable reconstruction (see fig. 3.1). Like most Augustea, the temple at Antioch was constructed in typical Roman fashion: Corinthian, prostyle, with four columns in the front row and two in the rear, resting on a high podium and monumental staircase.[63] The rock-cut foundation of the temple, which still remains largely intact, measures ca. 24.10 m long × 15.24 m wide × 3.5 m high (fig. 3.17).[64] Based on the surviving architectural fragments, Mitchell and Waelkens estimate that the temple stood to

[61] Tuchelt 1983, 509–511.

[62] Another semicircular portico does not appear in Asia Minor until the construction of the Baths of Capito in Miletus under the reign of the emperor Claudius (AD 41–54). See Tuchelt 1983, 509–510.

[63] On the general design of Augustan-era imperial cult temples, see Hänlein-Schäfer 1985, 39–78; Zanker 1988, 311–312. Scholars often compare the architecture of the imperial temple at Antioch to Western Augustea, such as those at Pola and Magalensberg. While these comparisons are apt, we should also take into account more local architectural antecedents. As Price has pointed out, there is nothing in-

trinsically "Roman" about the design of the imperial temple at Antioch (Price 1984, 168). Prostyle temples first appeared in the Greek world during the late classical period (Plommer 1954, 158–159). Although most featured a low, three-step stylobate, there are some examples with impressive monumental staircases and elevated podia—e.g., the temple of Dionysos at Pergamon (Radt 1999, 189–192). It is interesting to note that the podium of the imperial cult temple at Antioch also bears a certain resemblance to the rock-cut podia of the Lycian temple tombs, such as the Heroon of Perikle at Limyra (Borchhardt 1976, 112–114).

[64] Taşlıalan 1994, 246.

Fig. 3.18. Acanthus frieze from the cella of the Augusteum. Kelsey Museum Archives neg. no. 7.1601.

Fig. 3.20. West central akroterion with acanthus goddess. Kelsey Museum Archives neg. no. 7.1665.

Fig. 3.19 . Bucranium frieze from the cella of the Augusteum. Kelsey Museum Archives neg. no. 5.0250.

a total elevation of approximately 17–18 m, while Woodbridge favors a slightly lower elevation of approximately 14–15 m (see fig. 3.3).[65]

The temple of Augustus was lavishly decorated with sculptures and reliefs celebrating the Pax Augusta. Along the exterior cella wall was an unusual double frieze of acanthus scrolls and poppy flowers reminiscent of the vegetal imagery on the Ara Pacis in Rome (fig. 3.18).[66] A pedimental frieze of bucrania and garlands bearing local fruits, such as cherries and pomegranates, further emphasized the theme of peace and prosperity (fig. 3.19).[67] Mounted to the roof of the temple was a set of six white marble akroteria. The two central akroteria (ca. 1.8 m high) depicted a goddess rising up from a bundle of lush acanthus leaves and scrolls (fig. 3.20). On her head, she wore an elaborate crown—a high vertical *polos* surmounted by disk, which may have symbolized either the sun or moon.[68] The identity of this goddess is highly controversial, but she is probably best identified as

[65] Mitchell and Waelkens 1998, 138.

[66] Robinson 1926a, 12; Mitchell and Waelkens, 1998, 165; *contra* Taşlıalan (1994, 260–262), who favors a single block frieze.

[67] F. Rumscheid has suggested that the bucranium frieze normally associated with the imperial temple was, in fact, part of a late Flavian or early Trajanic altar erected somewhere in the Augusta Platea. Few scholars would agree, however, with either Rumscheid's proposed dating or identification of the frieze. See Rumscheid 1994, 2:5. For a more conventional interpretation of the frieze, see Robinson 1926a, 11–12;

Mitchell and Walkens 1998, 167.

[68] The design of the goddess's crown is similar to those worn by Egyptian deities, such as Isis and Hathor (e.g., Tiradritti 2000, 356 and 363). This may be intended as a subtle allusion to Octavian's victory over Antony and Cleopatra at the battle of Actium in 31 BC. For a discussion of Egyptianizing motifs in Augustan art, see Zanker 1988, 144–145; Swetnam-Burland 2010. Robinson argues the disk on the goddess's crown may also be interpreted as a *clipeus* similar to the one held by Victoria on the column of Trajan in Rome (Robinson 1926a, 18).

the Greek goddess Artemis.[69] Artemis would have made a fitting addition to the decorative program of the imperial temple given that she was both the protector of Antioch's mother city, Magnesia-on-the-Meander, as well as the sister of Apollo, Augustus's patron deity.

The Question of the Temple's Dedication

Scholars have long debated about the dedication of the imperial temple at Antioch. During the 19th century, the first visitors to the site identified the temple as the intramural shrine to Mên Askaênos, which Strabo mentions in his brief description of Antioch (*Geography* 12.3.31).[70] But as Ramsay's excavations commenced in 1913, serious doubts began to emerge. The discovery of the *Res Gestae* and the characteristically Roman design of the imperial temple both seemed incongruous with a dedication to the local Anatolian god, Mên Askaênos. Based on this new evidence, Callander argued for the first time that the temple was an Augusteum, whereas Ramsay vacillated between positions, sometimes identifying the temple as an Augusteum, other times as a shrine to Mên.[71]

As late as 1924, Ramsay and Robinson still hoped to find a dedicatory inscription, which would name the temple's dedicatee and bring an end to the ongoing debate, but none ever surfaced. Without the benefit of dedicatory inscription, scholars have had to rely on other methods of identification, such as architecture and iconography. As a result, a number of conflicting identification schemes have emerged, some more plausible than others.[72] I argue— based on the extant archaeological evidence—that the imperial temple was not dedicated to Mên but, rather, bore a tripartite dedication to Augustus, Jupiter Optimus Maximus, and the Genius of Colonia Caesarea Antiocheia, and that this tripartite dedication not only reflected but also reinforced the newly established colonial hierarchy at Pisidian Antioch. By worshipping a triad of gods closely associated with the ethos of Roman imperialism, the people of Antioch actively constructed a new civic identity predicated upon loyalty to the imperial family and a fundamental belief in the legitimacy of Roman colonial rule.

The arguments in favor of Augustus as the dedicatee of the imperial temple are relatively straightforward. We know that the propylon of the imperial sanctuary was dedicated to Augustus in the year 2

[69] Acanthus figures appear in a number of Hellenistic architectural contexts, e.g., the temple of Artemis at Magnesia and the tomb at Sveshtari in Bulgaria (Pfrommer 1990, 73–76; Webb 1996, 32–33). These figures are all thought to represent the goddess Artemis. Thus the same identification seems warranted here. Other possible identifications include Cybele (Tuchelt 1983, 516), Pax, Tellus, Victoria, and Roma (Robinson 1926a, 18). The ambiguous nature of the acanthus goddess's iconography prevents a single, definitive identification. This was likely intentional. The designers of the Augustan imperial sanctuary consistently relied on multivalent imagery to communicate their message effectively to a diverse colonial audience.

[70] Arundell 1834, 1:275; Hamilton 1842, 1:474.

[71] When he first arrived at Antioch, Ramsay did not even believe the imperial sanctuary was a temple but instead suggested it was an odeon or theater. In 1916, he wrote that he agreed with Callander that the temple was an Augusteum. By 1926, his opinion had changed yet again, and he argued that the priesthood of Augustus was nothing more than "the

survival of the old priesthood of Mên-Mannes, Romanized and imperialized." Later that same year he suggested that the temple dated to 189 BC and was dedicated to Mên. Finally, in 1930, he declared the temple was not Hellenistic but rather high Roman, built in the 2nd century AD. See Ramsay 1916, 107–108; 1924, 201; 1926, 111; 1930, 277. See also Callander's unpublished report of the 1913 excavations in the Kelsey Museum Archives.

[72] Tuchelt favors a dedication to Mên and Cybele (Tuchelt 1983, 515–522). Mitchell and Waelkens, Mellor, Güven and Demirer favor a dedication to Augustus (Mitchell and Waelkens 1998, 160; Mellor 1975, 144–145; Güven 1998, 35; Demirer 2002, 82). Robinson, Hänlein-Schäfer, and Taşlıalan identify the temple as an Augusteum but leave open the possibility of a joint dedication with Mên or Cybele (Robinson 1926a, 12 and 18; Hänlein-Schäfer 1985, 196; Taşlıalan 1995, 248). Levick and Magie identify the temple as a Capitolium (Levick 1968, 52; Magie 1950, 1:460, 2:1320). B. Burrell alone argues that the temple was dedicated to Julius Caesar (Burrell 2004, 170). I discuss the merits of these various theories at some length in Rubin 2008, 57–71.

BC.[73] This strongly suggests that the accompanying temple was also dedicated to Augustus or to a group of gods that included Augustus, such as the Dei Augusti.[74] As we have seen, the decoration of the imperial sanctuary supports this conclusion. The propylon was adorned with sculptures celebrating Augustus's victories on land and sea, as well as a Latin copy of the *Res Gestae*. It is significant for the purposes of identification that the only two other extant copies of the *Res Gestae* both come from Augustea in the province of Galatia: a Greek copy from the imperial *"temenos"* at Apollonia and a bilingual copy from the temple of Roma and Augustus at Ankara.[75] The imperial temple itself, as Mitchell and Waelkens have noted, also conformed to the standard Roman model used for Augustea.[76] The Corinthian, prostyle design testified to the grandeur and resources of the Roman Empire, while the lush acanthus frieze symbolized the copious bounties of the Augustan Peace.[77] *In toto*, this architectural evidence points directly at Augustus as the primary dedicatee of the imperial temple.

The cult of Augustus at Pisidian Antioch is further attested by an honorific inscription found reused in the wall of a house in modern Yalvaç. Although the inscription is highly fragmentary, the sixth line clearly mentions the title "Sacer(dos) Aug(usti)" or "Priest of Augustus."[78] The precise wording of the inscription is significant because it suggests that the priesthood was dedicated to the living emperor Augustus rather than the deceased emperor, in which case we would expect the title "Sacerdos Divi Augusti."[79] This synchronizes well with the date of the propylon dedication (2 BC), as well as the architectural dating of the temple, which is routinely assigned on stylistic grounds to the late Augustan period.[80]

Based on the architectural and epigraphic evidence, there is little reason to doubt that the imperial temple at Antioch was dedicated to the emperor Augustus prior to his death in AD 14. It is unlikely, however, that the temple was dedicated exclusively to Augustus given that the vast majority of Augustea in Asia Minor featured bi- or multi-partite dedications.[81] As Dio Cassius records (51.20.6–9), the tradition of honoring multiple dedicatees at imperial cult temples can be traced back to Augustus's proclamation

[73] Mitchell and Waelkens 1998, 147.

[74] The propylon of a Graeco-Roman sanctuary was normally dedicated to the same god (or gods) as the accompanying temple, but there were exceptions. For instance, at Aphrodisias, the propylon of the Sebasteion was dedicated to "Aphrodite, the *Theoi Sebastoi* and the *Demos*," while the temple itself was dedicated more specifically to "Tiberius and Livia (and probably also Aphrodite, Augustus and the *Demos*)." See Reynolds 1986, 114; 1995, 45; Smith 1987, 90; 1988, 51.

[75] The exact location of the fragmentary copy of the *Res Gestae* at Apollonia is unclear. The inscription is presumed to come from a statue base, which was displayed in the *"temenos"* of the Theoi Sebastoi. *MAMA* 4:48-50; Price 1984, 270.

[76] Mitchell and Waelkens 1998, 165.

[77] Robinson 1926a, 12; Mitchell and Waelkens 1998, 165.

[78] *CIL* 3.6848; Ramsay 1924, 179; Levick 1967a, 88. Unfortunately, the name of the priest was not preserved. There are also two extant inscriptions that attest to the existence of a priesthood of Dea Iulia Augusta, the wife of the emperor

Augustus. Ramsay and Levick assign the foundation of Livia's cult to the reign of the emperor Claudius (ca. AD 42), but the lack of "Diva" in her title suggests otherwise. The description of Livia as "Dea Iulia Augusta" rather than "Diva Augusta" is, in fact, consistent with a cult established during Livia's lifetime. See Grether 1946, esp. 228–232 and Fishwick 1970, 81 *contra* Ramsay 1939, 206; Levick and Jameson 1964, 98–99; Levick 1967a, 88 and 112.

[79] For the Latin nomenclature of imperial cult priests, see Gradel 2002, 85–91.

[80] Robinson 1926a, 11; Wiegand 1937, 420–421; Alzinger 1974, 125–126; Tuchelt 1983, 508–509; Waelkens 1986, 48–51; Mitchell and Waelkens 1998, 166–167; Waelkens et al. 2000, 580–582.

[81] The goddess Roma often drops out of epigraphic and numismatic references to *naoi* and priesthoods of Roma and Augustus. We should read this as nothing more than a space-saving abbreviation. See, for instance, the epigraphically attested *"naos* of Augustus" at Mytilene (Hänlein-Schäfer 1985, 179–180). For a discussion of numismatic abbreviation and the temple of Augustus at Nicomedia, see Burrell 2004, 148–149.

of 29 BC, in which he expressly forbade the cities of Asia and Bithynia from worshipping him or his adoptive father, the Divus Iulius, without the accompaniment of the Goddess Roma. Out of respect for Augustus's wishes, the majority of Augustea were consequently dedicated to Roma and Augustus; however, variations did occur.[82] The most common modification to the standard Roma-Augustus formula was the addition of a third or even fourth dedicatee. Typically, these dedicatees were personifications of cities (*Demos*), regions (*Patris*) or civic bodies, such as the Roman Senate. The first Augusteum to bear such a multipart dedication was the neokorate temple at Nicomedia dedicated to Roma, Augustus, the Senate, and the People of Rome.[83] During the later Julio-Claudian period, this type of multipart dedication became increasingly common, especially in Pisidia and Caria.[84]

It is also important to note that Roma's importance as a cult partner diminished over the course of the Augustan period.[85] As Augustus's proclamation of 29 BC slowly faded from memory, Roma's name began to be omitted from inscriptions referring to longstanding cults and priesthoods of Roma and Augustus.[86] Other gods and goddesses began to usurp her role as a cult partner to the emperor. For example, at Priene, the *demos* (i.e., the people) voted to rededicate a temple to Augustus and Athena Polias, the city's patron deity.[87] By the reign of the emperor Tiberius, Roma's name effectively ceased to appear in imperial temple dedications, even those dedicated posthumously to the emperor Augustus. As a result, dedications like the one at Priene became the norm, where a local patron deity occupied the place formerly reserved for Roma.[88]

Thus it seems quite likely that the Augusteum at Antioch was also dedicated to multiple gods. Since the early 1900s, a number of scholars have proposed that the imperial temple may have been

[82] For a full listing of temples dedicated to Roma and Augustus in Asia Minor, see Taylor 1931, 273–277; Price 1984, 249–274; Hänlein-Schäfer 1985, 164–197.

[83] The fullest version of the temple's dedication on city coins reads, "*Rom. S. P. Aug.*—Rom(ae) S(enatui) P(opulo) Aug(usto)." This is sometimes shortened on coins to "Rom(ae) Aug(usto)," but "S(enatui) P(opuli) Q(ue)" is still included in the fields. Some coins also depict a male figure worshipping at an altar, which is probably meant to represent the *genius* of the Roman People (Hänlein-Schäfer 1985, 164–165; Burrell 2004, 147–151). The dedication of the temple in Nicomedia is comparable to the altar of "Roma, Augustus and the *Demos*" at Hierocaesarea in Lydia (Taylor 1931, 276).

[84] See, for instance, the Sebasteion at Carian Aphrodisias dedicated to "Aphrodite, the *Theoi Sebastoi* and the *Demos*" (Reynolds 1986, 114; Smith 1987, 90; 1988, 51). The neokorate temple at Smyrna in Ionia was dedicated to Tiberius, Livia, and the Senate (Price 1984, 258; Burrell 2004, 38–42). Sebasteia with multipart dedications are also firmly attested at Erythrae, Asar Tepe, Alabanda, Hyllarima, Rhodiapolis, Adada, Pednelissus, Sagalassos, Lamos, and Near Cestros in Cilicia. See Price 1984, 249 ff., nos. 37, 49, 63, 67, 119, 128–130, 151, and 148. There are also probable examples at Selge (Nollé and Schindler 1991, 78 and 80) and Kremna (Mitchell 1995, 108–109; Horsley and Mitchell 2000, 43–44). Undoubtedly, many of the epigraphically attested temples that are described simply as Caesarea, Sebasteia, or Augustea also bore multipart dedications.

[85] For the cult of Roma in the imperial period, see Mellor 1981, 976 ff.

[86] This was done simply as a space-saving measure, but the omission of her name does show her diminished importance in relation to Augustus himself. This process of inscriptional omission is best documented at Ankara. See Hänlein-Schäfer 1985, 185–190; Burrell 2004, 166–174.

[87] Von Gaertringen 1906, 129; Carter 1983, 24–38; Price 1984, 258. See also the dedication to Augustus and Apollo Thermios at Thermae (Taylor 1931, 274).

[88] The convention of replacing Roma with the patron deity of the city often led to the seemingly unlikely combinations of Anatolian gods with Roman emperors: for example, at Adada, the Theoi Sebastoi were worshipped alongside "Zeus Megistos Sarapis and the *Patris*" (Price 1984, 269) and at Near Cestros in Cilicia, where Trajan shared a cult with "*Theos Megalos* and the *Demos*" (Price 1984, 273). By contrast, the combined worship of "Apollo Klarios, the *Theoi Sebastoi* and the *Patris*" at Sagalassos (Price 1984, 270; Talloen and Waelkens 2004, 183) seems more in keeping with traditional Roman ideology. See also the temple of "the *Theoi Sebastoi*, Apollo Isotimos and the *Demos*" at Alabanda (Bean 1980, 160; Price 1984, 261). For the frequent association of Apollo with Augustus and later Roman emperors, see Zanker 1988, esp. 79–102; Talloen and Waelkens 2005, 221–225; L'Orange 1953.

Fig. 3.21. Possible dedicatory inscription of the Augusteum. Photo: B. Rubin.

dedicated to Roma and Augustus.[89] This is a logical assumption given that many, if not most, of the imperial cult temples in Asia Minor were dedicated to Roma and Augustus. However, an inscription currently located in the Tiberia Platea suggests otherwise.[90] The inscription (fig. 3.21), which is carved on a monumental block of white limestone (ca. 1.5 m × .6 m × .3 m), preserves two full lines and one partial line of a Latin dedication:

IOVI · OPT · MAX
AUG · ET · GEN · COL

[*vacat*] EVEI

To Jupiter Optimus Maximus
Augustus[91] and the Genius of the Colony
[   ] the son of Eueius

[89] Ramsay 1916, 108; Mellor 1975, 144–145; Hänlein-Schäfer 1985; Mitchell and Waelkens 1998, 160.

[90] Special thanks to Ünal Demirer for permission to examine the inscription, which awaits fuller publication elsewhere.

[91] The word "Aug(usto)" in line 2 of the inscription can be translated either as an adjective modifying Jupiter or as a proper noun referring to the emperor Augustus. I have translated "Aug(usto)" in this context as a proper noun for the following reasons: (1) The inclusion of Augustus's name in this dedication would be in keeping with local epigraphic practice in Asia Minor. (2) A local Antiochene, a certain "son of Eueius," helped to pay for the inscription (see below). (3) The inscription is associated with the propylon of the imperial sanctuary, which was also dedicated to Augustus in his lifetime. (4) Augustus and his family figure prominently in the sculptural program of the imperial sanctuary. (5) As noted above, there are epigraphic references to a priest of

Augustus (Sacerdos Augusti) at Antioch (Levick 1967a, 88). And finally, (6) the Roman emperor was also worshipped in tandem with Jupiter Optimus Maximus at the nearby Augustan colony of Kremna in Pisidia (Horsley and Mitchell 2000, 43–44).

If interpreted as an adjective, the word "Aug(usto)" would translate as "August" or "Imperial." During the Roman period, many gods in the western provinces—particularly Spain and Gaul—were given the epithet "Augustus" or "Augusta." The meaning of this epithet is much debated and likely depended on context. According to J. Edmondson, the epithet "associated the divinity with the emperor and his family and sought the god's protection for the ruling Caesar" (2007, 543). While popular in the West, the term "Augustus" is only rarely used as a divine epithet in the eastern provinces. See, for example, the temple of Jupiter Augustus at Cyrene (Goodchild, Reynolds, and Herington 1958, 36–37). For further discussion of "Augustus" as divine epithet, see Clauss 2001, 280–289; Fishwick 2002, 446–454; Gradel 2002, 104–105.

The first two lines of the inscription have survived almost completely intact—only the very tops of the words "OPT" and "MAX" are lost.[92] By contrast, the lower half of the block has sustained substantial damage, which has obliterated almost the entire third line with the sole exception of the word "EVEI," a Latinized form of the Greek name Euios.[93] The description of Augustus in line 2 as "AUG" rather than "DIV AUG" suggests that this inscription dates to Augustus's reign (ca. 27 BC–AD 14).[94] This dating is confirmed by the letterforms, which are consistent with the Augustan period.[95]

　　Without a secure excavation context, it is difficult to know for certain where this inscription was originally displayed; however, its size, date, and composition all point to the nearby temple of Augustus. Given its dimensions, the inscription most likely derives from a monumental altar located at the base of the temple similar to the one depicted in Woodbridge's drawing from 1924 (figs. 3.1 and 3.22).[96]

　　As we have seen, tripartite dedications were a regular feature of imperial cult temples in Asia Minor. This was particularly true in the region around Pisidian Antioch. Out of twelve imperial cult temples known to have had tripartite dedications, seven (ca. 58 percent) are located in Pisidia and western Caria.[97] The rest are spread out along the southwestern coast of Asia Minor in the provinces

[92] The letters of the first line average ca. 15 cm tall, while those in the second and third lines are ca. 10 cm tall. There is a ca. 10 cm space between the second and third lines. The upper edge of the inscription was reworked—presumably for reuse in the construction of one of the Byzantine shops in the Tiberia Platea. It is this reworking that removed the very tops of the letters in the first line.

[93] The Latinized version of the Greek name Euios is attested once in a manumission inscription from Rome dated to the 1st or 2nd century AD. The owner of the slaves is named as "C(aius) Eueius C(ai) l(iberatus) Felix." See Chastagnol, Leglay, and Le Roux 1984, 40, no. 140. The "son of Eueius" mentioned in the Tiberia Platea inscription is probably one of the donors who contributed to the construction of the imperial cult temple or its altar. See below.

[94] The Roman Senate awarded Augustus the title of "*Divus*," or "Divine," following his death in AD 14. This title consequently appeared in most posthumous Latin dedications to Augustus. For the dating of imperial cult priesthoods, see Gradel 2002, 85–91. Augustus is also addressed on the propylon dedication simply as "AUG," followed by his current offices (Mitchell and Waelkens 1998, 147).

[95] The letters are carefully carved and have sharp, pointed ends similar to those seen in other inscriptions from the Augustan period at Antioch, such as the altar of the Augustan Peace discovered in the imperial sanctuary by Ramsay in 1914 (Ramsay 1916, 177, no. 2.) The use of elongated I's to mark long vowels, such as the final "I" in "EVEI," is also a common characteristic of Augustan and early Julio-Claudian inscriptions. Much like the preamble of the *Res Gestae*, the opening line of the Augusteum dedication is also enlarged. This is a small stylistic point, but it adds to the body of circumstantial evidence, which dates the dedication to the

time of Augustus. See Robinson 1926e; Drew-Bear 2005.

[96] The dimensions of the inscribed block are comparable with those of other altar blocks in Asia Minor. See, for instance, the altar of Demeter at Pergamon, which is composed of blocks approximately 1–1.5 m long and .3 m deep (Bohtz 1981, pl. 55). See also the altar to the emperor Claudius between Myra and Limyra in Lycia (Marksteiner and Wörrle 2002, esp. 547–548). The inscription is simply too large to have come from a statue base or votive dedication. As J. Højte has pointed out, Latin inscriptions on statue bases rarely exceed 8 cm in height (Højte 2005, 33). The letters of the inscription in the Tiberia Platea measure between 10 and 15 cm. Moreover, the two small holes at the top of the inscribed block in the Tiberia Platea are neither large enough (ca. 3 cm radius) nor spaced appropriately to hold the support struts of a statue (or statues). The holes were used instead for the insertion of building clamps, which were chipped out, presumably at the same time the block was recarved for secondary use.

[97] The temples are located in Smyrna, Erythrae, Rhodiapolis, Lamos, Near Cestros, Alabanda, Aphrodisias, Hyllarima, Adada, Kremna, and two at Sagalassos. Six of these temples (ca. 50 percent) have dedicatory inscriptions that conform to the same epigraphic formula used at Antioch, i.e., "to X god, the emperor, and the city." The dedications at Sagalassos, Aphrodisias, and Near Cestros conform exactly, while the dedications at Alabanda, Adada, and Hyllarima place the name of the emperor before the god, i.e., "to the emperor(s), X god, and the city." There are also numerous smaller dedications in Pisidia and Caria that conform to this formula. See, for instance, the dedication to the "*Theoi Sebastoi*, Artemis and the *Polis*" from Selge (Nollé and Schindler 1991, 69–70). For the late Republican dedications at Aphrodisias, see Reynolds 1980, 72–74.

Fig. 3.22. Digital reconstruction of the temple and altar; ground level view from in front of the altar looking towards temple. Digital model: B. Rubin and J. M. Harrington.

of Lycia, Cilicia, and Asia. This distribution pattern implies that the inscription in the Tiberia Platea not only could, but probably did, serve as the dedication of the Augusteum. It also raises fascinating questions about the ethnicity of the men who prepared the Augusteum's dedication. To my knowledge, there is not a single Augusteum anywhere in the western provinces with a tripartite dedication like the one at Antioch.[98] The absence of tripartite dedications in the western provinces suggests that the Roman colonists living at Antioch did not formulate the dedication of the Augusteum on their own but instead collaborated with members of the local Greek-speaking elite.[99] Otherwise, we would not expect the dedication to conform so faithfully to an epigraphic formula indigenous to the "Greek" cities of Asia Minor.

Not coincidentally, the dedication of the Augusteum preserves what appears to be the name of one of these elites—a certain Eueius or Euios. His name is written in the genitive case ("Euei"), which is significant because it suggests that the Augusteum was dedicated not by Eueius himself but rather by one of his children, who included his father's name in the dedicatory inscription as a patronymic, i.e., "so and so, the son of Eueius." Unfortunately, the section of the inscription that presumably listed the full name and titles of Eueius's son is now missing, so we are forced to speculate about his identity based on his patronymic alone.[100]

Although names do not necessarily reflect ethnic identity, there can be little doubt, in this case, that Eueius and his son were members of the local Graeco-Phrygian elite of the former Hellenistic colony. The Latin "Eueius" appears only once in the Roman epigraphic record: a single manumission inscription from Rome mentions a Greek freedman by the name of Caius Eueius,

[98] During the reign of Augustus, Augustea in the West are normally dedicated to Roma and Augustus or to Augustus and the City (e.g., Beneventum) but never to Roma, Augustus, and the City. For a list of dedications in the West, see Taylor 1931, 267–283; Hänlein-Schäfer 1985, 115–152; Gradel 2002, 376–379. The formula is somewhat reminiscent, however, of the tripartite dedication of the Capitolium in Rome to Jupiter Optimus Maximus, Juno, and Minerva—perhaps intentionally so.

[99] *Contra* Mitchell, who maintains that the colonists built the Augusteum without any help from Antioch's indigenous inhabitants. See Mitchell 1993, 102–103; Mitchell and Waelkens 1998, 163.

[100] The full name of Eueius's son presumably ran across the entire third line of the dedicatory inscription, the majority of which is now lost. If Eueius's son were a Roman citizen with a *tria nomina* and a host of civic titles, his name may have even continued onto a fourth line.

son of Caius.[101] By contrast, the Greek name Euios is commonly attested throughout the eastern Mediterranean.[102] The name occurs most frequently in Scythia and Thrace, which may indicate that Eueius descended from Thracian immigrants who settled at Antioch during the Hellenistic period.[103] Regardless of his precise genealogy, it is probably safe to assume that Eueius's son was not a Roman colonist but rather a local euergetist who participated in the construction of the Augusteum in order to win political prestige both for himself and his home city of Antioch.

The Gods of the Imperial Cult Triad

I propose, then, that the dedication of the Augusteum honors three gods: Jupiter Optimus Maximus, Augustus, and the Genius of the Colony. In accordance with local epigraphic practice, the gods are listed in descending order of importance. The Roman colonists recognized Jupiter Optimus Maximus as the city's patron deity. Jupiter was the supreme god of the Roman pantheon, who ensured the safety and security of the Roman state. As a matter of course, Roman colonies were traditionally outfitted with their own Capitolium modeled on the temple of Jupiter Optimus Maximus in Rome.[104] It appears that Antioch was no different, but Antioch's "Capitolium" deviated from the standard model in one very important respect.[105] In the dedication of the temple, the Roman colonists replaced Jupiter's usual cult partners, Juno and Minerva, with the gods of the Roman imperial cult, Augustus and the Genius of the Colony. The decision to pair these gods with Jupiter Optimus Maximus effectively allowed the imperial sanctuary to function simultaneously as both a Capitolium and an Augusteum.[106] Through this hybridization of two distinct religious institutions, the Roman colonists found a way to

[101] With a name like Caius Euieus, son of Caius, this freedman must have been of Greek origin. Surprisingly, there are no attestations of the Greek name Euios in Sicily or southern Italy. Fraser and Matthews 1997, 166.

[102] The name Euios was originally a cult epithet for the god Dionysos. It was also used as a personal name throughout Greece and the Greek islands. There are twenty-three attestations in all listed in the *Lexicon of Greek Names*. Most are relatively early in date, i.e., the Hellenistic period or earlier. See, for instance, Fraser and Matthews 1987, 176; 1997, 166. The name Euios is conspicuously absent, however, from the epigraphic record in Antioch's mother city, Magnesia-on-the-Maeander. See Kern 1900, 183.

[103] There are fourteen attestations of the names Euios and Euion along the northern coast of the Black Sea. See Fraser and Matthews 2005, 131-132. Large numbers of Thracians are known to have resided at Apollonia, Arykanda, and in the nearby region of Milyas, where they helped the local inhabitants erect an altar to Roma and Augustus (von Aulock 1977, 20–21; Hall 1986, 139). There is a general consensus that the Thracian *kolonoi* living in southern Asia Minor were once military veterans, but it is unclear whether they served under Amyntas or one of the earlier Seleucid or Attalid kings. See Ramsay 1922, 184; Jones 1932, 412; Magie 1950, 2:1315.

[104] This Republican tradition of building Capitolia in Roman colonies began to give way during the Augustan period. Most Augustan colonies chose to build an imperial cult temple dedicated to their colony's founder, Augustus, rather than a more traditional Capitolium. On the diminished role of Jupiter Optimus Maximus in Roman religion during the Augustan period, see Fears 1981, 56 ff.

[105] Magie and Levick were the first to identify the imperial sanctuary as a Capitolium (Levick 1968, 52; Magie 1950, 1:460, 2:1320). However, neither Magie nor Levick articulates clear arguments in favor of the identification. They appear to base their identification primarily on the existence of an attested priesthood of "J.O.M." at Antioch (*ILS* 7200; Ramsay 1924, 178). This is probably a reference to the same priesthood that oversaw the cult of Augustus. There are also numerous attestations of unspecified *pontifices* (e.g., Cheeseman 1913, 253–254), *flamines* (e.g., *CIL* 3.6837), and *sacerdotes* (e.g., *CIL* 3.6831, 6841) who could have potentially overseen the imperial cult. See Levick 1967a, 87 ff.

[106] It is interesting to note that Horsley and Mitchell have recently restored a parallel imperial cult dedication at the Augustan colony of Kremna in Pisidia, which reads: "(For Jupiter [*sic*] Optimus Maximus and the emperor) Caesar Marcus Aurelius (Antoninus Augustus, brother) of the divine Verus (and to Lucius Aurelius Commodus) Caesar…" (Horsley and Mitchell 2000, 43–44). The presence of "J.O.M." in this 2nd-century inscription (ca. AD 169–177) suggests that a tradition of worshipping J.O.M. had developed alongside the emperor in the Pisidian colonies founded by Augustus in the 20s BC.

balance tradition (the worship of Jupiter Optimus Maximus) with contemporary political necessity (the Roman imperial cult).

We can be fairly certain that the joint worship of Jupiter Optimus Maximus and Augustus also appealed to Antioch's pre-Roman local population. Although the evidence is somewhat sparse, it seems likely that Zeus was worshipped alongside Mên at the original Seleucid colony of Antioch.[107] If this was indeed the case, the local Greek-speaking population already had a longstanding tradition of worshipping Jupiter Optimus Maximus, only in a different guise. Furthermore, it is important to note that in the Hellenistic world, the goddess Roma was most commonly worshipped in tandem with a local variant of the god Zeus (e.g., Eleutherios, Polieus etc.).[108] The close association between these two deities would have made Jupiter Optimus Maximus an ideal candidate to replace the goddess Roma as Augustus's cult partner in the dedication of Antioch's new Augusteum.

The dedication of the Augusteum lists the third member of the imperial cult triad as the "*Genius Coloniae.*" In the dedication of the Augusteum, the term "*Genius Coloniae*" probably refers to the collective spirit of the colony's inhabitants (*genius populi*), as well as the spirit of the city itself (*genius loci*). As we have seen, the dedications of imperial cult temples in Asia Minor often featured joint dedications to personifications such as the *Demos* (People) or *Patris* (Fatherland).[109] The dedicators of the Augusteum at Antioch simply replaced the usual Greek personification with a suitable Latin equivalent, i.e., the Genius of the Colony. As Gradel has observed, the *genii* of cities and colonies were worshipped throughout Italy, but particularly in the region of Campania just south of Rome.[110] It seems that once again the dedicators of the Augusteum found a way to merge Roman religious beliefs with indigenous ritual practice to create a supernatural figure that appealed to all members of Antioch's disparate, multicultural population.

When worshipped together as a group, the gods of the imperial cult triad projected a hierarchical vision of the cosmos designed to legitimize the Roman rule at Pisidian Antioch. At the top of the cosmic hierarchy was Jupiter Optimus Maximus, the king of the gods. According to the poet Vergil, Jupiter Optimus Maximus had ordained that the Romans should one day rule the entire world: "*tu regere imperio populo, Romano, memento*" (*Aeneid* 6.788 ff.). This mandate extended even to the far-flung region of Pisidia, where Augustus settled the veterans of Legions V and VII. The colonization of Pisidian Antioch, therefore, came about as the direct result of Jupiter's divine plan for the Roman people. In the cosmic hierarchy of the imperial cult, the emperor Augustus occupied a liminal position between mankind (*Genius Coloniae*) and the gods (Jupiter Optimus Maximus). By spreading Roman law and institutions to Pisidian Antioch, Augustus acted, in effect, as Jupiter's

---

[107] Zeus Sosipolis was one of the principal gods of Magnesia-on-the-Meander, Antioch's mother city. The Greek colonists undoubtedly brought this deity with them to Antioch. As Ramsay has pointed out, Zeus was also traditionally worshipped at Seleucid colonies (Ramsay 1918, 183, no. 138; Buckler, Calder, and Cox 1924, 30–31). Seleucid coins depicting Zeus seated with a scepter have been discovered on site. See Demirer 2002, 20. For the prevalence of Zeus worship in Pisidia during the Hellenistic period, see Waelkens 1999, 199–201.

[108] Mellor 1981, 973–974. Zeus and Roma were also occasionally worshipped together in imperial cult contexts during the early imperial period. See, for example, the epigraphically attested cult of Zeus, Roma, and Augustus in the Macedonian town of Kalindoia (ca. AD 1). *SEG* 35.744. For commentary, see Beard, North, and Price 1998, 360.

[109] Cities and colonies rarely appear in the dedications of Augustea in the western provinces. See, for instance, the Augusteum at Beneventum, Italy. Taylor 1931, 169 and 279; Hänlein-Schäfer 1985, 141–142; Gradel 2002, 182.

[110] Gradel 2002, 81. Gradel specifically cites an example of a temple dedicated to the Genius of Pompeii. The temple was formerly associated with the *Genius Augusti*. See also Hänlein-Schäfer 1985, 133 ff.

Fig. 3.23. Torso of Augustus as Jupiter from the attic of the propylon. Photo: Kelsey Museum Archives neg. no. 7.1432.

chosen agent on earth.[111] In recognition of his privileged status, the people of Antioch worshipped Augustus as a sort of living god worthy of all the same honors as his Olympian counterparts. Despite his immense power, Augustus could not carry out Jupiter's divine plan on his own. He needed the help of his colonial subjects at Pisidian Antioch. The Antiochenes appear in the dedication of the Augusteum personified as a single unified entity, the Genius of the Colony.[112] This personification served as a potent symbol of civic unity in a community divided along social, political, and ethnic lines. By worshipping the Genius of the Colony as a god, Antioch's various political factions actively participated in the construction of a new group identity predicated upon loyalty to the emperor and submission to the will of the gods. The Roman colonists retained a leadership role in the colonial administration due to their "close" personal relationship with the divine Augustus, but ultimately every man, woman, and child at Pisidian Antioch had his or her own part to play in the preservation of the new imperial order. This included members of the Graeco-Phrygian elite, like Eueius and his son, who must have been eager to reenter civic politics after being stripped of their citizenship rights in 25 BC. For these disenfranchised elites, the Roman imperial cult offered a way to integrate themselves into the new imperial bureaucracy while regaining a measure of their former political prestige. Through their intellectual and monetary contributions to the construction of the imperial cult sanctuary, Eueius's son and his colleagues asserted an active role as partners, rather than victims, in the Roman project of empire building.

[111] It is worth noting that among the statues that adorned the attic of the Augustan propylon was one that likely depicted Augustus in the guise of Jupiter (fig. 3.23) (Robinson 1926a, fig. 56). The statue is badly damaged, but its basic iconography is clear: the figure wears a cloak, and his right breast is bare in a manner typical of Jupiter. Augustus often appeared in the guise of Jupiter, especially in contexts associated with the Roman imperial cult (Burrell 2004, 147–151; Gradel 2002, 94–95). At Antioch, this form of syncretization would have eloquently symbolized the partnership between Augustus and the city's patron deity, Jupiter Optimus Maximus. For further discussion of this statue, see Rubin 2008, 42–43.

[112] If we accept that the Genius of the Colony appeared in the dedication of the Augusteum, it seems irresistible not to identify the winged *genii* on the propylon spandrels as per-

sonifications of Pisidian Antioch (see fig. 3.11). What better way to represent the benefits of Roman rule than to show a personification of the colony literally holding the fruits of the Augustan Peace? In Roman art, *genii* were normally depicted as nude or partially draped male figures holding a cornucopia and patera (a small bowl used for pouring libations). However, there is also a tradition of representing *genii* with wings. These winged *genii* often hold small leafy branches and trays of fruit rather than a patera or cornucopia. See, for instance, the second style wall painting of a winged *genius* from the Villa of Fannius Synistor at Boscoreale (ca. 60–40 BC), now at the Louvre. Tuchelt's suggestion that the *Genius Coloniae* is depicted on the propylon frieze as a helmeted warrior should be firmly rejected. The image he is referring to (see fig. 3.13) is clearly a representation of Mên. See Tuchelt 1983, 519.

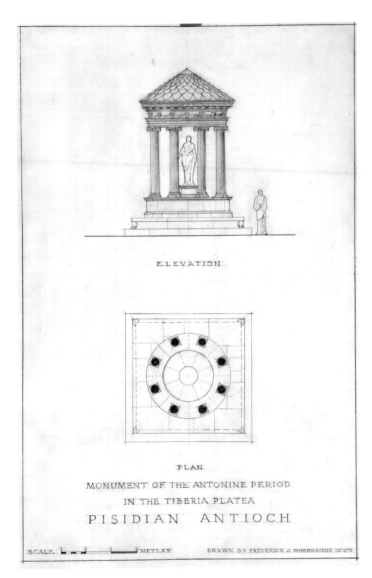

Fig. 3.24. Woodbridge's reconstruction drawing of the *tholos*. Photo: Reprographic Services of Drawings & Archives Department, Avery Architectural & Fine Arts Library, Columbia University. By permission of the library.

Note on a Severan Monument in the Tiberia Platea

The Tiberia Platea, like the rest of the imperial cult sanctuary, remained an important locus for elite display well into the early 3rd century AD. Evidence of this comes in the form of a round commemorative building, or *tholos*, located in the southeast corner of the Tiberia Platea (fig. 3.24).[113] In 1924, Robinson uncovered a round concrete foundation containing an aggregate of "greenish stone," as well as a number of rounded architrave blocks, column capitals, and a piece of a bench with lion's feet.[114] Using the existing fragments, Woodbridge reconstructed the *tholos* as a small rotunda with a tapered roof supported by eight slender columns, all on a 5.2 m square plinth. The function of the monument is unclear, but it most likely served as an architectural frame for an honorific statue of

[113] See the entries for May 17 and 18 in the Journal of Excavations.

[114] See the entries for May 17 and 18 in the Journal of Excavations. For further discussion, see Mitchell and Waelkens 1998, 154–157.

the emperor Caracalla or the Goddess Fortuna.[115] A single fragment of the dedicatory inscription from the *tholos* has survived on a badly weathered cornice block. The block preserves the words: "*-]-i Antonini Aug.*" Mitchell and Waelkens have argued convincingly that the inscription refers to Marcus Aurelius's adoptive grandson, Marcus Aurelius Antoninus Augustus, better known as the emperor Caracalla.[116] The fact that Caracalla's name appears in the genitive case suggests that the *tholos* was not dedicated to him directly but rather to one of his virtues or to a specific victory in his war against the Parthians (AD 215–216). During the Severan period, imperial victories, or *epinikeia*, often served as the impetus for constructing honorific monuments. This was especially true in Asia Minor, where imperial visits, or *adventi*, were a common occurrence because of the ongoing Parthian wars.[117]

---

[115] By the Roman period, canopy monuments were already relatively common in Asia Minor. Many included statuary. See, for instance, the early 3rd-century BC Ptolemaion at Limyra and the Augustan canopy monument at Sagalassos. Borchardt and Stanzl 1990; Waelkens 1993b, 16; Waelkens, Pauwels, and Van Den Bergh 1995, 24; Talloen and Waelkens 2004, 188–191. See also the 2nd-century AD *monopteros* at Pergamon (Koenigs and Radt 1979).

[116] Mitchell and Waelkens 1998, 154–157.

[117] See Talloen and Waelkens 2005, 235–238.

4 Architecture, Entertainment, and Civic Life: The Theater at Pisidian Antioch

Hima B. Mallampati and Ünal Demirer[1]

The theater at Antioch, like other theaters in the Graeco-Roman world, was a multifunctional venue for religious ceremonies, political meetings, and entertainments such as dramatic performances and wild beast fights. The theater's changing physical layout, revealed through archaeological investigation, provides a glimpse into the shifting patterns of its use throughout the site's history. These phases of construction, reconstruction, and finally abandonment of the theater also shed light on the religious, political, and social identities of the city's ancient inhabitants.

In 1833, Arundell identified the theater at Pisidian Antioch by noting, "[t]he remains of the theatre lie on the east of the church, on a little ascent. The seats are all removed, and the diameter not exceeding one hundred and fifty feet,"[2] a description proved inaccurate by later excavations. The first of these was conducted in 1913 by Callander, who unearthed a cistern in the theater that contained sculptural fragments. Callander also found a large inscribed arch nearby, but he failed to report his findings in any detail.[3] Although the University of Michigan excavation of 1924 did not include the theater, the team photographed it and made squeezes of the inscribed arch (fig. 4.1).[4] Mitchell and Waelkens's survey of the city in 1982 and 1983 produced an overall site plan, which maps the theater before it was excavated (fig. 4.2),[5] but it was not until 1991 that Taşlıalan excavated the scaena (stage building), cavea (seating area), and orchestra.[6] In 2003, Demirer continued excavations in the theater focusing on the orchestra and the stage building.[7] A magnetometric survey conducted by T. Smekalova and S. Smekalov in 2001 mapped the area to the west of the theater but did not include the theater itself.

The theater at Antioch still awaits full publication. The main accounts to date include Taşlıalan's informative report published in 1997; M. Christol and T. Drew-Brew's article of 1999 concerning several inscriptions found in the theater district; E. J. Owens's analysis of the cistern attached to the theater, published in 2002 as part of his ongoing study of the city's water supply; and the results of

---

[1] The authors are grateful to Diana Ng for her contributions to the section of this chapter subtitled "Civic and Social Roles" and to Robert Chenault for his assistance with the section subtitled "The Theater in the Late Antique Period."

[2] Arundell 1834, 273.

[3] Mitchell and Waelkens 1998, 108–109. In a letter to Francis Kelsey, T. Callander discusses the 1913 excavation: "we also dug an exploring trench along the proscenium of the theatre and at the corner of the theatral area cleared out a cistern containing a lot of sculptured fragments (some good pieces) and uncovered the remains of a large archway." T.

Callander letter to F. Kelsey, September 1, 1924, 2. The arch may be the one dedicated by Marcus Valerius Diogenes, discussed below.

[4] Journal of Excavations, 26 notes that the squeezes of the arch were made on June 9, 1924.

[5] Mitchell and Waelkens 1998, xiii.

[6] Taşlıalan 1997, 325.

[7] Demirer 2003.

Fig. 4.1. Unexcavated site of the
theater in 1924, captioned "Theatre
from West." Photo: D. M. Robinson,
Kelsey Museum Archives neg. no.
KR051.09.

Smekalova and Smekalov's magnetometric survey, published with Taşlıalan and Bagnall in 2003.[8]
Demirer drafted two governmental reports from his 2003 and 2004 seasons that outline his excavation
results.[9] In this chapter, we analyze the physical remains of the theater and attempt to envision the
structure at different periods of its history. We also explore unresolved questions about the dating,
architectural form, seating capacity, and the decorative program of the theater, and we propose that
the theater was a heterogeneous mix of Eastern and Western architectural styles, perhaps reflecting
the diverse makeup of Antioch's population. Finally, we examine the changing role of the theater
over several centuries of the city's life and argue that throughout much of its history the theater was
an important site for displays of loyalty to the Roman emperor.

Architectural Remains of the Theater and Its Chronology

As one of the largest structures in the city, the theater was an imposing feature in the urban landscape. Facing westward, it was located adjacent to the main east-west thoroughfare, the *decumanus
maximus*. In all periods of its history it would have been visible shortly after entering the city from
the southwest (fig. 4.3).

The date of the theater's initial construction is disputed. Taşlıalan contends that it was built
either in the Hellenistic period, given what he identifies as a horseshoe-shaped seating area and its
construction into the natural slope of a hill, or at the founding of the Roman colony in ca. 25 BC.[10]

[8] Taşlıalan 1997. Taşlıalan published a guidebook in 1991 with
a brief discussion of the theater. Taşlıalan 1991, 27. In 2002,
Demirer updated Taşlıalan's guidebook by detailing some
of the results of the earlier 1990s excavations of the theater.
Demirer 2002, 56–59; Christol and Drew-Bear 1999; Owens
2002, 341; Taşlıalan et al. 2003.

[9] Demirer 2003; 2004.

[10] Taşlıalan 1997, 325; 1991, 27. Bieber 1961, 189 notes that

Greek-Hellenistic theaters are characterized by the following
features based on her reading of Vitruvius book 5: (a) they are
built against a hillside without vaulted substructures; (b) they
contain a cavea that extends past the shape of a semicircle;
(c) they have a circular orchestra; and (d) they possess two
open passages allowing access to the theater; she lists the
following features as emblematic of Roman theaters: (a) a
cavea that is raised on vaulted substructures or sometimes
built on a hillside, (b) a semicircular cavea, (c) a semicircular
orchestra and a low stage; and (d) performances that no

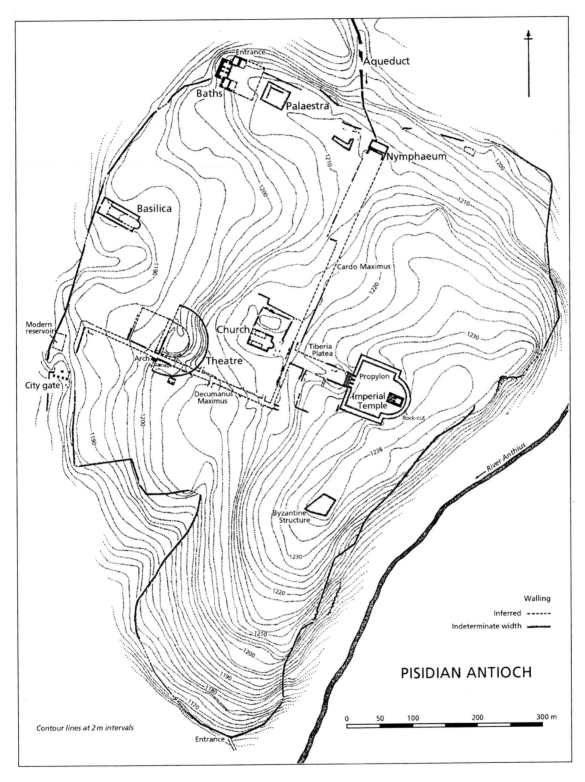

Entrance

Aqueduct

Baths

Palaestra

Nymphaeum

1210

1200

Basilica

1210

1190

Cardo Maximus

1220

1230

Modern
reservoir

Church

Tiberia
Platea

Arch

Theatre

Propylon

City gate

Decumanus
Maximus

Imperial
Temple

Rock-cut

1236

1190

1200

River Anthius

Byzantine
Structure

1230

1230

1220

1210

Walling

Inferred ------

Indeterminate width

1200

1190

1180

1170

PISIDIAN ANTIOCH

0   50   100   200   300 m

Contour lines at 2 m intervals

Entrance

Fig. 4.2. Site plan of Pisidian Antioch showing site of the theater before excavation.
After Mitchell and Waelkens 1998, 92, fig. 18. By permission of Classical Press of Wales.

Fig. 4.3. View of the theater with *decumanus maximus* at left (2004). Photo: B. Rubin (T52–BR).

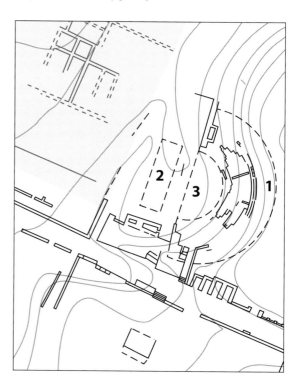

Fig. 4.4. Revised plan of the theater showing
(1) the cavea, (2) the scaena, and (3) the orchestra.
Drawing: A. J. Ossi.

Demirer's recent archaeological work, however, suggests that the theater was built first in the early 1st century AD. Architectural and decorative components were modified throughout the theater's history, complicating the attempt to date its major phases of construction and use. We argue here that new seats most likely were added in the 2nd century AD; the stage building was refashioned, and the orchestra was converted into an arena in the late 3rd–early 4th century AD; a possible chapel was constructed on site in the late 4th century AD; and, finally, that the structure was probably abandoned in the 8th

longer take place in the orchestra. Dodge (1999, 219–223), however, warns that in Asia Minor many Greek theaters were adapted and modified, almost always with the addition of a Roman-style stage building. Regardless of the dating of this particular theater at Antioch, it is highly likely that there was a theater somewhere in Hellenistic Antioch, given the theater's importance in Greek cultural and political life.

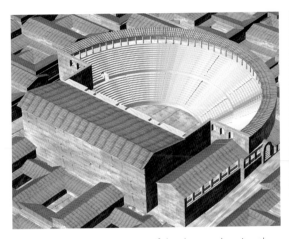

Fig. 4.5. Digital reconstruction of the theater showing the cavea. Digial model: J. M. Harrington.

Fig. 4.6. Lower seating section of the theater showing seats and staircase (2004). Photo: J. M. Harrington (T107).

century AD. These phases of the theater's history become clear when one analyzes its three components: the cavea, the scaena, and the orchestra (fig. 4.4).

Cavea/Seating Area. Various phases of rebuilding are apparent in the theater's cavea. Many theaters in Roman Asia Minor, including the one at Antioch, were built into the natural slope of a hill in the earlier Hellenistic fashion, with only the wings projecting as freestanding structures.[11] The cavea is divided horizontally by three semicircular *diazomata*, or walkways, in the front, center, and back of the theater (fig. 4.5). They were used to order the seating plan of the theater and to guide spectators to their seats.[12] A wall probably surrounded the *diazoma* at the back of the theater to shield the spectators seated in the uppermost section from the precipitous drop behind them.[13]

The lower level cavea seats, located between the front and central *diazomata*, are divided by seven staircases, which form six wedges of seating sections (fig. 4.6), or *cunei*.[14] Theaters in Asia Minor were commonly divided into five, seven, or nine *cunei* in their lower caveae, but those in Italy and in the western part of the empire generally were divided into four, five, or six *cunei*.[15] Antioch's lower cavea with its six *cunei* suggests that the architects who designed the theater were from the West, or at least were familiar with Western theater design.[16] The theater's Western-style semicircular cavea,

[11] Bieber 1939, 373. For example, the theaters at Perge and Myra are built into the slope of the hill, while the wings are supported by infill. Most Roman theaters outside of Asia Minor, however, were freestanding constructions. Taşlıalan asserts that the northern half of Pisidian Antioch's cavea was set against the hill behind it, and the southern portion was reinforced by vaults and arches. Taşlıalan 1991, 27. In contrast, Demirer suggests that the entire cavea was set against the natural slope, which was reinforced with rubble, on top of which the seating blocks were set.

[12] The first *diazoma*, located at the front of the seating area, is 0.75 m wide; the second, in the center of the cavea, is 1.20 m wide; and the third *diazoma* at the back of the theater is 3 m wide. Taşlıalan 1997, 327–328.

[13] Taşlıalan 1997, 328. Many other theaters in Asia Minor have colonnades at the back of the theater, for example, the ones at Aspendos and Hierapolis, but the preserved evidence at Antioch does not indicate the existence of such a colonnade. These colonnades at the top of the cavea are mentioned in Vitruvius 5.6.4.

[14] Taşlıalan 1997, 327 for the dimensions of the stairs: h. 0.25 m and w. 0.35 m. Railing holes are visible near these stairs in the lowest section of the cavea.

[15] Sear 2006, 24.

[16] For a discussion of the veteran colonists, see Rubin, chap. 3, this volume.

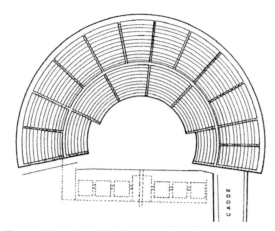

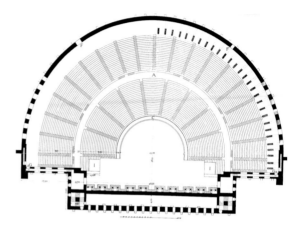

Fig. 4.7. Older plan of the theater at Antioch.
After Taşlıalan 1997, plan 2.

Fig. 4.8. Plan of the theater at Aspendos. After
Lanckoroński 1890, pl. XXI.

rather than the horseshoe-shaped cavea commonly found in theaters in Asia Minor, also hints at Western influence on the theater's design. It is striking that the Augustan-era theaters at Kremna and Ankyra both appear to have Western semicircular caveae.[17] The large influx of Romans into these cities during the Augustan period may well have influenced the architectural structures of these growing communities.[18] This is not to discount the importance of the local architectural tradition, which was clearly evident in Antioch's theater. The horizontal division of Antioch's cavea into two zones, an upper and lower zone, which was a typical feature of theaters in Asia Minor, rather than into the three zones found in theaters in the western half of the empire, implies that the architects were also familiar with Greek architectural styles.[19]

The shape of the theater and its cavea changed in the course of its history. Taşlıalan suggested that the cavea was altered into a horseshoe-shaped design typical of other theaters in Asia Minor after two side sections of seats, each measuring 19.50 m in length, were added to the lowest level at an unspecified later period and that these additions were placed behind the older, central semicircular section of the cavea (fig. 4.7).[20] A somewhat comparable plan is well preserved in the late 2nd-century AD theater at Aspendos (fig. 4.8). There, the lowest ring of seats does not extend to the wings of the cavea. In the theaters at both Aspendos and Antioch, there is evidence of a sloping roof over the stage building, which may have enhanced the acoustics.[21]

[17] Sear 2006, 368. In addition to the semicircular cavea, the Kremna theater's cavea, with a diameter of 80 m and its 26–30 rows of seats, is remarkably similar to the theater in Antioch in size and shape. Mitchell 1995, 76 (suggesting a possible 1st-century AD date for the abandonment of construction of the Kremna theater given the shortage of funds and remoteness of the city during this period).

[18] Sear 2006, 112.

[19] Sear 2006, 24–25.

[20] Taşlıalan 1997, 327.

[21] Demirer unearthed terracotta tiles, probably from the roof of the stage façade, during his excavation of the orchestra and the stage building. These tiles may have been attached to the stage building roof at a later period of the theater's use or possibly were placed over the wooden roof. Wooden stage floors and wooden doors on the stage façade were common in many Roman theaters and were presumably built for acoustic purposes as well. See Sear 2006, 90 on roofs over the stage building and their likely acoustic function. Sear finds evidence for such roofs only at Arausio, Aspendos, and Bostra but believes that these roofs were probably regular features at other theaters (Sear 2006, 8, 90). The probable wall at the top of the cavea might have aided in circulating sound at Antioch as well; Vitruvius 5.6.4 also mentions that the colonnades around the tops of theater caveae improved the acoustics.

Fig. 4.9. Profile view of theater seats at Antioch (2004). Photo: J. M. Harrington (T61).

Taşlıalan reports that the seats in the lowest level, which were made of white limestone, were attached to each other with durable mortar, unlike the few surviving upper level seats, which used no mortar.[22] Differences in the profiles of the seats and the materials used to construct them indicate that the seat blocks were altered and repaired or replaced over time (fig. 4.9).[23] Many of the surviving seats in the lowest section of Antioch's theater resemble the flat, smooth form of the theater seats in the odeion at Aphrodisias and the theater at Aspendos. Both these theaters were constructed in the late 2nd century AD, suggesting a similar date for a refurbishment of Antioch's theater. In addition, seats with backs—perhaps *prohedria*, seats of honor—were found in the lowest level of the cavea at Antioch,[24] and some of the seating rows preserve Greek inscriptions.[25]

Scholars have debated the capacity of the theater. The measurements of the cavea are crucial to estimating the size of the audience of a given theater. Rosetto and Sartorio propose that a length of 1.5 feet should be calculated for each spectator.[26] Taşlıalan reconstructs the first phase of Antioch's semicircular cavea to measure 105 m in diameter, and he believes the cavea most likely contained 26 rows of seats. Taşlıalan claims that the theater held 5,000 spectators at this point, while 4th-century additions enlarged the space to accommodate 15,000.[27] These 4th-century dimensions are larger than those of other nearby theaters, but the number of seating rows is smaller than, or comparable to, the theaters at Sagalassos (diam. 97 m, 40 rows, estimated capacity of 6,000);[28] Termessos (diam. 65 m,

[22] Taşlıalan 1997, 326, 328.

[23] Taşlıalan 1997, 327.

[24] With the exception of their height, the dimensions of these backed seats were commensurate in size with other seats in the theater, measuring 0.90–.91 m long, 0.60 m wide, and 0.75 m high. Taşlıalan 1997, 328.

[25] Taşlıalan 1997, 327. *SEG* 50 (2000) reconstructs these inscriptions to read "for the citizens of the Apollonia" and "homonoia," the latter of which was also found as a seating section designation in Ephesos (*SEG* 1290 and 1291). *SEG*

reconstructs the Antioch theater inscriptions from photographs "in a report on his survey in Antiochia" by T. Drew-Bear (2000) and dates them to the Roman imperial period.

[26] Rossetto and Sartorio 1994, 1:80. Regionary catalogues that detailed the seating capacity of the theaters in Rome often specified the length of the seating rather than the number of seats. Sear 2006, 25.

[27] Taşlıalan 1997, 334.

[28] Rossetto and Sartorio 1994, 3:351.

Fig. 4.10. Bucrania frieze from the theater at the Yalvaç Museum (2004). Photo: H. B. Mallampati (M16).

26 rows, estimated capacity of 4,000–5,000);[29] and Selge (diam. 102 m, 44 rows, estimated capacity of 8,700).[30] Taşlıalan does not indicate whether his measurements take into account his claim that the theater cavea spanned the *decumanus*. If so, the actual dimensions of the theater and audience capacity in the 4th century at Antioch might have been smaller than those projected by Taşlıalan; Mitchell and Waelkens give a diameter of roughly 95 m for the front of the theater in its last phase.[31] Demirer rejects Taşlıalan's proposed 4th-century dimensions based on evidence discussed below; considering the results of the excavation and the comparative examples, he suggests that the capacity of the Antioch theater might have been about 5,000.

Two main arched entrances, or *paradoi*, linked the cavea to the stage building on the north and south sides.[32] Taşlıalan suggests that two other entrances on the south side belonged to the hypothetical Hellenistic theater on this site. He further suggests that one of these entrances was turned into a cistern in the late antique period, a date based on the presence of inscribed crosses on some of its blocks. The other entrance became a passageway with five steps leading onto the lowest *diazoma*.[33] Owens agrees in part with this hypothesis but claims that the original Hellenistic entrance to the theater was converted into a small fountain house with two adjoining tanks rather than a cistern.[34] The presence of waterproof cement covering the terracotta tiles on the floor of the tanks supports Owens's case for either a cistern or a fountain house.[35] While Owens warns against attempting to date the piping leading to this proposed fountain house, he tentatively suggests that it was part of the original design of the aqueduct system, which may date to around 25 BC, when the Augustan colony was founded.[36] If the water distribution system dates to this early period, it is possible that the fountain house had been part of the original theater, given Demirer's dating of the structure to the early 1st century AD. In this case the inscribed blocks with crosses mentioned by Taşlıalan would have replaced earlier blocks.[37]

[29] Rosetto and Sartorio 1994, 3:443.

[30] Mitchell and Waelkens 1998, 106; Rossetto and Sartorio 1994, 3:534.

[31] Taşlıalan 1991, 27; Mitchell and Waelkens 1998, 106.

[32] Taşlıalan 1999, 333 provides the dimensions of the south *parados* (3.25 m wide × 11.50 m long) and the larger north *parados* (3.25 m wide × 28.50 m long). The gray limestone bases of these two entrances still survive.

[33] Taşlıalan 1997, 333–334, 338.

[34] Owens 2002, 341.

[35] Owens 2002, 341.

[36] Owens 2002, 339, 341.

[37] A water source near a theater occurs in other theaters in Asia Minor such as at Perge, where a nymphaeum was added to the back of the stage building in ca. 200 (Rosetto and Sartorio 1994, 3:357). Farther afield, at Ostia, two fountain houses bordered the eastern and western entrances to the theater (Calza 1926, 112).

Scaena/Stage Building. Along with the cavea, the stage building (scaena) at Antioch saw major changes in its design over time. The stage building at Antioch, measuring 25.50 m × 55 m in its latest phase, consisted of a basement, a stage floor, and a stage façade (*scaenae frons*). Unfortunately, few remnants of the stage building and the stage façade at Antioch survive intact. Analyses of material retrieved from excavations by Taşlıalan and Demirer and comparison to other theaters in Asia Minor, however, provide clues regarding its original appearance. In the basement of the stage building at Antioch, Taşlıalan records seven rooms covered by vaulted arches, which he believes connected the orchestra to an agora to the west (see fig. 4.7).[38] He projects the height of the stage façade as equal to the height of the cavea, a feature found in other Roman theaters in Asia Minor.[39] The focal point of the theater for seated spectators was the decoration of the stage façade. From the surviving fragments, Taşlıalan reconstructs the lower level of the stage façade as adorned with columns with white marble Ionic bases, flat granite shafts, and yellow marble Corinthian capitals with an architrave decorated with a frieze of theater masks, bucrania, and elaborate garlands (fig. 4.10).[40] On the level above he places Corinthian columns and a floral frieze.[41]

Unlike theaters in other parts of the Roman Empire, which contained stage façades with deep central niches and low stages, stage façades in Asia Minor often had shallow niches cut into straight walls.[42] The high stages in these theaters often rose 7 to 10 feet above the orchestra floor.[43] Roman theaters throughout Asia Minor, such as those at Ephesos, Priene, Miletos, Aezanoi, Aspendos, Sagalassos, and Termessos, all have stage buildings with shallow niches as well as an elevated stage, suggesting that the stage at Antioch was of a similar design. Between five and seven doors pierced the stage façades in most theaters in Asia Minor,[44] and a comparable number of doors most likely adorned the theater at Antioch.

Among decorative elements, masks were a common motif of Roman theaters starting with early imperial structures, such as the theater of Marcellus in Rome, ca. 20–10 BC, which was decorated on the exterior with marble masks representing characters from tragic, comic, and satyric plays.[45] Theater masks were also widespread decorative features in Asia Minor to judge by those on the 2nd-century theater at Side (fig. 4.11) and on the late 2nd-century theater at Aspendos (fig. 4.12). The mask at Aspendos is thought to illustrate a female pantomimic figure,[46] whose long braided hair, dour expression, and closed mouth resemble features on some of the masks found on the frieze at Antioch (fig. 4.10). The popularity of pantomime in the 2nd and 3rd centuries AD may suggest that the heads from Antioch's theater also represent pantomimic imagery and date to this period. In addition to masks and bucrania, lions' heads also adorned a frieze on the stage façade (fig. 4.13).

[38] Taşlıalan 1997, 335, 337. The presence of an "agora" is merely conjectural because the area to the west of the theater has not been excavated. A magnetometric survey of this area did not reveal the presence of an agora but rather found a kiln, a possible metalworking shop, as well as a possible road (Smekalova and Smekalov 2001, 4).

[39] Taşlıalan 1997, 338. Taşlıalan surmises that the first story of the stage façade reached a height of 9 m, and that the second story rose an additional 8.5 m. In addition, Taşlıalan suggests that the height of the stage from the orchestra floor was 3 m. Taşlıalan 1997, 335. Taşlıalan's estimate of the height of the stage façade and stage building seems inflated when compared to the height of the stage façade of the much larger theater at Aspendos, which rose to a height of 23 m. See Brothers 1989,

104 for a discussion of the stage façade at Aspendos.

[40] Taşlıalan 1997, 335.

[41] Taşlıalan 1997, 335.

[42] Bieber 1939, 379.

[43] Bieber 1939, 379; Sear 2006, 112.

[44] Isler 1994, 120.

[45] Green 1994, 143.

[46] Jory 1996, 17.

Fig. 4.11. Frieze of theater masks from the theater at Side (2004). Photo: D. Ng.

Fig. 4.12. Portion of frieze of a theater mask from the theater at Aspendos. After Moretti 1993, fig. 19. By permission of *RÉA*.

The nonfigural decorative elements appear to be from a later phase of the façade decoration. The carving style of the tendril friezes, rosettes, and egg-and-dart moldings from the stage façade unearthed in Taşlıalan's excavation have been compared by Mitchell and Waelkens to that of analogous motifs from the 4th-century phase of stage building at Hierapolis.[47]

Demirer's excavation uncovered many more features of the stage building, especially decorations belonging to its reuse in later periods. Among these is an elaborate mosaic depicting partridges, peacocks, and a duck standing near a cage, two trees, and a double-handed vase, all set against a white background (fig. 4.14).[48] A Greek inscription, ΕΥΧΕΚΟΣ ΤΑΝΤΙΝΟΥ ΚΑΙ ΔΙΟΝΥΣΙΟΥ, "in prayer from Tantinos and Dionysios," written in three lines within a decorative frame (*tabula ansata*), is situated above the two-handled vase, and a plaited braid design frames the entire mosaic. The rich variety in the color of the tesserae, the style of the inscription, and especially the images on the motif lead Demirer to conclude that the mosaic dates to the 4th century AD.[49] Typical mosaic decoration of the 4th century consists of a simple border surrounded by faunal or vegetal designs, which often illustrates two-handled vases, peacocks, doves, and pheasants. These diverse, colorful subjects are sometimes thought to suggest the richness of early Christian views of paradise.[50] The presence of the mosaic with peacocks, a common motif in Christian imagery, and an inscription may indicate that the stage building was converted into a chapel; the mosaic, however, contains no overtly Christian symbols, such as monograms or common representations of α or ω, that are typically found in mosaics from chapels or churches of this period, and peacocks and other birds also occur in non-Christian contexts.[51]

[47] Mitchell and Waelkens 1998, 109.

[48] Demirer 2004, 3.

[49] Demirer 2004, 3. Demirer suggests that the date of this mosaic is similar to that of the mosaics in the basilica. See Herring-Harrington, chap. 6, this volume.

[50] Dunbabin 1978, 189–190, 193–194.

[51] A peacock also appears in the nave mosaic of the 4th-century Church of St. Paul; see Herring-Harrington, chap. 6, this volume.

Fig. 4.13. Lion's head (lying upside down) from theater architrave at Antioch (2004). Photo: B. Rubin (T39).

Fig. 4.14. Peacock mosaic from the theater at Antioch (2004). Photo: Ü. Demirer.

Fig. 4.15. Theater mask found during 2004 theater excavation. Photo: E. K. Gazda (M160).

Fig. 4.16. Face and torso of statue found during 2004 theater excavation at Antioch. Photo: Ü. Demirer.

In addition to the mosaics, in the basement of the stage building or in its vicinity, Demirer found two ceramic theater masks (fig. 4.15), torsos of several statues used as supports in Byzantine walls, Sasanian silver coins dated to the 7th–8th century AD, wine glasses, and pottery. An oval lime kiln, inside of which were found remains of partially burned statues, was unearthed in the middle of the stage building.[52] At present, the date of the kiln is unknown, but Demirer proposes that the presence of the statue fragments inside the lime kiln indicates the intentional destruction of the stone fragments at a later date in the theater's history.[53] Demirer's 2004 excavation in the orchestra also uncovered a female torso and a female head (figs. 4.16). Future analysis of these statue fragments may determine their date and the reason why they were deposited within the orchestra. Given the evidence of the lime kiln, it is possible that the stage building was transformed into a workshop that was connected to Demirer's proposed chapel.

[52] Demirer 2004, 3.

[53] Demirer 2004, 3.

Fig. 4.17. "Shops" in the theater district at
Antioch (2004). Photo: H. B. Mallampati.

Orchestra. The horseshoe-shaped orchestra at Antioch measures 35.50 m in diameter and 1.74 m in depth.[54] The depth of the floor of the orchestra suggests that it was lowered to convert the theater into an arena during the 3rd or early 4th century.[55] By the end of the 3rd century many theaters in Asia Minor, such as those at Ephesos (mid-2nd century), Myra (3rd century), Perge (ca. mid-3rd century), and Side (3rd century), were converted into arenas for games by surrounding the orchestra with a high balustrade wall for the spectators' safety and sometimes by removing the lowest rows of seats in the cavea and creating chambers beneath the cavea or inside the stage building to house animals and supplies.[56] Some modification along these lines at Antioch is indicated by the presence of a balustrade wall with blocks connected with iron joints.[57] Taşlıalan suggests that wild beasts may have been caged in the vaulted chambers below the stage building since no chambers existed below the cavea.[58]

Demirer found that the ground of the orchestra in Antioch's theater is made of compressed soil and that a canal system surrounded the orchestra to prevent rainwater from accumulating in the area rather than for piping water into the theater.[59] Substantial drainage works, water pipes, reservoirs, and waterproof plaster on the orchestra floor often suggest the presence of a pool within an arena.[60] Such pools, or *colimbethra*, were for staging water ballets and mock naval battles and are found at theaters throughout Asia Minor from the 3rd century onwards, such as the ones at Hierapolis (4th century) and Myra (beginning of 4th century).[61] The compressed soil floor of the orchestra at Antioch

[54] Taşlıalan 1997, 334.

[55] When the theater at Aphrodisias was converted into an arena, the level of the orchestra was lowered 1.53 m. Sear 2006, 44.

[56] On these changes, see Isler 1994, 1:122. See also Welch 1998, 121–122. Welch focuses on the conversion of stadia into oval amphitheaters. She suggests that stadia were the initial location of gladiatorial shows, *venationes* or wild animal shows, and executions in the Greek East before the conversion of theaters into arenas.

[57] Taşlıalan 1997, 334. Other examples of walls around the

orchestra include a 1.20 m high wall at the acropolis theater in Pergamon, a 3.50 m high wall at the theater in Corinth, a 2.40 m high podium wall at the theater of Ephesos, a 2.80 m podium wall at the theater at Dodona, and a 3.30–3.40 m high podium wall at Xanthos. Sear 2006, 43–44.

[58] Taşlıalan 1997, 335.

[59] Demirer 2003, 7.

[60] Sear 2006, 44.

[61] Isler 1994, 1:122–124.

Fig. 4.18. So-called agora at Antioch, with theater in left foreground (2004). Photo: B. Rubin (T57).

would negate the presence of a pool, at least in the very last period in the theater's life. On the one hand, given the various reconstructions that occurred within the theater at different periods, the absence of paved stone or other water repellent on the arena floor does not preclude the possibility that the arena was used as a pool at some point. The presence of the drainage system, water pipes in the theater, and nearby fountain house or cistern could support such a hypothesis. On the other hand, it is possible that the extant drainage system and pipes were only used to supply water for the fountain house or cistern rather than for the arena.

The Theater District. The precinct surrounding the theater preserves evidence of a variety of activities that occurred near this popular social venue. Along the *decumanus*, a series of four small rooms, probably shops, lined the southwestern exterior wall of the theater (fig. 4.17).[62] Taşlıalan conjectures that the open square (20 × 30 m) directly west of the theater (fig. 4.18)[63] may have served as an agora.[64] Colonnaded squares also occur in conjunction with a number of other theaters in Asia Minor—for example, at Aphrodisias, Pessinus, and Side—as well as in the western provinces, as at Ostia, Pompeii, Augusta Emerita, Balbus, and Tusculum.[65] In Aphrodisias, after a series of earthquakes in the 4th

[62] We have measurements for three of these rooms or shops; the dimensions of the largest shop are l. 3.75 m, w. 2.90 m, and h. 3.80 m. Taşlıalan 1997, 331. Taşlıalan suggests that the rectangular holes along the walls of the shops, which are all equidistant from each other and from the ground, indicate that the shops were two stories tall.

[63] Taşlıalan 1997, 337.

[64] Taşlıalan 1997, 324 and n. 38 above. Alternatively, this proposed square may have served as part of the theater structure

where theater-related activities took place. Gallo-Roman theaters sometimes contained adjacent squares that hosted theatrical performances, but this feature is not found in other theaters in Asia Minor. Rosetto and Sartorio 1994, 1:140.

[65] See Sear 2006, 9, 93–94 for a discussion of Vitruvius's description of the quadriporticus adorned with statues and wall paintings behind the theater of Pompey in Rome. Sear also notes that a shrine with a head of a veiled Augustus was found in the quadriporticus at the theater of Augusta Emerita in Spain.

century flooded the old agora, the governor of the city built a new agora called the *tetrastoön* (four *stoa*s or porticoes) on higher ground to the east of the stage building.[66]

At Antioch, the situation may have been similar. The early 4th century inscription on an arch that spanned the *decumanus* near the south entrance of the theater mentions porticoes donated by Marcus Valerius Diogenes, the governor of the new province of Pisidia.[67] The location of these porticoes, however, is uncertain. They may not have surrounded the theater square but instead may have lined the streets. It is possible that at some phase of its history the theater square area housed commercial enterprises. The magnetometric survey results revealed the presence of a large pottery kiln and a workshop, possibly for metalworking.[68]

The Question of a Tunnel beneath the Cavea. Although Taşhalan's excavation report of 1997 provides us with the bulk of information for reconstructing the appearance of the theater, this same report raises some puzzling questions. Taşhalan asserts that a vaulted tunnel measuring 56 m long, 5 m wide, and 6.50 m high ran beneath the southern part of the cavea, a feature found in three other Roman theaters in Italy (Tusculum), Tunisia (Bulla Regia), and France (Toloso), but it is, at present, unknown elsewhere in Asia Minor.[69] Taşhalan claims that this tunnel was created when the cavea was extended over the *decumanus maximus*[70] and that the archway at the entrance of the "tunnel," as well as architectural elements in the surrounding area, provide evidence for its location.[71] Mitchell and Waelkens accept Taşhalan's hypothesis, given the narrowing width of the *decumanus maximus* to 5 m in this area and the alleged presence of foundations of the southern part of the cavea across the street.[72] In his excavation, however, Demirer found no archaeological evidence for a tunnel, nor did he locate foundations for the enlarged cavea on the south side of the *decumanus*, thus casting Taşhalan's theory into doubt. Moreover, a tunnel requiring additional seats on the southern side of the theater would have disturbed the symmetrical arrangement of the cavea, which, in turn, would have caused problems with the roofing of the stage building and with the acoustics. Also, as was discovered when a virtual model of the theater was built, an enlarged building that spanned the *decumanus* would have had to be exceedingly tall. Further excavation, especially of the area south of the *decumanus*, may clarify the issue. For the present, we reconstruct the theater as having a smaller diameter than Taşhalan projects.

Civic and Social Roles

In antiquity, the theater was among a handful of buildings whose presence was perceived as a basic marker of urban status. Ample evidence from Rome to Asia Minor illustrates the importance of theaters in defining and displaying a city's social structure and hierarchy and in reinforcing social and political relationships between different segments of a city's population.

[66] Erim 1986, 89. The *tetrastoön* was constructed by the governor of Caria, Antonius Tatianus, in an effort to expand Aphrodisias's role as a metropolis of Phyrgia and Caria. The various styles of columns from the porticoes of the *tetrastoön* were likely spolia from other buildings at the site. Erim 1986, 90–91.

[67] Mitchell and Waelkens 1998, 108–109. The inscriptions on the archway are discussed at length later in this chapter.

[68] Smekalova and Smeklov 2001, 4.

[69] Taşhalan 1997, 326; Mitchell and Waelkens 1998, 106–107; Sear 2006, 25.

[70] Taşhalan 1997, 329; Mitchell and Waelkens 1998, 107.

[71] Taşhalan 1997, 329.

[72] Mitchell and Waelkens 1998, 106–107. Taşhalan, however, does not mention foundations across the *decumanus* in his excavation report, but it is possible that the earlier Mitchell and Waelkens survey identified this evidence.

The seating arrangements in the cavea played a role in imposing social order on the audience according to civic status, gender, or tribal affiliation. In classical Greece, tribal groups were seated in different *cunei*, as the different tickets that were assigned to different tribes in Athens attest.[73] In a fragment of a comedy by 4th-century BC writer Alexis of Thurii, a woman comments that she had to take a seat in the outermost *cunei/kerkis*, like a foreigner.[74] Seating based on tribal affiliation persisted into the Roman period. When Hadrian visited Athens in AD 126, each tribe dedicated a statue to the emperor in their section of the theater of Dionysos. In Asia Minor at the Roman theater at Hierapolis, the steps of the cavea were inscribed with names of the city's tribes.[75]

In Rome itself, where theater and drama were viewed skeptically by the authorities, a host of legislation from the Republican period onwards regulated theatrical activity by, for instance, segregating the audience by gender and mandating dress codes for the audience.[76] In addition, Roman theater seating was arranged according to social hierarchy, with senators occupying the seats closest to the orchestra, in front of the members of the lower social ranks.[77] It is possible that the unstudied seat inscriptions at Antioch designated tribal units and prescribed a mode of audience organization that was more closely related to the customs of the Greek theater, despite the heavy influence of Western architectural forms on the structure of the building itself.[78]

The theater was also a key location for euergetistic activities through the sponsorship of festivals and games and donations of architectural or sculptural works. A primary motive for benefactions in the theater, and in cities in general, was to court public opinion and thereby further personal political and social aspirations.[79] The visibility of the donors, who were often segregated from the rest of the audience in reserved seats such as the high-backed chairs at the orchestra,[80] and of their donations,

[73] Bieber 1961, 71.

[74] Bieber 1961, 71.

[75] Small 1987, 86–87; Mitchell and Waelkens 1998, 99–100; Ritti 1985, 118–122.

[76] Beacham 1992, 154 states that the production of new plays and formal comedies and tragedies had been supplanted by other stage spectacles by the end of the 1st century BC.

[77] Augustus's *Lex Julia Theatralis* specified that social class and gender were the main segregating principles in the theater. Rawson 1987, 83–114; Edmondson 1996, 90; Sear 2006, 11. While the structure of a Roman theater reinforced the social hierarchy of the city, at the same time it highlighted the cohesion among the different groups that formed communal units. Edmondson observes that "the presence of freeborn non-citizens, slaves, and prostitutes [at the theater] ipso facto gave even the poorest members of the *plebs Romana* a heightened sense of their civic and social identity" (1996, 97). As elsewhere, the spectators in the theater at Antioch would have represented a cross-section of the community ranging from citizens to slaves, governors to peasants, soldiers to foreign merchants, and priestesses to prostitutes (Edmondson 1996, 82). See Beacham 1992, 21–22, noting that citizens, women, and slaves, who were not allowed a seat, were free to attend the games, and while the games

were primarily religious, an important part of their social function was their entertainment value.

[78] See n. 25 regarding the reconstruction of the Antioch cavea inscriptions in *SEG* 50 (2000). Chaniotis 2007, 61 classifies the Antioch inscriptions alongside those at Ephesos as tribal designations. It is possible that additional inscriptions no longer preserved may have provided names that were linked to the Roman *vici* established with the founding of the Augustan colony.

[79] Cicero claimed that there were "three venues where the opinion and feeling of the Roman people could be most directly expressed about public affairs: at a meeting, at the Assembly, and at a gathering for plays and gladiatorial shows." Cicero, *Pro Sestio*, 50–59 cited in Beacham 1992, 160.

[80] Özgür 1990, 30. Bieber 1961, 70–71. Certain seats seem to have been reserved for particular members of Antiochene society, as do ones at Aspendos and Termessos, in the provinces of Pamphylia and Pisidia, respectively. Drew-Bear 2000, 209; Small 1987, 90. Drew-Bear (2000, 210) believes additionally that *homonoia* relationships, or civic alliances, with other neighboring cities were also commemorated by the seat inscriptions in the theater. See n. 78 for a different interpretation of these inscriptions; see also Mitchell and Waelkens 1998, 99–100.

which were on constant display on the stage building, the stage façade, in the orchestra, or in another part of the theater, made theaters a prime venue for euergetism in the city.

In the theater at Antioch, as at theaters in other cities of the Greek East, euergetistic activities probably often served as well to proclaim the patron and the city's loyalty to the Roman emperor.[81] Augustus, who had created the Actium games in honor of his own naval victory, initiated a fashion in the East for games dedicated in honor of the emperor and his family. In the theater at Hierapolis in Phrygia, for example, a cylindrical altar, dated to between 1 BC and AD 4, names a patron, Zozimos, who dedicated the altar to Gaius, the grandson of the *princeps*, and to Rome. Ritti identifies Zosimos as a victor in as yet unidentified games that were likely dedicated to Gaius and Roma or to Augustus himself.[82] During the Tiberian period, in the Laconian city of Gytheion, the theater was the destination of a ritual procession that marked the commencement of its festival in honor of the imperial family and of two prominent local citizens who had been allies of Augustus.[83]

Though not all festivals and games held in a city's theater were dedicated to the emperor, the emperor's presence was still felt indirectly. In many theaters in the Greek East portraits of the emperor, and sometimes of his family, were placed in different spots, most often on the stage building, along with portraits of private citizens.[84] In addition, certain dignitaries would be given the honor of wearing crowns with busts representing the Roman emperor alongside other deities. Such is the case at the Lycian city of Oenoanda, where the Demostheneia musical festival was established in the time of Hadrian. Here, the *agonothete*—the official in charge of organizing the festival—was distinguished from the crowd by his purple robe and silver crown featuring the portrait of Hadrian and the local ancestral deity, Apollo. This festival was a benefaction of the local patron Demosthenes, and its founding was approved by Hadrian himself.[85]

Neither Gytheion nor Oenoanda was a major civic center, and neither one had the privilege of hosting an official imperial cult as did Antioch.[86] Nevertheless, through extravagant displays of loyalty in the form of theatrical games and festivals, each city was able to forge a closer connection with the mighty imperial house and consequently to burnish its civic credentials.[87] The epigraphic record detailing the games and festivals at Gytheion and Oenoanda reveals that the patron at Oenoanda and the councils of both cities had petitioned the emperor and established a record of imperial correspondence that preserves, in the case of Gytheion, an expression of detached, dutiful attention on the part of Tiberius and, in the case of Oenoanda, a more appreciative response on the part of Hadrian to the activities proposed by the local communities.[88] These dossiers of correspondence

[81] Potter 1999, 278.

[82] Ritti 1979, 183–197; 1985, 78–84.

[83] This procession at Gytheion is described in a Greek inscription from the city, *SEG* 11:923. Translations can be found in Ehrenberg and Jones 1955, no. 102; Lewis and Rheinhold 1951, no. 168; Sherk 1988, no. 32.

[84] Sturgeon 2004, 29–33 provides a short survey of imperial portraits and imagery in the theaters of the Greek East. See also Ng 2007, chap. 5; Ritti 1985, 59–77; D'Andria and Ritti 1985; Gebhard 1996, 113–127. Potter 1999, 278–282 discusses the influence of imperial tastes and the occasional physical presence of the emperor in the provinces on the establishment of local festivals and games.

[85] The Greek inscriptions related to the establishment and the protocols of the Demostheneia are published in monographic form by M. Wörrle (1988). Mitchell translated this dossier into English in 1990. Rogers 1991a and 1991b examine the aspects of patronage of this festival; the lines pertaining to the costume of the *agonothete* are described at Rogers 1991b, 51–53, 56–58.

[86] Price 1984, 60–61.

[87] Ng 2007, chap. 5.

[88] Tiberius refused the honor of the festivals but accepted some honors on behalf of his father, Augustus, as seen in the inscription in Sherk 1988, no. 31. Hadrian's response to the Demostheneia is recorded in the dossier cited above, lines 1–6.

Fig. 4.19. Frieze from the imperial cult temple now at the Yalvaç Museum (2004). Photo: B. Rubin (A07).

Fig. 4.20. Cornice with lion's head from city gate at Antioch (2004). Photo: H. B. Mallampati (CG26).

were published in prominent places so that the cities could advertise that they had enjoyed the interest of the Roman emperor, however restrained the expression thereof. Such records gave these places and patrons importance and prestige. The associations among the local elites, cities, and the emperor were broadcast to the crowds that came from other cities and streamed into the theaters for the festivals. The theater thus played a singularly important role in the cities' demonstration of civic status and identity.[89]

Though there is no known archaeological or epigraphic evidence of such imperially sanctioned festivities at the theater at Antioch, there appears to be a link between the theater and the emperor in visual elements common to Antioch's theater and parts of the imperial cult sanctuary.[90] If Demirer's date of the early 1st century AD for construction of the theater is correct, then it was built not long after the construction of the imperial cult sanctuary. The curved form of the theater's cavea is echoed in the hemicycle of the imperial cult sanctuary, and both structures conform to the same axial alignment, which perhaps alludes to a symbolic relationship between the two structures (see fig. 4.2).[91] The theater and the imperial cult sanctuary are also related through their sculptural ornaments. The decorative bucrania and garland friezes on the imperial cult temple and the theater are of similar design. While the earlier, deeply carved bucrania and garlands are separated by rosettes on the imperial cult temple (fig. 4.19) and are stylistically different from the theater's flatly carved bucrania and garlands (see fig. 4.10), the bulls' long broad snouts, the tufts of hair between their eyes, and the locking pattern of garlands above their heads are strikingly similar on both friezes. The evocation of imperial imagery also appears in the lion's head frieze unearthed by Demirer in the theater. Lions' heads also occur on the imperial cult temple. The lion's head from the theater, which projects forward from a background of vegetal forms, is also reminiscent of the lions on the cornice of the Arch of Hadrian and Sabina built during the emperor Hadrian's reign in the 2nd century (fig. 4.20).

[89] Ng 2007, 161–163, 171–174.

[90] The westward, sunset-facing orientation of the theater at Antioch may suggest that performances either occurred during the morning or, more likely, that the theater was covered with an awning, as was the 2nd-century theater at Aspendos, so that spectators were screened from the afternoon light. This westward orientation of the theater and the imperial cult sanctuary is also repeated in the apses of the later churches that dotted the city.

[91] Similarly, the quasi-theatric structure at Pessinus, a temple, and a colonnaded square were built along the same axis and situated within a few steps of one another. The physical proximity and axial arrangement of the temple and quasi-theater have led some to suggest that these structures functioned as a single architectural unit. Waelkens 1986, 39.

Ossi, in chapter 5 of this volume, conjectures that the theater was a stopping point in ritual processions related to the imperial cult in Antioch, a procession that would have connected the imperial cult sanctuary to other important monuments in the city, including the Hadrianic triple-arched city gate that clearly emulates the triple-arched Augustan propylon of the sanctuary. This is an intriguing hypothesis. Well-attested processions in other cities of the Greek East stopped in the theater; however, not all such processions were connected to the imperial cult.[92] Regardless of whether a religious and ritual connection between the theater and the sanctuary existed at Antioch, the decorative scheme at the theater drew upon the precedent of the imperial cult sanctuary. Its unmistakably imperial character would have visibly underscored the city's identity as an imperial colony.

The different groups of the city, still in the process of blending and merging in Augustan times, would have had their assigned places within the theater. The entire community here would have been contained in an imperially marked space. Their theater, like the sanctuary, as Rubin argues in chapter 3 of this volume, would have served as an architectural metaphor for the Roman imperial project in Pisidia.

The Theater in the Late Antique Period. The theater at Antioch remained an important locus for displays of elite status, generosity, and imperial loyalty well into late antiquity. The inscriptions found in the area of the theater shed light on the political and religious identities of the city's patrons and the honors that were bestowed upon them. The earliest of these inscriptions dates to the first half of the 3rd century AD; it informs us that C. Arrius C. f. Quirina Calpurnius Frontinus Honoratus, a patron of the colony and a consul, was honored *postulante populo in theatro*—"by a request of the people in the theater"—meaning the popular assembly that met in the theater to conduct civic business. The reason for this honor is unknown.[93]

The largest surviving inscription—the early 4th-century inscription mentioned above, which names Marcus Valerius Diogenes, governor of Pisidia—implies a benefaction that related to the theater (fig. 4.21):[94]

> To the concord of the emperors. For the most happy times of our masters Galerius Valerius Maximianus, and Galerius Valerius Maximinus, and Flavius Valerius Constantinus and Valerius Licinianus Licinius, the most devout emperors, Marcus Valerius Diogenes, a most perfect man, governor, devoted to their spirit and majesty, at his own initiative took charge of the construction of the arch (with the) porticos (and all the) decoration from the foundation.[95]

[92] Processions took place at Gytheion and Oenoanda, as noted above. At Gytheion, especially, the influence of the imperial cult is quite strong. The most widely discussed civic procession that had a stop in the theater is the one established by C. Vibius Salutaris in Ephesos in the Trajanic period; in this procession, the main emphasis was on the cult of Artemis and local history rather than on the imperial cult. See Wankel 1979–1984, no. 27, with German translation; Rogers's monograph (1991b) on this inscription includes an English translation. Chaniotis 2007, 52 discusses these processions briefly and makes the important point that such cult rituals were especially suited for the theater because the spectators were witnesses to the relations between cities and emperors that were reinforced by ceremony.

[93] Mitchell and Waelkens 1998, 224 (citing *CIL* 3.6810–6812).

[94] T. Callander first described the archway in 1913. Mitchell and Waelkens 1998, 106–108; Christol and Drew-Bear 1999, 46–50 argue that the style of the epigraphy as well as the ordering of the emperor's names suggests that the archway was erected in AD 310 or 311. Most of the inscribed blocks are in their original location near the theater (fig. 4.21) or in the Yalvaç Museum.

[95] Christol and Drew-Bear 1999, 54; Mitchell and Waelkens 1998, 108–109. Mitchell and Waelkens's translation does not mention Galerius Valerius Maximinius, as the name was not found among the fragments, but it is likely that it was merely lost rather than not included in the original inscription. Christol and Drew-Bear's insertion of this name is probably accurate given its inclusion in other imperial documents of

Fig. 4.21. In situ remnants of the Valerius Diogenes arch at Antioch (2004). Photo: H. B. Mallampati (T12).

Christol and Drew-Bear argue that the erection of porticoes and the arch, with its dedication to the emperors, points to the importance of the imperial cult even in this later period.[96] The dedication of the new works to the "spirit and majesty" of the emperors, however, is part of an epigraphic formula that was used in imperial dedications after Constantine, when the worship of the emperor as a deity was discouraged from the top.[97] In addition, because Diogenes was himself an agent of the emperors as the governor of Pisidia, it is not surprising that his dedication should be to the tetrarchs to whom he answered. As for the porticoes themselves, Price notes that porticoes sometimes contained shrines that may have been used for practicing the imperial cult, but the porticoes he refers to were in the main squares of cities.[98] The location of Diogenes's porticoes is unknown; as mentioned earlier, they may have stood in the putative square adjacent to the theater,[99] along the *decumanus maximus*, or in another part of the city altogether. It is certainly possible, but speculative given the available evidence, that Diogenes erected porticoes to serve the imperial cult's purposes. Even if these particular donations were not related to the worship of the emperor, they nonetheless provide evidence of the influence of the emperor and his representatives in the imperial administration in the lives of the cities of Asia Minor at this time. This trend of imperial involvement occurred as private benefaction of major construction projects dropped precipitously in the second half of the 3rd century.[100]

Another theater inscription naming Diogenes was found in Demirer's 2004 excavation of the orchestra, indicating that, in addition to the construction of the archway and porticoes, Diogenes

this period. The emperors discussed in the inscription by their most recognizable names are Galerius, Maximinus Daia, Constantine, and Licinius.

[96] Christol and Drew-Bear 1999, 55 cite Price 1984 and Gros 1990.

[97] This epigraphic formula is also often abbreviated and acts more as a parenthetical than as a device to underline the importance of imperial worship. This exact phrase, "devoted to his spirit and majesty," is used also for Constantine and

emperors after him, who were Christian and who clearly were not being worshipped. For examples of this phrase, see *ILS*. This phrase can occur in any dedication to the emperors regardless of venue (baths, circus, stand-alone statues, etc.).

[98] Price 1984, 140.

[99] See n. 38 above for the area west of the theater.

[100] Mitchell 1993, 206–211; Zuiderhoek 2009.

Fig. 4.22. Diogenes inscription (lying upside down) found in theater orchestra at Antioch (2004). Photo: H. B. Mallampati (T01).

probably contributed to a remodeling of the theater itself (fig. 4.22). The incomplete inscription reads: (1) D N IOVIO MAXIMIANO INVICTO AUG; (2) VAL DIOGENES VP PRAES PROVINCO PISID, which may translate as (1) "to our lord Jovian Maximinus unconquered Augustus;"[101] (2) "Valerius Diogenes, a most perfect man, governor of the province of Pisidia." Diogenes's benefactions in and around the theater seem to fit into the general pattern of imperial governors who took over the role of local elite patrons during this period.[102]

Our strongest evidence for postulating a ritual relation between the 4th-century theater and the imperial cult comes from the structural modification to the cavea that took place in this period. As described above, balustrade walls that were set up around the perimeter of the orchestra suggest gladiatorial and animal games took place in the theater. The *munera*, or gladiatorial games, were undoubtedly popular early in the history of the Roman military colony at Antioch, whose citizens in the late 1st century BC and early 1st century AD included numerous Roman veterans. Not all *munera*, however, were connected to emperor worship. Augustus's account of his own deeds, the *Res Gestae*—a copy of which was displayed on or near the propylon at the entrance to the imperial cult sanctuary complex at Antioch—lists his own expenditures for hugely popular gladiatorial shows and wild beast hunts in Rome. Augustus proclaims:

> Three times I gave shows of gladiators under my name and five times under the name of my sons and grandsons; in these shows about 10,000 men fought. . . . Twenty-six times, under my name or that of my sons and grandsons, I gave the people hunts of African beasts in the circus, in the open, or in the amphitheater; in them about 3,500 beasts were killed.[103]

[101] The inscription may refer to Maximian, who held the title of Augustus from 286 to 305, or more likely to Galerius Valerius Maximianus, who was named Caesar by Diocletian in 293 and gained the title of Augustus from 305 to 311 after the abdication of Diocletian. For a detailed account of Galerius's deeds, see Potter 2004, 288, 340–346, 348–351, 355–356. In either case, the inscription dates somewhere

between AD 286 and 311.

[102] Roueché 1991, 101 notes that governors were expected to appear at these public events and facilitated the performance of the shows.

[103] *Res Gestae Divi Augusti* 22.1 (Bushnell ed. 1998) available

Gladiatorial games highlighted the military ethic and emphasized the martial basis for Rome's domination of foreign territories.[104] This most Roman form of entertainment had no parallels in the Greek East, and though the first games had been held in Syrian Antioch in the 2nd century BC, it was not until the early imperial period, the same period during which Pisidian Antioch was founded, that gladiatorial games became a more regular feature of public entertainment in Greek cities.[105] Pisidian Antioch, having been settled by Italian veterans and other Roman colonists, might have served, like Roman Corinth, as a point of entry for gladiatorial games in its region.[106] Unlike the theatrical performances or the animal games, the gladiatorial games did not have a defined religious connotation early in Roman history but later were directly linked to emperor worship in the eastern provinces.[107] Often the imperial priests owned their own troupes of beasts, gladiators, and beast fighters for these various spectacles,[108] and they along with public officials were expected to sponsor gladiatorial games.[109] Such shows remained staples of public entertainment around the empire into the 4th century, along with plays, mimes, and pantomimes.[110]

Though the Christianization of the empire had certainly put an end to the imperial cult by the Byzantine period, cities such as Antioch continued to honor the emperor and to declare their fealty to him. Statues and inscriptions adorned the main thoroughfares of Antioch, including those near the theater, during this later period. A large inscribed block located on the *decumanus maximus* by the south entrance of the theater was probably a statue base for the image of the Byzantine emperor Justinian (r. AD 527–565) (fig. 4.23).[111] Zuckerman translates the Greek inscription as follows:

at: http://classics.mit.edu/Augustus/deeds.html. An undated inscription from Pisidian Antioch attests that games were also subjects of testamentary documents:

> Dedicated to Gaius Albucius Servius Firmus son of Gaius, aedile and douvir, who designated money in his will to provide for an athletic contest to be held every year at the feast of the Moon. *ILS* 5070, *CIL* 3S.6829 cited in Mahoney 2001, 44.

It is likely that this athletic contest was held in the small theater of the sanctuary of Mên Askaênos rather than the theater at Antioch given that sanctuary's role in celebrating the feast to Mên. See Katchadourian and Raff, chaps. 7 and 8, this volume. The inscription reveals that such games and other forms of entertainment were sponsored by various members of society, in this case a former *douvir* and aedile. Most importantly, individuals, whether they were emperors or local citizens of Antioch, wished to be remembered for their patronage of these games.

[104] Edmondson 1996, 72. Possibly, the display of organized public violence within the confines of the theater was an outlet for aggression and a vehicle for controlling civic disorder as well. It is unknown whether such games would have taken place in the theater at this early a date in Pisidian Antioch. For a discussion of gladiatorial games, see Potter 1999, 311–317.

[105] Potter 1999, 306. Polybius gives an account of the games sponsored by Antiochus IV (30.25–26).

[106] Welch 1999, 136–138.

[107] Dodge 1999, 206, 225 notes that the earliest gladiatorial games were part of aristocratic funerals and during the Empire occurred in amphitheaters, circuses, and only occasionally in theaters. Mitchell 1993, 105, 111 notes that during Tiberius's reign half of the Galatian priests of the Divine Augustus and the Goddess Roma in Ankyra (Ankara) provided gladiatorial games, or *venationes*, during their tenure; also that the design of the theater at Pessinus accommodated gladiatorial shows and wild beast fights, which were often associated with emperor worship. The most important epigraphical source for gladiators in the Greek East is Robert 1940.

[108] Welch 1998, 123. An interesting note in the *Acts of Paul and Thecla* reveals that Alexander, the imperial priest who attacked Thecla, owned his own beasts, which were used in shows in the theater.

[109] Mitchell 1993, 110 notes that the majority of gladiatorial inscriptions are connected with the imperial cult.

[110] Balsdon 1969, 251 observes that Constantine's decree limiting gladiatorial fights was ineffective. Gladiatorial fights continued until the end of the 4th century, while wild beast fights continued until the end of the 5th century.

[111] Zuckerman 2002, 243. The block measures 136 × 83 × 90 cm.

Fig. 4.23 (left). Inscription block/statue base outside theater (2004). Photo: H. B. Mallampati (T30).

Fig. 4.24 (above). Seat from the "Round Building" (*tholos*) at Antioch (1924). Photo: G. R. Swain, Kelsey Museum Archives neg. no. 7.1207.

> The city of Antiochenes erected
> a rampart crowned by God:
> The divine Justinian, the orderer of the rules of the world.[112]

The "orderer of the rules of the world" probably refers to the codification of law in the *Digests* during Justinian's reign.[113] Zuckerman suggests that the citizens of Antioch put up the statue some time after legislation relaxed an earlier policy against erecting imperial images,[114] to express their collective loyalty by according honors to the emperor, to celebrate his divinely mandated power to rule, or to call attention to Justinian's own piety.[115]

Reuse and Preservation of the Theater

Recent excavation and current preservation efforts at the theater are just as interesting as its ancient history. Taşlıalan felt that the theater was "the most ruined of all structures scattered over the site."[116] The missing upper rows of the cavea seating as well as the destroyed entrances and damaged stage façade led Taşlıalan and others to believe that the theater had become a quarry whose rectilinear building blocks could be easily reused for other structures.[117] The reuse of the theater's components may have occurred in numerous phases of Antioch's history and for different reasons. Michigan's excavation in the Tiberia Platea unearthed corner seats with lions' paws at their base in the "Round

[112] Zuckerman 2002, 244. The epithet "divine" in this inscription, as Zuckerman notes, connotes the venerable but not divine nature of the emperor and his image, in a manner akin to the veneration of saints.

[113] Zuckerman 2002, 246–247.

[114] Zuckerman 2002, 248–253.

[115] Zuckerman 2002, 252.

[116] Taşlıalan 1991, 27.

[117] Rossetto and Sartorio 1994, 1:82 discuss the destruction of Graeco-Roman theaters in Asia Minor, specifically stage façades and steps.

Fig. 4.25. Fragment of mask frieze from the theater at Antioch reused in a wall (1924).
Photo: G. R. Swain, Kelsey Museum Archives neg. no. 7.1125.

Building," later referred to as the *tholos*,[118] leading Robinson to ask whether these seats were reused from the theater or were imitations of seats in the theater (fig. 4.24). Although similar seats with lions' paws have not been uncovered in the theater, this form occurs in other theaters in Asia Minor, such as those at Side and Kremna. It is possible that some of the seats in the *tholos* were taken from the theater after new seats were added to the latter in the 2nd century, or even at a much later period.

On July 2, 1924, George R. Swain of the University of Michigan's excavation team at Antioch photographed a portion of a then unidentified theater frieze, which he saw along a road leading to the town of Yalvaç (fig. 4.25). The frieze, adorned with theater masks, bucrania, and garlands, matches the sculptures found during Taşlıalan's excavation of the theater in the 1990s. In addition, the finds from Demirer's more recent excavation of the orchestra include a plethora of building blocks made of various stones, inscriptions, and carvings that adorned the stage façade and arena walls. Taken together, these blocks should allow a larger portion of the stage façade to be reconstructed than was previously thought possible (fig. 4.26).

Conclusion

From its founding in the 1st century BC or AD until its eventual abandonment in the 8th century, the theater at Antioch underwent many architectural modifications to accommodate changes in its use. Starting as a site for dramatic performances, later used as an arena, then possibly a chapel, and finally a stable,[119] the theater was influenced by changes in the economy of the city and in the

---

[118] See the note appended to Rubin, chap. 3, this volume, for a discussion of the *tholos*.

[119] As observed by Demirer during his excavation of the theater.

Fig. 4.26. Excavation of the stage building of the theater at Antioch (2004). Photo: Ü. Demirer.

religious viewpoints and political attitudes of its inhabitants. Most of the architectural features of the theater in its present state appear to date to the late 3rd–early 4th centuries AD, when Antioch was experiencing an economic boom connected to the city's rise in status as the capital of the province of Pisidia and its patronage under the governor Marcus Valerius Diogenes.[120] Further research, especially on the many inscriptions and sculptural decorations unearthed during Demirer's 2004 excavation and earlier, will undoubtedly yield new insights into the theater's political, religious, and social significance to the city's residents.[121]

[120] Mitchell and Waelkens 1998, 12; Christol and Drew-Bear 1999, 70.

[121] See Özhanlı 2009b, 73–74 for continuing work at the theater.

5 The Arch of Hadrian and Sabina at Pisidian Antioch: Imperial Associations, Ritual Connections, and Civic Euergetism

Adrian J. Ossi[1]

In AD 129, the Roman emperor Hadrian traveled through Asia Minor in order to become better acquainted with the peoples, cultures, and cities that he ruled. In the same year, the citizens of Pisidian Antioch built at the entrance to their city a monumental arch that was dedicated to Hadrian and his wife Sabina (fig. 5.1). Hadrian is known to have passed close by Antioch, and, given the prominent location of the arch, it is highly likely that he visited the city. The honorific arch would have presented a monumental welcome to the emperor as he entered the city, and for centuries to come it would have remained as a permanent reminder of his prestigious visit. This chapter presents an examination of the political and social motivations for the construction of the Arch of Hadrian and Sabina, based on a reading of its architectural form and iconographic content.

Past Research and Current State of the Remains

In 1833, Francis V. J. Arundell was the first to identify the site of Pisidian Antioch. During his visit, he seems to have noticed the remains of the arch, but he incorrectly identified them as a temple of Bacchus.[2] The form of the monument was first identified as an honorific arch when the University of Michigan team began its excavation on July 7, 1924.[3] As originally excavated, the fragments of the superstructure of the arch were in a jumbled mass lying on top of, between, and around the bases of the four piers that remained partially in situ (fig. 5.2). The team moved many of the blocks into the surrounding fields for further study and identified the location of each of the four piers. A few meters north of the arch's central passageway, the team uncovered the foundations of a semicircular fountain (fig. 5.3).[4] They also opened two test trenches farther north, ca. 35 and 70 m from the arch, and uncovered a small part of the paved street that passed through the arch.[5]

In the course of excavations, architect Frederick J. Woodbridge and his assistant Horace F. Colby documented the remains of the arch in a series of notebooks and drawings, and photographer George R. Swain took numerous photographs. While in Yalvaç, Woodbridge sketched several preliminary reconstructions of the arch, revising and improving his conception of the monument as new evidence was uncovered.[6] In the following year, Woodbridge drafted a final detailed reconstruction of the arch

[1] This study is based on a chapter of my doctoral dissertation (Ossi 2009, 108–185). I am indebted to the Kelsey Museum of Archaeology for permission to publish archival materials pertaining to the 1924 Michigan excavations at Pisidian Antioch, and to Ünal Demirer, former director of the Yalvaç Museum, for permission to study the remains visible at the ancient site in 2004.

[2] Arundell 1834, 268.

[3] Journal of Excavations, entry for July 7, 1924.

[4] Robinson 1924a, 443.

[5] Journal of Excavations, entry for August 12, 1924. The approximate location of these two trenches is indicated on Woodbridge's plan of the site (see fig. 2.3). For a photograph of the small area of paved street revealed, see Ossi 2009, fig. 163.

[6] For discussion of Woodbridge's process of reconstruction illustrated with several of his working drawings, see Ossi 2005–2006.

Fig. 5.1. Digital reconstruction of the Arch of Hadrian and Sabina and its surroundings, with a hypothetical nymphaeum at upper left. Digital model: A. J. Ossi and J. M. Harrington.

Fig. 5.2. Excavation of the Arch of Hadrian and Sabina in 1924. Enoch E. Peterson leans against the base of pier 2. Today, the orthostats of this pier are no longer in situ. Photo: G. R. Swain, Kelsey Museum Archives neg. no. 7.1624.

using the data he had collected (fig. 5.4). In 1926, David M. Robinson, the director of the Michigan excavations, published two of Woodbridge's reconstruction drawings of the arch along with a discussion of the sculptural reliefs that decorated the upper portion of the monument.[7] Robinson did not provide a detailed explanation of the archaeological basis for Woodbridge's reconstruction. Based on a fragment of the dedicatory inscription, Robinson suggested a date of construction around AD 212.[8] For a long time thereafter, scholarly interpretations of the arch relied on this date,[9] but recent research (discussed further below) has proved this date to be incorrect.

  After the Michigan team departed, the site of Pisidian Antioch lay fallow for nearly seventy years. In 1982, a team led by Stephen Mitchell and Marc Waelkens performed an architectural survey at the site.[10] By this time the architectural fragments and foundations of the Arch of Hadrian and

[7] Robinson 1926a, 45–56 (discussion) and figs. 1 and 67 (reconstructions).

[8] Robinson 1926a, 45.

[9] Güven 1983, 66–70; Vermeule 1968, 78–79; Ward-Perkins 1980, 280.

[10] Mitchell and Waelkens 1998.

Fig. 5.3. The semicircular fountain (in foreground) aligned with the central opening of the Arch of Hadrian and Sabina (at center), viewed from the north in 1924. Photo: G. R. Swain, Kelsey Museum Archives neg. no. 8.0017.

Fig. 5.4, Woodbridge's reconstruction drawing of the Arch of Hadrian and Sabina (1925). Kelsey Museum Archives AAR-2421.

Fig. 5.5. The Arch of Hadrian and Sabina today, viewed from the northeast. Pier 4 is closest to the viewer at lower left. The white blocks at right surround the semicircular fountain (2007). Photo: A. J. Ossi.

Sabina had become mostly reburied, so that Mitchell and Waelkens could draw only a partial plan of the monument.[11] In the mid-1990s, excavations were resumed under the auspices of the Yalvaç Museum, first directed by Mehmet Taşlıalan and later by Ünal Demirer. The Turkish excavators reexposed the arch, uncovered much of the surrounding area for the first time (fig. 5.5), and discovered several previously unknown decorated blocks from the arch.[12]

When the new Michigan team visited the site in 2004, the locations of all four piers of the Arch of Hadrian and Sabina could be identified. For the purposes of this discussion I number them 1–4 from west to east, following the convention established in the 1924 Journal of Excavations.[13] Piers 3 and 4 are the best preserved (fig. 5.6). Both have orthostats in situ on top of a complete base molding course, and on pier 4 the orthostat course is fully preserved.[14] For pier 2, fragments of the base molding course, as well as two lower foundation courses, are preserved. In 1924 many of the orthostats of this pier were in place (fig. 5.2), but they have since been displaced. Pier 1 has almost completely vanished, but a low foundation course is visible in situ (fig. 5.7). The pier bases were composed of dark gray limestone to a height of ca. 1.6 m above the street paving.[15] The many fragments of the gate's superstructure are of white limestone, indicating that the gray pier bases would have contrasted with the white superstructure.[16]

The remains of the arch visible at the site today allow a few conclusions. First, it seems that the arch was never fully finished in all of its architectural details. This is most obvious on pier 4, where the base molding is in various states of completion on all four sides,[17] and the faces of the orthostats

[11] Mitchell and Waelkens 1998, fig. 19a.

[12] Taşlıalan 2000; Bru and Demirer 2006.

[13] Journal of Excavations, entry for August 30.

[14] At the time of excavation in 1924, all but one of the orthostats that today are scattered around pier 3 were also in situ on the pier base.

[15] Measured using the scale in Woodbridge's reconstruction drawing (fig. 5.4).

[16] A similar colorific effect marks the Arch of Augustus (the propylon) at Antioch, where the steps in front were of gray limestone, while the parastades on the steps and the arch itself were of white limestone. Cf. also the Arch of Mazaeus and Mithridates in Ephesos, where gray voussoirs of the passageways contrast with the white marble of the rest of the structure.

[17] This unfinished molding provides a snapshot of the stone-carver's techniques. First, he carved the final profile of the molding in a narrow line at the joint between two stones. Then, with that carved profile as a register, he began to cut away the overlying stone across the whole length of the molding.

Fig. 5.6. Piers 3 and 4 of the Arch of Hadrian and Sabina today, viewed from the southeast. In the foreground, the remains of the statue base south of pier 4. In the background, the stepped cascade and the pavement of the entrance platea (2004). Photo: A. J. Ossi (CG 97).

Fig. 5.8. Pier 4, western face with unfinished lower molding and roughly tooled orthostats (2007). Photo: A. J. Ossi.

Fig. 5.7. The current state of pier 1, from the southeast. At upper right, unrelated blocks are stacked on the foundations of the pier. At lower left, the foundations of the statue base south of the pier (2004). Photo: A. J. Ossi (CG 101).

on the east and north faces are only roughly tooled (fig. 5.8). Unfinished carving is visible on several other blocks from the superstructure, particularly in certain details of the architectural moldings. Many of these unfinished details would have been located at the edges of the monument or on the short lateral faces, which would have been less visible to visitors.[18]

Next, certain details suggest that the Arch of Hadrian and Sabina, which as originally designed was a freestanding ornamental archway rather than a closeable gateway, was connected to a wall and converted into a true closeable gate in a later period.[19] The section of wall that abuts on the eastern face pier 4 (fig. 5.5, lower left) contains many reused stones mixed with coarse rubble masonry, suggesting

---

Several different stages of this process are preserved on this pier base. The stones of the east face and the northeast corner have only the register positions carved, while in the northwest corner and on the west face the molding has been roughed in.

[19] Here I disagree with Robinson (1924a, 443; followed by Bru and Demirer 2006, 583), who implies that the Arch of Hadrian and Sabina was connected to the city's fortification wall when it was first built.

[18] Ossi 2009, 110.

Fig. 5.9. Pier 2, profile view from west. At left, the foundations of the pier. At lower right, the molded statue base to the south (2004). Photo: A. J. Ossi (CG 103).

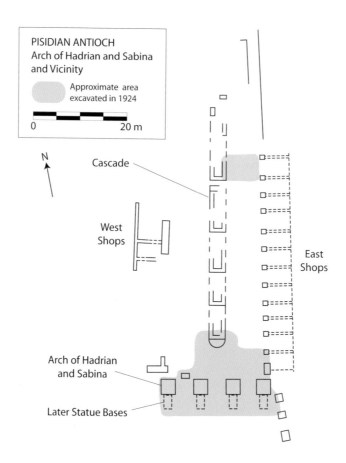

Fig. 5.10. Plan of the entrance platea at Pisidian Antioch. Drawing: A. J. Ossi, after an unpublished plan by I. Cowell, K. Hainswolf, B. Wolf, and M. Nikolic, with additional information from a drawing by F. J. Woodbridge in the Kelsey Museum Archives.

Fig. 5.11. Overhead view of several shops on the eastern side of the entrance platea, viewed from the southeast (2007). Photo: A. J. Ossi.

that it was built in a later period.[20] A line of apparently reused stones laid out south of the west passageway may have been the foundation of a wall that blocked access through the passageway (fig. 5.7, lower left). In addition, cuttings visible in the pavement of the east passageway and on the west face of pier 4 may have been for the insertion of a threshold and doorpost, by which the passageway could have been closed.[21] Other arches in the eastern Roman Empire underwent similar conversions, including the arch at Patara in Asia Minor and the arch at Isthmia in Greece.[22]

Recent excavations revealed the foundations of four rectangular bases immediately south of the arch, one aligned with each pier (figs. 5.6–7 and 5.9–10). The sequence of construction of the arch and the bases can be deduced using the characteristics of the preserved remains. The Ionic molding on the base south of pier 2 does not continue all the way around the stone; where it abuts on the foundations of the arch, the stone is flat (fig. 5.9). This suggests that the foundations of the Arch of Hadrian and Sabina were already in place when the base was installed.[23] Further excavation would be required to determine if all four bases were built at the same time. These four bases could have been for statues placed on axis with the piers of the arch; their dimensions are appropriate for statues of reclining animals, such as lions, or for small equestrian statues.

Recent excavations north of the arch exposed a broad street, or platea, with much of the paving preserved (fig. 5.10).[24] It was also discovered that the semicircular fountain uncovered by the Michigan team was the terminus of a long stepped cascade, the foundations of which can be seen today running northward from the arch along the central axis of the platea (figs. 2.11 and 5.6). On the eastern side of the platea a long row of shops was uncovered (figs. 5.10–11), the construction of which required carving back the bedrock of the hill in a number of places. Fragmentary remains on the western side of the platea suggest that a row of shops flanked this side of the street as well (fig. 5.10).

Since M. Taşlıalan's excavations reexposed the remains of the arch in 1998, scholarly interest in the monument has been rekindled.[25] A highly significant contribution to the study of the arch

[20] Other portions of the city wall also contain reused material (Mitchell and Waelkens 1998, 93–94). The modifications to the Arch of Hadrian and Sabina may be contemporaneous with these parts of the city wall.

[21] A base attributed to a large pilaster from one of the piers, now lying south of the arch, has an analogous cutting (Ossi 2009, figs. 172–174).

[22] Patara: Işık and Yılmaz 1989, 7. Isthmia: Gregory and

Mills 1984, 411.

[23] *Pace* Bru and Demirer (2006, 607–609), who suggest that the four bases may have been those of an earlier arch that was dismantled and replaced by the arch under discussion here.

[24] Taşlıalan 2000.

[25] See, e.g., Byrne 2002; Bru 2002; Bru and Demirer 2006.

Fig. 5.12. Frederick J. Woodbridge, architect of the 1924 excavations, holds bronze letters in place on an inscribed block from the Arch of Hadrian and Sabina. Tribune, abbreviated TRIB, was an office held by the arch's dedicator, C. Julius Asper Pansinianus. Photo: D. M. Robinson, Kelsey Museum Archives neg. no. KR107.12.

is that of Maurice Byrne, who was the first to read the dedicatory inscription by deciphering the pattern of sockets by which a series of bronze letters, now lost, were attached to the architrave (fig. 5.12).[26] Byrne's conclusion, that the arch was erected in AD 129 in honor of Hadrian and Sabina, has redefined the historical situation surrounding the creation of the arch.

My own research has partly focused on analyzing in detail the evidence for the accuracy of Woodbridge's reconstruction of the monument.[27] My analysis shows that Woodbridge's reconstruction drawing, which has become the standard reference for discussions of the arch,[28] is accurate in its architectural form, but that his representation of the decorative program can be improved.[29] Here I present a new reconstruction of the arch that for the first time includes the north and south façades, both of which had decoration in relief. On the outer, southern face (fig. 5.13), figures of bound captives with torches and wreaths were positioned in the spandrels of the central passageway, while winged nude male figures, or *genii*, decorated the side passages accompanied by garlands and bull skulls, or bucrania. The inscription on this face dedicated the arch to Hadrian and Sabina. Above the inscription stood a frieze of military implements and fantastic creatures, including hippocamps, tritons flanking trophies, and two winged figures carrying a shield. The inner, northern face (fig. 5.14) had figures carrying military emblems over the central archway, with winged victories, garlands, and bucrania over the side passages. The frieze on this face had an elaborate spiraling vegetal motif punctuated by palmettes, and the inscription credited Gaius Julius Asper Pansinianus with the construction and decoration of the arch. The following discussion provides an interpretation of the symbolic content of the arch based on this new reconstruction and Byrne's revised date of construction in AD 129.

Historical Context for the Creation of the Arch of Hadrian and Sabina

The historical situation in the early 2nd century AD provides essential contextual information for the interpretation of the Arch of Hadrian and Sabina at Pisidian Antioch. Compared to other cities in Pisidia, Antioch had a head start on its urban development due to the intensity of Augustan investment in the

[26] Byrne 2002 provides preliminary discussion, and Byrne's complete text is published in Demirer 2002, 51–54 and Mitchell and Waelkens 1998, 97–99. For a detailed comparison of Byrne's restored text with the inscribed blocks themselves, see Ossi 2009, 227–237.

[27] Ossi 2009, 108–143.

[28] Woodbridge's reconstruction has been reproduced repeatedly—e.g., Robinson 1926a, fig 1; Ingholt 1954, pl. 5.1; Mitchell and Waelkens 1998, fig. 19b; Bru 2002, pl. 11; Demirer 2002, 49; Landskron 2005, fig. 48.

[29] Rose (2005, 56) gives a one-sentence description of the decorative program of the Arch of Hadrian and Sabina that does not match Woodbridge's drawing, but he does not explain the archaeological basis for his description. My research agrees with Rose's brief description.

DRAWN BY FREDERICK J. WOODBRIDGE, 1925
REVISED BY ADRIAN J. OSSI, 2009

IMP. CAESARI. DIVI. TRAIANI. F. DIVI. NERVAE. NEP. TRAIANO. HADRIANO. AVG. PONT. MAX. TRIB. POT. XIII. COS. III. P. P. ET. SABINAE. AVG. (INREAD. COL.

0 1 2 3 4 5 METERS

Fig. 5.13. Restored south elevation of the Arch of Hadrian and Sabina. Drawing: A. J. Ossi.

C·IVL·ASP·PANSINIANVS·II·VIR·V·TRIB·MIL·LEG·I·PRAEF·AL·INREAD·STONE·D·S·P·FECIT·ET·ORNAVIT

DRAWN BY FREDERICK J. WOODBRIDGE, 1925
REVISED BY ADRIAN J. OSSI, 2009

0 1 2 3 4 5 METERS

Fig. 5.14. Restored north elevation of the Arch of Hadrian and Sabina. Drawing: A. J. Ossi.

city, starting with its refoundation as a Roman colony in 25 BC. Over the course of the 1st century AD Antioch to a certain extent maintained this preeminent status, but by the Hadrianic period other cities had caught up with and surpassed it in regional importance. Under Hadrian, the neighboring city of Sagalassos was declared the metropolis of Pisidia, and a massive temple to Hadrian and Antoninus Pius was built there to house the imperial cult.[30] By this time, Antioch had become one among many prosperous cities in Asia Minor as the region flourished in the early 2nd century, and cities competed with one another to be recognized as preeminent within their individual provinces and within the broader empire.

This civic competition was led by the members of a city's wealthiest, most influential, and most imperially connected families. Since its foundation as a colony, the leading citizens of Antioch had maintained a certain level of involvement in the imperial system. In the 1st century AD, four members of the imperial circle are known to have held magistracies in Antioch.[31] Before the turn of the 2nd century, Antioch already had two citizens who had risen to the senatorial order and who had been appointed consul in Rome, L. Sergius Paullus in AD 70 and C. Caristanius Fronto in AD 90.[32] While these examples illustrate Antioch's continued involvement in the imperial system, the high status attained by these individuals proves to be the exception rather than the rule. Into the early 2nd century, the advancement of Antioch's citizens beyond the equestrian order remained rare.[33] In the absence of advancement to the senatorial order, equestrians, such as C. Julius Asper Pansinianus, were the leading citizens of Antioch in the Hadrianic period.

In many ways, Hadrian himself set the tone in this age of civic competition. He took a personal interest in the cities of his empire and their unique and varied histories, an interest that was clearly manifested in his extensive travels. He desired to experience at first hand the many cultures, famous sights, and unusual cults encompassed by his empire. On a series of imperial *adventus* coins issued toward the end of his reign, seventeen provinces and regions are recorded as having been visited by the emperor.[34] A visit by the emperor was a prestigious event that could raise the status of a city in relation to its neighbors because the visited city could boast that the emperor deemed it to be the most significant in the region. Even if there was no chance of an imperial visit, many cities voted honors for the emperor, such as making him an honorary citizen, electing him to the city's highest civic position or priesthood,[35] establishing festivals and games in his honor,[36] or even renaming entire cities after him.[37] Asia Minor was one of the areas of the empire that Hadrian visited most. He made three trips through the region, first at the beginning of his reign in AD 117 as he traveled from Syria to the Danube to broker peace with local tribes,[38] and later in 123–124 and 129–131 as journeys undertaken for the purpose of visiting provincial cities.[39] As mentioned above, Hadrian's known route

---

[30] Waelkens 2002, 351.

[31] Levick 1967a, 81; Boatwright 2000, 63.

[32] Paullus: Mitchell and Waelkens 1998, 10. Fronto: *ILS* 9485.

[33] Levick (1967a, 107 n. 4) identifies eight senators from Antioch, most of whom date to the mid-2nd century and later (113–119).

[34] Magie 1950, 628–629.

[35] Boatwright 2000, 58–72.

[36] Boatwright 2000, 94. The practice of dedicating games and festivals in honor of the emperor began under Augustus and continued through the imperial period. See Potter 1999, 250–278 for a discussion of the intersection of spectacle and imperial loyalty.

[37] See Le Glay 1976, 357–359 for a list of cities in Asia Minor with some variation of Hadrian in their names. For discussion of this phenomenon, see Boatwright 2000, 104–105.

[38] Magie 1950, 611–612.

[39] Magie 1950, 613.

brought him close to Antioch in 129,[40] and considering the dedication date of the Arch of Hadrian and Sabina, he probably visited Antioch at this time.

Hadrian's involvement with provincial cities was not limited to mere tourism. He was a prolific benefactor of provincial cities, donating funds for public works projects, festivals, and grain distributions to more than 130 cities throughout the empire.[41] He was honored as benefactor, founder, or savior in many of these cities. In this way, too, he set the tone for the era. Wealthy citizens could enhance their social status by donating funds for public benefit.[42] Benefactions could include monetary distributions, grain subsidies, games, festivals, and buildings such as baths, aqueducts, gymnasia, porticoes, and theaters. Such buildings were often dedicated jointly to the people of the city and to the emperor. If a private citizen funded a building dedicated to the emperor, the benefits could potentially be twofold; the citizen's personal connections with the emperor might be strengthened, and his or her city might rise in stature within the imperial administration.

Benefactions would be proposed by an individual donor, but they had to be approved by the council and people of a city. If the benefaction was significant enough, the emperor himself or his provincial governor might also give his approval, even if no imperial funds were to be used.[43] Proposals would lead to discussion and negotiation at the local level.[44] If a dispute arose about some specific detail, there would have been a certain degree of compromise among the parties involved to achieve a mutually acceptable solution. Alternatively, one or both parties could turn to the emperor for arbitration.[45] Once the proposal was finalized, an embassy would be sent to the emperor to make the request, and the emperor would deliver his response by letter. Often, the text of the proposal and of the emperor's response would be recorded in an inscription in the city. When a city voted an honor to an emperor, such as naming him founder or erecting a statue of him, the emperor's approval was usually required. It was the emperor's prerogative to accept, modify, or decline any honor, and refusals were not uncommon.[46] Honorific arches occupy a unique space in the system of euergetism because they were constructed as urban embellishments but simultaneously acted as symbolic honors for the emperor. An honorific arch was perhaps the most elaborate type of symbolic honor, since it involved constructing a large stone structure as well as sculpting a number of portrait statues in stone or bronze for display on the monument. Accordingly, it is highly likely that the honorific nature of such a monument would have required imperial approval in nearly every case.

---

[40] Birley 1997, 224.

[41] Boatwright 2000, 5.

[42] Elite benefaction was extremely active in Asia Minor during the 2nd century AD but had been an important aspect of civic life in the region since the Hellenistic period, following the examples set by Hellenistic kings. See Mitchell 1993, 210–211 and chap. 1, this volume, for recent literature on euergetism in the Roman world.

[43] E.g., the foundation of lotteries and a procession in Ephesos under Trajan, approved by the governor (Rogers 1991b); the foundation of a musical festival at Oenoanda approved by Hadrian (Wörrle 1988, with further discussion by Mitchell 1990 and Rogers 1991a); and Hadrian's approval of an aqueduct at Aphrodisias (Reynolds 2000, 5–10 and 16–20).

[44] E.g., for the musical festival at Oenoanda, where local and imperial concerns required a year's worth of negotiation (Rogers 1991a, 91–100). Dio Chrysostom's orations shed light on the kinds of debates that surround such public gifts from elite citizens to their cities (*Orationes* 40 and 45).

[45] E.g., Hadrian's resolution concerning the aqueduct at Aphrodisias (Reynolds 2000, 17–19) and the resolution by Antoninus Pius of a dispute over a building project at Ephesos (Kalinowski 2002, 111–117). Pliny the Younger's letters also reflect the imperial government's involvement in major projects proposed by private citizens (10.37–41).

[46] E.g., Hadrian refused a gold crown offered by Aphrodisias (Reynolds 2000, 14–15), and Marcus Aurelius suggested that Athens should forgo the precious metal statues offered in favor of less costly bronze busts (Oliver 1941, no. 24, with discussion on 116–120).

Fig. 5.15a. Tritons flanking trophies from the Arch of Augustus. Photo: G. R. Swain, Kelsey Museum Archives neg. no. 7.1391.

Fig. 5.15b. Similar motif from the Arch of Hadrian and Sabina. Photo: G. R. Swain, Kelsey Museum Archives neg. no. 5.0232.

The system of euergetism outlined above ensures that the symbolic message of an honorific arch does not represent merely the autocratic whim of a lone donor. Rather, an arch embodies a communal message negotiated and mediated by several entities, including the donor, the city council, and the emperor himself. Accordingly, the symbolic content of a provincial honorific arch may be seen as a baseline statement of official civic identity within the imperial system. This is not to suggest that the message would have received universal support by the city's inhabitants. Even today, design by committee often produces a result palatable to all but preferred by none. Furthermore, we can be certain that the basic power structures of Antioch's colonial situation, even after more than 150 years of existence, would have kept some voices from being recognized in the discussion. We should, therefore, give consideration to other voices that may have been overshadowed by the arch's ostentatious display. An analysis of the symbolic content of the arch elucidates these local and imperial entanglements.

Imperial Associations: Hadrian and Augustus

A key characteristic of the Arch of Hadrian and Sabina is that its decorative program contained numerous sculptural references to its predecessor, the Arch of Augustus, erected in 2 BC as the propylon of the city's main urban sanctuary (see fig. 3.5).[47] As triple-bayed arches with side passageways slightly narrower than the central opening, the arches are similar in form, and they are comparable in size, ca. 20.5 m for the width of the Augustan arch and ca. 23 m for that of the Hadrianic monument.[48] Parallel imagery is contained in the figural frieze and the spandrel zone, with the spandrel decoration relating most closely. In the figural frieze, both arches have two preserved sets of tritons flanking trophies (fig. 5.15). On both monuments, the fish-tailed tritons hold rudders or other objects in one hand and reach out with the other to touch the helmet of the trophy that stands between them. Both friezes also contain weapons and armor of similar character: cuirasses, shields, bows, spears, etc. In the spandrels, both arches have preserved examples of two types of winged figures flanked by hanging garlands. The figures are nude winged males, or *genii*, depicted holding grapes in one hand (fig. 5.16), and draped winged females, or victories, holding emblems of victory such as wreaths or palm fronds (fig. 5.17). On blocks preserved from both arches, a swag of garland emerges from behind both types of winged figure.

[47] These decorative similarities have been noted in every discussion of the Arch of Hadrian and Sabina since the first preliminary publication in 1924 (Robinson 1924a, 438; 1926a, 46, 51, 56; Güven 1983, 67; Mitchell and Waelkens 1998, 97; Rose 2005, 54–57), but a brief summary of the similarities is necessary.

[48] Measurements taken using the scales in Woodbridge's reconstruction drawings, fig. 5.4 in this chapter for the Arch of Hadrian and Sabina and fig. 3.5 in Rubin, chap. 3, this volume, for the Arch of Augustus.

Fig. 5.16a. *Genius* figure from the Arch of Augustus. Photo: G. R. Swain, Kelsey Museum Archives neg. no. 7.1371.

Fig. 5.16b. *Genius* figure from the Arch of Hadrian and Sabina (2007). Photo: A. J. Ossi.

Fig. 5.17a. Victory from the Arch of Augustus. Photo: G. R. Swain, Kelsey Museum Archives neg. no. 7.1139.

Fig. 5.17b. Similar motif from the Arch of Hadrian and Sabina (2004). Photo: A. J. Ossi (CG 62).

Each of the similarities listed above has been noted in previous discussions, but I would add two parallels not previously observed, a pair of hippocamps from the frieze and a bound captive from the spandrel zone. A capricorn on the frieze of the Augustan arch probably inspired the hippocamps on the Hadrianic monument (fig. 5.18). Both of these fantastic animals have the forepart of a quadruped (a goat and a horse, respectively) and the tail of a fish. From the spandrel zone, at least one bound captive is preserved from both arches. Two complete bound captives were found in the excavation of the Augustan propylon,[49] and a block found in Yalvaç and plausibly attributed to the Arch of Hadrian and Sabina shows the lower half of a similar crouching figure (fig. 5.19).[50] A torch and a wreath hover in the pictorial space behind the Augustan version of one captive, and the tip of what is surely a similar torch is preserved on the Hadrianic block. Thus, we now have direct evidence that both arches contained similar representations of military implements (swords, bows,

[49] Robinson 1926a, figs. 41–42; Ossi 2009, figs. 139–140.

[50] Robinson 1926a, fig. 72; Ossi 2009, fig. 141. This stone was found by the Michigan team "near a stream in Yalivadj" and is attributed to the Arch of Hadrian and Sabina in Wood-

bridge's notebook, in the captions on the photographs in the Kelsey Museum Archives, and in Robinson's publication (1926a, 46). The dimensions of the block, its general shape, and the sequence of moldings on the pilaster capital verify its attribution to the Arch of Hadrian and Sabina.

Fig. 5.18a. Capricorn from the Arch of Augustus. Photo: A. J. Ossi.

Fig. 5.18b. Hippocamp from the Arch of Hadrian and Sabina. Photo: G. R. Swain, Kelsey Museum Archives neg. no. 5.0213.

Fig. 5.19a. Bound captive with wreath and torch from the Arch of Augustus. Photo: G. R. Swain, Kelsey Museum Archives neg. no. 7.1275.

Fig. 5.19b. Lower part of similar motif from the Arch of Hadrian and Sabina, with the bent leg of the figure and the end of the torch preseved (2004). Photo: D. Ng 2004 (CG 50).

shields, and cuirasses), two types of fantastic creatures (tritons flanking trophies and aquatic half-quadrupeds), and three types of spandrel figures (*genii*, victories, and captives). Comparative evidence from Augustan coins suggests that other decorative elements from the Hadrianic arch, such as a pair of figures carrying military emblems in the spandrels and a combined shield and wreath motif in the frieze, may also have been inspired by similar representations on the Augustan arch.[51]

The Arch of Hadrian and Sabina also contained several architectural features that I would argue are similarly related to the Augustan arch. Both arches have a socle with simple moldings that is positioned just below the main columnar order. This socle makes sense in the context of the Augustan arch, where it provides a visual foundation for the monument above the level of the stair-case that leads up to it (see fig. 3.5). By comparison, on the Hadrianic arch the gray pier bases alone would have been a sufficient visual foundation for the Corinthian pilasters above (see figs. 5.13–14). Thus, on the Hadrianic arch the socle course seems redundant—except as an architectural reference to its predecessor. The influence of the Augustan arch may have continued in the later life of the Hadrianic arch. As noted above, four bases were installed in front of the Arch of Hadrian and Sabina

[51] Emblem bearers: Rose 2005, 56; Rubin 2008, 41–42; and Ossi 2009, 75–76. Shield and wreath: Ossi 2009, 73–74.

at some point after its construction. These four bases, which projected in front of the arch (see fig. 5.10), would have been a clear visual parallel to the parastades that projected onto the steps in front of the Augustan propylon (see fig. 3.5).

Two factors likely led to the selection of the propylon of the imperial cult sanctuary as a source of inspiration for the new Arch of Hadrian and Sabina: a spirit of cultural renewal and local history encouraged by Hadrian, and a desire to make a favorable comparison between the reigning emperor and his imperial ancestor, Augustus. First, as M. T. Boatwright points out, "the actual interaction between Hadrian and many cities was associated with a renewal, preservation, or promotion of the unique history of that place."[52] In Asia Minor, cities advertised their connection to the shared Greek past, often by claiming Homeric heroes as founders in ongoing intercity competition for prestige.[53] Antioch's dominant political class, the descendants of the Roman colonists, may have perceived that, as a Hellenistic colony refounded by Romans, Antioch did not have the sort of deep Hellenic roots boasted by other cities in the region. The colonial elites turned this potential liability into an asset. Antioch was the oldest and most strategically important of the Pisidian colonies founded by Augustus, and the city's elaborate imperial cult complex was the crown jewel symbolizing Antioch's preeminent position among these colonies at the time of their foundation. The imperial cult sanctuary was, in effect, a locus of cult for the city's deified founder (see Rubin, chapter 3, this volume), and the propylon of the sanctuary highlighted this relationship with an array of iconographic symbols that summarized the deeds and virtues of Augustus.[54] By echoing certain salient features of the Arch of Augustus in the new Arch of Hadrian and Sabina, the city drew attention to the moment of its greatest historical importance as perceived by the dominant political class.

Furthermore, the close association between the Arch of Hadrian and Sabina and the Augustan propylon implies an intentional comparison between Hadrian and Augustus. This may reflect a broader empirewide political program because in many ways Hadrian styled himself as a new Augustus. In the 120s he minted coins that abandoned the usual lengthy dynastic titles in favor of the simple title "Hadrianus Augustus," drawing a close connection between himself and the first emperor.[55] In Rome, Hadrian rebuilt the Pantheon, a temple that originally had been constructed by Agrippa and that probably had a role in the fledgling imperial cult in the city of Rome.[56] Out of deference to the memory of Agrippa and Augustus, Hadrian famously did not change the building's inscription, which gave credit for its construction to Agrippa. Moreover, Hadrian's mausoleum on the banks of the Tiber was partly inspired by that of Augustus on the opposite bank of the river.[57] This iconographic and architectural association extended to the provinces. For example, a nymphaeum constructed under Hadrian in Sagalassos contained iconographic references to Augustus and the imperial cult. The central figure in the decorative scheme of the nymphaeum, a colossal statue of Apollo Clarios, was a direct reference to the temple of Apollo Clarios established in Sagalassos in the Augustan age, which probably also served as the city's first imperial cult shrine.[58] To emphasize

[52] Boatwright 2000, 13.

[53] An important example of the manifestation of cities' promotion of their own histories in the time of Hadrian is, of course, the Panhellenion (Romeo 2002; Spawforth 1985; 1986). Newby 2003 discusses artistic depictions of civic history during the reign of Hadrian and his successors. See Ng 2007 on depictions of civic history on public monuments and their role in intercity rivalries.

[54] These symbols are discussed in detail in Ossi 2009, 71–89.

[55] Birley 1997, 147.

[56] Boatwright 1987, 263; Zanker 1988, 141.

[57] Davies 2000, 158–163.

[58] Talloen and Waelkens 2004; 2005.

Fig. 5.20. Bucranium with garlands from the Arch of Hadrian and Sabina. Photo: G. R. Swain, Kelsey Museum Archives neg. no. 5.0223.

the Hadrianic association with the Augustan imperial cult, a gilded bronze statue of Hadrian stood in a niche directly above the colossal Apollo.[59]

Like their neighbors in Sagalassos, the citizens of Antioch likely perceived the associative power of their Augustan imperial cult sanctuary in the Hadrianic period. There is evidence of cult activities taking place at the sanctuary at a number of historical moments before and after the reign of Hadrian. An inscription uncovered in 1999 during construction activities in Yalvaç records the dedication of a statue, games, sacrifices, and a beast hunt in honor of Claudius's Brittanic victory.[60] Scholars have plausibly associated this series of rituals and festivals with the imperial cult.[61] Excavation in 1991 uncovered a portrait of Marcus Aurelius in the portico of the sanctuary itself (see fig. 3.16),[62] and excavation in 1924 revealed that a small Severan-era *tholos* was built in the platea in front of the propylon, probably in honor of Caracalla (see fig. 3.24).[63] Clearly, ritual activities in the imperial cult sanctuary would have been ongoing in the Hadrianic period as well. Creating a new version of the sanctuary's propylon at the very entrance to the city and dedicating it to Hadrian would announce the city's dedication to the emperor; it would stress Hadrian's association with Augustus; and it would exemplify the spirit of historical renewal that was promoted by the well-traveled emperor. Notably, each of these associations emphasized the colonial aspect of the city's identity, situating it within the past and present of the imperial system.

Local Ritual Connections

Certain details of the arch may also have highlighted a connection with the city's pre-Roman past, embodied in the extramural sanctuary of Mên Askaênos, a lunar deity with Anatolian roots (see Raff and Khatchadourian, chapters 7 and 8, this volume). One reading of the bucrania positioned above the side openings on the arch is as a direct reference to the cult of Mên (fig. 5.20). While representations of bucrania were common in many ritual contexts in Asia Minor,[64] the bull was very closely associated with Mên, partly because the horns of the bull resemble the crescent moon.[65] Late Hellenistic coins from Antioch show a bust of Mên on the obverse and a bull on the reverse (see fig. 8.3).[66] Representations of the cult statue of Mên Askaênos, preserved in statuettes and on coinage, show the god standing with one

[59] Mägele, Richard, and Waelkens 2007, 490–491.

[60] Christol, Drew-Bear, and Taşlıalan 2001.

[61] Christol, Drew-Bear, and Taşlıalan 2001, 20; Standing 2003, 281–282.

[62] Taşlıalan 1993, fig. 21; Rubin 2008, 48–49.

[63] -]*i antonini aug*[is all that is preserved of the dedicatory inscription of the *tholos*. Robinson (1924a, 441) identifies the honorand as Marcus Aurelius, but based on the style of the architectural decoration Mitchell and Waelkens (1998, 156–157) suggest a Severan date, with Caracalla as the most likely candidate. See the note appended to Rubin, chap. 3, this volume, for more discussion of this monument.

[64] Including on the frieze of the imperial cult temple in Antioch; see Rubin, chap. 3, this volume.

[65] Lane 1976, 102–104.

[66] Lane 1975a, pl. XXX.1–10.

foot resting on the head of a bull (see figs. 8.9–11),[67] and some dedications to Mên show a bull tied to a flaming altar.[68] No evidence survives to suggest that the bucrania on the Arch of Hadrian and Sabina were inspired by similar representations on the Arch of Augustus. Thus, the bucrania on the Hadrianic arch are the monument's strongest surviving iconographic link to the cult of Mên. In addition, given the amount of space on the arch devoted to the display of freestanding statuary, with up to eight statue niches in its piers and room for many more statues high atop the monument, it seems highly likely that Mên Askaênos would have been among the figures included. Such a direct connection between the imperial house and the cult of Mên had already been made on Antioch's Arch of Augustus, with its imperial iconography and a depiction of a bust of Mên Askaênos in relief (see fig. 3.13).

An examination of honorific arches built as ornamental city gates elsewhere in Asia Minor shows that a relatively small iconographic detail could be used to highlight the connection between city and extramural sanctuary, even if the greater part of the monument's imagery was devoted to imperial representations. At Xanthos in Lycia, an arch honoring Vespasian was added to a preexisting classical-era city gate.[69] The road through the arch led to the city's main extramural sanctuary, dedicated to Leto, the mother of Apollo and Artemis. To highlight this connection, busts of Leto, Apollo, and Artemis in relief decorated the metopes in the Doric frieze that capped the arch. Similarly, in the 2nd century AD at Mylasa in Caria an arch was built on the road that led to the extramural sanctuary of Zeus Labraundos.[70] Although no inscriptions survive from this arch, its connection with the sanctuary is confirmed by the representation of a double axe, the symbol of Zeus Labraundos, on its keystone. Finally, at Perge in Pamphylia in the Hadrianic period, a powerful woman named Plancia Magna remodeled a Hellenistic city gate and built a triple-bayed honorific arch just inside the gate.[71] Surviving inscriptions from the arch indicate that among numerous portraits of members of the imperial house stood a statue of Artemis Pergaia, the city's most important deity, whose sanctuary was located somewhere outside the city.[72]

For each of these cities, the respective extramural sanctuary was the site of the most important civic cult, and iconographic references to the deity on an ornamental city gate highlighted the spatial and ritual connection between the city and the sanctuary. In addition, at least two of the arches, at Xanthos and Perge, contained references to both the primary civic deity and the imperial household, thereby situating the relationship between city and sanctuary within the broader imperial framework. A person walking from city to sanctuary or vice versa would have enacted the relationship symbolized by the placement and iconography of these arches. Like the arches in Xanthos, Mylasa, and Perge, the Arch of Hadrian and Sabina monumentalized the transition between countryside and city and contained implicit, and likely explicit, references to the city's extramural sanctuary. With its overt iconographic connection to the intramural imperial cult sanctuary, the arch in effect stood as a symbolic link between Antioch's two major ritual centers.

Comparative evidence suggests that this symbolic link may have been enacted ritually by means of a procession from one sanctuary to the other. Two surviving inscriptions record processions in

[67] Statuette: Lane 1971, no. 175. Coin: Krzyzanowska 1970, pl. 2.5.1.1.

[68] Lane 1971, nos. 177 and 288.

[69] Cavalier 2005, 27–29.

[70] Kızıl 2009.

[71] Mansel 1956, 104–120. For discussion of the city gate complex, its donor, and its display of statuary, see Boatwright 1991 and Ng 2007, 47–57.

[72] Statues of the imperial household: Şahin 1999, nos. 91–99. Statue of Artemis Pergaia: Şahin 1999, no. 89. The exact location of the extramural sanctuary of Artemis Pergaia is unknown.

Greek cities that were used to link the worship of local deities with the imperial cult. The first inscription, from Gytheion, a small port town near Sparta in Greece, records the foundation of a musical festival during the reign of Tiberius.[73] The festival included a procession that linked a number of different religious and civic spaces in the city. Three painted imperial portraits, depicting Augustus, Tiberius, and Livia, were carried in the procession, which started at the temple of Asklepeios and Hygeia and proceeded to the imperial cult temple, where a bull was sacrificed. Further sacrifices took place in the agora, and the procession concluded at the theater, where the portraits were set up for the duration of the musical competitions that were the main attraction of the festival.[74]

In the Trajanic period, C. Vibius Salutaris founded a recurring procession in Ephesos.[75] This procession led from the extramural sanctuary of Artemis Ephesia, through the city with a stop at the theater, and back to the sanctuary.[76] Although the procession started and ended at the temple of Artemis Ephesia, it was overtly connected with the imperial cult by means of statues carried in the procession, which included several imperial portraits as well as pairings of imperial and local personifications.[77] Notably the Magnesia Gate, where the procession first crossed into the city proper, was an important point along the procession route.[78] Here the city's *ephebes*, or male adolescents, waited to escort the statues through the streets of the city to the theater, where the statues were temporarily set up for display. When the procession resumed, the *ephebes* escorted the statues to the Koressian Gate on the other side of town, where the procession departed the city and returned to the sanctuary of Artemis Ephesia. Scholars interpret these ritual processions as part of a process of negotiation between local civic identities and the imperial system, as expressed through the interaction between local religious practice and the imperial cult.[79]

If in Antioch a recurring procession like those at Ephesos and Gytheion linked cult activities at the extramural sanctuary of Mên Askaênos and the imperial cult sanctuary, the Arch of Hadrian and Sabina would have been a major architectural marker along the processional route. The route of such a procession would have followed the so-called Via Sacra, which starts at the sanctuary of Mên and leads down the slopes of Sultan Dağ. The path down the mountain can still be traced today by following the numerous dedications to Mên that take the form of aediculae carved into the bedrock.[80] At the base of the mountain the procession would probably have crossed the river Anthius and skirted the southern edge of the fortification wall to reach the easiest route of access to the city on the western side of town. As in many other ancient cities, tombs embodying the city's ancestral past would probably have lined the approach to the city's entrance. At this point the procession would have encountered the Arch of Hadrian and Sabina, standing as an elaborate marker of the boundary between countryside and urban space. The bucrania on the façade, and perhaps a statue of Mên Askaênos standing in a niche, would have reminded the participants of the procession's origin, while the overall form and decorative program would have presaged the destination at the imperial cult sanctuary. After passing through the arch, the procession would probably have turned east at

[73] *SEG* 11.923; translation in Sherk 1988, no. 33.

[74] For discussion of these rituals, see Ng 2007, 158–163; Gebhard 1996, 117–121; and Price 1984, 210–211.

[75] Rogers provides the Greek text with facing English translation (1991b, 152–185) and lists previous editions of the Greek text (34, n. 65).

[76] Rogers 1991b, 162–163 (text) and 85–111 (discussion).

[77] Rogers 1991b, 158–163 (text) and 83–85 (discussion).

[78] Rogers 1991b, 162–163 (text) and 86 (discussion).

[79] Gytheion: Ng 2007, 158–163; Price 1984, 210–211. Ephesos: Ng 2007, 163–167 and 218–232; Rogers 1991b, 136–149.

[80] Labarre and Taşlıalan 2002. See Raff, chap. 7, this volume.

the end of the platea and climbed the hill past the theater. As at Gytheion and Ephesos, the theater could have been a stopping point where a large crowd could gather to observe the procession and to take part in the ritual. From the theater, the procession would have continued east to the Tiberia Platea, where those involved would encounter a view of the Arch of Augustus framing the imperial cult temple behind it. Climbing the stairs and passing through the Arch of Augustus, the procession would reach its destination at the imperial cult sanctuary, where sacrifices could take place.

This portrait of a procession through the countryside and city of Pisidian Antioch is admittedly speculative. Nevertheless, the comparative evidence for monumental and ritual links between local and imperial cults suggests that the placement and iconography of the Arch of Hadrian and Sabina likely would have signaled these types of ritual associations. We might question whether the city's inhabitants of Hellenic and Phrygian descent would perceive these links as a positive integration of local and imperial interests or as a co-option of the city's pre-Roman history by colonial interlopers. No evidence survives to answer this question, but we should expect a range of such reactions from one person to the next. It is clear that these associations would have been reinforced each time a visitor entered the city, even if her purpose was merely to buy bread or to visit the baths. C. Julius Asper Pansinianus was certainly aware of this when he built the arch; after all, his name would be affixed to the monument along with those of the emperor and his wife. Further evidence suggests that Pansinianus designed his benefaction not simply as an expressive civic ornament but as part of a perpetually functional gift to the city.

Civic Euergetism: Arch, Platea, and Cascade

A number of architectural details suggest that the Arch of Hadrian and Sabina was built in conjunction with a major renovation of the platea to which it gave access. A glance at the city plan shows that the platea inside the arch is not aligned with the street grid (see fig. 2.4), which indicates that this stretch of roadway probably followed the topography of the hill to provide easier access to the city. This detail suggests that the arch, cascade, and platea with shops may have been a renovation and monumentalization of an earlier entrance to the city. To the north, the roadway is precisely as wide as the arch, and the cascading water channel is axially aligned with the arch's central opening. The rooms on either side of the roadway, which were certainly designed as shops, may also have been part of this renovation. The remains visible on the site today show that the shops on the east side of the street were partially cut out of the bedrock, which suggests that the renovation required a substantial construction operation.

Certain iconographic details of the Arch of Hadrian and Sabina, namely the hippocamps that were positioned at both ends of the frieze and the thyrsoi that decorated the upper pilasters, affirm its close association with the cascading water channel. As we shall see, these are decorative elements that are commonly associated with monumental hydraulic installations. As mentioned above, the hippocamps on the frieze of the Hadrianic arch may have been inspired by the capricorn from the frieze of the Augustan propylon (see fig. 5.18). The capricorn of Augustus was associated with Hadrian in other media,[81] so placing a capricorn on the Arch of Hadrian and Sabina would not have been inappropriate. Accordingly, the choice to replace the Augustan capricorn with hippocamps may have been an intentional iconographic change meant to redirect the associations of the aquatic elements of the frieze. In this revised framework, the triton groups positioned over the lateral passageways may also be read as generic aquatic symbols (see fig. 5.15b) rather than as references to the Battle of Actium, which they symbolize on the Augustan arch in Antioch. Moreover, in 1924 the Michigan team

[81] Grant 1952.

Fig. 5.22. Thyrsos decorating a pilaster in the upper zone of the Arch of Hadrian and Sabina. Photo: G. R. Swain, Kelsey Museum Archives neg. no. 5.0221.

Fig. 5.21. Sculptural fragment depicting the head of a dolphin, found during the excavation of the Arch of Hadrian and Sabina. Photo: G. R. Swain, Kelsey Museum Archives neg. no. 5.0211.

uncovered a statue of a dolphin in the vicinity of the Arch of Hadrian and Sabina (fig. 5.21), which the excavators associated with the semicircular terminal fountain of the cascade. If this attribution is correct, the aquatic imagery would have carried from the hippocamps and tritons on the frieze of the arch into the central passageway, where the dolphin statue would have complemented the sight and sound of actual flowing water—according to E. J. Owens, both cascading down the channel and flowing out of a pedestal fountain in the center of the terminal basin.[82] We find a comparable example of this type of imagery on the contemporary Hadrianic nymphaeum in Sagalassos, mentioned above. This monumental fountain was decorated with a number of aquatic symbols in relief, including tritons blowing shell horns, nymphs standing on dolphins, and reclining river deities.[83]

The thyrsoi that decorated the upper pilasters on the Arch of Hadrian and Sabina also belong to this web of aquatic associations (fig. 5.22). The thyrsos was a symbol of Dionysos, the god of wine and theater, who often appeared in the context of monumental nymphaea accompanied by statues of his companions, satyrs. In Perge, crossed thyrsoi decorated a frieze on the Hadrianic North Nymphaeum, which itself was the origin of a water channel similar to, but much longer than, the one in Antioch.[84] Statues of Dionysos and a satyr are preserved from the Trajanic nymphaeum in Ephesos,[85] and the Hadrianic nymphaeum at Sagalassos had a satyr and a nude male that may be Dionysos or Apollo.[86] With eight niches and more room for display atop the Arch of Hadrian and Sabina, there certainly would have been space on the monument for a statue of Dionysos to go along with the representations of thyrsoi. In fact, a "beautiful marble statue of a boy, with left breast and shoulder and part of right side preserved," is one of the few fragments of freestanding statuary found in the excavation of the arch,[87] and Dionysos is often depicted as just such a nude youth. Thus, when viewed in their

[82] Owens 2002, 342; Owens and Taşlıalan 2009, 315.

[83] Mägele, Richard, and Waelkens 2007.

[84] Mansel 1975, 367–372. The decoration of this nymphaeum is discussed by Chi 2002, 164–177; Longfellow 2005, 197–204; Ng 2007, 57–67; and Trimble 1999, 150–154.

[85] Aurenhammer 1995, 268–269.

[86] Mägele, Richard, and Waeklens 2007, 484 and 489.

[87] Journal of Excavations, entry for August 31. The statue could also have been Apollo or Hadrian's lover, Antinous.

Adrian J. Ossi

Fig. 5.23. Digital reconstruction of the
Arch of Hadrian and Sabina and its
surroundings. The arch, shops, and
cascade are based on archaeological
evidence; the nymphaeum at the far
end of the cascade is hypothetical.
Digital model: A. J. Ossi and J. M.
Harrington.

architectural and spatial context, these sculptural details communicate the association between the Arch of Hadrian and Sabina and the cascading water channel to the north. Visitors approaching from the south would see and hear the water flowing down the cascade visually framed in the arch's central passageway (fig. 5.23), and they would recognize the aquatic associations of the hippocamps, tritons, thyrsoi, and dolphins that decorated the complex and encouraged visitors to refresh themselves at the semicircular fountain.

The position of the inscriptions on the arch may have emphasized that the entrance platea complex was a gift from Pansinianus to the local population. As noted above, the dedication to Hadrian and Sabina was displayed on the southern, outer face of the arch, and the dedication by Pansinianus was on the northern, inner face. This arrangement suggests that, symbolically, the imperial inscription addressed the outside world, while the Pansinianus inscription addressed the local population.[88] While symbolically addressing the city, the dedication by Pansinianus would literally have been visible from the platea inside the Arch of Hadrian and Sabina, which would have been filled with bustling activity centered on the shops lining the roadway. If, as at Perge, the cascading water channel originated from a monumental nymphaeum at the unexcavated north end of the entrance platea,[89] the complex would have been bracketed by monumental façades at both ends (see fig. 5.1). The platea would act as a visually defined space with a coherent organization. The combination of the dedicatory inscription and the probable association among the Arch of Hadrian and Sabina, the platea, and the cascade suggests that Pansinianus's benefaction was not simply the construction of a personally aggrandizing honorific imperial monument. Rather, Pansinianus apparently created a highly functional urban space that was crowned by the imperial honorific monument, the presence of which might raise the profile of the city within the regional political landscape and in the eyes of the imperial administration.

If we widen our perspective beyond the immediate vicinity of the Arch of Hadrian and Sabina, we see that the renovation of the entrance platea may have been part of a larger program of improvement

[88] Newby (2003, 201) proposes a similar conceptual arrangement for the South City Gate and Hadrianic triple arch at Perge, whereby the Hadrianic triple arch was targeted to nonlocal visitors from across the empire, and the South City Gate, with its sculptural depictions of legendary founders of Perge, was meant to appeal to the citizens of Perge.

[89] A possibility suggested by Owens (2002, 341), although he has since backed away from this hypothesis, citing a lack of evidence and problems with siting a large nymphaeum at the intersection of the entrance platea and the main east-west street (Owens and Taşlıalan 2009, 316).

to the city's hydraulic infrastructure. Owens suggests that the cascade at the Arch of Hadrian and Sabina may have been built in conjunction with the bath building, so that the overflow from the bath could feed the cascade.[90] He cites a similar arrangement in Rome, where the overflow from the baths of Agrippa fed the Euripus, an artificial canal.[91] Furthermore, while the city's monumental aqueduct has been known since Antioch was first identified in 1834, Owens recently has identified a second aqueduct composed of terracotta pipes that brought water to the city from a different source.[92] He suggests that this aqueduct may have been built specifically to feed the bath building.[93] This type of project, whereby a new water source is tapped in order to supply a new monumental bath complex, was a fairly common occurrence throughout the imperial period.[94] Hadrian personally funded at least three such projects, in Greece, Syria, and Spain.[95] Thus, Antioch's terracotta aqueduct, bath building, and cascade may have been part of a massive expansion of the city's hydraulic infrastructure under Hadrian, although further field research is required to confirm this hypothesis. It is just such a project that would probably have required the approval of the emperor, and imperial assistance in the form of engineering consultations or even direct funding would also have been possible. If the construction of these hydraulic installations proves to have occurred under Hadrian, it is conceivable that the Arch of Hadrian and Sabina was a thank offering from the city for these infrastructural improvements. Funding or otherwise supporting such practical urban improvements often earned an emperor the title of *ktistes*, or founder, as voted by the city council.[96] The arch's overt comparison of Hadrian with the city's original Roman founder, Augustus, symbolically positioned Hadrian as just such a new founder.

Conclusion

The Arch of Hadrian and Sabina at Pisidian Antioch is a monument uniquely inspired by its colonial situation. In the 2nd century AD, the cities of Asia Minor competed with one another for regional prestige in order to increase their status within the imperial administration, which could lead to social and economic benefits. One major field of competition involved claims of ancient Hellenic history, manifestations of which were of interest to and often subsidized by emperors, including Hadrian himself. Cities searched for and even invented local links to legendary Greek figures and claimed particular heroes as founders. In this competitive situation, Pisidian Antioch used its own local history to follow a different route. The city had been founded as a Seleucid colony in the Hellenistic period, and the cult of Mên Askaênos may have been a manifestation of a more ancient past, but the symbolic content of the Arch of Hadrian and Sabina favors the city's more immediate colonial history. Pansinianus, the donor of the gate, may have realized that, if the goal of such intercity competition was recognition within the imperial community, an emphasis on the first and greatest emperor as

[90] Owens and Taşlıalan 2009, 316.

[91] Owens and Taşlıalan 2009, 316–317.

[92] Owens and Taşlıalan 2009, 307–312.

[93] Owens and Taşlıalan 2009, 312.

[94] Coulton 1987, 82; Hodge 1989, 128; Owens and Taşlıalan 2009, 314.

[95] At Corinth in Greece (Pausanias 2.3.5; Boatwright 2000, 117 n. 23; Lolos 1997, 300), Antioch-on-the-Orontes in Syria (Boatwright 2000, 137 n. 113), and Italica in Spain (Boatwright 2000, 163–164). The aqueduct project that Hadrian funded at Alexandria Troas in Asia Minor might also have included the construction of baths (Boatwright 2000, 116–117, with n. 23). Compare also the case of Aphrodisias, where Hadrian approved the city's request to build a new aqueduct (Reynolds 2000, 5–10 and 16–20), and baths and a large ornamental pool were also built during Hadrian's reign (Ratté 2002, 22–23).

[96] Boatwright 2000, 29–32; Mitchell 1987, 358.

the city's founder may well have been the city's most notable claim—especially compared with other cities in the region that were advertising Homeric hero after Homeric hero as founders. The imperial cult sanctuary was the primary monumental manifestation of Antioch's foundation by Augustus, and ongoing ritual activities at the sanctuary would have given this imperial past a tangible presence in Antioch's civic and religious life right up to the time of Hadrian and beyond. By incorporating numerous references to the propylon of the sanctuary into the new Arch of Hadrian and Sabina, Pansinianus emphasized the foundation by Augustus as one of the primary characteristics of the city's externally projected identity. References to the Arch of Augustus on the Arch of Hadrian and Sabina implied a favorable comparison between the reigning emperor and his imperial forefather, a comparison that Hadrian clearly welcomed and fostered. The placement of the Arch of Hadrian and Sabina at the very entrance to the city may even have implied greater loyalty to and appreciation for Hadrian over and above the memory of Augustus. While the Arch of Augustus marked the imperial cult sanctuary as a shrine to Augustus, the Arch of Hadrian and Sabina effectively rededicated the entire city to Hadrian and symbolically positioned him as a new founder.

The overt imperial and colonial associations of the arch subordinated the city's pre-Roman history as part of the city's official civic identity even while maintaining iconographic and possibly ritual links to the local cult of Mên Askaênos. The interaction between these two facets of the city's identity is a fascinating subject for future study. In Antioch, Roman citizens would have lived alongside descendants of the original Greek settlers and native Anatolian inhabitants.[97] While the colonial situation may have provided Greeks and Phrygians with some tangible benefits, including an extensive urban infrastructure, they might not have been wholly satisfied with the political situation. It is possible that the sanctuary of Mên Askaênos would have been a locus of expression for these alternative interests. The god's Anatolian roots could have provided inhabitants with an outlet for the expression of the city's pre-Roman identity. The iconography of the Arch of Hadrian and Sabina makes a strong statement in favor of the preeminence of the imperial cult sanctuary in AD 129, but we also know that within a decade of Hadrian's visit the santuary of Mên Askaênos began to undergo a revival (see Raff and Khatchadourian, chapters 7 and 8, this volume). This may be no coincidence. The cult of Mên is precisely the kind of deeply rooted cultic tradition that interested Hadrian. Whether or not Hadrian provided the impetus for the revival, which appears in the archaeological record during the reign of his successor, Antoninus Pius, the evidence shows a clear shift in the city's civic cultic emphasis. From the reign of Antoninus Pius on, the sanctuary of Mên Askaênos became a more prominent symbol of the city, as advertised especially on its coinage. Had the Arch of Hadrian and Sabina been constructed even ten years later, it is possible that its form and decoration would have privileged an entirely different facet of the city's complicated civic identity.

[97] Mitchell and Waelkens 1998, 8; Rubin 2008, 28–30.

6 The "Church of St. Paul" and Religious Identities in 4th-Century Pisidian Antioch

Lydia Herring-Harrington[1]

The visits made by the missionary Paul to Antioch of Pisidia in the middle of the 1st century, during his journeys across Asia Minor, marked the beginnings of the expansion of Christianity from its origin in the regions around Jerusalem to the rest of the Roman world.[2] According to the book of Acts, chapter 13, Paul and his companion Barnabas encountered a thriving Jewish community in Pisidian Antioch, many of whose members were at first open to the message that they delivered in the synagogue. As the numbers of converts increased, however, the Jews grew antagonistic. Their contentious interaction, and opposition from Antioch's high-ranking civic leaders, caused Paul to shift his missionary activities to the non-Jewish populations of Asia Minor, among whom he met with greater success.

The account of Paul's conflict with the Jews of Pisidian Antioch in the 1st century belongs only to the first chapter of the history of Christianity in the city. Three centuries later, Christians who assembled at the basilica church, recently named the "Church of St. Paul,"[3] would play an active part in a complex interplay among Christian, Jewish, and polytheist communities in the city and beyond.[4] The Church of St. Paul, along with other religious monuments in Antioch, provides the architectural and historical evidence for this chapter's exploration of the evidence for Christianity within the pluralistic religious context of Antiochene society in the 4th century, a period that saw a crucial shift in the balance of power in Pisidian Antioch.

By the 4th century, Pisidian Antioch was home to a wide variety of religious structures, including churches, temples, and perhaps also a synagogue. There is archaeological evidence of at least three other (poorly preserved) Christian churches in addition to the Church of St. Paul (fig. 6.1).[5] The

[1] Many thanks are due to the colleagues who read all or part of this essay or previous versions of it (in chronological order): Elaine Gazda, David Potter, Rossitza Roussanova Schroeder, Diana Ng, Ellen Muehlberger, Benjamin Rubin, Robert Chenault, and James McIntosh. Thanks also to Özgen Felek for translating Turkish sources. Any errors that remain are, of course, my own.

[2] All dates are AD unless otherwise stated. For recent work on Paul's life and mission, see Dunn 2003; Hinson 1996; Murphy-O'Connor 1996; Wilson 1997; Witherington 1998. For Paul's experience at Pisidian Antioch specifically, see also Grech 2002; Snyder 2002; Trebilco 1991, 21–24.

[3] So called by Taşlıalan (2002) on the basis of a stone baptismal font inscribed with the name of St. Paul (ὁ ἅγιος Παῦλος; see below for further discussion). I use the nickname, despite

the sparse evidence for such an attribution, to distinguish this church from the second basilica church recently found in the northern area of the city (Taşlıalan et al. 2003).

[4] I use the term "polytheist," and not "pagan" (*paganus*) because of the latter's pejorative connotations. It was a slur used by Christians meaning "civilian" or "rustic," to describe those who had not enrolled themselves as "soldiers of Christ" (*miles Christi*). "Pagan," in its modern usage, is also incorrect, as it wrongly suggests a unity among non-Christians in their beliefs, or lack thereof. Cf. Lane Fox 1987, 30–31; *OCD*[3] s.v. *pagans, paganism*.

[5] I do not believe that the 4th-century mosaic found in the stage building of the theater is possibly evidence of a chapel having been built there (cf. Mallampati and Demirer, chap. 4, this volume). The iconographic combination of two

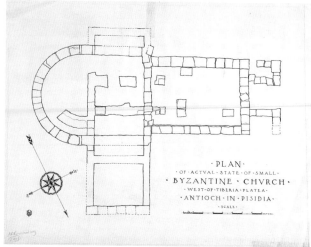

Fig. 6.1 (above left). The churches within the city perimeter. Drawing: A. J. Ossi.

Fig. 6.2 (above right). Woodbridge's plan of the central church (post-1924). Kelsey Museum Archives AAR-2411, neg. no. 7.1334.

Fig. 6.3 (right). View east from the apse of the central church to the imperial cult temple in the background (1924). Photo: G. R. Swain, Kelsey Museum Archives neg. no. 7.1301.

first of these other churches, the central church, is so called because of its placement in the center of the city, to the west of the Tiberia Platea. Its remains were first observed by Arundell during his expedition in 1833. In 1924, the plan of the church was partially cleared by Robinson and drawn by Woodbridge, and in 1927 further excavation was undertaken by Ramsay. The central church was not studied again until Mitchell and Waelkens surveyed the entire city in 1982 and 1983. Although it does not include the features that Mitchell and Waelkens detected in 1982/1983 or those seen by Ramsay in 1927, Woodbridge's plan is still the most accurate representation of the basic form of the church (figs. 6.2–3).[6] The remains of another church lie unexcavated on the hillside just below the sanctuary of Mên Askaênos. Although this church site was briefly examined by Ramsay, the sole reliable archaeological account of it is that of Mitchell and Waelkens (figs. 6.4–5).[7] In 2001, the magnetometry survey commissioned by Bagnall and carried out by Smekalova and Smekalov identified the plan

---

confronted peacocks, an amphora, trees, and other species of bird is a variation of a type popular in both Christian and non-Christian contexts throughout the Roman period and is not itself indicative of a Christian association for the space, given the absence of any other Christian elements (see Dunbabin 1978, 166–169; Kondoleon 1995, 109–117 for the type). Furthermore, it is unlikely that the theater would have

been put completely out of use as early as the 4th century.

[6] Even today, only the bare outlines of the central church are visible, and the full outline of the church is unknown.

[7] Ramsay 1911–1912, 43 n. 1; Mitchell and Waelkens 1998, 201–206. Cf. Raff, chap. 7, this volume.

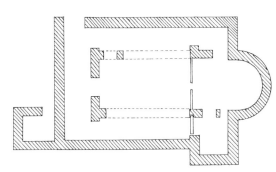

Fig. 6.4. Plan of the church built near the sanctuary of Mên. After Mitchell and Waelkens 1998. By permission of Classical Press of Wales.

Fig. 6.5. Unexcavated ruins of the church near the sanctuary of Mên, view west from the temple (1924). Photo: G. R. Swain, Kelsey Museum Archives neg. no. 7.1581.

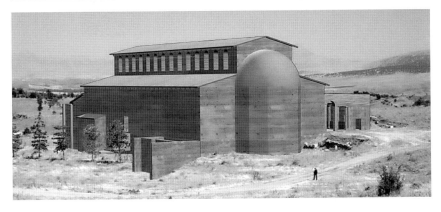

Fig. 6.6. 6: Digital reconstruction of the Church of St. Paul superimposed on the physical remains. Not all of the rooms along the south side of the basilica are reconstructed. Digital model and photo: J. M. Harrington 2004 (B 27– From Theater–MH).

of a large basilica, the north church, in the area of the Roman bath building to the northeast of the Church of St. Paul. The excavators date its first phase to the end of the 6th century.[8]

The Church of St. Paul is by far the best documented of Antioch's four churches, and its history provides a window onto Christianity's place in the religious life of the city (fig. 6.6). In this chapter, I examine the archaeological reports that document the remains of the Church of St. Paul, along with comparative evidence from other churches in Asia Minor, in an attempt to reconstruct the building's

[8] Taşlıalan et al. 2003 on the magnetic survey. Harmankaya and Gümüş 2006, 148–149 on the excavation.

Fig. 6.7. The Church of St. Paul as seen from the east (2002). Photo: Ü. Demirer.

ancient appearance, which had both a 4th-century and a 5th- or 6th-century phase. This reconstruction provides a basis for considering the significance of the Church of St. Paul in Pisidian Antioch. While most of the archaeological remains described below belong to the second phase of construction, in my interpretation of the social significance of the church I focus on the 4th-century phase because there is more evidence relevant to Antioch in that period. I argue that this church sheds new light on the rapid ascent of state-sanctioned Christianity in the city and in the multifaceted religious landscape of Roman Asia Minor in this period.

Archaeological Investigations of the Church of St. Paul

The Church of St. Paul lies on the western edge of the city (fig. 6.7). Like the central church, the Church of St. Paul was first recorded by Arundell in 1833 on his site plan. Robinson undertook the first excavation of the building in 1924, but he published only a general description of it.[9] He was primarily concerned with the inscribed 4th-century mosaic pavement of the nave and several graves beneath the floor. Woodbridge's plan of the church and portions of its mosaic best records Michigan's work at the Church of St. Paul (fig. 6.8). To this we must now add information from Mitchell and Waelkens's survey in 1982 and 1983 and from the excavations conducted by Taşlıalan from 1985

[9] Robinson 1924a; 1926b. Robinson's unpublished Journal of Excavations provides more information, but it is in no way a complete record of the excavation of the basilica.

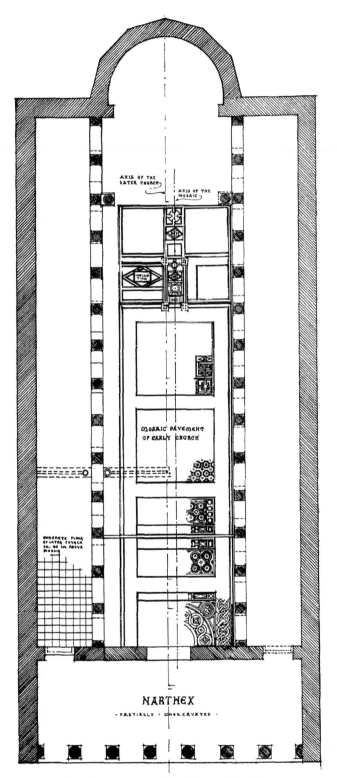

AXIS OF THE
LATER CHURCH

AXIS OF THE
MOSAIC

INSCRIP-
TION

INS

MOSAIC PAVEMENT
OF EARLY CHURCH

CONCRETE FLOOR
OF LATER CHURCH
CA. 60 CM. ABOVE
MOSAIC

NARTHEX

· PARTIALLY · UNEXCAVATED ·

· PLAN · OF · THE · BASILICA ·

· AT · ANTIOCH · IN · PISIDIA ·

Fig. 6.8. Woodbridge's plan of the Church of St. Paul (1924). Kelsey Museum Archives AAR-2405. Photo: G. R. Swain, Kelsey Museum Archives neg no. 7.1247d.

Fig. 6.9. Drawing of the full preserved extent of the nave mosaic of the 4th-century church (2002). Illustration: Ü. Demirer.

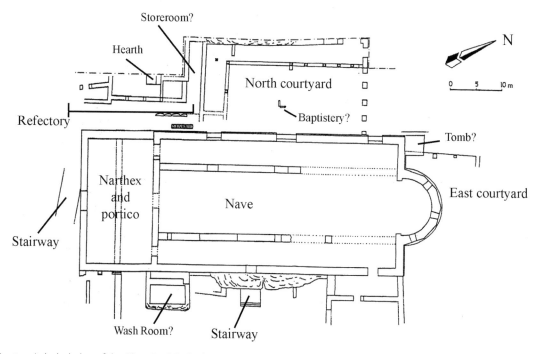

Fig. 6.10. Labeled plan of the Church of St. Paul in its second phase (5th–6th century). Illustration: L. Herring-Harrington after Taşlıalan 1997 = Taşlıalan 2002.

to 1995.[10] Taşlıalan's excavation not only uncovered further structures to the north and south of the basilica but also clarified the structure of the narthex, resulting in a new plan of the ecclesiastical complex. Demirer has since consolidated what remains today of the mosaic floor[11] and uncovered another grave beneath the basilica (fig. 6.9).[12]

[10] The latter were originally published in Turkish in 1997 and translated into English for the First International Conference on Antioch of Pisidia in 1997, the proceedings of which were published as Drew-Bear, Taşlıalan, and Thomas 2002.

[11] Much damage occurred after Robinson's excavations ended in 1924, while the mosaic was being studied prior to being covered over for protection: Journal of Excavations, July 10–August 11, 1924. The mosaic suffered still further damage over the succeeding seventy years prior to Demirer's consolidation in 2002.

[12] Ünal Demirer, personal communication, August 4, 2004.

Fig. 6.11. Digital reconstruction of the interior of the Church of St. Paul in its 5th–6th-century phase. Possible galleries above the side aisles not depicted. Digital model: J. M. Harrington.

Description of the Architecture of the Church of St. Paul: The Archaeological Remains and Their Reconstruction. The main body of the Church of St. Paul in its 5th- or 6th-century phase (27 m × 71 m on the exterior) comprises a nave, two side aisles, an apse, and a narthex, which are all hallmarks of a canonical basilica form (fig. 6.10).[13] Each side aisle is separated from the nave by a row of thirteen columns set on a stylobate that runs the length of the nave (fig. 6.11). Fallen column drums at the eastern end of the nave indicate that at least some of the original twenty-six columns were of colored marble. The stylobates themselves are constructed of white limestone blocks reused from other buildings.[14] The semicircular apse at the eastern end of the church has six facets on its exterior but is a smooth curve on the interior; one of its blocks is reused from an unknown structure.[15] With the exception of the stylobates and other weight-bearing elements, the basilica is constructed of local gray limestone.[16]

    The narthex at the western end of the nave ran the entire width of the basilica. It is uncertain whether it was fronted on its west side by six columns as Woodbridge's plan indicates.[17] A wide central doorway connected the narthex to the nave and was flanked by two smaller doors that opened onto the side aisles. Little remains today of either this narthex or another, outer narthex to the west, said by Arundell to have been formed by extensions of the two long east-west walls of the main body of the church.[18] Although Robinson does not mention the outer narthex in his account, nor does it appear on Woodbridge's plan, Taşlıalan's excavation has recently confirmed its presence.[19] The discovery of a foundation ramp confirms that there was a stairway leading up from ground level to the narthex.

---

[13] These dimensions exclude the structures to the north and south of the basilica itself.

[14] As recognized by Taşlıalan 2002, 10 and Mitchell and Waelkens 1998, 214. Mitchell and Waelkens believe, on the basis of the markings on the blocks, that they were initially intended for use as architrave sections. Otherwise, there is no evidence for where the blocks originated.

[15] Mitchell and Waelkens 1998, 213–214.

[16] Brick was used in the interior foundations of the basilica.

[17] Taşlıalan 2002, 11 states that the narthex was fronted by six

columns. It is not clear from his report, however, whether he found actual columns or is relying on Woodbridge's record of six columns. Mitchell and Waelkens 1998, 214–215 did not see any evidence of columns in their 1982/1983 survey, and they note that the colonnade on Woodbridge's plan is conjectural. The Journal of Excavations mentions ongoing work in the west end of the basilica but does not provide more detail. Some number of columns would not be unexpected, however, as the combination of a portico-narthex and outer narthex was a common one.

[18] Arundell 1834, 306.

[19] Taşlıalan 2002, 11.

Comparison of the Church of St. Paul with churches in the Cilician region along the southern coast of Asia Minor suggests that the narthex could have been two-storied, with a second story connecting to galleries above the side aisles in the main body of the church.[20]

Even though no element of the church is preserved for more than a few courses of blocks above present ground level, there is some evidence for the roof. Flat and curved terracotta roof tiles that fell into the building when the roof collapsed indicate that the main body of the church once had a pitched wooden roof to which the tiles were affixed.[21] The narthex seems to have been roofed by a single tile-covered surface at a shallow incline.[22] The apse, in contrast, may have been covered by a stone half-dome, supported in part by an arch carried on two columns.[23] There is, unfortunately, little other archaeological evidence for the architecture of the 5th–6th–century church. Various carved blocks that today lie in a field south of the Church of St. Paul and in the courtyard of the museum in Yalvaç suggest that the church was ornamented with relief sculpture at some point in its history, whether in the 5th–6th centuries or later.[24] One of the blocks still lying in the vicinity of the church depicts two rams flanking a cross.[25]

From 1985 to 1995 Taşlıalan unearthed several structures to the north, south, and east of the church. Three doorways in the north wall of the church opened onto a paved courtyard with a colonnade around its northern and western sides (figs. 6.12–13); a carved capital found here suggests that the colonnade may have been ornamented with crosses.[26] According to Taşlıalan, the central threshold between the north aisle of the church and the north courtyard once bore a now-lost inscription, which read: "the vow of Aberkios, courtier and civic administrator."[27] Opposite the central doorway to the church, in the center of the courtyard, are the remains of a basinlike structure with a stone water channel, possibly a baptistery, as proposed by Taşlıalan.[28] The courtyard was also accessible from the east through a triple doorway surmounted by two arches supported on pillars. A series of four rooms on the west side of the courtyard yielded a hearth with traces of coal and ash, terracotta household utensils, and fragments of large storage jars. Taşlıalan believes that these rooms belonged to a refectory.[29]

On the south side of the church, the ground level drops away sharply to a series of seven rooms of uncertain function. In the middle of these rooms there was a stairway leading up to the church. To

[20] See Hill 1996, 16–19 for discussion of the churches in Cilicia.

[21] Taşlıalan 2002, 14.

[22] Taşlıalan 2002, 14 reconstructs this roof from the method of construction of the preserved elements of the narthex.

[23] Taşlıalan 2002, 14 concludes this from the blocks found in front of the structure.

[24] Ruggieri's 2004 and 2005 articles cataloguing Byzantine sculpture in the museum at Yalvaç list one or two pieces that potentially come from either the second phase of the Church of St. Paul or the central church, or from elsewhere in the ancient site. The first is a 6th-century capital of a type intended for use in a window (2004, no. 16); the second is a fragment that might be part of a pluteus of the late 6th or 7th centuries, though its decoration suggests a date later in the 10th–11th centuries (2005, no. 17). Most of the extant

Christian sculpture dates to the 10th–11th centuries. Ruggieri (2004, 261–262) laments that he cannot identify exactly where any of it originated, though some of it is known to have come from outside Yalvaç. The 2005 article purposefully omits the late Roman and early Byzantine material in order to focus on the medieval corpus, so there might be other early pieces.

[25] Ruggieri makes no mention of this block.

[26] Ruggieri does not mention this capital.

[27] εὐχὴ Ἀβερκίου κόμητος καὶ οἰκονόμου, as quoted by Taşlıalan 2002, 12, who did not see the inscription himself. He does not provide an accurate source for it, and I have not been able to locate the original publication.

[28] Taşlıalan 2002, 15.

[29] Taşlıalan 2002, 17.

Fig. 6.12. The north courtyard. Column bases along the L-shaped portico are visible in the background. The basin and quatrefoil font in the center of the courtyard may be the remains of a baptistery (2004). Photo: L. Herring-Harrington (B 39–Nave–LH).

Fig. 6.13. Digital reconstruction of the Church of St. Paul, as seen from the northwest. The refectory and the stairway on the west side of the basilica are not reconstructed. Digital model: J. M. Harrington.

the west of this stairway lay a cistern with a stone spout connected by a terracotta pipeline, probably to one of the two known aqueducts.[30] A room with marble revetment on its floor and walls, which adjoins the cistern to the south, may have been used for washing.[31]

At the east end of the church, Taşlıalan found a wall running perpendicular to the apse, which he claims was the northern boundary of a rectangular courtyard.[32] In the courtyard he uncovered a stone baptismal font.[33] Taşlıalan proposes further that a "small cell" in the northwest corner of this presumed courtyard, next to the apse of the basilica, might have been a tomb. Whether or not this area was a courtyard, the presence of such features to the east as well as to the north and south of the Church of St. Paul is consistent with the general architectural form of other basilican churches in western Asia Minor.[34]

The 4th-Century Nave Mosaic. The mosaic, which ran the length of the nave, is important both artistically and culturally. Woodbridge's plan of the church includes representative sections of its design as it was preserved in 1924, and he drew some of these sections in detail (fig. 6.14). The entire design of the mosaic was never fully recorded, and much of what survived in 1924 has since been destroyed.[35] In 2002, Demirer drew a plan of the full extent of the mosaic as it was then preserved (fig. 6.9). Demirer's plan, studied along with Woodbridge's drawings and archival photographs, gives us a good idea of

[30] Described by Taşlıalan 2002, 12 as "a construction built to hold water," it is termed a cistern by Mitchell and Waelkens 1998, 217. See Ossi and Harrington, chap. 2, this volume for discussion of the aqueducts and water distribution system.

[31] Taşlıalan 2002, 13, 18. Similar facilities have been found at the early Byzantine episcopal basilica in Xanthos: des Courtils and Cavalier 2001, 168.

[32] Taşlıalan 2002, 18.

[33] This font is in addition to the one dedicated to St. Paul that Taşlıalan (2002, 18) claims also originated in the "east courtyard." Calder, however, who first published the inscrip-

tion (1912, 98, no. 29), reports that the font sat in the baths in Yalvaç at the time when the inscription was copied. Mitchell and Waelkens (1998, 215) relate how Taşlıalan was told that it originated at the site of the church; Ruggieri 2005, 84–87 also tells how it was later taken to the museum in 1960. The font dedicated to St. Paul appears to belong to the 10th or 11th century AD (Ruggieri 2005, 87).

[34] See below.

[35] When Demirer uncovered the mosaic for study and conservation, he calculated that 20 percent of the tesserae had been lost in the intervening years: Ünal Demirer, personal communication, August 4, 2004.

Fig. 6.14. Woodbridge's drawing of a section of the nave mosaic (1924). Photo: G. R. Swain, Kelsey Museum neg. no. 1247c.

Fig. 6.15. The north side of the nave mosaic (1924). Photo: G. R. Swain, Kelsey Museum neg. no. 7.1348.

original overall design. What remains of the composition of the mosaic is predominantly nonfigural, consisting of geometric and some vegetal motifs in white, red, yellow, blue, and pink tesserae (fig. 6.15).[36] The design consists of repeated motifs, some of which, such as Solomon's knot (fig. 6.16), could have served a magical or apotropaic function to protect the church.[37] Repetition of the image may in fact have been thought to increase its potency.[38] This decorative scheme, which largely excludes representational

[36] Although the mosaic is now covered over, there are numerous sources for its appearance. First among them are the Journal of Excavations (July 7, 1924) and Woodbridge's and Demirer's drawings and photographs from 1924 and 2002, respectively. Woodbridge's material is held at the Kelsey Museum of Archaeology; Demirer's material remains among his personal papers. There are also several published descriptions of the mosaic. These are Kitzinger's (1974), which is based on the excavation notes and photographs; Mitchell and Waelkens's (1998), though it is not clear whether they viewed the mosaic themselves or relied on the original notes and photographs; and Taşlıalan's (2002), which is based on sondages he conducted, in addition to the data from Robinson's excavations. There are also four small fragments of the mosaic in the collection of the Kelsey Museum of Archaeology (KM9.3861, KM9.3862, KM9.3863, KM9.3864).

[37] See Kitzinger 1970 for discussion of Solomon's knot.

[38] Maguire 1994. The specific meaning of any motif in a mosaic is dependent upon its context. The location of the Solomon's knot drawn by Woodbridge is unknown, but there are others in the first and second panels from the west of the nave; those in the first panel appear in the semicircle ringing the entry through the main door into the nave. Thresholds and graves are among the areas in a church most often accompanied by apotropaic motifs (Kitzinger 1970). Unfortunately, the locations of the graves in the nave of the Church of St. Paul are not known with enough accuracy, and the mosaic is too fragmentary, to determine whether there is a spatial association between the graves and Solomon's knots.

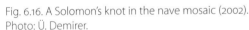

Fig. 6.16. A Solomon's knot in the nave mosaic (2002).
Photo: Ü. Demirer.

Fig. 6.17. The peacock in the *solea* (2002).
Photo: Ü. Demirer.

imagery, conforms to other 4th-century pavements in churches in Asia Minor.[39] The only figural image to survive is of a peacock, which might have signified abundance, prosperity, and good fortune (fig. 6.17).[40]

Starting at the western end of the nave, four successive square panels are surrounded by a continuous frame that links them in a long rectangular composition covering about four-fifths of the length of the nave. Occupying the eastern fifth of the nave floor is an unusual square panel, which is divided into four smaller panels with a central band of seven smaller panels running east-west down the middle (fig. 6.18). The third and sixth of the small panels in the central band are inscribed with Psalm 43:4 from the Bible. The relation of these inscribed panels to their architectural context is unusual, as they played more than an ornamental role. A person walking toward the altar from the west end of the nave would have first read the inscription in the third panel, "and I shall go to the altar of God" and, proceeding to the second inscription in the sixth panel, "unto God who gladdens my youth" (fig. 6.19).[41] The inscriptions thus anticipate and mirror the actions of the person reading

[39] Such as the mosaics of the Martyrion of St. Babylas at Antioch-on-the-Orontes in Syria. See Kitzinger 1970, 639.

[40] Dunbabin 1978, 166–169; Kondoleon 1995, 109–117. Other contexts in which peacocks appear include private houses and synagogues (see Avi-Yonah 1963, fig. 5 for the latter); another mosaic of a peacock in Antioch was found by Demirer in the theater. See Mallampati and Demirer, chap. 4, this volume. The peacock in the Church of St. Paul occurs

in the *solea* (see my discussion of this *solea* below).

[41] καὶ εἰσελεύ- / σομαι πρὸς / τὸ θυσιαστή- / ριον τοῦ Θεοῦ and πρὸς τὸν θε[ὸν / τὸν εὐφ[ραί- / νοντα τ[ὴν / νεότητ[ά μου. Taşlıalan's (1997, 231 = 2002, 14) mistake in his publication of the latter is most likely the consequence of his not having uncovered the entire mosaic when he excavated (see Taşlıalan 2002, 10). Robinson (1926b, 234–235) provides the correct transcription.

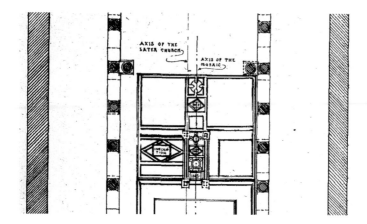

Fig. 6.18. Enlargement of Woodbridge's plan of the east end of the Church of St. Paul (1924). Kelsey Museum Archives AAR-2405. Photo: G. R. Swain, Kelsey Museum Archives neg. no. 7.1247d.

Fig. 6.19. The inscription of Psalm 43:4 in the *solea* (2002). Photo: Ü. Demirer.

them. No other comparable arrangement of inscriptions is known in the late Roman or early Christian periods, though there is evidence suggesting that the Psalm was read aloud during the liturgy of this time.[42] Just as the repetition of images in the nave mosaics gave them greater force, the reinforcement of liturgical ritual by the reading (both silent and audible) of the text of the Psalm inscription could have heightened the religious experience of the worshipper. The central band, which forms a path, or *solea*, along which the clergy walked toward the altar, was marked off visually from the rest of the mosaic by a low barrier. This *solea* at Antioch seems to be the earliest one known.[43]

Two additional inscriptions are important because they provide evidence for the date of the mosaic. The first, in the northwest of the four paired panels at the east end of the nave, reads, "in the time of the most venerable bishop Optimos, Eutuchianos, having made a vow to God, fulfilled it." The second, in the first panel of the *solea*, similarly proclaims, "in the time of the most venerable bishop Optimos, Eidomeneus, public secretary, having made a vow to God, rendered it."[44] Optimos, according to Theophanes, was bishop of Antioch from AD 374 until sometime after AD 381, when he represented Antioch at the Council of Constantinople; he was also a correspondent of Basil of Caesarea during that time.[45]

The Chronology of the Church of St. Paul. The mosaic, laid in the time of Optimos, provides a guideline for reconstructing the chronology of the Church of St. Paul. The physical location of the mosaic indicates that it belongs to an earlier phase of construction than the rest of the architectural remains

---

[42] As cited by Kitzinger 1974, 393: Ambr., *De myst.* 8.43, *De sacram.* 4.2.7 in J. Quasten, *Monumenta eucharistica et liturgica vetustissima* 3 (Bonn 1936) 131, 156; F. C. Burkitt, "The Early Syriac Lectionary System," *Proceedings of the British Academy* (1921–1923) 313, 328.

[43] Kitzinger 1974, 392.

[44] ἐπὶ τοῦ αἰδεσ(ιμωτάτου) ἐπισ(κόπου) / Ὀπτίμου

Εὐτυχιανὸς / ε]ὐξάμενος ἐπλήρωσε / τ]ὴν εὐχὴν τῷ θε[ῷ] and ἐπὶ τοῦ αἰδεσιμωτάτου / ἐπισκόπου Ὀπτίμο[υ / Εἰδομενεὺς ἀναγνώστη[ς / εὐξάμενος τῷ θεῷ / τὴν εὐχὴν ἀπέδωκε (Robinson 1926b, 234).

[45] Optimos as bishop of Antioch: Theophanes 61.18; Theodoret 4.27. Optimos as participant in the Council of Constantinople: Theodoret 5.8.

Fig. 6.20. Terracotta piping cut into the mosaic in the nave of the Church of St. Paul during the second phase of construction (1924). Photo: G. R. Swain, Kelsey Museum Archives neg. no. 7.1448.

described above. In his excavations, Robinson found portions of the concrete floor of a later church some 60 cm above the 4th-century mosaic floor, clearly indicating a second phase of construction.[46] Moreover, in the second phase the longitudinal axis of the body of the church was shifted slightly northward from that of the 4th-century mosaic, as shown on Woodbridge's plan, which combines the two phases of construction.[47] Also in the later phase of construction, walls were built over the mosaic at the west end of the nave, and a drainage system was set into the floor, cutting through the mosaic (fig. 6.20).[48] The physical evidence, then, indicates two phases of construction—the first represented only by the ornamental mosaic floor of the 4th century and the second by the architectural

[46] This concrete floor had a simple mosaic pavement of black and white tesserae. Robinson mentions its existence in the Journal of Excavations (June 7, 1924), but the first full description of it is reported in *The Michigan Alumnus* (31:701; cited by Kitzinger 1974, 389). A fragment of this pavement was located in the north aisle of the basilica by the door to the narthex. Robinson believed the concrete floor to have once covered the entire nave as well. That the excavators in 1924 believed this concrete floor to have been of later date than the mosaic is also evident in a report written by George R. Swain (1924), the expedition photographer. Taşlıalan (2002, 13) also mentions this floor. The depth of the mosaic floor below the concrete pavement is recorded on Woodbridge's plan. Since

Demirer's consolidation, the mosaic has been covered over for protection and the floor filled in, so the discrepancy in the floor depths of the two phases is not evident today.

[47] The Journal of Excavations (July 7, 1924) also notes that the mosaic is "out of line with the apse."

[48] The terracotta piping of the drainage system is connected to the cistern to the south of the basilica, indicating that it, at least, among the southern rooms, is associated with the latest phase of the complex. See the Journal of Excavations, June 23, 1924, for the discovery of the piping.

remains.[49] Assuming that the 4th-century church was destroyed, perhaps by an earthquake such as those that damaged Aphrodisias in the 4th century,[50] many of the fallen blocks may have been reused in building the new church. Judging from the continued use of ashlar masonry in the construction of the basilica visible today, Mitchell and Waelkens believe that this second phase of construction most likely dates to the 5th or 6th centuries.[51]

The Architectural and Historical Contexts of the Church of St. Paul

The Form and Function of the Church of St. Paul. A mid- to late 4th-century date for the original construction of a church with an elaborate mosaic is consistent with other evidence for the development of church architecture in Asia Minor. Both archaeological and literary sources, such as correspondence between church officials, suggest that the first public monumental Christian architecture appeared in the mid-3rd century.[52] Known as *aulae ecclesiae*, these hall-like structures had only some of the features of a basilica.[53] Scholarly consensus attributes the adoption of the fully developed basilican form to Constantine in the first half of the 4th century.[54] Once accepted for use as churches, basilicas quickly became the standard church form; thus it is most likely that the church associated with the mosaic at Antioch was of basilican form like its 5th–6th–century successor. Beyond sharing the characteristics of apse, naves, aisles, and narthex, however, early Christian basilicas in Asia Minor varied greatly in form, and classifying them by architectural type is difficult.[55] Nor is it always possible to link a church's form to the liturgical and theological principles of the particular patriarchate or other administrative unit with which it was associated.[56] In any case, the fact that the original Church of St. Paul is one of only two securely dated churches in ancient Asia Minor belonging to the 4th century[57]—the other being

[49] There is no support for Robinson's (1924a, 443) and Taşlıalan's (2002, 19) suggestions that the Church of St. Paul underwent three phases of construction. Robinson himself provides no evidence for his argument in the publication of his excavation, nor is there any corroborating evidence in the Journal of Excavations. The primary flaw in Taşlıalan's chronology is that he does not allow for a phase after the laying of the mosaic. The church clearly underwent significant changes after the mosaic was placed, as evidenced by the pipe that cuts through the mosaic, the later walls built over it, and the shift in the longitudinal axis of the church.

[50] See Ratté 2001, 140–144 on earthquake damage at Aphrodisias.

[51] Mitchell and Waelkens 1998, 213.

[52] See White 1990, 11–25, 102–139; Blue 1994; Krautheimer 1986, 23–67 for overview and discussion of the development of Christian architecture. The first Christians met in the houses of individual members, and beginning in the mid-2nd century, some houses were remodeled to serve exclusively as Christian meeting places (*domus ecclesiae*). Both private and public larger buildings and halls appeared in the 3rd century.

[53] White 1990, 22, 128. He cites the churches of SS. Giovanni e Paolo and San Clemente at Rome as examples (later built

over with standard basilican churches). The so-called Canonical Letter of Gregory the Wonder-Worker, a Neacaesareian bishop, describes what seems to be an *aula ecclesia* in Pontus in the 250s: Mitchell 1993, 2:56; Lane Fox 1987, 539.

[54] See Ward-Perkins 1954; White 1990, 17–20, 137–139; Lane Fox 1987, 587; Krautheimer 1986, 37.

[55] Hellenkemper (1994) demonstrates the varied nature of Christian architecture for the region encompassing Lycia, Pamphylia, Isauria, and Cilicia, regions that resemble the area in which Pisidian Antioch lies. By the beginning of the 4th century, most cities in this region, like Antioch, had bishops and other clergy, though there was a strong polytheist presence until the 6th century. See also Hill 1996; Mitchell 1993, 2:57–63.

[56] Given that Roman provincial divisions, along which the Church operated its own administrative structure, cut across cultural and other preexisting boundaries, and that provincial boundaries were redrawn throughout the imperial period, it is not surprising that local preference could have been a more influential factor in determining architectural choices. See Mitchell 1993, 2:151–163 for discussion of provincial boundaries in Asia Minor.

[57] As noted by Mitchell and Waelkens (1998, 213), who credit the observation to H. Hellenkemper.

the Church of St. Babylas in Antioch-on-the-Orontes in Syria, which also had an elaborate floor mosaic—is significant for understanding the politically and religiously elevated status of Pisidian Antioch in the 4th century (discussed below).

Before discussing the Church of St. Paul's broader significance, however, further analysis of its preserved remains can provide insight into how the building functioned as a place of worship in each phase of its existence.[58] In the 4th-century church, for example, the *solea*, the pathway set off by a low wall, preserves two pairs of small square bases along its long edges. These bases were probably connected by rails, suggesting that the path was reserved for the clergy to walk along as they approached the altar. While moving along this path, they might well have read the passages of Psalm 43 inscribed on the mosaic panels.

The evidence for liturgical usage of the church in the 5th–6th–century phase is considerably more extensive. A round concrete foundation built over the mosaic at the east end of the nave may have been part of an *ambo* in the later church.[59] Typically, an *ambo*, or pulpit, was placed at the end of the *solea* in the middle of the nave. (Though there is no visible evidence of a *solea* in the later 5th–6th–century church, one might well have existed.) The *ambo* was one of the main focal points of the church, and processions connecting it with the *bema*, the area of the church containing the altar (usually in front of the apse), were common. A photograph taken in 1924 shows this foundation before it was removed to expose the mosaic floor beneath.[60] Also in this area of the church, protrusions still visible on either side of the apse of the second phase most likely supported the chancel barrier separating the apse from the nave as the holiest part of the church.[61]

The three doorways in the exterior wall of the north aisle of the second phase of the Church of St. Paul, when considered along with the three entrances to the nave from the narthex and the single entrance from the south into the south aisle, offer another example of how use may be indicated by architecture. As in churches in Syria, which had two or three side doorways, the multiple doorways at Antioch could have been used for segregated entry, with clergy passing through one door and laity another.[62] The lack of evidence for screens between the stylobate columns suggests that once lay worshippers were inside the Church of St. Paul, they were allowed in the nave, as was common in Constantinople but not in Greece.[63]

As the largest church in the city, the Church of St. Paul was probably the episcopal basilica, the seat of the bishop of Antioch.[64] As such, it would have needed space for residential quarters as well as

[58] Cf. Mathews 1971; see also Hellenkemper 1994 and Poulter 1994 for the idea that doctrinal belief, liturgy, and other specific activities had an effect on a church's form. I thank R. Schroeder for bringing Mathews's work to my attention.

[59] See the Journal of Excavations (July 1, 1924) for reference to this feature. The foundation is identified as a concrete base, perhaps for a pulpit. At 19.6 m from the extreme eastern end of the apse, it is in the right position for an *ambo*. The Journal further notes that it resembled the round foundation in the middle of the Tiberia Platea in front of the propylon, which led to the imperial cult sanctuary.

[60] The caption for the photograph (Kelsey Museum Archives KR63.06) states that the "round altar or pulpit" is in the middle foreground.

[61] The function of the protrusions is suggested by Mitchell and Waelkens 1998, 214.

[62] The Syrian evidence is discussed by H. C. Butler, as cited in White 1990, 200 n. 124: cf. R. Garrett et al., eds., *Syria: Publications of an American Archaeological Expedition to Syria in 1899–1900*, vol. 2 (New York: The Century Co. 1903). Alternatively, topography may have been a factor in the way the doors were used. At Kremna, the topography mandated that the narthex of Church D be entered through a door in its short north side rather than through the wide west end: Mitchell 1995, 226, 229.

[63] Mathews 1971, 118–121. I am grateful to R. Schroeder for pointing this out.

[64] The basilica recently found to the north of the Church of

administrative and utilitarian support services. Perhaps the rooms Taşlıalan discovered to the north of the Church of St. Paul served as the bishop's residence or were used by other church personnel.[65] As noted earlier, Taşlıalan identified a stone basin in the middle of the north courtyard as a baptistery, and the rooms on the west side of this courtyard seem to have been a refectory, judging by the household utensils, storage jars, and hearth found in them.[66] Some of the rooms to the north and south of the basilica could also have been used for the preparation of clergy and of the vestments, implements, and *prosphora* (loaves consecrated for the Eucharist) used in the liturgy.[67]

Social and Religious Implications of the Church of St. Paul in Pisidian Antioch. For the Christians who gathered at the Church of St. Paul, practicing their religion was easier than it had been for Christians earlier in the history of the Roman Empire. In AD 313, Constantine legalized Christianity and put it on equal footing with the traditional cults of the Roman Empire, so that Christians could worship openly without fear of repercussion.[68] Constantine also passed legislation to benefit Christians, such as laws regulating the bequest of property, though he had to be circumspect in his treatment of both Christians and non-Christians in this early period. Many prominent Romans, including the provincial governors on whom Constantine relied to enforce his edicts, were polytheists, and he could not afford to lose their support. His successors were more aggressive in checking the religious practices of non-Christians, in addition to promoting the welfare of Christians.

In the 4th century, Antioch itself was flourishing. It had been named the capital of the newly formed province of Pisidia around the turn of the century. The refurbishment of the stage building of the theater and the conversion of its orchestra into an arena suggest that a spate of building activity accompanied the city's rise in political status. As Mallampati and Demirer point out in chapter 4 of this volume, the renovation of the theater is all the more significant given that only a small number of theaters were refurbished on such a large scale in this period. Antioch's Church of St. Paul was constructed in the third to fourth quarter of the 4th century, as the inscription naming Optimos attests. The fact that the Church could afford such a basilica at so early a date indicates that Antioch's Christian community was prospering as well. Antioch's historical connection to St. Paul probably attracted pilgrims who would have contributed to the prosperity of the church and the city. In addition, the city's connection to an important Christian apostle must have played a significant role in the community's sense of its own identity.[69]

The 4th-century donor inscriptions of Eidomeneus and Eutuchianos, in the mosaic floor of the basilica, along with the later 5th–6th–century one of Aberkios, on the marble threshold of the center

---

St. Paul is slightly smaller; it measures about 25 m by 50 m (Taşlıalan et al. 2003). Antioch may have gained its bishop when it became the capital of the province of Pisidia. Lequien (1740, 1035–1037) names six bishops who presided over Antioch before Optimos. Mitchell and Waelkens (1998, 217) believe that there is "no doubt" that the Church of St. Paul was "the seat of the metropolitan bishop at Antioch."

[65] Taşlıalan (2002, 15–17) suggests that the rooms served as lodgings for personnel and were set aside for the use of church officials to carry out their administrative duties. A comparison is a house associated with Church C at Kremna that Mitchell (1995, 16) suggests may have functioned as a bishop's residence, due to its large size and lavish decoration with mosaic and marble revetments. See above for Taşlıalan's

work in the rooms to the north of the Church of St. Paul.

[66] Taşlıalan 2002, 16–17 suggests these room functions.

[67] Cf. Taft 1998, 53 ff.; Mathews 1971, 107, 161.

[68] See Potter 2004, 364–581 for the history of the Roman Empire in the 4th century after the victory of Constantine in 313; also Lane Fox 1987, 17–18, 622–624, 663–682.

[69] The 10th–11th–century stone baptismal font dedicated to St. Paul demonstrates that Antioch's association with Paul continued to be commemorated centuries after his sojourns there.

doorway between the north aisle and courtyard, attest to the wealth of some members of the Antiochene congregation. The vows recorded in these inscriptions most likely refer to donations of money to pay for building improvements.[70] The epitaph on the sarcophagus of Eugenios, the bishop of Laodiceia Katakekaumene in southeast Phrygia in the mid-4th century, proudly proclaims that he, as bishop, "built the entire church from its foundations, and . . . provided the adornment of the whole."[71] Such donations by members of the wealthy elite indicate a change in focus in the patterns of euergetism at Antioch, as elsewhere, over the course of the 3rd and 4th centuries.[72] Because traditional outlets for elite benefaction—such as baths, theaters, and games—were now frowned upon by the Church owing to their incompatibility with a Christian way of life and because these lavish expenses were thought to have been motivated by vainglory, Christian euergetism focused on the construction of churches and other doctrinally and ethically sanctioned activities.[73] Now, in addition to the construction and ornamentation of churches by wealthy members of the congregation, the new forms of benefaction included distributing property and money to the church and delegating the church as an intermediary in the administration of social services.[74] The patronage of elites helped to promote Christianity and to weave it tightly into the fabric of the community when churches became important community centers.[75]

One might expect that a church as important to the community as the Church of St. Paul would be placed in a more prominent location rather than directly adjacent to the city wall. However, large basilicas do not begin to appear in city centers until the end of the 4th century and the early 5th century[76]—just after the Church of St. Paul was built in its earliest form. In the first phases of church building—that is, before the later 4th century when imperial legislation began to encourage the destruction of polytheistic sanctuaries—it was probably difficult to find space for large churches in an urban center already filled with temples and civic buildings, and this circumstance, coupled with a desire to avoid offending prominent non-Christians, may explain why many early churches are either outside the city walls or within them but located along the edges of the community, like the Church of St. Paul.[77]

The presence of multiple churches in Pisidian Antioch—two large basilicas and the smaller central church inside the city itself, as well as the church outside the city at the sanctuary of Mên—all built during the 4th–6th centuries,[78] also demonstrates a high level of Christian building activity that

[70] Taşlıalan (2002, 13) and Mitchell and Waelkens (1998, 213) suggest that Eidomeneus and Eutuchianos donated money for the laying of the mosaic floor. Alternatively, perhaps they paid for the right to be buried in or beneath the church and are among those interred under the nave of the Church of St. Paul. What evidence there is for the location of the graves found by Robinson in 1924 suggests that they were placed in proximity to the inscriptions (Journal of Excavations, June 25, 1924; July 1, 1924).

[71] Recently republished by Tabbernee (1997, 426–436) with English translation, line drawings, and photographs.

[72] Potter 2004, 395–397; Mitchell 1993, 2:82–83; Brown 1992, 120; Lane Fox 1987, 323–325, 591. Potter discusses the evidence that decline in the performance of civic *munera* (duties, services) was caused by imperially granted exemptions; this decline left a gap that Christians were able to fill.

[73] Jones 1986, 971–972. My thanks to Robert Chenault for his

perspective on Christian euergetism.

[74] Van Dam 2002, 48–52; Mitchell 1993, 2:82–83; Lane Fox 1987, 323–325, 591.

[75] Lane Fox 1987, 669–670.

[76] Mitchell 1993, 2:67.

[77] Cf. Krautheimer 1983, 2–3, 28–31 on the choice of location for the cathedral of S. Giovanni in Laterano in Rome. See also Mitchell 1995, 229–230; 1993, 2:67; Lane Fox 1987, 672; Deichmann 1939 for some discussion of patterns in church placement and related imperial legislation. The location of a church could be highly provocative, as the placement of the central church demonstrates: see below.

[78] See below for the dating of the church at the Mên sanctuary and the central church.

is consistent with the picture for Asia Minor in this period. Multiple churches in a single population center were the norm, even for smaller cities and towns. In Xanthos in Lycia, Aphrodisias in Caria, Hierapolis in Phrygia, and Kremna in Pisidia, churches were scattered throughout the city and outside the walls as well. Even small communities such as Korykos, a small city in Cilicia along the coast, had more than twelve churches between the 5th and 6th centuries.[79]

The reasons that a city would house multiple churches are many. At Antioch, the wealth of the city and its inhabitants, its status as a bishop's seat, and its historical importance no doubt played influential roles in the location and number of churches since these would have increased the need of physical outlets for piety, pilgrimage, and patronage.[80] Churches in antiquity served a variety of purposes. The multiple apses on either side of the western end of Church F at Kremna, for instance, suggest that the church was dedicated to martyrs' cults, while a house associated with Church C at the same site probably served as a bishop's residence or as a hostelry for pilgrims.[81] Pilgrimage, an important part of early Christian life, aided the spread of Christianity. As previously stated, a city such as Antioch, with connections to a figure like St. Paul, would have been an important destination for pilgrims in antiquity.

The presence of different Christian sects was also a potential factor in the decision to build multiple churches. At Kremna, for example, the size and relatively central position of Church C, in a city that had another basilica, may be evidence of a different sect of Christianity.[82] In Antioch, the newly identified basilica near the bath building suggests the possibility of a rival Christian sect there as well.

If there was more than one Christian sect in Antioch, some may have held views on Christian theology that differed from Orthodox doctrine.[83] During the 4th century, there were numerous variants of Christianity in Asia Minor. Phrygia, for example, is known to have been more heterodox than Orthodox.[84] The depth of feeling behind differences in theological stances often played itself out in bitter intra-Christian conflict. The seesawing struggle for control of the bishopric at Ankyra from 314 to 360 between the bishops Marcellus, who was an Orthodox proponent, and Basil, who was not, was accompanied by riots.[85] Complicating the situation further, a nominally Orthodox bishop could be sympathetic to heretics; in 320, for example, Eusebius of Caesarea sheltered the exile Arius, a major proponent of the heatedly debated heresy that Christ the Son was created by God the Father and inferior to him rather than equal in status as in Orthodox theology.[86] Attempts at reconciliation occurred throughout the 4th century, but the controversy was not resolved until the Council of Constantinople in 381, at which nearly two hundred bishops convened by the emperor Theodosius ratified a new creed that proclaimed the victory of Orthodoxy.[87]

[79] Hellenkemper 1994, 215.

[80] See Poulter 1994, 266–267 for discussion of the factors behind the presence of multiple churches in a city.

[81] Mitchell 1995, 225–226, 228.

[82] Mitchell 1995, 230. See above for Mitchell's claim that Church C was suited for a bishop's seat.

[83] See Pagels 2003 for a thoughtful exploration of how Orthodoxy was shaped amidst the political and religious concerns of the 2nd through 4th centuries, and its relationship with other Christian belief systems. Potter 2004, e.g. 402–422

provides a historical account of the primary sectarian conflicts of the 4th century.

[84] Mitchell 1993, 2:59, 71.

[85] Mitchell 1993, 2:91–93.

[86] See Davis 1983, 53–55 and L'Huillier 1996, 17–19 for more detailed discussion.

[87] Potter 2004, 560; Davis 1983, 119–133. Given human nature, it ought not to be surprising that new disputes arose in later years (see Norris 2007, 94–94 on Miaphysitism).

Optimos, the Orthodox bishop who provides the date for the mosaic from the earlier phase of the Church of St. Paul, represented Antioch at this council, and it is his presence there that provides us with a narrow window into Antioch's position and role in Christian politics of the 4th century.[88] As bishop, he almost certainly wielded significant influence within the imperial administration.[89] Bishops of prominent cities, such as Ambrose of Milan, commonly had the ear of the emperor himself. As part of his duties, Optimos would have instituted an imperially sanctioned court of arbitration (*episcopalis audientia*) at Antioch that adjudicated disputes for all who sought assistance.[90] The presence of an Orthodox bishopric, in addition to the basilica itself and the three other churches, clearly signals Antioch's status within the overlapping spheres of Roman imperial government and ecclesiastical administration.

Jews, Polytheists, and Christians in the 4th Century AD

Even as the numbers of Christians and support for Christianity grew, there remained throughout the empire a vast majority of polytheists, many of whom took no notice of what was happening to Christians.[91] Though faced with increasingly stringent restrictions on their religious practices, polytheists continued to play significant roles in their communities in the decades after the victory of Constantine in 313.[92] The Roman Empire's transformation into a Christian empire did not happen overnight. At Antioch, the evidence for other religious buildings in the city also provides us with evidence for the existence of Jewish as well as polytheist communities.

The Antiochene Jews and Their Synagogue. It is clear from the account of Paul's visit to Antioch recorded in the book of Acts, chapter 13, that there was a Jewish synagogue in the city in the mid-1st century. Several scholars have speculated that either the central church or the Church of St. Paul was built on top of it.[93] Indeed, it is tempting to think that the reused blocks in both churches may have come from the synagogue.[94] Unfortunately, neither the published reports nor the unpublished

[88] Theodoret 5.8.

[89] See Mitchell 1993, 2:72–81 and Brown 1992 and for discussion of bishops and their roles. Arundell 1834, 308 makes the statement that Optimos "was delegated by the synod to re-establish the churches which had been devastated by the factions of the Arians," perhaps referring to Socrates, *Historia ecclesiastica* 5.8.

[90] Brown 1992, 100; Lane Fox 1987, 500–501, 667; Potter 2004, 424.

[91] Lane Fox 1987, 592 touches on the ratio of Christians to non-Christians.

[92] Polytheists faced successive bans on the forms of traditional cult, including sacrifice, though the degree of restriction and the intensity of enforcement varied. See Potter 2004, 402, 431–435, 485–488, 555.

[93] Although Taşlıalan (2002, 19) acknowledges that the physical evidence is lacking, he argues for the existence of a 1st-century synagogue on the site of the Church of St. Paul.

Ramsay (1928, 51–53) bases his argument for the central church on the excavations he carried out at the site in 1927, during which he saw more than the one apse visible during Robinson's excavations in 1924. The new, smaller apse supposedly contained a stone foundation for a bench and a desk facing the congregation to mark the spot where Paul gave his sermon. Cf. Mitchell and Waelkens's (1998, 208) more skeptical observations. It is unlikely that we can pinpoint the location of the synagogue without further excavation at the site since there does not seem to have been a pattern to a synagogue's location in the community. The synagogues in Capernaum and Sardis, for example, are in the city center, while that at Chorizaum is on a high hill outside the city. The one at Priene was placed in the domestic quarter.

[94] In addition to the apse and stylobates, Taşlıalan (2002, 10, 12, 15, 17) identifies the north courtyard and its associated rooms, the south wall of the nave, and the rooms to the south of the Church of St. Paul as containing reused blocks. The apse of the central church also contains a reused block: Mitchell and Waelkens 1998, 209. Synagogues are known to have been reused in churches elsewhere. At Jerash in Jordan, archaeologists have found an entire synagogue underneath

excavation journal indicates exactly where the reused stones were placed in each church or where the blocks originated. They could well have come solely from the 4th-century church if it had, in fact, been destroyed by an earthquake. The notion that the site of the 4th-century church appropriated that of a Jewish synagogue is nonetheless intriguing. If the builders of the Church of St. Paul had deliberately built on the site of a synagogue and used materials from the synagogue in their new church, it might imply that relations between the Christian and Jewish communities at Antioch were contentious.[95]

Evidence for Jewish-Christian relations throughout the wider landscape of Asia Minor in the 4th century, however, suggests that the situation in Antioch was probably more nuanced. Attacks on synagogues, for example, did occur despite official policy condemning them. The tension between Jews and other groups in the 4th century stemmed from the imperially sanctioned, traditional privilege that allowed Jews to abstain from important obligations of community life such as participation in the imperial cult.[96] In some cities of Asia Minor, however, Jewish practices were accepted and even emulated by many Christians. In Apamea in southern Phrygia, for example, Jewish practices were so appealing to Christians that the Council of Laodiceia in the late 4th century instituted several canons mandating that Christians not adopt them.[97] The situation at Antioch may be clarified by further excavation and discovery.

The Imperial Cult Temple and the Sanctuary of Mên. Fortunately, the archaeological evidence for polytheistic religious practices at Antioch is more extensive. It does not, however, indicate how long the imperial cult temple was in use.[98] The one piece of evidence for the continued practice of the imperial cult at Antioch in the 4th century—whether or not it was associated with a functioning temple—is found in the previously mentioned epitaph on the sarcophagus of Markos Ioulios Eugenios, bishop of Laodiceia Katakekaumene. The inscription records that as a young man Eugenios served as an officer in the civil service of the Roman army under the governor of Pisidia, in Antioch.[99] He was in the service when Maximinus ordered that Christians perform a sacrifice (311 or 312) and not be allowed to resign instead.[100] Eugenios was tortured before managing

one of the churches at the site—much of it incorporated into the later church constructed in 530 (Shanks 1979, 41–42). At Stobi in Macedonia, a synagogue was transformed into a Christian basilica in the 5th century (White 1990, 71).

[95] Cf. Papalexandrou 2003. At Hierapolis, the extramural baths to the north of city, adjacent to the agora, were converted into a Christian church (see Parrish 2001, 31). Also, the basilica at Kremna known as Church A, which is probably the earliest church at the site, was converted from a Hadrianic civic basilica (Mitchell 1995, 220–222). Mitchell (1995, 230) suggests that the conversion of civic buildings occurred when Christians were not yet strong enough to oust polytheists from their temples.

[96] For attacks on synagogues in the 4th century, see Ambrose, *Epistles* 41.27 and *Codex Theodosianus* 16.8.9; also Brown 1992, 108, 115. See also Williams 2000 for Jews' relationship to Roman society. See Winter 2002; Potter 2004, 424; Trebilco 1991, 9–11 for Roman privileges granted to Jews. Constantine and his successors were less likely to grant new favors to Jews, but they generally upheld those privileges that had

already been granted and limited governmental restrictions on Diasporan Jews to controlling their community's growth. The Diasporan Jews did not participate in the Flavian and Bar-Kochba revolts alongside their homeland counterparts and thus were not targeted in many of the repercussions: Mitchell 1993, 2:36; Trebilco 1991, 32–33. It is not clear whether the laws passed by Theodosius in the 5th century to ban the building of new synagogues applied to Asia Minor as well: *Codex Theodosianus* 16.8.25, 27.

[97] Canons 16, 29, 37, 38: see Trebilco 1991, 101.

[98] The archaeological evidence indicates that the imperial cult was in operation at least into the Severan period in the early 3rd century, when the *tholos* of Caracalla was built in the Tiberia Platea. See Rubin, note to chap. 3, this volume.

[99] See above for the text of the inscription.

[100] See Tabbernee (1997, 426–436), who also sketches the debate surrounding the date of Maximinus's order. Mitchell 1988, 105 n. 4 discusses the arguments for 311 or 312.

to leave the service.[101] It is not surprising that he was tortured since Christianity was not legalized until 313. The key fact is that although adherence to official dictates was not consistent across the empire, Eugenios was unlucky enough to have lived in an area of the empire where persecution edicts were more stringently enforced than elsewhere. Perhaps diligence in enacting such dictates related to the worship of the emperor suggests there would have been interest in continuing to maintain the imperial cult temple into the early 4th century.

Developments elsewhere over the course the of the 4th century, however, imply that the imperial cult temple probably ceased to serve a religious function by the end of that century, as the emperors themselves began to discourage, and then to outlaw, worship of themselves as divine beings.[102] The emperor Constantine may have allowed some Umbrians in Italy to build a temple to himself and his family in the 330s, but he mandated that no sacrifices take place there.[103] The curbing of sacrifices to the emperor culminated during the reign of Theodosius (347–395), when all forms of animal sacrifice, the aspect of traditional cult most problematic for Christians, were officially banned.[104]

As for the cult of Mên Askaênos, we can be fairly certain that the Antiochenes continued to frequent the sanctuary on the hill of Kara Kuyu into the 4th century.[105] Paradoxically, however, the only definitive evidence we have for its use beyond the continued establishment of dedications at the sanctuary in the late 3rd–early 4th century is the destruction of the temple of Mên, probably before the turn of the 5th century, for which Christians may well have been responsible.[106] Not long afterwards, the church that now stands near the sanctuary site was built with blocks taken from it.[107] A message of victory over polytheism seems clearly intended here.

Taken together, the evidence for polytheistic religious practices suggests that Christianity was not the predominant religion in Antioch in the early 4th century but that the picture soon changed. Like the church on Kara Kuyu, the highly charged placement of the central church—opposite the *cardo maximus* from, and on axis with, the imperial cult temple—suggests a conscious challenge to, if not a deliberate declaration of victory over, the old state cult (see fig. 6.3).[108]

[101] Tabbernee 1997, 435 suggests that Eugenios's high social status aided him in his eventual resignation.

[102] See Potter 2004, 401–402, 431–434, 485, 488, 555–556, 560, 573–574 for the policies of individual emperors toward traditional cult practices. They represent varying degrees of tolerance and preference for peaceful coexistence.

[103] Price 1984, 227.

[104] Potter 2004, 573–574.

[105] See Khatchadourian, chap. 8 and Raff, chap. 7, this volume for further discussion of the sanctuary and its functions.

[106] Lane 1976, 59; Hardie 1912, 147. Ramsay's (1906; 1912) and Anderson's (1913) theories about activity in the sanctuary in the early 4th century must be discounted. Ramsay's claim that the inscriptions with the word τεκμορευειν represent the presence of an anti-Christian society is groundless. Not only is his argument based on leaps of logic and does it lack sufficient evidence, but Lane (1976, 61) has shown that there was not an exclusive connection between the anti-Christian

society posited by Ramsay and the crescents on the inscriptions, which Ramsay took to be the sign, or τεκμορ, that the society's members used in a ritual manner. Furthermore, Mitchell and Waelkens (1998, 12–13) have disproved Anderson's assertion that agonistic inscriptions referring to the revival of a series of festivals and games at the sanctuary can be dated to the early 4th century; they attribute them to the 2nd century.

[107] Ramsay (1918, 121) says that the destruction of the temple of Mên occurred ca. AD 400; the entrance was blocked up deliberately, and almost all the votive stelai in open spaces were broken into pieces, also deliberately. Mitchell and Waelkens (1998, 206) date a custom-made frieze in the church to the 5th century, at the latest, based on its stylistic characteristics, though they believe that this frieze (and thus the church) is, in fact, from an earlier period. They (1998, 85–86) concur with Ramsay regarding the deliberate destruction of the sanctuary. See also Raff, chap. 7, this volume.

[108] Ramsay dates the central church to the 4th century, and Mitchell and Waelkens (1998, 210) tentatively agree based on the stylistic properties of the architectural decoration.

Conclusion

The 4th century, thus, was a crucial period for shifts in the balance of power in the religious life at Pisidian Antioch. Several tentative conclusions can be drawn regarding the interaction of different religions in that period. First, the Christian community had enough strength to mobilize the financial and political support to build four churches when it became politically feasible to do so. Second, although nothing is yet known about the survival of Judaism at Pisidian Antioch beyond the 1st century, polytheism did survive into the 4th century and in fact seems to have had a healthy participant base.

This situation changed, however, as Christianity became an officially recognized religion and greater numbers of churches and Christian institutions filled in the urban landscape. The destruction of temples and shrines was legally mandated by Constantine's successors. By 361, polytheism had declined sufficiently across the empire that when the emperor Julian set out to revitalize it through a series of purposeful campaigns to boost interest in the ancient gods and arrest the growth of Christianity, he was disappointed in the lack of a great upwelling of enthusiasm.[109] The Christian community at Antioch, with its large basilicas and symbolically valuable connection to Paul, dominated the city's physical and religious landscape over the course of the 4th century. It was not until the end of that century, however, when the temple of Mên was destroyed and a Christian church was built from its ruins, that there is clear archaeological evidence for a decisive shift in the power relations between these religions.

The houses to the east of the central church are described by Robinson and Peterson in the Journal of Excavations (June 16, 1924; June 21, 1924) as "Byzantine" and "late Byzantine," although without reference to actual centuries or dates.

[109] See Potter 2004, 510–516.

7 The Architecture of the Sanctuary of Mên Askaênos: Exploration, Reconstruction, and Use

Katharine A. Raff

At the summit of the high hill of Kara Kuyu located 3.5 km due southeast of the Roman colony of Pisidian Antioch (see fig. 8.1), the sanctuary of Mên Askaênos looks out across the Yalvaç plain. In antiquity it was connected to the city by a rough road whose traces can still be seen in a number of places today. Over the course of more than five centuries, the sanctuary of Mên played a vital role in the religious and political life and civic identity of Pisidian Antioch.[1] From the time of the foundation of the sanctuary in the Hellenistic period, through the apparent resurgence of cult activities in the mid-2nd century AD,[2] to the construction of a Christian church on the site in the 5th century from stones from the temple of Mên,[3] numerous structures were erected on the sanctuary's grounds to meet the changing needs of worshippers. These structures, now in varying states of ruin, include two temples, one within a large *temenos* or sacred enclosure, a small theater or odeion,[4] and at least eighteen single- and multi-room buildings that served a variety of purposes (fig. 7.1).[5]

In this chapter, I draw upon previous studies of the architecture of the sanctuary of Mên Askaênos—the temples and all known subsidiary structures—relying primarily on the detailed archaeological publication of 1998 by Stephen Mitchell and Marc Waelkens.[6] I reconsider the functions proposed by Mitchell and Waelkens for a number of the subsidiary buildings, and I present a slightly revised version of their plan of the sanctuary. In an attempt to visualize the entire complex as a functioning environment experienced by worshippers, I compare this once-famous religious destination in Anatolia with more fully studied and better known sanctuaries in both Asia Minor and Greece, thus extending the interpretive work of Mitchell and Waelkens.[7] It is beyond the scope of this chapter and the available archaeological evidence to document the origins of the sanctuary and its development over time.[8]

[1] For an in-depth discussion of the interplay of religion, identity, and politics at the sanctuary of Mên Askaênos, see Khatchadourian, chap. 8, this volume.

[2] See Khatchadourian, chap. 8, this volume, on the cult's resurgence under Antoninus Pius; Labarre 2009 on the origins of the cult in general.

[3] Mitchell and Waelkens 1998, 86.

[4] Basing its layout and location on Mitchell and Waelkens's plan of the sanctuary, I propose that what they refer to as a "stadium" is a small theater or an odeion.

[5] Mitchell and Waelkens 1998, 72–86; Mitchell and Waelkens refer to the various structures as "Houses," "*oikoi*," and the "Andron." In this essay I use an alternative terminology to describe the possible uses of these structures.

[6] My description of these structures is based on the survey data collected by Mitchell and Waelkens in 1982/1983 and published by them in 1998, 37–90.

[7] This reconstruction is part of the larger project to reconstruct the ancient appearance of the city of Pisidian Antioch and its sanctuary of Mên Askaênos. See Harrington, chap. 9, this volume.

[8] For the dating of the original construction of the temple of Mên in the Hellenistic era, I rely on the arguments of Mitchell and Waelkens 1998, 66–68.

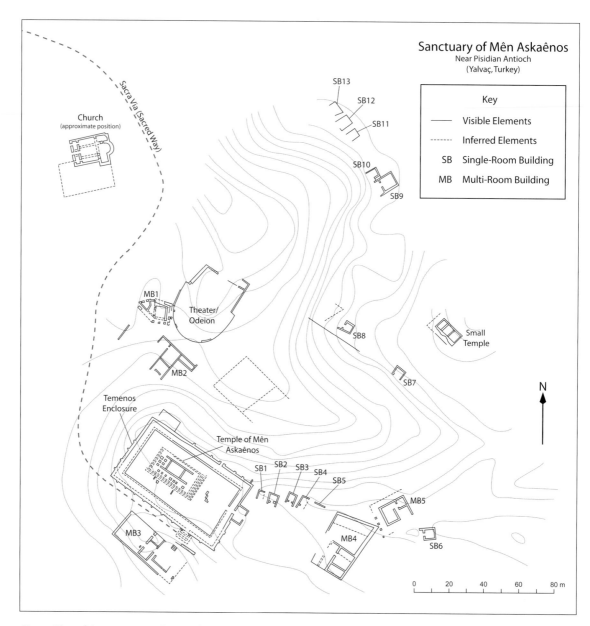

Fig. 7.1. Plan of the sanctuary of Mên Askaênos. Drawing: A. J. Ossi and K. A. Raff.

Rather, I focus on the sanctuary in its Roman imperial heyday—from the Antonine period through the 3rd century AD—a time when most, if not all, of its now-ruined structures would presumably have been in use.

Location of the Sanctuary

Long before the first 18th- and 19th-century travelers set out to explore the ancient city of Antioch of Pisidia, Strabo, writing in the latter half of the 1st century BC or in the early 1st century AD, made reference to the city and its temple of Mên, a deity worshipped in Anatolia but whose origins are uncertain.

> And this is also the temple of Selenê, like that among the Albanians and those in Phrygia, I mean that of Mên in the place of the same name and that of Mên Ascaeus near the Antiocheia that is near Pisidia and that of Mên in the country of the Antiocheians.[9]

The ambiguity of Strabo's passage has puzzled scholars for over a century and no doubt contributed to the difficulty in locating and identifying the sanctuary on the nearby promontory of Kara Kuyu as one devoted to Mên Askaênos.[10] As early as 1913, however, J. G. C. Anderson postulated that Strabo's passage indicates that there were two temples of Mên Askaênos: one located near the city of Antioch (on Kara Kuyu as discussed below) and the other located either in the territory of Antioch or the region of which the city of Antioch was the capital.[11] The latter sanctuary remains unidentified.

Previous Studies of the Architecture of the Sanctuary of Mên

The architecture of the sanctuary on Kara Kuyu has been studied sporadically since 1911, when Sir William and Lady Ramsay, accompanied by W. M. Calder and Margaret M. Hardie, made the ascent to the top of the high hill after receiving news of inscriptions and architectural ruins on a nearby mountain.[12] Calder tells of an agent of the Ottoman Railway in Yalvaç, M. Kyriakides, who "had heard from a Turkish peasant of 'written stones' on a neighbouring mountain-top, and persuaded the man to guide us [the Ramsay party] to the long-looked-for holy place."[13] Lacking a permit, the group was unable to excavate, but Calder, Hardie, and Ramsay made some notes on the remains and copies of numerous inscriptions, which they published in preliminary reports intended to raise awareness of the site and garner monetary support for future excavation.[14] In the summer of 1911, Ramsay published the first account of their discovery, noting the remains of a small church, a theater, the *temenos*, numerous dedicatory inscriptions, and the temple of Mên, which he mistakenly identified as an altar. At that time, Ramsay believed that there was no temple at the site.[15] The following year, Hardie provided a more thorough account, in which she identified the sanctuary as one devoted to the Anatolian lunar deity, Mên Askaênos. Hardie published the inscriptions and also reported evidence of numerous features, including a path through the sanctuary—the so-called Sacred Way—the remains of a small theater, the entrance to the sanctuary from the south, and the ruins of a building inside the *temenos*, which she identified as a "great altar" rather than a temple due to its relatively small size.[16]

In 1912, Ramsay and Hardie set out on another expedition to the sanctuary with Calder and Anderson. The sanctuary was in dire need of systematic excavation in part because local inhabitants

---

[9] Strabo, *Geographica*, 12.3.31, trans. H. L. Jones (G. P. Putnam's Sons, 1917) 431 and n. 8. According to David M. Robinson, *Ascaenus* (Ἀσκαηνός) is the regular spelling of the word, as is attested by hundreds of inscriptions, whereas *Ascaeus* (Ἀσκαίος) has been discovered in only two inscriptions.

[10] It is possible that Strabo actually refers to three different temples of Mên in this passage: one in Phrygia; one near Pisidian Antioch, which is likely the one situated on Kara Kuyu; and one in the region of Antioch (i.e., the temple in "the country of the Antiocheians"). David M. Robinson indicated in private communication with T. E. Page, editor of the Loeb translation of Strabo, *Geographica*, that this third temple "may have been . . . at Saghir," which is an area near Pisidian Antioch. Strabo, *Geographica*, 12.3.31–33, trans. H.

L. Jones (1917, 432–433 n. 2).

[11] Anderson 1913, 268.

[12] Mitchell and Waelkens 1998, 26.

[13] Calder 1912, 78. Ramsay 1918, 108 also describes the party's visit to the site. See also Mitchell and Waelkens 1998, 26–27.

[14] Ramsay 1911, 192–193; Calder 1912, 78–109; Hardie 1912, 111–150.

[15] Ramsay 1911, 192–193.

[16] Hardie 1912, 118.

Fig. 7.2. Stoever's plan of the
sanctuary of Mên Askaênos. After
Ramsay 1918, pl. 1.

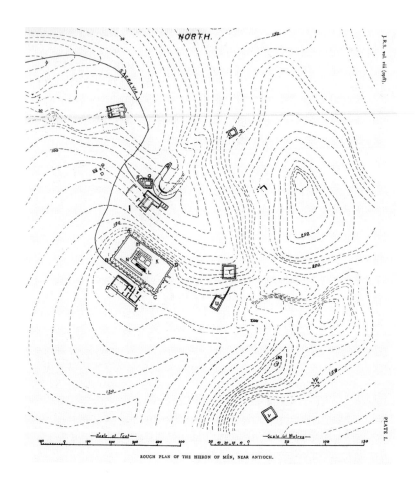

had disturbed the remains in search of building stone and other "valuables."[17] E. R. Stoever, the sur-
veyor for Princeton University's excavations at Sardis, joined Ramsay's expedition for several days
to produce the first ground plan of the sanctuary (fig. 7.2).[18] During this first excavation, Ramsay,
Calder, and Anderson observed structures that Ramsay described as an official residence of a priest
or "hieron," a small temple to Aphrodite, another small temple to Cybele, an "Initiation Hall," a small
church, a structure that Hardie had called a "theater" but that Ramsay later described as the "stadium," and a complex of buildings near this so-called stadium.[19] Ramsay returned to the sanctuary
in 1913 with Calder and Callander to continue the excavation of the *temenos*.[20] During this season,
Ramsay changed his mind about the identity of the temple on Kara Kuyu. He proposed instead that

[17] Ramsay 1918, 123.

[18] Ramsay 1918, 110. Mitchell and Waelkens 1998, 27. The
plan of the sanctuary, published in plate 1 of Ramsay's 1918
article, is reproduced here.

[19] Ramsay 1918, 107–123; Mitchell and Waelkens 1998, 37–86.
Mitchell and Waelkens discuss a number of Ramsay's errors
at length.

[20] During this season, the team concluded their excavation

on Kara Kuyu and then began work in the city on the semicircular portico, the imperial cult temple, and the so-called
Platea Augusti. Callander supervised the excavation and also
dug an exploratory trench at the corner of the theater area
and along the proscenium of the theater. Hopes for a third
season of excavation in 1914 were nearly dashed when Lord
Strathcona, the main provider of funding for the expedition,
died, but Sir William and Lady Ramsay refused to halt the
expedition and set out to excavate in the city on their own.
Mitchell and Waelkens 1998, 27.

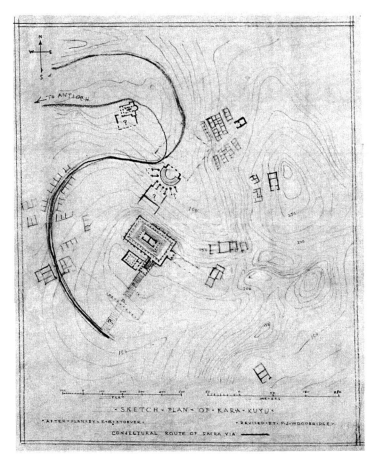

Fig. 7.3. Woodbridge's sketch plan of Kara Kuyu after a plan by E. R. Stoever. Bentley Historical Library, University of Michigan, Kelsey Museum Papers, Box 73.7.

it belonged to the imperial cult, a theory dismissed by subsequent scholars. In 1924 members of the Michigan team visited the site a few times. On the last visit the group photographed votive stelai and drew plans, one of which was a plan of the sanctuary sketched by Woodbridge (fig. 7.3). In revising the plan that Stoever had drawn for Ramsay, Woodbridge included many more structures. It is impossible to verify without further excavation whether he saw actual remains of them in 1924 or simply sketched structures where he thought they might logically have been.[21]

Several decades passed before scholars in the 1960s turned again to the study of the sanctuary of Mên Askaênos, but their work focused solely on the dedicatory inscriptions.[22] Further studies of the architecture were not undertaken until the early 1980s, when Mitchell and Waelkens conducted their meticulous archaeological survey of the topography and architecture of the sanctuary. Their book, published in 1998, provides our most detailed and reliable source of information for the site.[23]

[21] The Michigan team's Journal of Excavations records several day trips to Kara Kuyu, on June 6, 1924, on July 4, 1924, at some point between July 10 and August 11, and on August 29, 1924. Photographer George Swain, architectural assistant Horace Colby, and driver Easton T. Kelsey participated in the August 29 visit.

[22] Barbara Levick copied many of the inscriptions and published them in numerous articles. See Levick 1958a; 1958b;

1965; 1967a; 1967b; 1968; 1970; and 1971. E. N. Lane visited the sanctuary in 1961. Although he published inscriptions and discussed the relevance of the sanctuary of Mên of Antioch in his *Corpus Monumentorum Religionis Dei Menis,* he did not contribute any new archaeological observations of the sanctuary at Antioch. See Khatchadourian, chap. 8, this volume.

[23] Mitchell and Waelkens 1998. The authors refute a number of Ramsay's earlier observations, including his measurements

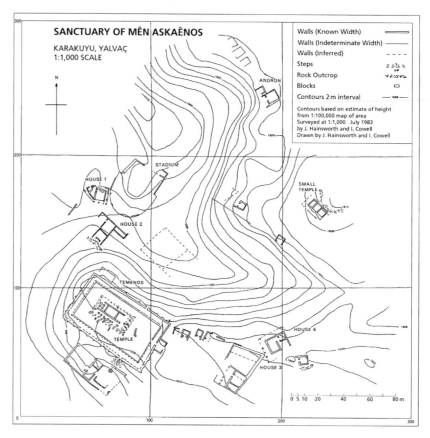

The goal of that survey was to reconstruct the sanctuary's building history and to locate its remains in a correct cultural and historical context. Mitchell and Waelkens made accurate measurements and descriptions of the *temenos* wall, the temple of Mên Askaênos, the small temple, and most of the other buildings scattered over the site; they also produced a new map of the sanctuary (fig. 7.4).[24] In 1989, Ismail Karamut conducted a brief survey of the sanctuary and published a plan of the temple.[25] No further architectural studies of the sanctuary have been undertaken since that time.[26]

My reconstruction of the sanctuary, partially represented in the virtual reality model presented in this volume, relies on a newly revised plan of the sanctuary (fig. 7.1).[27] This revised plan incorporates elements of Ramsay's plan (fig. 7.2)—namely the location of the small church and the postulated course of the "Sacred Way" within the sanctuary—into Mitchell and Waelkens's plan of

of the thickness of the *temenos* walls and his identification of a "cistern" that he believed had been used to provide water for the sanctuary.

[24] Mitchell and Waelkens 1998, xiii–xiv, 37–90.

[25] Karamut 1989, however, does not include the peristyle. Mitchell and Waelkens 1998, 32–33. In his introduction to Drew-Bear, Taşlıalan, and Thomas 2002, M. Taşlıalan notes, "excavations carried out since 1979 on the site of the ancient city and in the temple of Men by M. Taşlıalan," but it is not clear what kind of excavation he did at the temple of Mên

nor whether it is published.

[26] See also Mitchell 2002. This article summarizes the main conclusions regarding the sanctuary and the two temples that were previously drawn in Mitchell and Waelkens 1998, 37–90, but it does not present any new conclusions.

[27] This new plan was developed by Adrian Ossi and me. It served as the basis for the virtual reality reconstruction of the sanctuary.

[28] The University of Michigan's Journal of Excavations, 82,

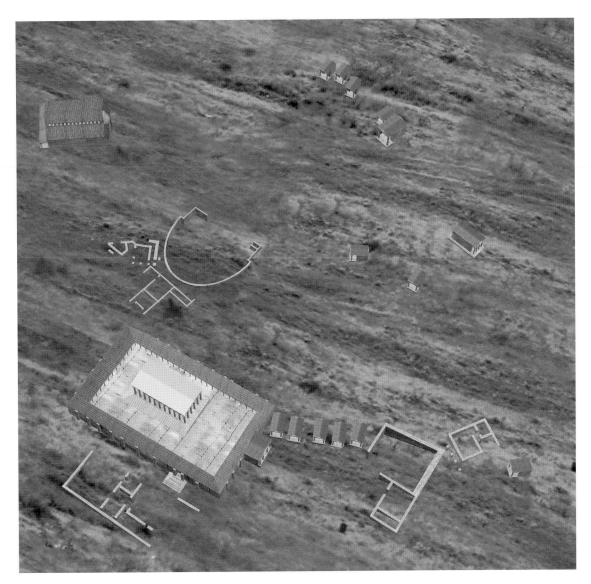

Fig. 7.5. Digital reconstruction of the sanctuary of Mên Askaênos, bird's eye view.
Digital model: J. M. Harrington.

1998.[28] By using this plan and comparing the individual structures at the sanctuary of Mên to similar ones at other sanctuary sites in the Greek world whose purposes are better known, one can gain a vivid idea of the appearance and use of the sanctuary of Mên, at least at the time of the latest period of its documented use, the last decade of the 3rd century (figs. 7.5–7).[29]

85 documents that Peterson, Swain, and Woodbridge found traces of roads leading from Antioch to the sanctuary on Kara Kuyu. Their finds upset the published statements of Ramsay, who said that the traces of the "Sacred Way" had disappeared completely. See also Labarre and Taşlıalan 2002 on the reliefs displayed along the Sacred Way. A map of the road is provided on p. 282.

[29] Mitchell and Waelkens 1998, 37 rightly believe that the Hellenistic temple of Mên would not have stood alone on Kara Kuyu; rather there must have been buildings of the types found there in ruins today. See Khatchadourian, chap. 8, this volume for a discussion of the inscription of C. Flavius Baebianus, which is datable to the last decade of the 3rd century AD.

Fig. 7.6. Digital
reconstruction of the
sanctuary of Mên
Askaênos, as seen from the
west. Digital model: J. M.
Harrington.

Fig. 7.7. Digital
reconstruction of the
sanctuary of Mên
Askaênos, detail of
temenos and temple.
Digital model: J. M.
Harrington.

The Buildings of the Sanctuary of Mên Askaênos: Their Form and Function

The area outside the *temenos* of a Greek sanctuary usually included structures such as *stoa*s, treasuries, storerooms, and buildings where feasting, athletic contests, and dramatic and choral performances took place.[30] Dining rooms, kitchens for preparing food and drink, rooms for washing and purification for initiation rites, theaters, stadiums, gymnasiums, baths, and overnight accommodations were common, though not all such facilities were required at every sanctuary.[31] The sanctuary of Mên conforms in many respects to Greek sanctuaries of the Hellenistic and Roman periods in Asia Minor and to earlier sanctuaries on the Greek mainland. Many if not all of the sanctuary's structures underwent different stages of development and rebuilding, but those stages have yet to be fully discerned, documented, and dated.[32] I therefore take into account only what is still visible of each structure, as described and measured by Mitchell and Waelkens, as the basis for envisioning its original appearance.

[30] Tomlinson 1976, 19.

[31] Pedley 2005, 8, 74–77.

[32] At present there is no stratigraphic evidence to assist in dating the various buildings. Aside from excavation in the temple of Mên by Taşlıalan (see n. 25), there has been no excavation in the sanctuary since 1913.

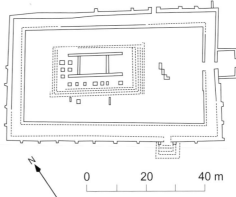

Fig. 7.8. *Naiskoi* in *temenos* of Mên Askaênos. Photo: Kelsey Museum Archives neg. no. 7.1579.

Fig. 7.9. Plan of the temple of Mên Askaênos, detail from plan of the sanctuary of Mên Askaênos. Drawing: A. J. Ossi and K. A. Raff.

Buildings for Worship

The **Temenos** *of Mên Askaênos.* An essential characteristic that all sanctuaries shared was a *temenos* (boundary), which separated the consecrated domain from the surrounding secular area.[33] Typically, within the *temenos* were one or more temples with altars. The roughly rectangular *temenos* of the sanctuary of Mên Askaênos, oriented on a northwest-southeast axis,[34] is built of large blocks of the dark gray limestone bedrock of Kara Kuyu. The *temenos* wall is adorned with *naiskoi* carved in relief and inscribed with dedications to the god Mên (fig. 7.8).[35] The majority of these votive dedications, which date to the Roman period, cover a substantial part of the outer face of the southwest wall and its buttresses.

The main entrance into the sacred precinct was through a propylon, or gatehouse, on the southeast side, on axis with the temple.[36] The temple was situated within the northwest part of the *temenos* on a *euthynteria* and a *crepidoma* of dark gray limestone slabs built over a bedrock foundation.[37] The interior of the cella measures 7.9 m, while the entire *naos* measures 18.52 m in length.[38] The temple was likely framed by an Ionic colonnaded portico of white limestone running along all four sides of the precinct's interior (fig. 7.9).[39] The white limestone in the portico colonnade, in the temple's Ionic columns, and in the frame of the cella's door provided a visual contrast with the dark

[33] Tomlinson 1976, 17; Pedley 2005, 6.

[34] Mitchell and Waelkens 1998, 37–38. Its external measurements are: 44 m southeast side; 73.1 m southwest side; 41.7 m northwest side; 71.5 m northeast side. See Mitchell and Waelkens 1998, 38–90 for measurements of the remaining sanctuary structures.

[35] Mitchell and Waelkens 1998, 37.

[36] Mitchell and Waelkens 1998, 53.

[37] On the gray limestone slabs, see Mitchell and Waelkens 1998, 45–48. On the use of bedrock in the foundation course, see Mitchell and Waelkens 1998, 41–42.

[38] Mitchell and Waelkens 1998, 65, table 1. Additional measurements of the temple of Mên are as follows: width of the *naos* (from the exterior): 8.63 m; width of the *naos* (from the interior): 5.9 m; length of the *pronaos* (from the interior): 5.3 m; length of the *opisthodomos*: 2.5 m.

[39] Mitchell and Waelkens 1998, 47. This entrance was initially flanked by two large rectangular blocks, although a propylon was later added at the front. The side walls of the propylon are not attached to the *temenos* proper, and the construction was erected according to a more rectilinear plan than the other *temenos* walls. Fragments of Ionic fluted and unfluted white limestone columns that were most likely from this colonnade were found in the debris.

Fig. 7.10. Plan of the temple of Athena Polias at Priene. After Mitchell and Waelkens 1998, 64, fig. 12. By permission of Classical Press of Wales.

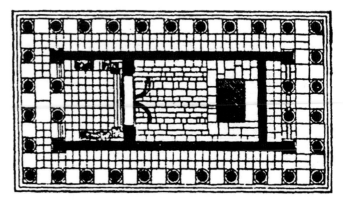

Fig. 7.11. Plan of the temple of Dionysos at Teos. After Mitchell and Waelkens 1998, 64, fig. 12. By permission of Classical Press of Wales.

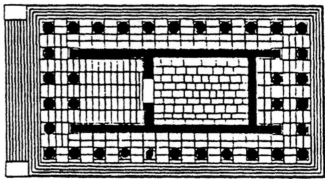

gray limestone *crepidoma*.[40] It has been suggested that the white limestone might have been the same as that which was used for the imperial temple in the city itself.[41]

Mitchell and Waelkens have shown that the ground plan of the temple of Mên is closely comparable to those of two temples in Asia Minor—the temple of Athena Polias at Priene built in 310 BC (or possibly over a period of many years into the 2nd century BC) and the temple of Dionysos at Teos built in 208–204 BC. All three temples are Ionic peripteral with six columns on the short sides and eleven on the flanks (figs. 7.10–11).[42] While the short sides of the temples at Priene and Teos are distyle in antis, the temple of Mên Askaênos at Antioch is distyle in antis only on its northern side, i.e., the back of the temple. The proportions of the stylobate of each of the temples are also fairly similar.[43] Mitchell and Waelkens propose that the temple had been dedicated by the Attalids of Pergamon sometime between 175 and 125 BC, during the reign of Eumenes II or Attalos III, when the Attalids had a strategic interest in securing the area.[44] It is possible, as Khatchadourian suggests in chapter 8 in this volume, that the temple whose remains are now visible was rebuilt in the Antonine period following its original Hellenistic ground plan.

No evidence of an altar has survived in the *temenos* of Mên, but there would surely have been one in front of the temple, probably on axis with the temple façade and the propylon. An altar was an

[40] Mitchell and Waelkens 1998, 51–53. Fragments of white limestone Ionic capitals and a portion of the cella door were recovered.

[41] Mitchell and Waelkens 1998, 51.

[42] Mitchell and Waelkens 1998, 63–66; Mitchell 2002, 314.

[43] According to Mitchell and Waelkens 1998, 65, table 1, the ratio of the length of the stylobate to its width for each of the temples is: 1.9:1 at Priene, 1.88:1 at Teos, and 2.01:1 at Antioch.

[44] Mitchell and Waelkens 1998, 68.

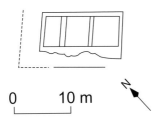

Fig. 7.12. Plan of the so-called small temple, detail from plan of the sanctuary of Mên Askaênos. Drawing: A. J. Ossi and K. A. Raff.

0   10 m

essential component of any functioning temple, for it was on the altar that sacrifices to the deity inside the temple were made.[45] A multitude of dedications—votive inscriptions, sculptural monuments, and other offerings—would have surrounded the temple and altar. Among the remains recovered by Ramsay were an impressive over-life-sized marble statue of Cornelia Antonia (see fig. 8.5), numerous marble votive stelai, and inscribed bases.[46] Such costly dedications would clearly have signaled to the worshipper that the cult of Mên was patronized by members of the local elite.[47]

The Small Temple. To the east of these structures and higher up the hill is the so-called small temple, erected on a terrace cut from natural rock overlooking the sanctuary from the northeast. The central axis of the small temple is almost parallel to that of the temple of Mên (fig. 7.12). Its cella, which measures 4.3 m in length at the interior, is similar in size to that of the temple of Mên, and the building also employs gray and white limestone.[48] The decoration and walls have completely disappeared, although it is thought that they were finished to a high standard.[49] Mitchell and Waelkens observe that the small temple's plan is similar to that of the temple of Zeus Sosipolis at Magnesia, which may reflect Magnesian influence on the small temple's design. This would not be surprising, given that Antioch was initially colonized in the Hellenistic period by settlers from Magnesia.[50] There are no physical remains of an altar, which must have faced the entrance to the small temple, but within the cella there is an octagonal limestone base that might have held a cult statue.[51]

Khatchadourian discusses two sculptures found in the sanctuary that may provide clues to the identity of the deity worshipped in the small temple. One of these sculptures, found in the *temenos* of Mên, has been thought to represent Demeter, Cybele, Artemis, Selene, or even Mên himself (see fig. 8.14). The other, a triple figure found in the small temple, has been called Artemis-Hekate (see fig. 8.16) by Anderson and Cybele by Ramsay. Khatchadourian notes the likelihood that the figure is Hekate. She calls attention to the pairing of Mên and Hekate in a funerary stele from either Cottiaeum or Thessaloniki, which portrays a triple Hekate with Mên (see fig. 8.17). While it cannot be positively

[45] While the temple was the building where the god resided, it was at the main altar that the public religious rituals enacted in the god's honor took place. In addition, private worship could take place throughout sanctuaries at smaller altars. See Tomlinson 1976, 16–17; Pedley 2005, 7–8.

[46] Mitchell and Waelkens 1998, 50 do not provide a date for the marble *naiskoi*, which surpassed in quality the roughly carved *naiskoi* cut into the limestone of the hill and on the outer walls of the *temenos*.

[47] Lane 1976, 113.

[48] Mitchell and Waelkens 1998, 59. See also Mitchell and

Waelkens 1998, 65, table 1 for additional measurements of the small temple, including the following measurements: width of the *naos* (from the interior): 5 m; length of the *pronaos* (from the interior): 3.35 m; length of the *opisthodomos*: 2.5 m. The length of the *opisthodomos* in the small temple is identical to that in the temple of Mên, and the measurements of the width of the *naos* from the interior and those of the length of the *pronaos* from the interior are similar for both temples.

[49] Mitchell and Waelkens 1998, 59.

[50] Mitchell and Waelkens 1998, 67.

[51] Mitchell and Waelkens 1998, 62.

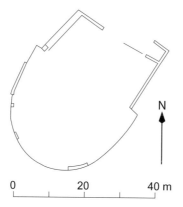

Fig. 7.13. Plan of small theater
or odeion, detail from plan of
the sanctuary of Mên Askaênos.
Drawing: A. J. Ossi and K. A. Raff.

N

0   20   40 m

determined that the small temple was dedicated to any of these female deities, it seems likely that
there would have been a place of worship for at least one of them, perhaps Cybele, who is identified
in an inscription from elsewhere as the mother of Mên. Cybele was also known as Demeter, and a
priest of Mên and Demeter is recorded in an inscription of the 3rd century.[52]

Buildings for Competitive Performances

Small Theater or Odeion (Mitchell and Waelkens's Stadium). Athletic, dramatic, and musical
competitions were common features of religious festivals at Greek and Roman sanctuaries, and
the sanctuary of Mên was no exception. The first structure that one would have encountered upon
entering the sanctuary along the Sacred Way must have accommodated such events. This structure
is one that Ramsay and Hardie both referred to as a stadium, although Hardie had at first proposed
that it was a theater (fig. 7.13).[53] The visible remains have small dimensions, with a cavea that measures
approximately 34 m in diameter and a stage building that measures approximately 30 m in width and
20 m in depth. This seems compatible with a theater or a recital hall (odeion),[54] which normally would
have been even smaller than a theater. Either a theater or an odeion would have been appropriate
for a sanctuary.[55]

Small theaters similar in size to the structure at the sanctuary of Mên are found at numerous locations throughout Asia Minor, although only a few of them appear to be associated with sanctuaries.[56]

[52] Khatchadourian, chap. 8, this volume.

[53] Ramsay 1918, 110 acknowledges that in when he, Calder,
Hardie, and Lady Ramsay visited the site in 1911, they initially
regarded the building as a theater. However, he notes that he
later altered his interpretation to that of a small stadium, of
which only the rounded western end had been constructed.
See also Hardie 1912, 113–114. Hardie identifies the structure
as either a theater or a stadium, also noting that if it were
the latter, only one end seems to have been built. Mitchell
and Waelkens 1998, 37, 72, pl. 46 refer to the structure as a
stadium, although they did not undertake an architectural
study of it during their survey.

[54] These dimensions are based on calculations made from
the plan of the "stadium" as represented in Mitchell and
Waelkens's plan of the sanctuary. Mitchell and Waelkens

1998, 38, fig. 5. They are only an approximation and not a
precise measurement of the structure's dimensions.

[55] According to Welch 1998, 118, stadia in antiquity were
generally at least 178 m in length in order to accommodate
footraces. See Rossetto and Sartorio 1994, 3:345–533 for a full
discussion of theaters and odeia in Asia Minor, including
dimensions of the structures. Following the comprehensive
dimensions provided by Rossetto and Sartorio, it is apparent that the measurements of the caveae of theaters in Asia
Minor range from 22 m to 150 m or larger. Structures that
are classified as small theaters or odeia, however, tend to be
smaller, with a cavea measuring between 22 m and 50 m.

[56] Rossetto and Sartorio 1994 provide brief descriptions of
small theaters not located in sanctuaries at the following locations in Asia Minor: Amos, Greek theater, Hellenistic (375);

Mitchell and Waelkens's plan records rectangular walls on the northeast side of the structure, which were located farther down the slope from the curved end in a relatively flat area (see fig. 7.4). These rectangular walls may have surrounded a stage building, as do those in the theater in the city of Antioch below,[57] or they may have enclosed an entrance court. If the structure was an odeion, however, the rectangular walls would have enclosed the entire semicircular seating area and stage, and the building would have been covered by a roof.[58]

As a theater, the building could have been used to hold athletic competitions, especially during the Roman period.[59] Twelve Greek inscriptions found within the *temenos* of Mên attest to festival activities such as gymnastic and wrestling competitions held during the reign of Maximian Galerius, who became Caesar in the late 3rd century.[60] The small orchestra could have accommodated such events since they required less space than the footraces, gladiatorial games, and wild beast shows (*venationes*) that normally took place in amphitheaters and stadia or in large theaters that were remodeled to accommodate them,[61] such as the theater in the city of Pisidian Antioch.[62] Alternatively, as an odeion, the structure would have accommodated musical recitals and competitions.[63] An agonistic inscription from the *temenos* of Mên describing contests of trumpeters and heralds suggests events that could have been held here.[64]

Buildings for Dining and Sleeping

Sanctuaries in the Greek world were frequented by people of all ranks and classes, including men and women, youths, slaves, and the poor.[65] For most of the worshippers communal dining, and also sleeping, took place in the open air.[66] A privileged few, however, could have dined and slept on couches inside houselike buildings or other dining facilities on the sanctuary grounds. Dining and sleeping arrangements for visitors at sanctuaries seem to have varied greatly, depending on the number of visitors as well as the proximity of the sanctuary to an urban center. Many may have returned home at night; others may have found accommodations in a nearby city.[67] Still others could have

Kolybrassos, a Roman theater or odeion (379); Pergamon, a Roman theater or odeion (401); Bubon, an unclassified theater (450); Herakleia ad Latmos, Greek theater, 3rd century BC (499); Balbura, Greek theater, mid-2nd century BC (460); Antiphellos, Greek theater, Hellenistic (465); Apollonia, Greek theater, Hellenistic (470); Idebessos, Greek theater, Hellenistic (473); Korydalla, unclassified theater (474); Rhodiapolis, Greek theater, Hellenistic cavea, Roman stage building (491); Olba, unclassified theater, 2nd century AD (517); Kadyanda, Greek theater, Hellenistic (523); Cyaneae, Greek theater, late 3rd/early 2nd century BC (529). Rossetto and Sartorio also mention two small theaters in sanctuaries at the following locations: Kastabos, Greek theater at the sanctuary of the Hemithea, late 4th to mid-2nd century BC (489); Diocaesarea, Roman theater, part of the sanctuary of Zeus, proscaenium dates to AD 164–165 (522). Large theaters, however, are located at numerous sanctuaries, such as the sanctuary of Apollo at Delphi, the sanctuary of Asklepios at Epidauros, and abutting the Athenian Acropolis. See also Pedley 2005, 35–36.

[57] Mallampati and Demirer, chap. 4, this volume.

[58] Rossetto and Sartorio 1994, 1:138.

[59] Most sanctuaries had some sort of stadium. If the sanctuary of Mên were lacking a stadium, it seems reasonable that athletic competitions would have been held in the theater. I thank Diana Ng for this comment.

[60] For wrestling contests, Anderson 1913, 286–287, fig. 62; for gymnastic contests, Khatchadourian, chap. 8, this volume.

[61] Welch 1998, 117–145, esp. 117–118, 121–122.

[62] Mallampati and Demirer, chap. 4, this volume.

[63] Rossetto and Sartorio, 1994, 76–78.

[64] Anderson 1913, 288–289; Khatchadourian, chap. 8, this volume.

[65] Pedley 2005, 10.

[66] Tomlinson 1976, 44; Pedley 2005, 75.

[67] Tomlinson 1976, 44.

Fig. 7.14. Dining rooms at sanctuary of Demeter and Kore at Corinth, ca. 400 BC. After Bookidis and Stroud 1997, plan 4. Courtesy of the Trustees of the American School at Athens.

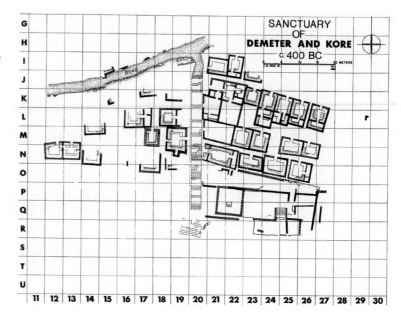

dined and perhaps even slept in temporary structures such as those described by Athenaeus in his *Deipnosophistae*, completed by AD 228. In his discussion of the Spartan feast known as the *Kopis* ("Cleaver"), Athenaeus states,

> Whenever [the Spartans] celebrate the Cleaver they first cause to be constructed booths beside the temple of the god, and in them they place rough couches of wood; upon these they spread rugs, on which they hospitably entertain all who have placed themselves in a reclining posture there—not merely persons who arrive from our country, but also any foreigners who have come to town.[68]

While such temporary structures have left no traces in the archaeological record, there are abundant remains of more permanent dining rooms at a wide variety of sanctuaries throughout the Greek world. The sanctuary of Demeter and Kore in Corinth on the Greek mainland provides the richest source of sanctuary dining rooms of various sizes. Dating from ca. 400 BC, more than thirty rooms with average dimensions of 4.5 × 5 m preserve evidence of up to eight built-in dining couches (fig. 7.14). Slightly larger rooms (6.5 × 6 m) at Corinth accommodated up to eleven couches.[69] Even larger (9.82 × 7.44 m) is a rectangular room known as the "Dining Establishment" at the Sanctuary of Zeus at Nemea in Greece (fig. 7.15).[70] Also typical of Greek dining rooms was an off-center entrance

[68] Athenaeus, *Deipnosophistae*, 4.138 ff., trans. C. B. Gulick (G. P. Putnam's Sons, 1928) 133.

[69] On the sanctuary of Demeter and Kore at Corinth, see Bookidis and Stroud 1997. On the dining rooms, see esp. pp. 393–421. At this sanctuary there are at least thirty-six presumed dining rooms, constructed between the late 6th and 4th centuries BC and used through 146 BC, when the arrival of the Romans following the Battle of Corinth led to a break in activity at the sanctuary. Pedley 2005, 85 notes that activities at the sanctuary resumed in the 1st century.

The dimensions of the dining rooms range from 3.0 m to 5.32 m in width by 3.95 m to 6.3 m in length. For overall dimensions of each dining room, see Bookidis and Stroud 1997, 414, table 2. These dining rooms also preserve evidence of built-in couches. For couch measurements, see Bookidis and Stroud 1997, 415, table 3. See also Pedley 2005, 75–76.

[70] Miller 1990, 167–168. This room yielded evidence of the preparation and consumption of foods, such as pig bones, a boar jaw, and a number of drinking vessels sealed within a vault inside the structure.

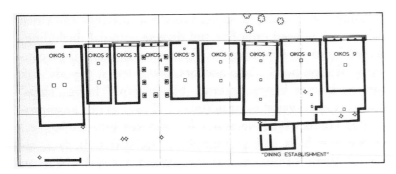 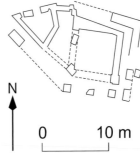

Fig. 7.15. "Dining establishment" at sanctuary of Zeus at Nemea. After Miller 1990, 119, fig. 42. By permission of the University of California Press.

Fig. 7.16. Plan of MB 1, detail from plan of the sanctuary of Mên Askaênos. Drawing: A. J. Ossi and K. A. Raff.

to accommodate the arrangement of the couches.[71] Bearing these examples and architectural features in mind, we can identify dining rooms in the multi-room buildings at the sanctuary of Mên.

Multi-Room Buildings. The multi-room buildings at the sanctuary of Mên have plans resembling Greek houses, and Mitchell and Waelkens label them as such in their publication.[72] Although these buildings would have fulfilled a number of the functions of houses, such as dining and sleeping, it is possible that they were houses for priests and priestesses or, as Mitchell and Waelkens suggest, for the activities of religious associations. Rather than refer to them as houses I prefer simply to describe them as multi-room buildings, leaving open the possibility that future excavation may show that these structures accommodated other functions as well.

Multi-Room Buildings 1 and 2 (Mitchell and Waelkens's Houses 1 and 2). Just south of the small theater or odeion and nearly abutting its curved outer wall is multi-room building (MB) 1.[73] This building has a nearly square interior chamber measuring 5.8 × 6 m and a crudely constructed triangular area to the west (fig. 7.16). It is possible that a road built prior to the construction of MB 1 dictated the irregular shape of the building. On Ramsay's plan, the hypothetical course of the Sacred Way diverges at MB 1 toward the northwest corner of the triangular part of the building and ends just south of that corner. The east and south sides of the building are distinguished by a row of rectangular piers, which face roughly in the direction of the *temenos* of Mên.[74] The square room, which was fronted partially by the row of piers, might have served as a dining room. Its dimensions are comparable to the standard 6.5 × 6 m dimensions of dining rooms in Greek sanctuaries.[75]

To the south of MB 1 is MB 2, located less than 1 m from the curved outer wall of the theater/odeion (fig. 7.17). A row of monumental piers on the south side of the building resembles those of the portico of MB 1, which suggests that the two structures might be contemporary.[76] A large vestibule lies opposite a doorway that leads to a rectangular room measuring 10.35 × 7.6 m which has an off-

[71] Tomlinson 1976, 44; Pedley 2005, 75.

[72] See n. 5 above.

[73] Mitchell and Waelkens 1998, 74 suggest that the "stadium" (my theater/odeion) was constructed at a later date, which helps explain why it encroaches so closely upon MB 1 and

on MB 2.

[74] Mitchell and Waelkens 1998, 74.

[75] Pedley 2005, 75.

[76] Mitchell and Waelkens 1998, 74–75.

Fig. 7.17 (near right). Plan of MB 2, detail from plan of the sanctuary of Mên Askaênos. Drawing: A. J. Ossi and K. A. Raff.

Fig. 7.18 (far right). Plan of MB 3, detail from plan of the sanctuary of Mên Askaênos. Drawing: A. J. Ossi and K. A. Raff.

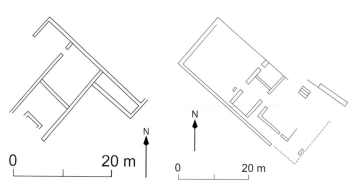

Fig. 7.19. Stone basin from MB 3. Photo: Kelsey Museum Archives neg. no. KR035.06.

center doorway in its southeast wall, evidence of its use as a dining room. This room and the square room in MB 1 compare in size and capacity to dining rooms at Corinth and Nemea.[77]

Multi-Room Building 3 (Mitchell and Waelkens's House 3).[78] On the southwest side of the *temenos* of Mên a doorway leads to a staircase of five steps that descend to a large terrace. From here another eight steps directed the visitor to the building complex of MB 3 and its peristyle courtyard (fig. 7.18).[79] Judging from its proximity to the *temenos* of Mên, MB 3 must have had special status. Like the exterior of the *temenos* wall, the walls of MB 3 are liberally adorned with carved dedications to Mên. MB 3 is significantly larger than the rest of the multi-room buildings in the sanctuary. It includes a spacious courtyard surrounded by a colonnaded portico composed of slender columns, a rectangular antechamber, and a large, almost square, room that measures 15.7 ×15 m.[80]

[77] On the dimensions of the rectangular room in MB 2, see Mitchell and Waelkens 1998, 75. On Nemea, see Miller 1990, 117–128, 161–168. On Corinth, see Bookidis and Stroud 1997, 414, table 2.

[78] In Mitchell and Waelkens's 1998 plan of the sanctuary on p. 38 (fig. 5), Houses 3, 4, and 5 are incorrectly labeled. House 3, which is located southwest of the Temple of Mên, is depicted in the plan in fig. 5, but it is not labeled. However, it is depicted and correctly identified as House 3 in Mitchell

and Waelkens 1998, 76, fig. 15. In Mitchell and Waelkens's fig. 5, the building that is identified as House 3 is actually House 4. Moreover, the building that is identified as House 4 is in fact House 5. House 5 is represented separately in Mitchell and Waelkens 1998, 80, fig. 16, but House 4 is not depicted in its own plan.

[79] Mitchell and Waelkens 1998, 76.

[80] Mitchell and Waelkens 1998, 76–77.

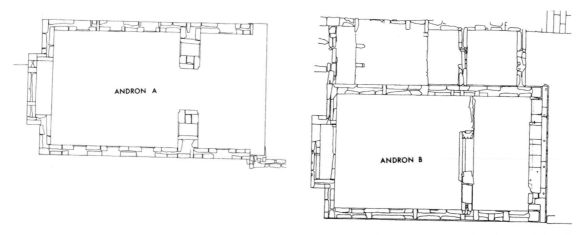

Figs. 7.20–21. Andron A and Andron B at the sanctuary of Zeus at Labraunda. After Westholm 1963, pl. 27. By permission of the Swedish Institute in Athens.

Ramsay called this building a "Hall of Initiation,"[81] while Mitchell and Waelkens propose that it was simply a large house "designed to accommodate the members of a cult association which might have held banquets or organized symposia associated with the god's festivals."[82] Mitchell and Waelkens's view is supported by several features that indicate MB 3 provided quarters for dining—a rock-cut bench in the large room, an off-center doorway, stone supports that may have been used for a table, and a rectangular stone basin possibly designed to collect rain water (fig. 7.19).[83] The size of the large room in MB 3 is comparable to that of two dining rooms at the Hekatomnid sanctuary of Zeus Labraundeus at Labraunda, Andron A and Andron B (figs. 7.20–21), each of which is approximately 12 × 20 m. Andron A was likely built by Idrieus between 351 and 344 BC, while Andron B was possibly built at an earlier date, no later than 353 BC, by his brother Mausolos. The rooms at Labraunda also have platforms along the inner walls, no doubt for dining couches.[84]

Structures located in or adjacent to a *temenos* have often been interpreted as priests' houses or, at the very least, rooms associated with ritual dining.[85] At the sanctuary of Artemis at Brauron, for example, a six-roomed structure is outfitted with stone tables and marked positions for dining couches around the walls. It seems likely that the young priestesses of the cult of Artemis dined, and possibly even lived, in this building.[86] A single stone seat near the northeast wall of MB 3, which carries the Greek inscription "Menelaos son of Attaos, also called Carpos offered a vow to Mên," may have been used by a high-ranking devotee of Mên, possibly a priest, during a meeting or a banquet (fig. 7.22).[87] A number of the dining structures at the sanctuary of Demeter and Kore at Corinth also contained lone seats, which may have been reserved for the supervisor of the meal. Another feature of MB 3, the basin, could have held the water necessary for a priest's ritual purification before entering into the divine presence of Mên in the temple in the adjacent *temenos*.[88]

[81] Ramsay 1918, 114.

[82] Mitchell and Waelkens 1998, 79.

[83] Mitchell and Waelkens 1998, 78–79.

[84] Hellström 1996, 164–168.

[85] Tomlinson 1976, 19.

[86] Tomlinson 1976, 110–111.

[87] Mitchell and Waelkens 1998, 78.

[88] On the importance of water at sanctuaries, see Tomlinson 1976, 45; Pedley 2005, 77.

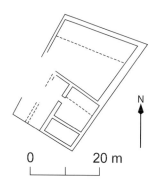

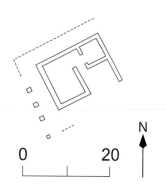

Fig. 7.22. Chair in MB 3. Photo: Kelsey Museum Archives neg. no. KR35.05.

Fig. 7.23. Plan of MB 4, detail from plan of the sanctuary of Mên Askaênos. Drawing: A. J. Ossi and K. A. Raff.

Fig. 7.24. Plan of MB 5, detail from plan of the sanctuary of Mên Askaênos. Drawing: A. J. Ossi and K. A. Raff.

Multi-Room Buildings 4 and 5 (Mitchell and Waelkens's Houses 4 and 5). East from the *temenos* of Mên, one comes upon MB 4, which was nearly as large as MB 3 (fig. 7.23).[89] The building comprises three spaces, and its plan, like that of MB 3, resembles that of a typical Greek house. The first space, a rectangular vestibule, leads to two adjacent rooms, a nearly square room of 9.5 × 8.5 m, and a smaller room of 4.5 × 8 m.[90] The sheer size of the structure and the fact that its entrance faces the propylon of the *temenos* suggest that, like MB 3, MB 4 was used primarily by elite worshippers, including priests and priestesses, who took part in activities inside the *temenos* of Mên. Perhaps the nearly square room functioned as a dining room, comparable to that in MB 3 but smaller in size.

Southeast of MB 4 is MB 5, which is similar in plan to MB 1. Around the north and west sides of MB 5, large rectangular piers form an external, southward-facing portico (fig. 7.24). The portico leads into a courtyard through which the visitor entered the inner rooms—a large rectangular room of 6.6 × 9.8 m connected to a smaller square room of 4.44 × 4.6 m.[91] The dimensions of the rooms, which are similar to those in the other multi-room buildings at the site, suggest that MB 5 also housed dining activities.[92]

Single-Room Buildings. Sanctuaries in the Greek world typically included a variety of single-room buildings that served purposes ranging from dining to storage. At the sanctuary of Zeus at Nemea, for example, Miller has suggested that a row of nine such buildings, which range in size from approximately 6 m to 14.5 m wide and 11.20 m to 22.40 m long, could have served as treasuries as well as storerooms. Moreover, their larger dimensions seem suitable for comfortably accommodating groups of worshippers at cult meals and banquets and perhaps also meetings.[93] There are remains of at

[89] I include the courtyards of MB 3 and MB 4 in my estimate of their relative sizes.

[90] Mitchell and Waelkens 1998, 79.

[91] Mitchell and Waelkens 1998, 81.

[92] See MB 1–4 above; Pedley 2005, 77.

[93] Miller 1990, 117–128, 161–168. The *oikoi* at Nemea were generally larger than the treasuries at Olympia and Delphi.

In fact, at least four of the Nemean structures are greater in size than the largest Olympian treasury. Miller 1990, 119 n. 69 goes on to suggest that the Nemean *oikoi* could be interpreted as simple *lesche* because of their large dimensions and their lack of a *prodromos*. Based on the parallel that he draws between the Nemean *oikoi* and those of the sanctuary of Apollo at Delos, Miller suggests that the former could have functioned as storerooms, meeting halls, treasuries, or embassies. Miller does not elaborate upon the "embassies" interpretation, although I believe that could be related to the fact that Nemea was the site of a Panhellenic festival,

least thirteen single-room buildings on the grounds of the sanctuary of Mên. Mitchell and Waelkens refer to twelve of them as *oikoi*, which they posit were used for smaller groups of diners and for a variety of other needs of organizations associated with the cult of Mên.[94]

Single-Room Buildings 1–5. Just outside the east side of the *temenos* of Mên is a row of five single-room buildings with chambers that were approximately 3 to 4 m wide and 4 to 5 m long.[95] These freestanding structures, some of which also had an antechamber, were entered through a central doorway flanked by two antae. Those with an antechamber have basic ground plans that are similar to that of Andron A at Labraunda.[96] At about half the size of the smallest *oikos* at Nemea, these single-room buildings at the sanctuary of Mên do not seem to have been suited for groups of people. Rather, they would probably have served as storerooms or treasuries for offerings to Mên. Individuals and entire communities requested divine help at sanctuaries and brought gifts in hopes of assistance as indications of piety and even as displays of social status. Such offerings varied in quantity and quality, depending on the affluence of the individual or the city that donated the gift.[97] Many of these were displayed within the *temenos*, but many others would have been stored safely in treasuries. Treasury buildings could serve as votive offerings in themselves and were often designed to appear as miniature temples.[98] They provided secure space for valuable offerings, often made of costly materials such as silver, ivory, and gold.[99]

The conspicuous location of this row of single-room buildings—just outside the main entrance to the *temenos* of Mên—is strongly reminiscent of that of the treasuries at the Panhellenic sanctuaries of Olympia and Delphi on the Greek mainland. Treasuries normally were small, rectangular structures with windowless walls.[100] Like those at the Sanctuary of Mên, the treasuries at Olympia are lined up in a row, facing a pathway. At Delphi they are situated along the Sacred Way or along paths connecting to it (figs. 7.25–26).[101] In contrast to the treasuries at Delphi and Olympia, which were built by cities in the Panhellenic League, those at the sanctuary of Mên might have been built by wealthy local families, given that this sanctuary was primarily for worshippers from the region of Antioch. One can well imagine that the family of Cornelia Antonia, whose statue Ramsay found in the *temenos*, might have had a treasury here.

---

beginning in 573 BC. See also Miller 1990, 1–12 on Nemea, the Panhellenic festival, and the temporary unification of differing political bodies for these regular athletic contests.

[94] Mitchell and Waelkens 1998, 73.

[95] These dimensions are an approximation based on Mitchell and Waelkens's 1998 plan of the site (p. 38, fig. 5).

[96] Hellström 1996, 166, fig. 3; Mitchell and Waelkens 1998, 82.

[97] Pedley 2005 10–11; See also Pedley 2005, 101–116 for a full discussion of the types of personal offerings given by individuals and states during different periods.

[98] Drees 1968, 120.

[99] Tomlinson 1976, 59; Pedley 2005, 74, 114–115.

[100] Pedley 2005, 74.

[101] The best evidence of treasuries is found at interurban Panhellenic sanctuaries such as Olympia and Delphi, where the treasuries were constructed to serve as gifts to the god on behalf of specific cities, to commemorate military victories, and also to indicate the wealth and power of a donating city through the decoration of its structure's façade. On Olympia, see Drees 1968. At Olympia, twelve treasuries were erected, eleven of which consisted of a rectangular room, with two columns and a small antechamber in the front. The treasuries vary in dimensions from approximately 6 to 15 m in width and 6 to 16 m in length. On Delphi, see Petrakos 1977, 13–20. At Delphi, there were no fewer than eight treasuries, which followed a fairly rectangular layout that consisted of a rectangular interior chamber and a small antechamber with two columns in antis. Two other treasuries followed the same basic layout, although they omitted the columns. The dimensions of the treasuries range from approximately 4 to 6 m in width and 5 to 10 m in length. See also Morgan 1990 on Olympia and Delphi.

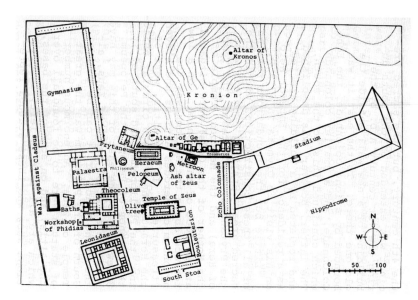

Fig. 7.25. Plan of the sanctuary at Olympia, ca. 200 BC.
After Holmberg 1979, 92, fig. 13.

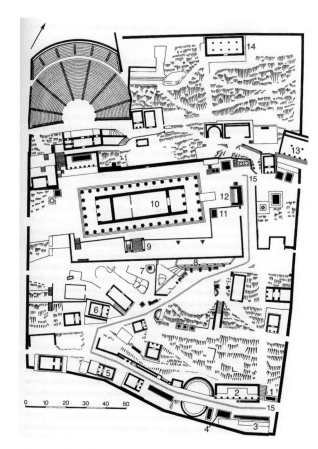

Fig. 7.26. Plan of the sanctuary at Delphi.
After Pedley 2005, 137, fig. 71.

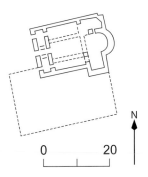

Fig. 7.27. Plan of SB 9, detail from plan of the sanctuary of Mên Askaênos. Drawing: A. J. Ossi and K. A. Raff.

0   20

N

Single-Room Buildings 6–8. Along the Sacred Way, southeast of MB 4 is another single-room building of similar dimensions, SB 6.[102] To the north of MB 5 are two small structures along the path, SB 7 and SB 8. Like the single-room buildings adjacent to the *temenos* of Mên, these buildings are approximately 3 m to 4 m in width by 4 m to 5 m in length and were probably also used as treasuries.

Single-Room Buildings 9–13. One single-room building at the sanctuary of Mên (SB 9), called the "Andron" by Mitchell and Waelkens, has architectural characteristics of a dining room. It is located at the northern end of the sanctuary amid a row of five single-room buildings. While similar in plan to nearly all the other single-room buildings at the sanctuary, it is nearly twice their size (fig. 7.27).[103] The almost square inner room of SB 9, measuring 8.25 × 7.8 m, and its off-center doorway are typical of dining rooms at the sanctuary and elsewhere. The proximity of this building to the much smaller SB 10 suggests that the latter served as a kitchen.[104] This arrangement of small, aligned structures accompanying dining rooms compares well with the one at the sanctuary of Zeus at Nemea, where two of the nine *oikoi* were attached by a wall to the "Dining Establishment." Oikos 9 at Nemea is believed to have functioned as a kitchen for the preparation of ritual meals.[105] The other single-room buildings in this zone of the sanctuary of Mên, SB 11–13, may have been treasuries, on analogy with SB 1–8.

Conclusion

The archaeological remains on Kara Kuyu indicate that the sanctuary of Mên incorporated many of the standard features of Greek sanctuaries. This similarity suggests that Mitchell and Waelkens may be right in proposing that the temple of Mên Askaênos was originally built in the 2nd century BC. However, as Khatchadourian points out in the following chapter, the visible remains of the *temenos*

[102] Ramsay's 1918 plan (pl. 1) of the sanctuary indicates walls south of SB 6 and farther down the hill due southeast. However, Mitchell and Waelkens do not note these walls. They may have been buried in the intervening years under debris falling from the hillside.

[103] Mitchell and Waelkens 1998, 81–82.

[104] These structures could have fulfilled a variety of additional functions, which include dining rooms for ritual banqueting, cooking areas, temporary sleeping accommodations, treasuries, general storerooms, meeting houses, embassies, rooms for ritual purification, and even workshops for sculptors creating objects to be dedicated at the sanctuary,

as evidenced by the bronze sculptor's workshop found in oikos 8 at Nemea. On the sculptor's workshop at Nemea, see Miller 1990, 162.

[105] Miller 1990, 119, 165–166. This hypothesis is based on the discovery of stones that seem to form a bench, a stone slab and grinder used in the preparation of flour, a clay-lined pit filled with carbon, ash, and bone that may have been used for roasting meat, and an unlined well. Miller suggests that two other *oikoi* (oikos 1 and oikos 8) at Nemea within the row of nine may have functioned partially as cooking areas, even though one of the two is not immediately connected to the Dining Establishment.

Fig. 7.28. Plan of the small sanctuary church, detail from plan of the sanctuary of Mên Askaênos. Drawing: A. J. Ossi and K. A. Raff.

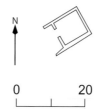

N

0   20

and temple may well belong to a structure of the Antonine period that was built on the plan of a Hellenistic predecessor. Clarification of the chronology of the temple of Mên and the other structures at the sanctuary must await excavation.

Despite its predominantly Greek appearance, the sanctuary exhibits the ethnic diversity of its worshippers in the Greek and Latin dedicatory inscriptions, with names indicating Roman, Greek, Etruscan, and possibly Anatolian backgrounds and a local taste for contrasting gray and white limestone in its architecture.[106] The coloristic effect of contrasting stones occurs both in the *temenos* and temple of Mên and in the small temple, and it appears again in monuments in the city of Antioch, including the imperial cult sanctuary and the Hadrianic arch. Sacred architecture and dedications commissioned by individuals and cities not only reflected the wealth and prestige of the donors but also established a sense of group identity, shared cult, and a collective cultural goal.[107] J. G. Pedley suggests, moreover, that the siting of a sanctuary can provide evidence of the social, political, and economic activities that took place alongside its religious activities.[108] Sanctuaries within a city, for instance, did not necessarily serve sociopolitical purposes, but sanctuaries located outside of a city would have done so by uniting scattered rural or smaller urban communities and connecting them to the main urban center.[109] As an extraurban sanctuary located away from the colony of Antioch, the sanctuary of Mên Askaênos would have served the interests and religious needs of the residents both of Antioch and of the surrounding region.

At times of religious festivals, the sanctuary of Mên, like similar sanctuaries of the Greek and Roman worlds, would have been filled with people performing sacrifices to the gods and dedicatory ceremonies and participating in athletic and other competitions and celebratory feasts. All this had ended, however, by the time the latest building constructed at the sanctuary, a small church, was erected to the northwest of MB 1 and 2 and farther down the slope (fig. 7.28) in the late 4th or early 5th century, apparently from the stone blocks of the cella walls of the temple of Mên.[110] The destruction of the temple to provide building materials for the church clearly signals the decline of polytheism in the period when Christianity gained a strong following at Antioch.[111]

[106] On the ethnic diversity of worshippers, see Khatchadourian, chap. 8, this volume.

[107] Pedley 2005, 42.

[108] Pedley 2005, 1, 39–56 notes the following six categories: sanctuaries in nature, interurban sanctuaries, urban sanctuaries, suburban sanctuaries, extraurban sanctuaries, and rural sanctuaries.

[109] Pedley 2005, 11–12, 42, 46–50.

[110] Until excavation verifies the chronology of the structures on Kara Kuyu, I accept with some reservation Mitchell and Waelkens's dating of the destruction of the temple of Mên around AD 400 and the construction of a Byzantine church in the late 4th or early 5th century.

[111] Mitchell and Waelkens 1998, 86; see also Herring-Harrington, chap. 6, this volume.

8 The Cult of Mên at Pisidian Antioch

Lori Khatchadourian[1]

The sanctuary to the lunar deity Mên Askaênos provided a forum for the heterogeneous community of Pisidian Antioch to celebrate the rites and festivals of a popular god, whose role as "patron deity" entailed the protection and representation of the nearby city.[2] The sanctuary, with its extant sacred precinct, scattered temple ruins, inscriptions, and tantalizing (if sparse) sculptural elements, was but one of a number of powerful religious institutions in Anatolia. Judging by their representations in the written record, these institutions played a critical role in the social, economic, and political life of the region in the Hellenistic and Roman eras. The sanctuary's distance from the city center symbolically, if not actually, elevated its importance as a potentially independent locus of social activity (fig. 8.1).

Mên Askaênos is commonly regarded as an "Anatolian" deity, due both to his absence from the Greek and Roman pantheons and to the way in which his portrayal in textual and artistic sources conforms to various classical conventions of Eastern representations. Beate Dignas has observed that the god Mên is "almost invariably represented in a purely oriental style."[3] Speaking of an "indigenous" Anatolian deity is a rather problematic enterprise, however. Such an essentializing notion could wrongly convey a sense of a timeless character to the cult of Mên Askaênos. Yet until now, our evidence for this enigmatic cult has been filtered for us through Greek and Roman textual and artistic media, and therefore what we regard as "purely oriental" is inseparable from the creative programs of the foreign communities who would come to inhabit the Anatolian landscape in the late first millennium BC.

There is relatively little firmly datable material evidence for the cult of Mên at Antioch prior to the reign of the Roman emperor Antoninus Pius (AD 138–161), and the evidence that is available after that time is narrow in scope. As a result, the understandable tendency in modern scholarship has been to consider the cult at Antioch within the broader context of religious activity in Hellenistic and Roman Anatolia and alongside other religious centers about which more is known.[4] The aim of this chapter, however, is to focus specifically on the evidence available at Antioch, which, despite limitations, is sufficiently rich to merit consideration on its own terms. The cult of the lunar god

[1] I would like to thank Elaine Gazda, Beate Dignas, and David Potter for their comments on earlier versions of this paper and Diana Ng for her contributions to the present version. Any remaining errors are entirely my own.

[2] A new study of the cult of Mên and its regional importance, Labarre 2009, appeared too late for me to take into account in this essay. Future work on the cult of Mên in Anatolia and the Roman Empire will undoubtedly address, among other things, Labarre's difference with Lane over aspects of this deity's worship at Pisidian Antioch. Similarly, Belayche 2008 could not be taken into account before press time. Belayche addresses the nomenclature of the deity worshipped at the Kara Kuyu sanctuary and argues that though private dedications were addressed to Mên Askaênos, the official name of the deity of this sanctuary was Luna. This new research would shed light on the discussion of the social versus political importance of this sanctuary.

[3] Dignas 2002, 225.

[4] See Debord 1982; Boffo 1985; Dignas 2002.

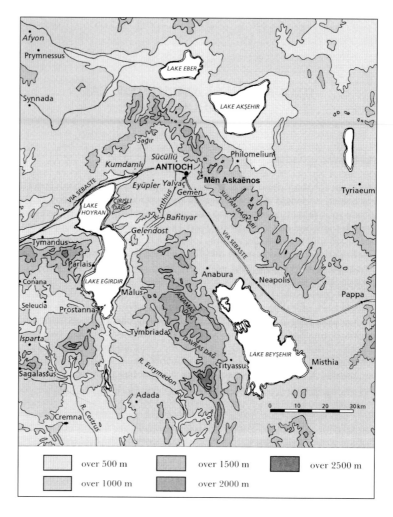

Fig. 8.1. Map of Antioch and surrounding territories, showing location of sanctuary of Mên Askaênos in relation to the city. After Mitchell and Waelkens 1998, fig. 2. By permission of Classical Press of Wales. Adapted by L. Sterner.

over 500 m   over 1500 m   over 2500 m

over 1000 m   over 2000 m

Fig. 8.2. Map showing temple-states of western Asia Minor. Drawing: L. Sterner.

Mên is rather exceptional and exhibits considerable variability from place to place.[5] To appreciate the particularities of the cult of Mên at Antioch we must first consider the broader ancient and modern discourses in which the sanctuary is situated.

Antioch in the Context of Anatolian Cult Centers

The sanctuary of Mên at Antioch generally figures in historical scholarship on the Roman East as one of the "temple-states" described by the ancient geographer Strabo sometime in the latter half of the 1st century BC or early 1st century AD. In their discussions of sanctuaries such as Antioch, historians have used Strabo's narrative both to define the phenomenon of temple-states and to categorize the representative sanctuaries discussed by this same ancient author.[6] These cult centers are said to represent the sacerdotal character of political authority in the pre-Roman period. By Strabo's account, the temple-states were Anatolian cult centers whose political prominence depended on powerful priesthoods (rather than civic institutions) and whose economic strength was based on the ownership of extensive territories. The power of these centers thus derived not only from the nebulous realm of the sacred but also quite pragmatically from temple finances, which were managed independently of civic finances and civic authorities.[7] In addition to priesthoods and temple lands, these temple-states as described by Strabo are thought to have possessed thousands of temple servants, known as *hierodouloi*.

The temple-states are usually distinguished from the major Greek coastal sanctuaries of western Asia Minor, such as that of Artemis at Ephesos, in two respects. Geographically, all of the sanctuaries that bear the characteristics of temple-states, including those of Antioch in Pisidia, Comana in Pontus, Zela in Pontus, Comana in Cappadocia, Pessinus in Galatia, and Olba in Cilicia, are located inland, in central and eastern Anatolia (fig. 8.2).[8] The temple-states are further differentiated from the Greek coastal sanctuaries by the supposedly Anatolian or Persian identity of the deity to whom they tend to be dedicated, although one should keep in mind the danger of ascribing deities to normative culture blocks. For example, the temple of Pessinus was dedicated to the so-called Anatolian mother-goddess Cybele; the temples of Comana in Pontus and Cappadocia to the Anatolian god Ma; and the sanctuary at Zela to the "Persian" deity Anahitis.

The temple-states are thus often treated as a separate category of religious institution, and one whose fortunes were closely linked to political developments. Scholars such as Pierre Debord have drawn a stark contrast between the status of the temple-states in the time of the Hellenistic kings and later, under Rome. In the former period, the priesthoods are thought to have been powerful, independent loci of authority, never fully controlled by the Hellenistic dynasts who ruled Asia Minor.[9] The traditional discourse envisions strong priestly control over sacred lands and the revenues they yielded for the temples in the Hellenistic period.[10]

The temple-states are thought to undergo a reorganization upon the emergence of Roman dominance in Anatolia in the 1st century BC. Although Strabo's description of the experience of each

[5] Dignas 2002, 225.

[6] Dignas 2002, 227.

[7] Dignas 2002, 4.

[8] Virgilio 1981. Though these distinctions exist, the physical components of the sanctuary do have similarities to elements at other major Greek sanctuaries such as ones at Nemea and Brauron; see Raff, chap. 7, this volume.

[9] Using Strabo, Debord (1982, 54) notes some nuances in the standing of these temple-states in the Hellenistic period: while Zela and Pessinus were regarded unfavorably by the kings of the Attalid dynasty, in Cappadocia the grand priest of Comana seemed to enjoy independence.

[10] Dignas 2002, 229.

of these temple-states allows for some variation, his remarks on Antioch reflect what is thought to be the general impact of the Roman encounter on many of the once-influential cult centers. Strabo writes: "Here there was also a priesthood of Mên Arcaeus,[11] which had a number of temple-slaves and sacred places, but the priesthood was destroyed after the death of Amyntas by those who were sent there as his inheritors" (12.8.14).[12] This and other such statements by Strabo have shaped our historical narrative, according to which the cult centers were, to varying degrees, neutralized and subsumed by Rome through control of the priesthoods and confiscation or reorganization of temple lands.

The Roman inheritors were motivated by economic and political concerns rather than an interest in the religious dimension of the sanctuaries.[13] Economic benefits would accrue from the reorganization and redistribution of temple estates and the discretionary control over temple revenues, exercised through the power of the priest.[14] The priesthoods would also represent an opportunity for political advantage to Rome, as powerful and well-established seats of authority with the capacity to mobilize supporters through the institution of the temple servants.[15] Such political advantages would be particularly useful in apparently fractious regions like Pontus and Pisidia. The notion that Antioch was colonized by the Romans for security reasons was expressed early on by G. L. Cheesman (1913), according to whom "the colony had been called into existence to check the incursions of marauders."[16] That same sentiment persists in scholarship from later in the century as well. According to T. R. S. Broughton (1938), "[t]he Pisidian colonies, from the first reinforcement of Antioch toward Pisidia, the strategic center of the region . . . were primarily intended to keep the unruly mountaineers in check."[17] Until recently, the temple-states were thus discussed primarily in terms of their economic, political, and military importance.

Recently, some scholars such as L. Boffo (2003) have called into question the utility of such concepts as the "temple-state."[18] Dignas, in her study, *Economy of the Sacred in Hellenistic and Roman Asia Minor* (2002), offers corrections to some features of the established discourse on the temple-states of Anatolia.[19] Contrary to the standard description, Dignas suggests that some Anatolian sanctuaries may have regained their powerful priesthoods and autonomous status in the Roman period, citing the admittedly unique case of the priesthood of Cybele at Pessinus, where there is evidence for a continuity of priestly independence from civic institutions.[20] In the reasonable search for patterns to

---

[11] "Arcaeus" is generally taken to be an error on Strabo's part or a corruption in the text. It should read "Ascaeus" or "Ascaenus."

[12] In contrast to the "destruction" (κατελύθη) of the priesthood at Antioch, Strabo tells us that the priesthood at Pessinus and Zela were not destroyed but "degraded" (μειόω) (Strabo 13.5.3 and 13.3.37).

[13] Debord 1982, 56.

[14] Strabo repeatedly mentions the economic clout of the cult sanctuaries as powerful emporia, conveniently located along prominent roads of the Achaemenid Persian network. Pessinus, for example, "is the greatest of the emporiums in that part of the world" (12.5.3). Comana in Cappadocia "is a noteworthy emporium for those from Armenia" (12.3.36), while "Zela's priest had great wealth" (12.3.37).

[15] In the case of Comana in Pontus, for instance, Pompey

appointed as priest Archelaos, whose father had enjoyed the support of Sulla and the Senate.

[16] Cheesman 1913, 256.

[17] Broughton 1938, 702.

[18] Boffo 2003, 259–267.

[19] Dignas (2002, 224) challenges the traditional distinction between the temple-states, or rural cults of central Anatolia, and the civic sanctuaries of western Asia Minor. She also emphasizes the difficulty of categorizing religious institutions based on the nature of the deities worshipped, the extent of a sanctuary's landholdings, the degree of surrounding urbanization, and the extent of "Hellenization," all of which have been factors that have been used to distinguish the central Anatolian cults from the sanctuaries of western Asia Minor.

[20] Dignas 2002, 229.

characterize Roman policies vis à vis Anatolian cult centers, scholars such as Dignas have turned to cult centers like Pessinus, which receive fuller treatment in Strabo's account and therefore assist in painting a big picture. On the basis of Pessinus, Dignas offers a new interpretation, which suggests the continuity of some degree of temple autonomy.[21]

From Strabo's Temple-States to the Case of Antioch

In the case of Antioch, as I shall demonstrate, we do see evidence for Rome making use of the influence of the sanctuary; however, without more precise evidence such as administrative records or imperial correspondence we cannot be sure that it was the administrative or economic strengths of the sanctuary that motivated the establishment of the nearby colony. Nor does the evidence shed light on the degree of autonomy enjoyed by the sanctuary from secular authorities, although it is likely that the administration of the sanctuary became the prerogative of the Roman colony, for we know that the colony appointed a *curator arcae sanctuarii* to oversee the sanctuary's financial management.[22] Nevertheless, Dignas's supposition concerning sanctuary autonomy is reasonable insofar as the complete subordination of an established local institution is unlikely. Numismatic, archaeological, and epigraphic evidence for cult activity at Antioch—along with the literary evidence provided by Strabo, on which scholars have relied so heavily—can further nuance our understanding of the political and ideological significance of the sanctuary of Mên at Antioch after the founding of the Roman colony in 25 BC. Such categories of evidence have been studied and well published by Eugene Lane, Stephen Mitchell, and Marc Waelkens, among others. By and large, however, scholarship on the sanctuary of Mên at Antioch is limited, in part because of the lack of excavations at the site since Ramsay's explorations of 1911–1913.[23]

Although Antioch is home to the only known archaeological remains of a temple to Mên, and was clearly a center of the cult of Mên in antiquity, inscriptions and coins from across Asia Minor demonstrate that devotion to this deity reached far beyond Antioch. The widespread evidence for the worship of Mên suggests that this cult may have been ideologically important for Roman policy in the Eastern empire, and that therefore this particular cult sanctuary may have been valuable to Roman elites in ways that extended beyond its local political and economic potential. Historians such as Debord and his predecessors have emphasized the economic, military, and political reasons for Roman incorporation of Strabo's temple-states, considering the instrumentality of these cult centers within the larger project of Roman expansion. The evidence for the cult of Mên, however, encourages us also to consider the meaning of the cult itself as a factor in its incorporation within Roman control. At least by the Antonine period, both imperial and local elites used the cult for purposes of propaganda and patronage, which perhaps suggests that the cult's appeal to Roman authorities extended beyond the economic and administrative institutions of the sanctuary.

Yet the state-sponsored, propagandistic use of the cult does not tell the whole story. If we are to consider the impact of Roman intervention on local cults, a natural corollary is to consider the impact of these cults on Rome, and particularly on the Roman colonists who inhabited the area of the cult centers. The widespread evidence for devotion to the god Mên throughout Asia Minor in the

---

[21] Dignas 2002, 244.

[22] Dignas 2002, 226.

[23] Margaret Hardie's (1912) and J .G. C. Anderson's (1913) publications on the inscriptions are largely superseded by

Lane's comprehensive treatment of Mên inscriptions (1971; 1975a; 1976; 1978), just as Sir William Ramsay's publications (1911–1912) are superseded (and largely discredited) by Mitchell and Waelkens (1998). See Raff's reconstruction of the sanctuary, chap. 7, this volume.

first few centuries AD and the numerous dedications at Antioch in Greek and Latin by individuals with Greek, Latin, Etruscan, and possibly local Anatolian names suggest that the cult was popular and meaningful to a heterogeneous profile of adherents. Among these adherents, a form of communal parity may have characterized the public expression of devotion to the deity, as I will argue below. The Anatolian cults, and particularly the cult of Mên, were thus probably more than just co-opted loci of power; for Romans and non-Romans alike, they were also arenas for communal and religious expression. The sanctuary of Mên at Antioch provided a forum for the display of individual and group identities. Evidence for ritual practice at the sanctuary suggests that despite the likely social and cultural heterogeneity in Pisidian Antioch and its environs, devotion to the cult transcended local or ethnic differences, whose articulation is entirely absent from the evidence. This apparently accommodating nature of the cult extends to the very nature of the deity himself, who was easily associated with other divinities, as the sculptural evidence, to be discussed below, attests.

The "Italian Connection"

On the basis of epigraphic evidence, Lane has offered a provocative approach to the cult of Mên under Roman rule that addresses the significance of the cult itself rather than the opportunities offered by its governing institutions. The crux of Lane's argument depends upon the most widespread of Mên's many epithets, Askaênos, which happens also to be the epithet associated with Mên at Antioch. The derivation of this word is uncertain. In two inscriptions it refers to a place name, Askaie.[24] The word also has broader resonances, however, particularly with Ascanius, son of Aeneas of Troy, the celebrated protagonist of one of Rome's foundation myths. From this Lane posits that, at least after the release of Vergil's *Aeneid* in the last quarter of the 1st century BC, the epithet would have had distinctly Roman overtones and would have created a strong putative link between Anatolians and Romans. "It is reasonable to suppose," Lane writes, "that the cult found official Roman favor by reason of the supposed Italian connection outlined above, and that that may even have been a factor in the selection of the site for a Roman colony in the time of Augustus."[25] Further support for Lane's argument comes from an inscription found near Dorylaion in northern Phrygia, in which Mên is modified by the epithet Italko.[26] In his most confident statement on what he terms the "Italian Connection," Lane posits:

> [T]he cult of Mên seems deliberately to have been fostered as a unifying force by the Roman rulers of Asia Minor, and a mythology deliberately created, which, through epithets laden with legendary lore and clever use of word-resemblances, underscored the cult of Mên as an integral part of the supposed racial relationship between the subject Anatolians and their Italian masters.[27]

Lane's argument is intriguing because it alters the "co-opt and control" model proposed by Debord and others by suggesting an ideological rather than material motive for Roman involvement in the cult of Mên. According to Lane's formulation, Roman emperors sought to take advantage of the identity of this particular cult. Lane's proposal is appealing because his emphasis on the cult as a "unifying force"—rather than merely as a political and economic resource to be extracted by Roman authorities—accommodates the plentiful evidence for widespread engagement with the cult of Mên across Asia Minor and among disparate social groups. In order for Lane's argument also to be compelling, however, we might expect to see certain additional conditions met: first, engagement with the

[24] Lane 1971, 101–102, nos. 162 and 163.

[25] Lane 1975b, 236.

[26] Lane 1975b, 235.

[27] Lane 1975b, 239.

Fig. 8.3. Example of one of the seventeen coins from Antioch that predate the founding of the Roman colony. Obverse: Bust of Mên with lunar crescent and head of rooster. Reverse: Humped bull. Paris, Le Cabinet des Médailles. After Lane 1975, pl. XXX, Antioch 10.

cult and its sanctuary in the earliest phase of the Roman colony's existence; and second, widespread, official use of the symbolism of Mên.

Patterns of Use

It is on the first front that Lane's argument falters, although the problem appears to be one of insufficient archaeological investigation rather than a clear indication that there was no worship of Mên in the age of Augustus. It is worth reviewing the evidence for the worship of Mên at Antioch up to Augustus's reign. Strabo's account, cited above, offers clear indication of the existence of extensive cult apparatus prior to the establishment of the colony. This is further corroborated by seventeen coins, which, according to Lane's analysis,[28] were minted locally before the founding of the Roman colony (fig. 8.3). Lane dates the coins, which bear the bust of Mên, a humped bull, the name of the city, and the names of magistrates, to some time after the treaty of Apamea in 188 BC, when Seleucid control over Antioch ended.[29] The appearance of coinage bearing iconic imagery of the cult may mark a transformation from "indigenous cult" to "state cult," although Dignas has warned of the limitations of such a dichotomous formulation.[30]

Architectural remains may also suggest a Hellenistic occupation at the sanctuary itself, although absolutely dated evidence is sparse. Mitchell and Waelkens (1998) provide a thorough discussion of the temple structure at the sanctuary, the details of which will not be covered here (but see Raff, chapter 7, this volume).[31] Briefly, on the basis of a comparison of temple ground plans from across Asia Minor, they conclude that the temple of Mên at Antioch dates to between 175 and 125 BC. Two caveats should be raised with respect to this dating, however. First, though the coins mentioned above attest to the worship of Mên in the 2nd century BC, there is no material evidence from the sanctuary for the use of the temple itself in the Hellenistic period. This may simply be the result of unsatisfactory attention to stratigraphy in the course of excavations and poor preservation of the site in antiquity, hastened by destruction in the early Christian period. Another point to bear in mind when considering a Hellenistic dating of the temple is the clear evidence for archaizing temple architecture in Asia Minor in the Roman imperial period. For example, the temple of Rome and Augustus at Ankyra and the temple of Zeus at Aezani—both once thought to be Hellenistic in date and attributed to Hermogenes—were in fact built under Hadrian and Antoninus Pius, respectively.[32] The fact that the latter was built by Antoninus Pius is particularly germane to a consideration of the

---

[28] Lane 1976, 55.

[29] Nothing is known of the attitude of Seleucid kings to the sanctuary at Antioch, although Dignas's study, based on other sanctuaries, suggests that Hellenistic kings at times served as mediators between cities and cults (Dignas 2002, 36–110).

[30] Dignas 2002, 10.

[31] See Mitchell and Waelkens 1998, 37–72.

[32] Mitchell and Waelkens 1998, 67.

Fig. 8.4: Example of early imperial coin from Antioch. Obverse: Bust of Mên with lunar crescent and head of rooster. Reverse: Rooster. Evelpides Collection, Athens. After Lane 1975, pl. XXXI, Antioch 18.

temple at Antioch since it is during his reign that the cult of Mên enjoyed a marked resurgence. It is therefore tempting to suppose that the temple of Mên may be yet another archaizing construction of the Roman imperial period, although in all such cases it is entirely possible for the archaizing monument to conform to the footprint of a predecessor, particularly in the context of potentially conservative cult practice. In any event, regardless of the date of the temple itself, which must for now remain an open question, there is sufficient evidence from literary and numismatic sources of the importance of Mên at Antioch prior to the founding of the Roman colony.

It is for the subsequent phase of the site's history, in the early imperial period when Antioch became a Roman colony and when the city was engaged in the construction of a sanctuary to the imperial cult, that evidence for the practice of the cult of Mên at the extramural sanctuary has not yet emerged. In his *Res Gestae*, a copy of which was inscribed at Antioch (see Rubin, chapter 3, this volume), Augustus maintains that he restored votive offerings to the Asian temples, and an inscription from Kyme of Augustan date does suggest a benevolent policy toward sanctuaries on the part of the *princeps*.[33] Pausanias portrays Augustus as more aggressive.[34] At Antioch, neither view can be verified. Indeed, there is almost no indication that the sanctuary was in use during the empire before the reign of Antoninus Pius, making it difficult definitively to situate Antioch within the broader pattern observed by Dignas of Roman benevolence and euergetic activities toward religious institutions.[35]

With the evidence currently available, Lane's suggestion that the colony was established in part "for the propaganda value that could be drawn from its principal cult" begins to lose ground given the silence concerning the cult during the early empire.[36] The one possible exception to this lack of early evidence is a small round *cippus*, or post, that was found at the sanctuary during Ramsay's excavations in 1912.[37] The inscription is by a dedicant named Ti. Claudius Epinicus, who may have been a freedman of Claudius and came to hold an important position in the civil administration at Antioch.[38] However, this *cippus* seems to be of 1st-century AD date and therefore does not solve the problem of the evidentiary lacuna for the period of the colony's founding. Nor is the gap filled by a series of small coins, all of which have the word COLONIAE on the reverse and Mên iconography on the obverse (fig. 8.4). Lane is open to the possibility that these coins date to the pre-Antonine period; however, in the absence of an emperor's name it is difficult to know, and Krzyzanowska (1970) has dated these same coins to the reign of Antoninus Pius.[39]

Lane's suggestion that the cult provided the impetus for establishing the colony does not hold up to scrutiny given the current state of our evidence. At the same time, it should be noted that if his

---

[33] Dignas 2002, 121. Although there is no evidence of activity at the extramural sanctuary in this period, Mên was depicted on the propylon of the Augustan imperial cult sanctuary. See Rubin, chap. 3, this volume.

[34] Pausanias 8.46.1–5.

[35] Dignas 2002, 219.

[36] Lane 1964, 56.

[37] Lane 1971, 100, no. 160.

[38] Cheesman 1913, 258.

[39] Krzyzanowska 1970 examines all die links and weights of the colonial coins of Pisidian Antioch.

proposal falls because of lack of evidence for use of the sanctuary in the time of Augustus, then the more traditional notion that Rome assumed control over the "temple-state" to use it as an instrument for pacifying rebel Pisidians falls, too. Indeed, by the time the cult is revived under Antoninus Pius, pacification is presumably no longer a pressing concern. None of the scholarship on the sanctuary ventures to explain this long hiatus in its use. In the absence of a definitive explanation, it becomes tempting to understand quite literally Strabo's comment that the independent priesthood was "destroyed" when the Romans arrived.

In any event, we can retain Lane's idea that the cult offered suitable ideological underpinnings for Rome's involvement in Anatolia and a handy symbolic repertoire through which powerful messages could be deployed. It seems that in later publications Lane himself shifted the emphasis of his claim. "Although the temple of Mên lost its temporal importance when the Roman colony was sent out," he writes, "the Romans do not seem to have been too long in becoming aware of the value of Mên Askaênos as a god who could comfortably be worshipped both by the natives and by the colonists."[40] Whatever the reasons for Antioch's original colonization and the cult's apparent decline there, arguably by the mid-2nd century the sanctuary of Mên was revived, becoming more than a military, economic, or political instrument.

Propaganda and Patronage

Overt indication of the propagandistic use of the cult of Mên in the Roman imperial period appears on coins from across Asia Minor. In his comprehensive publication of known coins associated with Mên, Lane lists over sixty separate imperial issues with iconography of the deity on the obverse. At Antioch, the coins range in date from the reign of Antoninus Pius (AD 138–161) to that of Trebonianus Gallus (AD 251–253). These coins provide unmistakable proof of the public character of the cult of Mên at Antioch during this period. The substantial collection of Antonine coins also attests to the resurgence of the cult in the period. Pius was not the first emperor to employ the iconography of Mên on the coinage of Asia Minor, and occasional instances of such coins, minted outside of Antioch, date as early as the reign of Augustus.[41] However, there is a clear spike in the number and spread of coins with images of Mên under the Antonines, which suggests that this dynasty systematically harnessed the symbols of the cult in a way that had not been done before. The confusion over how to render the god's name in Latin, as evident on some coins from Antoninus Pius until Septimius Severus in which the god's is named "Mensis" rather than "Luna," also suggests perhaps that the cult had not previously been a significant factor in Roman imperial policies, for presumably this basic matter of naming would already have been resolved.[42]

Given the general paucity of sculpture from Pisidian Antioch, let alone individualized portraiture, the inscribed statue of Cornelia Antonia, dated to the middle Antonine period and found at the sanctuary of Mên, also offers compelling support for the notion of heightened Mên patronage under

[40] Lane 1976, 65. See Rubin, chap. 3 and Ossi, chap. 4, this volume.

[41] Lane 1975a. Augustus: one from Hydrela, one from Philomelium, one from Siblia. Tiberius: one from Philmelium, one from Siblia. Nero: two from Maeonia, one from Nysa, one from Hydrela, two from Julia. Vespasian: one from Sardis. Nerva: one from Galatia. Trajan: two from Gordus-Julia, five from Galatia. Hadrian: one from Paleobeudos, one from Comana, two from Sagalassos, one from Seleukeia.

[42] Eventually the Romans ignore the awkwardness of gender rather than maintain the awkwardness of meaning and will render Mên as Selene. Lane posits that the gender problem is abbreviated out of the way by the formula LVS, which closely corresponds to the Greek Μηνι ευχήν, a phrase that appears on many of the votive inscriptions (Lane 1976, 57). Thus Lane argues that LVS is not *libens votum solvit* but rather *Lunae Votum Solvit*. See also Belayche 2008, which deals with this naming issue.

Fig. 8.5 (near right). Statue of Cornelia
Antonia. Istanbul Archaeological Museum
inv. no. 2645. After Inan and Rosenbaum
1966, pl. CLXII.1. By permission of the
museum.

Fig. 8.6 (far right). Statue of a woman
from Acmonia. Afyon Museum inv. no.
3267. After Inan and Rosenbaum 1966, pl.
CXXXVI.3. By permission of the museum.

Antoninus Pius and his successors (fig. 8.5). Cornelia is draped in a chiton and himation, the latter
acting as a veil. Parallels for this form of drapery can be found on other portrait statues from Asia
Minor, such as that of a woman from Acmonia (fig. 8.6), which is also dated to the Antonine period.[43]

Outside of Antioch, the imperial coins found throughout Asia Minor offer strong testimony
to the importance of the cult in Roman imperial policy in the East. It should be noted that it was not
common practice to harness every Anatolian cult in this way. According to Lane, there are very few
Roman coins with other Anatolian deities depicted on them. He notes one issue of the city Tarsos
that carries representations of Mithras, but this is Lane's only comparison for the phenomenon we see
in the case of Mên.[44] His omission of coinage bearing iconography of the goddess Cybele is notable.
There is ample evidence that images of Cybele were also used in the service of imperial propaganda.[45]

Nearly all of the coins from Antioch depict Mên with what Lane has termed his "Antiochene
attributes."[46] Mên is shown standing with a rooster at his feet and a bucranium at his shoulders—the latter symbol perhaps subtly signaling a link to this deity when it appears on Antioch's temple of Augustus
(see Rubin, chapter 3, and Ossi, chapter 5, this volume). In his outstretched hand Mên carries a statuette
of Nike, herself carrying a trophy (fig. 8.7). An alternative to the Antiochene type is seen on three coins
from the reigns of Marcus Aurelius, Septimius Severus, and Gordian III, in which the obverse carries
only a bust of Mên with a crescent and starry cap (fig. 8.8). But the Antiochene type dominates, and it

[43] Inan and Rosenbaum 1966, 184 and 208.

[44] Lane 1990, 2162[?].

[45] Turcan 1983.

[46] Lane 1975a, 90.

Fig. 8.7. Example of a coin with Antiochene attributes. Obverse: Bust of Septimius Severus. Reverse: Standing figure of Mên. Aulock Collection. After Lane 1966, pl. XXXIII, Antioch 34.

Fig. 8.8. Alternate Antiochene type coin. Obverse: Bust of Marcus Aurelius. Reverse: Bust of Mên with crescent. Aulock Collection. After Lane 1966, pl. XXXII, Antioch 28.

Fig. 8.9. Coin of Gordian III. Obverse: Bust of Gordian III. Reverse: Statue of Mên standing in a temple. London, British Museum After Lane 1966, pl. XXXVI, Antioch 56. London © The Trustees of the British Museum.

Fg. 8.10 (near right): Drawing of a model of the cult image of Mên from Antioch. After Anderson 1913, fig. 54.

Fig. 8.11 (far right): Bronze statuette of Mên said to be from Antalya. Rijksmuseum van Oudheden, Leiden. After Lane 1971, pl. LXII. By permission of the museum.

seems to have influenced the coinage of other cities of Asia Minor such as Seleukeia, Parlas, Nysa, and Priene. Some cities such as Julia and Sagalassos carry on their coin obverses an image of Mên riding an animal, often a bull, an association that hearkens back to the earliest, pre-Roman coins from Antioch.

The numismatic images of Mên with Antiochene attributes are generally thought to depict a version of the cult statue that stood in the temple. Support for this notion can be found on a coin of Gordian III, where Mên with Antiochene attributes is standing inside a hexastyle temple (fig. 8.9). The absence of the Antiochene type on pre-Roman coins from Antioch suggests that the cult image as it is rendered on the coins was a Roman innovation, which may offer weak support for a later date for the temple. By a stroke of serendipity, a small marble statuette found at the sanctuary itself seems to be modeled on the cult statue (fig. 8.10). The statuette depicts a draped figure whose left leg is raised and rests on an animal's head (probably a bull's), while its left arm leans on a column.[47] This configuration of Mên's drapery and the high belt can also be observed on other statuettes of the deity, including a bronze example from Antalya (fig. 8.11). In both cases there is an androgynous quality to the renderings—namely, in the suggestion of breasts—which may be intended to draw

[47] Anderson 1913, 275.

connections between Mên and Cybele (see below). The bronze statuette is published by Anderson (1913) and Mendel (1912–1914), but neither ventures to date it.

The propagandistic use of the cult of Mên continues until the middle of the 3rd century AD; however, even after the last known imperial coin, that of the Caesar Phillip II, there is further evidence for the patronage of the cult of Mên at Antioch, this time by local elites. A series of twelve hexagonal columns engraved with inscriptions pertaining to athletic competitions and found within the *temenos* wall offer rare evidence for the kinds of festival activities, including gymnastic contests and a contest of trumpeters, that would have taken place at the unexcavated theater or odeion (formerly called the stadium) in the northwestern part of the sanctuary. Anderson was the first to publish these inscriptions in his 1913 article, "Festivals of Men Askaenos in the Roman Colonia at Antioch of Pisidia." Among the inscriptions is an official decree honoring G. Ulpius Baebianus, a prominent citizen of Antioch, for making a gift to the city, presumably the finances for the festival.[48] On the inscriptions themselves, Baebianus appears as presiding priest. He is also described as augur and lifetime priest of Mên and Demeter.[49] Following G. Ulpius Baebianus, the games fall under a double *agonothete*, with one person, G. Flavius Baebianus, described as pontifex, patron of the colony, and lifetime high priest of Mên.[50] On all of these inscriptions Mên appears with the epithet *patrios*, which Lane believes "fits in well with the Roman propagandistic purpose of convincing people of the inherent Anatolianness of Mên, as well as of his Roman connection."[51] The games were consistently named after Maximian Galerius and are therefore dated to the last decade of the 3rd century, after he became Caesar. As with the coins, the inscriptions pertaining to athletic competitions point to the public nature of the cult, in this case patronized by "rich grandees of the community"[52] rather than distant emperors. It is curious that there is no evidence for games earlier than the late 3rd century, particularly in the Antonine period. Excavation of the theater or odeion itself would surely reveal more about patterns of use and the structure's role in the life of the sanctuary.

The renaissance of the cult of Mên in the Antonine period and beyond is demonstrable, but the reasons for it remain obscure.[53] It is possible that investment in the cult was in response to some exterior threat to Roman values (i.e., Christianity), and its pan-Anatolian resurgence, apparently centered at Antioch, part of an attempt to foster a unifying mechanism to bind Roman and non-Roman communities internally and to one another. This is speculation. However, with Lane's "Italian Connection" thesis in mind, it is not entirely implausible that, if emperors such as Antoninus Pius were looking to reinforce Roman authority in Anatolia, reviving the cult of Mên Askaênos would be one way to do it. Mên's epithet, with its recollections of Roman descent from Aeneas, offered one resonance through which Roman association with Asia Minor could be claimed as appropriate and enduring.

Individuals and Groups at the Sanctuary of Mên

The inscriptions pertaining to athletic competitions tell only a partial story about the social experience of the cult of Mên at Antioch. Through the various other inscriptions found at the sanctuary it is possible to speak about individuals who, in experiencing the sanctuary, may not have recognized

---

[48] Anderson 1913, 285.

[49] Lane 1976, 65.

[50] Lane 1976, 65.

[51] Lane 1976, 64.

[52] Lane 1976, 66.

[53] Ossi, chap. 5, this volume raises the possibility that this cult revival might have begun under Hadrian, in whose reign the iconography of Mên was already being used on prominent structures such as the Arch of Hadrian and Sabina at Pisidian Antioch.

the larger, state-sponsored imperial imperatives that were pursued through the cult. An examination of these individuals—with their great variety of Greek, Roman, Etruscan, and possibly Anatolian names, all rendered variously in Greek and Latin scripts—reveals the heterogeneous nature of participation at the sanctuary of Mên. The search for ethnic identities is futile given the present state of evidence at the sanctuary, and such an essentializing endeavor, given the layered complexities of cultural and personal identities noted throughout this volume, would be unproductive even if more evidence were available. Yet we can, to a certain extent, consider individual identities as they are articulated through the inscriptions at the site. At the same time it is worth remembering that the inscriptions themselves present static snapshots—the putative identity of individuals or families at the performative moment of producing an inscription. The dynamic process of identity construction as it was played out at the sanctuary complex itself, with its temples and surrounding buildings, might only be elucidated upon further archaeological excavation. Although there is a wide range of names and professions among the inscriptions, they are for the most part remarkably redundant. In focusing on these individuals, we are also observing their choices to exercise a form of conservatism and conformity that is perhaps unsurprising in ritual practice.[54]

Group affiliations are also detectable in the inscriptions. Among the dedicants we can identify families and an enigmatic cult association that emerges in the 3rd century AD known as the *xenoi tekmoreioi*.[55] It is not at all certain what this group was, nor what the activity they performed, attested in inscriptions as *tekmorousantes*, entailed. Lane and others have dismissed Ramsay's speculations that the action involved holding up a crescent-shaped object to an image of the god as baseless.[56] In any event, this association of *xenoi tekmoreioi* and the dedicating families sheds light on a less institutionalized aspect of the cult than one might expect from a "typical" civic sanctuary.[57] The practice of group identity, at least in the case of the *xenoi tekmoreioi*, appears to be closely linked to ritual performance at the sanctuary of Mên at Antioch.

The inscriptions found at the sanctuary fall broadly into two categories, those that were inscribed on the *temenos* wall and those that are on freestanding monuments (fig. 8.12). None can be closely dated, but the letter-forms point to a date in the second half of the 3rd century.[58] The inscriptions on the *temenos* wall are known as *naiskoi*. These usually consist of a temple-shaped front on a base, carved in relief, with pilasters and a pediment topped with an akroterion (fig. 8.13).[59] Very often crescents are carved inside the *naiskoi*, and some of these have lugs at the bottoms, perhaps replicating the votive offerings that were set up at the temple. Inscriptions have also been found on marble and limestone plaques and stelai, and limestone columns.

There are approximately fifty dedications by families that appear on both *naiskoi* and freestanding monuments. Family members mentioned include brothers, sisters, children, wives, cousins, and foster children, who, apparently, are curiously frequent in the inscriptions.[60] Worshipping Mên at Antioch

[54] The repetitive quality of the inscriptions was clearly a source of great disappointment to Anderson, who writes: "The epigraphic finds made during the earlier stages of the excavation were dedications to the god identical in type with those engraved on the enceinte, dreary repetitions of the same unimaginative, stereotyped formula Μηνι Ασκαηνω ευχήν, all showing an amazing lack of that spontaneity and individuality that is the natural expression of real religious experience" (Anderson 1913, 270).

[55] Dignas 2002, 226.

[56] Lane 1976, 61.

[57] Dignas 2002, 226.

[58] Lane 1976, 59.

[59] Hardie 1912, 115.

[60] Lane 1976, 60.

Fig. 8.12. Inscriptions on the wall of the *temenos* of Mên Askaênos near Antioch. Photo: E. K. Gazda.

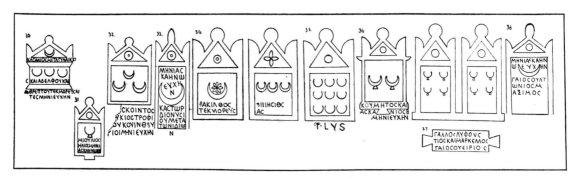

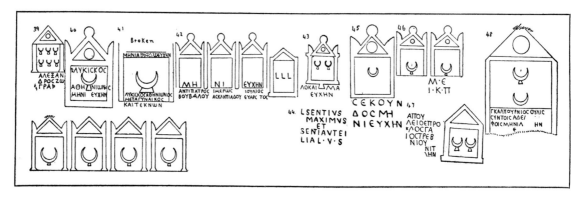

Fig. 8.13. Drawing of *naiskoi*. After Lane 1971, 126.

appears to have been a family affair, and this aspect of Mên as a protector of the family is seen elsewhere in the large corpus of evidence for the worship of Mên from beyond Antioch, as far as Attica.[61] One example of the familial dedications reads: "K. Lollios, with his wife and brother and adopted child, all of them, while being *tekmoreioi*,[62] make a vow to Men."[63] In another familiar inscription, a woman is the prime dedicant: "Hostilia Oresteina makes a vow to Mên with her children."[64] Finally, in a third example, the dedicant says that because he did wrong (sinned?), he makes a vow to Mên while being *tekmoreioi* with his wife and children.[65] The use of the word *hamartano* (sin, err) is conspicuous, for it is rarely found on these inscriptions. Hardie suggests that the dedicant's "sin" may have something to do with Christianity, since a violation of pagan ritual would be indicated by a different word.[66]

As is apparent from the above examples, and as Lane has observed, there is overlap between the familial inscriptions and those using the word *tekmoreusantes*. Identifying with this group was clearly important to the dedicants of Mên, particularly to those who also made an effort to identify with their families. In these otherwise terse and formulaic inscriptions, certain individuals make a point to advertise their associations and mark their differences. At least at the sanctuary of Mên, we might even suggest that family identity, and one's identity as a member of the *xenoi tekmoreioi*, trumped all other associations, whether ethnic, professional, or governmental. Assuming that ethnic differences mattered at all at Antioch (or even existed in the way we conceive of ethnicity today), it is possible that the sanctuary was an arena where such distinctions were dissolved by the communality of the cult.

In the case of the individual dedications, although they too follow the strict formula that Anderson finds so "unimaginative" (see n. 54), dedicants often make an attempt to mark their identity and set themselves apart from the dedicant of the neighboring *naiskoi* or stelai. One way in which they do this is by proclaiming their occupation. On one of the *naiskoi*, the dedicant, P. Viteilius (who has a Latin name, written in Greek), describes himself as *tektor*, or craftsman. On another, a certain Alexandros calls himself a *zographos*, or painter. Protion made two dedications on *naiskoi* and describes himself with the phrase, "whom the Muses foster"—apparently a man of education.[67] Between professions declared on *naiskoi* and those declared on freestanding marble or limestone monuments, there is no apparent status distinction. Among the latter group, one unnamed dedicant calls himself a *koptopoles*, or confectioner,[68] while T. Claudius Pasinianus Naos wants his audience—probably the deity and the community—to know that he is *summa rudis*, a head referee. Individual dedicants are overwhelmingly male, though in one instance a woman is the sole dedicant. Once again, there is no detectable trace of a concern for ethnic difference. Nor, incidentally, is there a concern with geographic identification. Place names never appear on these dedications. This does not necessarily mean that only inhabitants of Antioch visited the sanctuary, given that it was clearly the center of a cult that was widespread throughout Asia Minor. It does suggest, however, that involvement in the cult of Mên transcended local commitments, just as it may have transcended ethnic ones.[69] If the Roman

[61] See Lane 1971, 1–2, nos. 2 and 3.

[62] Since the meaning of this word is unknown, rather awkward translations are unavoidable.

[63] Lane 1971, 124, no. 208.

[64] Lane 1971, 117, no. 189.

[65] Lane 1971, 135, no. 242.

[66] Hardie 1912, 142.

[67] Lane 1976.

[68] The meaning of this previously unattested word is explored in Davies and Levick 1971.

[69] In different regions Mên did possess different epithets, and his iconography also takes on different points of emphasis from one region to the next. I do not mean to imply that the cult was identical across all of Asia Minor.

Fig. 8.14. Demeter/Cybele with *kalathos*. Yalvaç Museum.
Photo: E. K. Gazda.

Fig. 8.15. Stele depicting Mên and Cybele. Izmit Museum.
After Lane 1976, pl. 1, A8.

imperial intention in promoting the pan-Anatolian cult of Mên was to foster a sense of unity, it may
very well have succeeded at the sanctuary. One could interpret the "unimaginative" conformity of
the inscriptions as an indication of mechanical dedication rather than true devotion, a problematic
distinction that Anderson seems to imply. Alternatively, as I have argued, this conformity can be
interpreted to mean that the sanctuary of Mên was not an arena for playing out differences or status
competition, although it did leave room for displays of elite status, in the form of some exceptional
displays of wealth such as the statue of Cornelia Antonia and gestures of public generosity such as
the gifts of Baebianus. While it is probable that the freestanding marble dedications would have
required a greater investment than the inscriptions on the soft stone of the *temenos* wall, the content
of the dedications and the dedicants' relationship with the deity was no different for the craftsman
inscribed on the *temenos* wall than for the head referee mentioned on the freestanding monument.

Association and Syncretism

The unifying effect of the cult of Mên may also have been achieved by the accommodating and multivalent nature of the god himself. Mên's association with other deities, including Nike, Cybele, Hekate, and Anahitis, is apparent at Antioch and elsewhere. Among the few surviving sculptures found at the sanctuary of Mên, two fortuitous finds bear on Mên's relations with other deities. These sculptures are the only evidence for such associations at the sanctuary of Mên. All other evidence comes from sites outside of Antioch.

The first of these sculptures is a marble, half-life-sized head of a female resting against a high *kalathos*, or crown—one of a Janus-like pair (fig. 8.14). The sculpture was supposedly found in the southwest corner of the *temenos*.[70] Both Ramsay and Anderson identified the woman as Demeter and conjecture that the second head may have been Artemis, Selene, Mên, or a duplication of Demeter.[71] Ramsay feels confident that Demeter may be a Hellenized form of Cybele. Both Cybele and Demeter designations could be correct, and indeed both could be implied at the same time, as Ramsay suggests. The Demeter designation recalls the agonistic inscription noted above that mentions Baebianus's status as lifetime priest of Mên and Demeter. In addition, there are inscriptions and coins from outside Antioch that reveal this association between Mên and Demeter.[72] However, support for a designation as Cybele can also be found in the fact that the Mother Goddess is very often depicted with a *kalathos*. An intriguing comparative example can also be found in a stele of uncertain provenance that probably depicts Mên and Cybele (fig. 8.15). Mên is here identified by the crescent that emerges from behind his shoulders, while Cybele bears her hallmark attribute—the patera. Only Mên is named in the inscription, but the iconography of Cybele is unmistakable. What is remarkable about this monument is the relationship between the two figures as described by the inscription, in which Cybele is designated as Mên's mother (*tekousa*). This designation is especially unusual because Cybele is usually associated with a young consort, such as Attis. Lane remarks that this mother-son relationship "has striking parallelism to Christianity, which Mên-cult was competing with,"[73] but he goes no further.

The second sculpture is a small marble statuette, 6 inches high, which Ramsay may have found at the so-called small temple in the sanctuary of Mên at Antioch (fig. 8.16).[74] Ramsay takes the statue to be Cybele, while Anderson regards it as Artemis-Hekate. The triple form certainly suggests an identification with Hekate. In the six hands of the sculpture, Ramsay identifies hawks, which cannot be confirmed from the published images available. In any event, there is a compelling comparison for this association between Mên and Hekate, namely a marble funerary stele found either at Cottiaeum or Thessaloniki, which depicts Mên alongside a triple Hekate, both identified on the basis of iconography alone (fig. 8.17). Mên's association with other divinities does not stop here.[75] His capacity to be coupled with other "Anatolian" and "Greek" deities made the cult more flexible and accommodating to the heterogeneous community that participated in it.

---

[70] To my knowledge Anderson (1913) is the only one to have published an image of the sculpture, although Ramsay discussed it in an article published the year before.

[71] Ramsay 1911–1912, 56.

[72] See Lane 1971, 49, no. 75, where Mên is associated with Demeter in mysteries. Also, Lane 1975, 46, Silandus 3 is a coin depicting Mên and Demeter, the latter identified by grain and poppies.

[73] Lane 1976, 81.

[74] Ramsay (1911–1912, 59) says the statuette was found at a temple of Artemis Cybele at Antioch. It is not clear which temple he meant by this, but the only other known temple at the sanctuary besides the main structure to Mên is a temple just to the northeast.

[75] See Lane 1976, 81–98 for a full discussion.

Fig. 8.16. Marble statue of Hekate. After Anderson 1913, figs. 56 and 57.

Future Directions

This chapter has focused on the literary, epigraphic, numismatic, and sculptural evidence for the cult of Mên at Antioch. I have suggested that this local cult, although belonging to a broader discourse on temple-states, also ought to be considered on its own terms. I have further suggested that at Antioch we can give nuance to our traditional understanding of the importance of these temple-states by moving beyond their economic instrumentality to recognize the propagandistic and ideological benefits that this particular sanctuary of Mên offered. The cult was geographically widespread, easily engaged alongside other deities, and perhaps bore Italian connotations. The evidence for individual and group identifications in the context of ritual practice at the sanctuary in the Roman imperial period also adds a new dimension to our thinking on the former temple-state as a realm of social experiences and not only a factor in the calculations of high politics.

I have given little attention to the archaeological remains. Insufficient archaeological investigations at the sanctuary and its destruction in antiquity have limited material approaches to its interpretation. This state of affairs has made it difficult to consider the wider experience of the sanctuary as a place where dedicatory inscriptions were only one instantiation of a process of spiritual and social ritual. It is clear from Mitchell and Waelkens's (1998) discussion of the sanctuary that the temples

Fig. 8.17. Funerary stele with Mên and Hekate. Istanbul Archaeological Museum. After Lane 1971, pl. XLIII. By permission of the museum.

and *temenos* have received the most archaeological attention (see also Raff, chapter 7, this volume). It is at the theater/odeion and the subsidiary multi-room and single-room buildings, however, where further excavation could perhaps be most fruitful in shedding light on the experience of ritual practice at the sanctuary (see fig. 7.1). Excavation of the theater/odeion could further inform patterns of use at the sanctuary as a whole and the spatial relationships between this and other structures, which conditioned the experience of the sanctuary. Indeed, Raff's analysis of these structures in this volume leads to a fuller picture of the activities that may have occurred at this sanctuary, which appear to be comparable to those that took place at other sanctuaries in the Greek world.

Moreover, the remaining structures of the sanctuary—five larger multi-room buildings and thirteen smaller single-room ones—might, if excavated, also clarify patterns of use, practice, and perhaps group identification.[76] Mitchell and Waelkens have already suggested that the larger, more complex buildings may have served "the needs of organizations and associations connected with the

[76] In 1912, Ramsay excavated [MB] house 3, located southwest of the *temenos*. He termed it the Hall of Initiation (see Raff, chap. 7, this volume). On the finds from the excavation he comments: "[T]hose which we excavated were not thought by the officials worthy of transport to Constantinople, but were left in the cellar of the government house at Yalowadj" (Ramsay 1911–1912, 39). He goes on to say that the pottery that was found was reburied since it was all "valueless." Ramsay offered his "conclusive" conviction that the initiatory rites that took place here were those of the "Phrygian Mysteries and not special Mysteries of the god Men" (Ramsay 1911–1912, 43). Ramsay's discussion of this house is unreliable and his probable discarding of ceramics deeply problematic for any future investigation of the site.

cult of Men."[77] The smaller structures, which probably housed small groups of worshippers who spent longer periods at the sanctuary, may also reveal forms of group identity and the production of social differences. Some of these buildings seem to have been venues for the celebration of cult meals and banquets, or they could have been treasuries and embassies of families and neighboring cities.[78] The fact that some of the larger buildings located close to the theater/odeion seem to have had multiple building phases, while others do not, suggests that the excavation of these buildings might permit a diachronic understanding of the use of the sanctuary and perhaps offer some archaeological indication of a pre-Roman presence at the site. In short, Lane's invocation still holds today: "The site is crying out for an adequate and responsible archaeological reexamination."[79]

[77] Mitchell and Waelkens 1998, 73.   [79] Lane 1976, 58.

[78] Mitchell and Waelkens 1998, 73; Raff, chap. 7, this volume.

9

Rebuilding Pisidian Antioch: A Virtual Model and a New Mode of Research and Exhibition

J. Matthew Harrington

After the Michigan expedition to Pisidian Antioch in 1924, Francis W. Kelsey brought back to Ann Arbor only a small number of artifacts. Individually, these items project little of the quality that is sometimes termed "aura" in the field of Museum Studies. Even the fragment of the inscription of the *Res Gestae Divi Augusti* (the official autobiography of the emperor Augustus) that now resides in the Kelsey may seem obscure and insignificant to all but the specialist. Rather than depend on the Kelsey's limited array of fragmentary artifacts to mount an exhibition that would engage specialist and nonspecialist alike, we turned to the 1924 expedition's rich photographic record and the impressive drawings of Frederick J. Woodbridge, the expedition's architect. To these we added thousands of digital images from the on-site study at Antioch that our team conducted in summer 2004 to prepare for the exhibition and this book.[1] When the opportunity later arose to work with Dr. Klaus-Peter Beier at the University of Michigan's 3-D Laboratory (UM3D) in the Duderstadt Digital Media Commons, we realized that our photographic documentation of the site, combined with the 1924 photographic archive, could serve as a basis for a virtual rendition of Antioch and its monuments.

To begin the digital reconstruction process, we compared our photographs of the site taken in 2004, from multiple points of view, with prior plans and reconstructions by Woodbridge and others. Where a given feature was parallel with the film plane, we were able to take some proportions directly from the images. Then, in summer 2005, we went through initial training on the use of the 3-D Studio Max® program. That fall Adrian Ossi, Benjamin Rubin, and I participated in Engineering 477: Principles of Virtual Reality, taught by Dr. Beier. Although by early fall we had completed research on the six monuments of Antioch that we intended to reconstruct, it took until early November for us to acquire the skill-set required to complete the virtual models.

I completed the first of these reconstructions, the Church of St. Paul, based on research done by Lydia Herring-Harrington. This first effort consumed more than fifty hours of machine time. Digital images from the site were a constant resource during this process. Excluding the terracotta tiles of the roof, all of the textures mapped across the geometry of the church were taken from images of the actual materials on site. In fact, the completed model of the city and its surroundings (even the sky and the vegetation on the hills) uses nothing but digital images from our 2004 expedition.

Next, Adrian Ossi modeled the city gate complex while Ben Rubin worked on the temple of Augustus and the propylon from the sanctuary of the imperial cult, both using their own research data. Meanwhile, I modeled the theater complex, based on research by Hima Mallampati and Ünal Demirer. The semicircular seating area was easily reconstructed due to the repetitive nature of its

[1] Our work with the UM3D Lab was supported by a grant from the Summer Collaborative Research Program of the Horace H. Rackham School of Graduate Studies and the Institute for the Humanties. Thanks are also due to J. W. Humphrey, T. Smekalova, S. Smekalov, R. Bagnall, and Ü. Demirer for sharing their research on the city plan.

Fig. 9.1. Imperial cult sanctuary within the
topographic model of Antioch, as rendered
by the 3-D printer. Photo: J. M. Harrington.

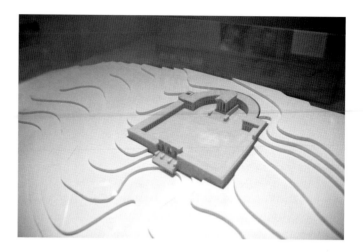

design; all the remaining elements, however, took much longer to integrate. Problems in the published measurements and prior reconstructions became glaring as the 3-D model took shape. It became clear, for example, that the seating area could not have extended across the main east-west street, as previously surmised, once we established how tall such a structure would have to have stood, since supports of the type required for the vaulted substructures of such a theater were not in evidence on either side of the cavea.[2]

With our digital reconstructions of the individual monuments completed, we turned our attention to the 3-D printing of each of the city's six monuments. The 3-D printers used for these models spray glue from a mechanism like an inkjet printer onto a fine powder, building up a 3-D model layer by layer, over the course of several hours. Brett Lyons, at the UM3D Lab, performed the printing and final preparation of the 3-D prints, as well as advising us on the parameters of the technology and the preparation of the 3-D file format required by the printer. In anticipation of their use within a tangible topographic model built by Adrian Ossi with foam-core board to represent the contour lines of the site, the scale of the 3-D prints was set to match the scale thickness of the board: 1:507 (fig. 9.1). The 3-D printing required us to adjust our digital models somewhat: to ensure the structural integrity of printed features at such a small scale, it was necessary to thicken roofs and columns and eliminate the slightest invisible—but structurally damaging to a print—gaps between architectural elements in the 3-D models.

As each of the individual monuments was modeled and refined, work began on a virtual reconstruction of the urban area and its surrounding topography. In all, the global model of Antioch with its topography went through eighty-seven versions, which were archived to prevent a catastrophic mistake from ruining the work of many hours. Invaluable during this process was the new site plan of Antioch researched and created by Adrian Ossi, which combined all of the archaeological information available to us in 2005. This plan made it possible to take scaled measurements and angles directly from a single source. Making use of this resource, the source file of each monument was digitally merged into the global model of the site and moved into its correct orientation and position. Of all the monuments, only the aqueduct was modeled as part of the global model of the city, as its construction was intimately tied to the topography north of the city. With the topography, walls,

---

[2] Using a measure of 0.3 m rise and 0.75 m run per row of seating, the difference in elevation between the orchestra and the top row of seating would have been approximately 13 m, with a minimum radius from the orchestra to the far edge of the *decumanus* of ca. 35 m and allowing for a *diazoma* of 3 m. See Mallampati and Demirer, chap. 4, this volume.

aqueduct, and several monuments in place, it became possible to fill in the unexcavated urban space of Antioch with imagined, but representative, streets, houses, apartment blocks, a few temples, and one public restroom, in order to give a vivid impression of the city as a functioning whole within which the monuments served as landmarks.[3]

Midway through the process of combining the monument models and filling in the city with representative structures, the Antioch model became so complex that every attempt to go further resulted in a complete system crash. An expansion of the RAM for the computer solved the immediate problem, but the issue of the model's complexity and its consequent demands on the various computer systems remained a primary concern. Before extensive efforts at optimization were undertaken, the city model approached 1.5 million polygons. Even after the number of polygons was reduced to less than a million, the final city model remained massive in relation to the computing resources available in 2005.

The final element to be integrated into the global model was the sanctuary of the Anatolian god Mên Askaênos, located 3.5 km (as the crow flies) east of Antioch on the hill of Kara Kuyu. Adrian Ossi finished the temple of Mên and its precinct wall, while I added the buttresses and steps to the exterior of the precinct wall and some of the other structures on the site, according to the specifications of Katharine Raff.[4] This addition of the sanctuary to the model required the expansion of the virtual world within which Antioch was placed, giving an amplified sense of the city within its surroundings, which was conveyed to visitors to the exhibition in the movie fly-out to the sanctuary of Mên or the flight along the path of the aqueduct.

In scale, the final version of Virtual Antioch is a disk 6 km in diameter, with over 420 m of vertical relief. The world could be no smaller and still include Antioch, the portion of its aqueduct that is visible from the city, and the hill of Kara Kuyu with the temple of Mên Askaênos. An overarching sphere has an image of the bright July sky of Antioch mapped across its interior surface. Due to the issues of lighting a virtual world, we used three lights in the sky of Antioch to counterbalance one another and eliminate excessive shadows.

From this final global file containing the model data it was possible to create both fly-over movies and the interactive reconstruction in the CAVE (Cave Automatic Virtual Environment) facility of the UM3D Lab. The high-resolution fly-over movie for presentation in a specially constructed three-panel theater in the exhibition gallery was composed from two sources. The discrete segments centered on each individual monument required three days to produce on desktop computers, while the long fly-out/over/around/in of the city was produced using a set of more than thirty linked computers (a render farm) at the UM3D Lab, with assistance from Scott Hamm. The CAVE mode of presentation allows viewers to immerse themselves in a full-scale (1:1) 3-D model of Antioch. Visitors wore specialized goggles that electronically blocked vision to alternate eyes in sync with the projection. In practice, the experience was so immersive that it was necessary to moderate the apparent speed at which we took visitors through the model in order to avoid motion sickness. Eric Maslowski, Scott Hamm, and Lars Schumann further optimized Virtual Antioch for the CAVE, and they set up the facility for each demonstration. We continued to refine the entire city model so that it would operate as smoothly as possible within the CAVE's six linked computers until two days before the

---

[3] For a discussion of the role of programmatic monuments within an urban fabric, see Favro 1996, 217 ff. The *latrina* (latrine) was placed in the model as an Easter egg, i.e., an inside joke for users of a program with the knowledge of how to discover the "egg."

[4] This model is not yet complete. A number of the single- and multi-room buildings will be added in future work on the model. See the plan by Ossi and Raff, chap. 7, this volume for these additional structures.

exhibition opened; it was crucial to maintain a sufficient frame rate in the CAVE simulation, again, to avoid motion sickness. Virtual Antioch could not functionally have grown more complex than it was at the time of the opening of the exhibition, given the available technology, nor could the digital model of the city and its monuments be further refined without the incorporation of additional data from a new series of excavations or site study. The UM3D Lab retains a copy of Antioch for future demonstrations in the CAVE, while the Kelsey Museum retains all of the source files and 3-D renders created for the exhibition and this book.

The online version of "Building a New Rome" contains 2,735 files, including the entire content of the exhibition as it was installed in the Duderstadt Gallery, as well as a significant number of additional images and movies. In my view, the fade-in movies—in which a reconstruction fades into an image of the remains of a monument—best represent the bridging of the gap between archaeologist and nonspecialist. In the course of 15 seconds, these fade-ins show the fragmentary remains of the buildings that are still on site being transformed into a reconstruction of the complete monument, allowing the viewer to see the alignment of the semi-transparent reconstruction with the on-site remains.

The positive response to the various forms of our virtual reconstruction of Antioch, especially from nonspecialists, has been highly encouraging. While the more immersive experience of Virtual Antioch, like the drawings of Woodbridge or other forms of scholarly reconstruction, relies on conjecture to a greater or lesser degree, I believe that this technology allows archaeologists to transmit their highly elaborated conception of sites and artifacts to those who do not have years of specialist training. In concert with the artifacts, images, and text, this mode of presentation allows the nonspecialist and the student to make a quantum leap upward in their comprehension of the links between fragmentary artifacts and their original ancient contexts.

By 2007, the rapid advance of computing equipment often called "Moore's Law" had allowed even a powerful laptop computer with an independent graphics card to open a global file and render images more quickly than the desktop workstations of 2005.[5] In late 2010, the speed of the software and hardware available have made verisimilitude, even photorealistic rendering, more readily accessible to those without the resources of major film studios. The questions related to the use of virtual reality as a tool of scholarship and communication have similarly become more acute. I would argue that 3-D modeling should in both concept and practice be more than illustration. The Roman poet Horace was correct when he opined: "The poet, who mingles the useful with the sweet, carries off every vote / by delighting his reader just as much as by advising him."[6] To be effective as a means of persuasion and education, 3-D or any other type of representation must capture the imagination as much as it directs it. Nevertheless, from the perspective of peer-reviewed scholarship, the argumentative aspect of the image should not be elided.

While rendering effects like depth-of-field, advanced lighting, or elaborate texture maps can increase the visual impact of an image, they may also obscure the argumentative point of the image by making portions of the image, in effect, out of focus and by distracting the viewer from the visual argument presented by the image. In my view, verisimilitude should not be an end in itself but should exist in dialogue with other communicative goals: 3-D models can subsume all available data, but like all forms of academic argument they must remain open to question. It is in the interest of the academic and museum communities to take steps to educate the viewer to read the images critically, as

[5] In 1965, Gordon Moore postulated that innovation would enable the amount of transistors that could be produced within a given area to double about every two years (Moore 1965, 115).

[6] Horace, *Ars Poetica* 343–344.

arguments. When viewed in this manner and encapsulated in a museum exhibition or in the general publication of an excavation, 3-D modeling is, I suggest, entirely desirable as a means to promote the clarity of textual and other visual arguments. Further, 3-D modeling is a uniquely effective tool for integrating and researching archaeological data and for subsequently reaching the nonspecialist audience in the setting of the museum, the classroom, and online.[7] For Antioch, the process of 3-D visualization proved particularly effective in making the esoteric specialized materials of the original expedition broadly accessible to the exhibition visitors and in advancing new arguments by suggesting research questions and by guiding the recovery of the ancient spatial system within which particular architectural monuments were linked to daily practice.

---

[7] Using these techniques, it has been possible for me to combine the documentation of the preserved architectural elements of the Sanctuary of the Great Gods on Samothrace with a new topographic survey of the site and its in situ stones to produce both a new plan of the sanctuary and a 3-D research tool with which to investigate the use of space within the site: http://www.samothrace.emory.edu/.

Appendix:
Archives Related to University of Michigan
Research on Pisidian Antioch

In their fundamental book on the archaeology of Pisidian Antioch (1998), Stephen Mitchell and Marc Waelkens include an appendix entitled "Papers and Archival Material Relating to Epigraphical and Archaeological Work at Pisidian Antioch," which contains a list of archives related to the 1924 expedition to Antioch that were known to them at that time. That appendix was compiled by Steven Mitchell and Maurice Byrne, and we are grateful for their permission to reproduce information they published and to expand it to include further documents that have come to our attention during the past several years.

Mitchell and Byrne's appendix 2 listed much of the archival material held in the Kelsey Museum of Archaeology and Bentley Historical Library at the University of Michigan in Ann Arbor and also briefly noted the contents of the collection of field notebooks and architectural drawings, mainly the work of Frederick J. Woodbridge, which at that time was at the American Academy in Rome. That collection was transferred by the Trustees of the American Academy to the Kelsey Museum in 2005, and we include a fuller description of its contents here. We also include lists of materials relevant to the Michigan expedition of 1924 found in the David M. Robinson Collection and Papers at the University of Mississippi in Oxford, Mississippi, and in the Frederick J. Woodbridge Papers at Columbia University in New York. In addition, we list artifacts from Antioch in the Kelsey Museum and in the University Museum in Mississippi.

Following the format devised by Mitchell and Byrne, the contents of the present appendix are organized by collection as follows:

I. Kelsey Museum of Archaeology, University of Michigan (with new sections prepared by Adrian J. Ossi, Benjamin Rubin, Elaine Gazda, and Gavin Strassel)
II. Bentley Historical Library, University of Michigan (with information added by Elaine Gazda)
III. David M. Robinson Collection in the Archives and Special Collections of the J. D. Williams Library, University of Mississippi, Oxford, Mississippi (prepared by Adrian J. Ossi)
IV. David M. Robinson Collection in the University Museum, University of Mississippi (prepared by Adrian J. Ossi)
V. Frederick J. Woodbridge Architectural Records and Papers in the Avery Architectural and Fine Arts Library, Columbia University, New York (prepared by Adrian J. Ossi)
VI. Ashmolean Library, Oxford, England
VII. Public Library, Belediye or Museum of Yalvaç
VIII. British Institute of Archaeology, Ankara
IX. Institute of Advanced Study, Princeton, New Jersey

On the Kelsey Museum Web site is a visual archive of the exhibition of the same title as this book, which was on display in Ann Arbor in January and February of 2006. The 3-D model and movie of the city and sanctuary of Mên prepared in conjunction with the exhibition is available online at http://www.lsa.umich.edu/Kelsey/antioch. The movie is also included in DVD format at the back of this book.

I. At the Kelsey Museum of Archaeology, University of Michigan, Ann Arbor

A. <u>Professional photographs taken by George R. Swain</u> and his "Index of all negatives made . . . during the season of 1924" (title page and pp. 1–46), which includes a short caption to each negative. The index does not include his Kodak photographs (see I B 3).
Negatives were made on American standard glass plates of the following sizes: 5" × 7", 7" × 11" and 8" × 10", using cameras with lenses of up to 28× focal length. The negatives are referred to by their smaller dimension. The relevant exposures are: 5.1 to 5.294, of which 5.1 to 5.94 were taken at Sizma by Easton T. Kelsey, 7.1106 to 7.1692, and 8.1 to 8.106. Panoramic views were also taken on a Cirkut camera: C.50 to C.66. There are fuller captions for all these, but not all the prints survive.

B. <u>Captions and prints (4" × 3") from Kodak film</u> of up to twelve exposures. These are of poorer quality.
  1. D. M. Robinson. Captions and prints from 110 rolls (ref. KR)
  2. E. E. Peterson. Captions only (no prints) from 29 rolls (ref. KP)
  3. G. R. Swain. Captions and prints from 14 rolls (ref. KS)

C. <u>A collection of digital images of Antioch and several other sites in Turkey</u>, taken in 2004 by the authors of this book.

D. <u>Correspondence, additional photographs, and publication reprints</u>
  Box 1
    1.1. Photographs of sculptures by Thomas Callander (1913) and duplicate prints by George Swain (1924)
    1.2. Composite of 6 photos of the *Res Gestae* of Augustus prepared by D. M. Robinson
    1.3. Enoch E. Peterson, Photographic Logs, 1924
    1.4. Frederick J. Woodbridge field notes and sketches:
      Thirteen 3 × 5 index cards with field notes and sketches from Antioch of Pisidia by Woodbridge
    1.5. Correspondence of 1924:
      Arthur Evans to Sir William Ramsay (9/20/1924); D. G. Hogarth to Professor Kelsey (10/21/1924); Francis Kelsey to Professor John G. Winter (12/9/1924); W. M. Ramsay to Professor Kelsey (10/19/1924)
    1.6. Publications, *Michigan Alumnus*, 1925 (5 articles by Francis W. Kelsey). Originals and photocopies
    1.7. Reprints of articles by David M. Robinson on Antioch, Sizma, and Apamea
    1.8. Correspondence, 1965–1984:
      Stephen Mitchell to Pamela Reister, registrar; Letters between Stephen Mitchell and John Griffiths Pedley (4/10/1984)
    1.9 Correspondence and publications of Mehmet Taşlıalan, 1990–1991:
      Letters between director John G. Pedley and Mehmet Taşlıalan from 1988, 1991; Robin

Meador-Woodruff to Dr. Mehmet Taşhalan (5/20/1991);
Three snapshots of excavations of imperial cult temple (temple of Augustus), 1990, taken by Mehmet Taşhalan; *The Journeys of St. Paul at Antioch of Pisidia*, by Mehmet Talslialan, Ankara, 1990 (booklet); *Pisidian Antioch: The Journeys of St. Paul to Antioch*, Dr. Mehmet Taşhalan (photocopy)
Box 2: 85 paper squeezes of Greek and Latin inscriptions including masons' marks

E. Materials transferred in 2005 to the Kelsey Museum from the American Academy in Rome
The architect F. J. Woodbridge was a visiting student at the American Academy in Rome in 1923–1925, and in 1971 he returned as a visiting scholar in order to finish his architectural drawings of Antioch.[1] The archives were rediscovered by Marc Waelkens in 1984. At that time they were in a hanging metal file folder in a filing cabinet in the Archaeology Suite of the Academy. The list below is organized according to the building or urban space depicted in the drawing. The subheadings employ the names of structures used in this volume along with older or alternative names in parentheses:
- 1–26: Imperial Cult Sanctuary (Augusta Platea) and Imperial Cult Temple (Augusteum; Temple of Augustus)
- 27–30: Tiberia Platea
- 31–50: Arch of Augustus (propylaea; propylon)
- 51–56: Arch of Hadrian and Sabina (city gate)
- 57–67: Molding Profiles (various buildings)
- 68–70: Miscellaneous Plans
- 71–73: Architectural Field Notebooks

Drawings are numbered continuously; the inventory number given by the American Academy in Rome (AAR) is also listed.[2]

Imperial Cult Sanctuary and Temple
1. Final restored plan of imperial cult sanctuary and Tiberia Platea. Blueprint. Undated. (AAR 2444)
2. Copy of #1. On transparency. (AAR 2420)
3. Copy of #1, in reverse. On paper. (AAR 2445)
4. Copy of #1. On paper. (From KM archives; no AAR number)
5. Plan of imperial cult temple. Pencil on paper, original. Possible 1924 field drawing. (AAR 2402)
6. Plan of imperial cult temple and hemicycle, with doodles of male and female portraits. Pencil on paper, original. Possible 1924 field drawing. (AAR 2403)
7. Plan of imperial cult temple and hemicycle, with temple oriented incorrectly. Pencil on paper, original. Possible 1924 field drawing. (AAR 2408)
8. Plan of imperial cult temple and hemicycle. Pencil on tranparency, original. Likely working drawing for final plan and elevation, ca. 1971. (AAR 2382)

[1] See Ossi 2005/2006 for a detailed discussion of Woodbridge's work on Antioch.

[2] The materials were inventoried and assigned AAR numbers in 2003 by Christine Murray with the support of the Weissman International Program under the supervision of Archer Martin.

9. Illustration of angle of divergence between the axes of the imperial cult sanctuary and the Tiberia Platea. Pencil on transparency, original. Undated. (AAR 2441)

10. Similar to #8. Pencil on paper, original. Possible 1924 field drawing. (AAR 2406)

11. Elevation of imperial cult temple, conjectural restoration. Oil pencil (?) on paper, original. Published in Robinson 1926. (AAR 2446)

12. 2-sided. Side 1: elevation of pediment of imperial cult temple. Side 2: section through pediment of imperial cult temple, including molding profiles of sima and window frame. Both sides: pencil on paper, original. Possible 1924 field drawings. (AAR 2442)

13. Study for elevation of imperial cult temple. Pencil on tranparency, original. Undated. (AAR 2410)

14. Copy of #12. (AAR 2443)

15. Study for elevation of imperial cult temple and hemicycle. Ink on transparency, original. Dated March 1, 1971. (AAR 2383)

16. Copy of #15. (AAR 2434)

17. Copy of #15. (AAR 2433)

18. Copy of #15. (From KM archives; no AAR number)

19. Study for elevation of roof tiles of hemicycle; includes a plan of the hemicycle roof. Pencil on transparency, original. Likely 1971-era working drawing. (AAR 2392)

20. Final restoration drawing of elevation of imperial cult temple and hemicycle. Ink on transparency, original. Dated August 7, 1971. (AAR 2385)

21. Copy of #19. Paper is turning pink. (AAR 2450)

22. Copy of #19. Paper is turning pink. (AAR 2429)

23. Elevation of stone facing at rear of hemicycle, 1:10 scale. Pencil on paper, original. Possible 1924 field drawing. (AAR 2404)

24. Plan of the fluting of one column from hemicycle. Pencil on transparency, original. Possible 1924 field drawing. (AAR 2426)

25. Plan of block with engaged column; building attribution uncertain. Pencil on transparency, original. Possible 1924 field drawing. (AAR 2419)

26. Section through imperial cult sanctuary, approx. west-east, looking north. Pencil on transparency, original. Possible 1924 field drawing. (AAR 2418)

27. Similar to 25, section through imperial cult sanctuary, looking north. Pencil on paper, original. Possible 1924 field drawing. (AAR 2425)

Tiberia Platea

28. Sketch of east-west section through Tiberia Platea, staircase, and imperial cult sanctuary. Pencil on paper, original. Possible 1924 field drawing. (no AAR number)

29. Sketch of east-west section through Tiberia Platea; includes location of *tholos*, does not include staircase. Pencil on transparency, original. Possible 1924 field drawing. (AAR 2417)

30. Plan of unknown series of blocks, possibly Tiberia Platea; includes measurements. Pencil on paper, original. Possible 1924 field drawing. (AAR 2407)

31. Plan of Tiberia Platea. Pencil on paper, original. Likely 1924 field drawing. (AAR 2415)

Arch of Augustus

32. Plan of Arch of Augustus, working drawing for #35. Pencil on transparency, original. Undated. (AAR 2391)

33. Plan of Arch of Augustus, working drawing for #35. Pencil on paper, original. Undated, possibly 1971 era. (AAR 2413)

34. Section through Arch of Augustus in profile. Pencil on paper, original. Undated, possibly 1971 era. (AAR 2414)

35. Combined plan and section of Arch of Augustus, final version. Pencil on transparency, original. Dated July 27, 1971. (AAR 2384)

36. Copy of #34. (AAR 2432)

37. Elevation of Arch of Augustus. Oil pencil (?) on paper, original. Published in Robinson 1926. (AAR 2447)

38. Elevation of Arch of Augustus, final version. Pencil on transparency, original. Dated July 27, 1971. (AAR 2386)

39. Copy of #37. (AAR 2431)

40. Elevation of Arch of Augustus, possible working drawing for #37. Pencil on paper, original. Possible 1971 era. (AAR 2437)

41. Elevation of Arch of Augustus, possible working drawing for #37. Pencil on paper, original. Possible 1971 era. (AAR 2381)

42. Similar to #39 and 40, includes partial plan and elevation of staircase. Pencil on transparency, original. Possible 1971 era. (AAR 2388)

43. Similar to #39 and 40, apparently a reworking of the columns and their bases. Pencil on transparency, original. Possible 1971 era. (AAR 2389)

44. Simlar to #39 and 40, though very schematic and apparently unfinished. Pencil on transparency, original. Possible 1971 era. (AAR 2390)

45. Partial elevation of Arch of Augustus, possibly a tracing of #36. Pencil on transparency, original. Undated. (AAR 2427)

46. Copy of #44. (AAR 2435)

47. Study for elevation of colonnades flanking Arch of Augustus. Pencil on transparency, original. Likely 1971-era working drawing. (AAR 2440)

48. Architrave with words "The Arch of Augustus." Pencil on transparency, original. Undated. (no AAR number)

49. Detail drawings of weapons frieze blocks. Pencil on transparency, original. Undated. (AAR 2439)

50. Similar to #47, drawings of weapons frieze blocks; with reconstructed inscription from architrave of Arch of Augustus. Pencil on transparency, original. Undated. (AAR 2438)

51. Detail of arch voussoir; diagram of radius of archway; and voussoir profile. Pencil on transparency, original. Undated. (AAR 2416)

52. Large-scale plan of engaged column from Arch of Augustus; and measured, detailed drawing of springer block. Pencil on transparency, original. Undated. (AAR 2412)

Arch of Hadrian and Sabina

53. Conjectural restoration of elevation of Arch of Hadrian and Sabina and environs, including fountain just north of central passage. Charcoal or oil pencil (?) on paper, original. Published in Robinson 1926. (AAR 2448)

54. Preliminary study for elevation of Arch of Hadrian and Sabina, restored as a single-bayed arch. Pencil on transparency, original. Likely 1924 era. (AAR 2409)

55. Copy of #54. (AAR 2436)

56. Final reconstructed elevation of Arch of Hadrian and Sabina. Ink and wash on paper, original. Published 1926. (AAR 2421)
57. Final restored plan of Arch of Hadrian and Sabina and fountain to the north. Ink on paper, original. Undated. (AAR 2424)
58. Sketch plan of Arch of Hadrian and Sabina and fountain. Pencil on paper, original. Possible 1924 field drawing. (AAR 2423)

Molding Profiles (various buildings)

59. Drawing of a series of profiles from various monuments, aesthetically arranged. Ink on paper, original. Likely 1924-era drawing. (AAR 2422)
60. Profile of pilaster base from imperial cult temple, possible tracing of #59, side 2. Pencil on transparency, original. Undated. (AAR 2428)
61. 2-sided. Side 1: profile drawing of "corona and cymatium cornice of temple," 1:1 scale. Side 2: profile of base of temple, 1:1 scale. Both sides oil pencil on paper, original. Possible 1924 field drawings. (AAR 2401)
62. 2-sided. Side 1: profile of architrave of arch (unspecified), 1:1 scale. Side 2: profile of cornice of Arch of Augustus, 1:1 scale. Both sides oil pencil on paper, original. Possible 1924 field drawings. (AAR 2400)
63. 2-sided. Side 1: profile of molding at top of pier of arch (unspecified), 1:1 scale. Side 2: three profiles, (1) pedestal cornice of Arch of Augustus, (2) molding of seat around *tholos*, (3) bench molding of imperial cult temple cella; no scale given. Both sides oil pencil on paper, original. Possible 1924 field drawings. (AAR 2399)
64. 2-sided. Side 1: 2 profiles, (1) frieze of imperial cult temple and garland, (2) bed mold of temple cornice; no scale given. Side 2: profile of Doric capital of hemicycle, 1:1 scale; and plan of Doric column near capital, 1:4 scale. Both sides oil pencil on paper, original. Possible 1924 field drawings. (AAR 2398)
65. 2-sided. Side 1: profile of base of pedestals in front of Arch of Augustus, 1:1 scale. Side 2: moldings on large block in front of chamber south of Arch of Augustus; no scale given, likely 1:1. Both sides oil pencil on paper, original. Possible 1924 field drawings. (AAR 2397)
66. 2-sided. Side 1: profile of architrave of imperial cult temple, no scale given, likely 1:1. Side 2: profile of frame of window in tympanum (pediment) of temple, no scale given, likely 1:1. Both sides oil pencil on paper, original. Possible 1924 field drawings. (AAR 2396)
67. Possible tracing of #62, side 2 (profile of Doric capital of hemicycle). Pencil on transparency, original. Undated. (AAR 2396)
68. Possible tracing of #62, side 1 (bed mold of temple cornice). Pencil on transparency, original. Undated. (AAR 2393)
69. Tracing of unknown profile. Pencil on transparency, original. Undated. (AAR 2394)

Miscellaneous Plans

70. Plan of central church (also known as the Byzantine church). Ink on paper, original. Undated. (AAR 2411)
71. Plan of unknown blocks, possibly from Tiberia Platea. Pencil on paper, original. Possible 1924 field drawing. (AAR 2405)
72. Sketch plan of Pisidian Antioch. Pencil and ink on paper, original. Possible 1924 field drawing. (AAR 2387)

Architectural Field Notebooks

73. Notebook AAR 2378, titled "Architecture." The architecture inventory notebook, written by Enoch E. Peterson, was discontinued upon the arrival of the excavation architect. The inventory contains verbal descriptions of ca. 165 fragments, accompanied by measurements. The fragments were uncovered during the excavation of the Arch of Augustus and the imperial cult temple. Each fragment is given a category code and a unique number. Eight categories are listed on the final page: seats, voussoirs, cornices, columns, capitals, pilasters, architraves, and miscellaneous (undetermined). About 120 of the entries have a sketch of the block in plan or in section. In practice, many of these sketch drawings are of minor value, especially if the block in question is missing or cannot be identified today. Several blocks have multiple explanatory drawings, and these are more helpful. The photographs in the Kelsey Museum Archives show that in 1924 the inventory number was painted directly onto each block, so sometimes an inventory entry can be matched with a photograph of the corresponding block. The photography, however, was not comprehensive. Pages in the inventory are not numbered.

74. Notebook AAR 2380, titled "Antioch of Pisidia, Measured details of the City Gate, Temple of Augustus & Stoa, and the Propylaea (Arch of Tiberius) by Frederick J. Woodbridge." Contains measured plans, elevations, sections, and profiles of architectural and decorative blocks. Twenty pages are devoted to the Arch of Hadrian and Sabina and 21 to the imperial cult temple. Other structures also represented (see breakdown below). Pages are hand numbered, and many list the 1924-era name of the monument depicted.

- Arch of Hadrian and Sabina (referred to by Woodbridge as "City Gate," "Triumphal Arch" or "Arch"), pp. 1–18, 24–25 (20 total pages). Primarily elevations of architectural elements and figured blocks.
- Monumental aqueduct, pp. 19, 21 (2 pages). "Typical bays" in elevation, plan, and section; *specus* in section.
- Church of St. Paul (referred to by Woodbridge as the "Basilica"), p. 23 (1 page). Architrave and column base.
- Imperial cult temple (referred to by Woodbridge as the "Augusteum"), pp. 30–35, 37–39, 41, 43, 45–47, 52–58 (21 pages). Primarily elevations of architectural elements and decorated blocks.
- Hemicycle colonnade (referred to as the "semicircular stoa"), p. 60? (1 page). Frieze and column details.
- Rubbing (of a mason's mark?), pp. 49, 51 (2 pages). The same rubbing made with different crayons. Possibly from imperial cult temple, considering the subject of drawings on the surrounding pages.
- Arch of Augustus (referred to by Woodbridge as the "Propylaea"), pp. 67–72 (6 pages). Plans and elevations of architectural elements.
- *Tholos*, p. 73 (1 page). Section of seat and its claw foot.
- Elevation and profile of unknown wall with upper molding, p. 75 (1 page). Likely the south wall of the Tiberia Platea.

75. Notebook AAR 2379, titled "Measured Details from Antioch of Pisidia made in the summer of 1924 by Horace Colby and Frederick J. Woodbridge." Contains measured plans, elevations, sections, and profiles of architectural and decorative blocks, as well as drawings of two sculptures. Most pages pertain to the Arch of Augustus (see breakdown below). Pages

are not numbered, and rarely titled. The following totals are given based on Adrian Ossi's identification of fragments on each page and, occasionally, labels on the page.

- Arch of Augustus, 19 pages. Elevations of decorated blocks and plans and elevations of architectural elements.
- Unknown columns and cornices, 3 pages.
- *Tholos*, 2 drawings. Elevation of cornice, top surface of ceiling fragment.
- Unknown fragments, including Byzantine coffered ceiling fragment, 1 page.
- Nike statue, 1 page. Front view.
- Arch of Hadrian and Sabina, 2 pages. Elevations and profiles of architectural and decorative elements.
- Portrait head of Augustus, 2 pages. Restored front and profile views.
- Central church, several loose pages inside back cover. Large-scale plan spanning multiple pages, with accompanying notes.

F. Objects from Pisidian Antioch in the Kelsey Museum
See the Kelsey Museum Web site for a link to images of the objects.

1. Ceramics

3072	Late Helladic III bowl sherd of pinkish buff clay. Found in 1929 by Sir William Ramsay, who gave it to Francis W. Kelsey. Restored by the British Museum in 1924.
93898	Roman or early Christian terra sigillata sherd with relief decoration of fishermen in a boat
93899	Late Roman/Byzantine clay lamp

2. Mosaic fragments

93861–64	Four early Christian mosaic fragments from the 4th-century AD floor mosaic in the Church of St. Paul (basilica). White, black, red, yellow marble tesserae.

3. Votive relief fragments

93868, 93878	Joining fragments of a white marble Roman votive relief
93894, 1966.2.3	Joining fragments of a white marble Roman votive relief with remnants of a Latin inscription. A note in the Kelsey Museum accession book reads: "Fragment of marble dedicatory inscription, a surface find at Antioch of Pisidia, before the excavations on that site by the University of Michigan in the spring of 1924. Sir William Ramsay of Edinburgh, Scotland, declared the fragment to be First Century. Peterson, Enoch E."

4. Fragmentary inscriptions

93880	White marble fragment of a Latin inscription
93881	White marble fragment of a Greek dedicatory inscription
93896	White limestone fragment of the *Res Gestae Divi Augusti*

5. Carved architectural ornaments

93865–7	Three non-joining white marble molding fragments of similar profile

93869	Fragment of a white marble relief with a meander decoration
93870	Fragment of a white marble volute from a Corinthian pilaster capital, probably from the imperial cult temple (temple of Augustus) or the Arch of Hadrian and Sabina (city gate)
93871	White limestone palmette fragment, possibly from an architrave
93872	White marble acanthus leaf fragment
93873, 93876	Joining fragments of a white limestone palmette from the left corner of the architrave of the imperial cult temple (temple of Augustus)
93874–5	Two white limestone rosettes, possibly from a Corinthian capital
93877	White limestone palmette fragment, perhaps from the corner of an architrave
93879	White marble drapery fragment
93892	Gray limestone palmette fragment, possibly from an Ionic capital
93893	Gray limestone egg and dart fragment, from a cornice or Ionic capital
93897	White limestone acanthus fragment
93895	White limestone or marble fragment of a double-sided guilloche

6. Samples of local limestone

| 93882 | White limestone from the imperial cult temple (temple of Augustus) |
| 93883 | Gray limestone from the Tiberia Platea |

7. Fragments of wall veneer or floor pavement

93884	Pavonzetto/Phrygian marble fragment
93885	Portasanta /Chian marble fragment
93886–90	Five pieces of white marble veneer or flooring
93891	Gray and white streaked marble (Proconnesian?) fragment
93901	Porphyry fragment

8. Miscellaneous metal objects

93900	Solidified molten lead, possibly for securing an iron clamp
93902	Bronze tube, possibly part of a letter from a monumental inscription
93903	Encrusted metal (bronze?) circle; flat surfaces with scattered rust stains

9. Plaster cast reproduction

| 4733 | Head of Augustus. Modern plaster reproduction of a marble head found in a Byzantine house near the imperial cult sanctuary. The original is in the Istanbul Archaeological Museum. The cast, including its conjectured nose, was made by the British Museum in 1924. |

II. At the Bentley Historical Library, Ann Arbor, Michigan
There are relevant papers under three classes.

A. <u>Correspondence of F. W. Kelsey. Class mark Aa 2, boxes 1 and 2</u> (see http://bentley.umich.edu/research/guides/anthropology/anthro_search.php?id=14). The correspondence is arranged chronologically with, in many cases, copies of Kelsey's reply. These replies, however, are separated from the letters to which they refer by the time taken for delivery. This arrangement, which has led to the breaking of Kelsey's original filing system by correspondent, is to be regretted.

B. Kelsey Museum Papers, class mark BIMY C450 2 (see http://bentley.umich.edu/research/guides/anthropology/anthro_search.php?id=15). These are arranged under various headings, of which the following are relevant:

1. Institute of Archaeological Research
   This includes in box 4 numbered Memoranda by Kelsey covering the period 20 March 1924 to 30 May 1925. These report to the Chairman (who was also the University President) of the Near Eastern Research Committee on the excavations, the post-excavation work and plans for the future. Box 5 contains correspondence of E. E. Peterson from 1927.

2. E. E. Peterson
   This section is preceded by a useful P/2-page biography of Peterson.
   Box 1: correspondence and an ectopic copy of Kelsey's Memorandum no. 5 (cf. II B 1)

3. Kelsey Museum
   Box 73. A gray file box containing a set of files as follows:
   73.1. Documents containing an application for a permit to excavate at Sizma.
   73.2. Labeled "Cilicia." In fact the contents mainly concern practical arrangements for the 1924 season. They show that Kelsey planned to reapply for a permit in 1925 in his own name to resume the excavation and that he anticipated a season of similar length to the first.
   73.3. Typescript of a report written by George Swain, dated August 12, 1924, giving details for the press of progress up to that date.
   73.4. Index to all the photographs made by Swain during the 1924 season (for the resultant prints see 1 above).
   73.5. Details of photographs printed and sent to various destinations.
   73.6. Two press cuttings on conditions in Turkey.
   73.7. Extract from a letter of July 12, 1926, from the architect F. J. Woodbridge and several drawings made by him:
      a. Original (pencil on transparency) and copy of a sketch plan of the sanctuary of Mên, Kara Kuyu, after E. R. Stoever with revisions by Woodbridge
      b. Original sketch (pencil on transparency: torn) and two copies of a plan of the Augusta and Tiberia Plateae by Woodbridge
      c. Original sketch (pencil on transparency) and copy of Woodbridge's rough sketch of the plan of the city, labeled Antiochia Pisidiae
      d. Two copies of Woodbridge's map of Antioch at close of excavations
   73.8. Press cutting of July 1, 1925, describing Michigan Near East Research, with two maps.
   73.9. A collection of press cuttings from 1924 reporting on the excavations and using many of Swain's photographs.
   73.10. More press cuttings.
   73.11. Typewritten copies of earlier reports on Antioch. A long typewritten memorandum in German from the Austrian traveler von Luschan, "fur eine amerikanische Ausgrabungs-Expedition in Nord-Syrien."
   73.12. A collection of offprints and memoranda concerning Antioch, including notes on Roman coins, a letter of T. Callander to Kelsey on the excavations of 1913 and 1914, a

memorandum on inscriptions, and a memorandum from the veteran Turkish classical archaeologist Macridy Bey, a blueprint of Woodbridge's basilica plan with mosaic details, and a bound copy of the Journal of Excavations.

73.13. Typescript and printed copies of D. M. Robinson's report on the excavation published in *AJA* 1924; a record of sculpture found by Callander in 1913; a second copy of the sculpture inventory (see II.C); two typed transcripts of radio broadcasts about the excavation; offprints from descriptions of the expedition published in *The Michigan Alumnus* by Francis W. Kelsey, "The Second Michigan Expedition to the Near East" (Parts I–V).

73.14. Large file of press cuttings.

73.15. A further file of press cuttings.

C. <u>Papers formerly in the Special Collections of the University of Michigan Library</u>. Class mark and contents unknown except that it includes a copy of the Journal of Excavations with a complete copy of the Architectural Inventory. This was a typescript journal, entitled *University of Michigan Near Eastern Research. Excavations in Asia Minor in 1924. Yalovatch, September 2 1924*. There are three sections with separate pagination: pp. 1–88 Journal of Excavations, Antioch of Pisidia (written by D. M. Robinson, except pp. 55–58, 60, 65, and 67–69 which are by E. E. Peterson); pp. 1–26 Journal of Excavations, Sizma (Robinson); pp. 117 Journal of Excavations, Sculpture Inventory (Robinson).

III. David M. Robinson Collection in the Archives and Special Collections of the J. D. Williams Library, University of Mississippi, Oxford, Mississippi

Materials pertaining to the excavations at Pisidian Antioch in 1924, which was sponsored by the University of Michigan; David M. Robinson was the director of excavations hired by Francis Kelsey. Robinson was teaching at the Johns Hopkins University at the time. Later in his career he moved to Oxford, Mississippi, where he taught in the Department of Classics. Biographical information for Robinson is reported as part of the history of the Department of Classics, which is available at http://classics.olemiss.edu/robinsoncollection/.

A. Box 36. Pisidian Antioch Excavation Notes, inside a folder labeled "Excavation Notes Antioch-Posidian" [*sic*].
Contents: small notebook, ca. 4" × 7", labeled "Yalovach note-book no. 2 Starting from July 17th." Notebook contains a handwritten daily log of excavation, similar to the typed log of excavations currently in the Kelsey Museum Archives in Ann Arbor, Michigan. The typed log book in Michigan might be an edited version of the handwritten notebook in Mississippi. Notebook contains many transcribed ancient inscriptions. Entries start July 17 and continue through to the end of excavations. The last few pages contain bibliographic notes compiled by Robinson.

B. Box 37. Materials for publishing the Pisidian Antioch statue of Victory, inside an old manila envelope labeled "Sardis Photograph of D. M. Robinson . . ."
Contents: manuscript and illustrations collected for Robinson's publication of a statue discovered at Pisidian Antioch in 1924, entitled "A Figure of Victory from Pisidian Antioch." Has some

plates depicting similar statues, possibly torn out of books as comparanda. Also contains an ink sketch of the statue drawn by Mustapha Tourgoud of Yalvaç, the modern town adjacent to the site of Pisidian Antioch.

C. Box 51
- 51.1. Photographs taken by Robinson during the 1924 excavations, in a large black photo album. Contents: Robinson's photographs of the excavations at Pisidian Antioch and at Sizma in 1924, from the beginning of excavations until June 29. There are copies of many of these photographs in the Kelsey Museum Archives, but some of those present in Mississippi are not present in Michigan.
- 51.2. Description of the 1924 excavations at Sizma. Typed manuscript, stored loose (not in a folder). Contents: A discussion of the excavations performed at Sizma in the middle of the summer of 1924 during a break in excavations at Pisidian Antioch. Twenty pages.
- 51.3. Records of the basilica at Pisidian Antioch, in an old manila envelope addressed to "Professor D. M. Robinson, The Hawthorne Inn, Gloucester, Mass." and labeled "basilica" in small letters on the back. Contents: materials pertaining to the basilica church excavated at Pisidian Antioch in 1924. Has a plan of the basilica drawn by architect F. J. Woodbridge on tracing paper (rolled up and pressed flat), and a smaller drawing with details of columns found in the basilica excavations. Also includes 15 large and 3 small photographs, which are stamped on the back with a University of Michigan stamp and inventory number and which probably have copies in the Kelsey Museum Archives.

D. Various boxes. Correspondence concerning the 1924 Pisidian Antioch architectural drawings, in 2 series dated 1941 and 1953.
- 1. 1941 series (Boxes 14a–b and 19): E. K. Rand invites Robinson to speak at a seminar at Dumbarton Oaks in October 1941. Robinson chooses "Transition from Roman to Byzantine at Pisidian Antioch" as his topic. After the seminar, Robinson says he feels that he could "work up three unpublished subjects in that paper, the basilica, the coins, and the magic tablet" (letter dated Nov. 27, 1941). Robinson asks Woodbridge if he has the colored restorations of the mosaics from the basilica, and asks Woodbridge to mail all the architectural records of the basilica to him (letter dated Oct. 14, 1941).
- 2. 1953 series (Boxes 5, 8, and 13): Harald Ingholt (one letter misspells it "Engholt") asks Robinson for copies of the plates of the standard bearers from the city gate at Pisidian Antioch, for use in a publication about Parthian sculptures. Robinson asks Peterson to send copies of the photos to Ingholt and expresses his frustration that he cannot find either the original drawing itself or his original photographs of the drawing (the letter is unclear on this point).

IV. In the David M. Robinson Collection in the University Museum, University of Mississippi
Materials pertaining to Pisidian Antioch:
Three fragments of *Res Gestae Divi Augusti* excavated during the 1924 season. Inv. nos. 1977.3.576 a, b, and c. Published by Robinson in *AJP* 67 (1926) and noted in the collection edited by John P. Bodel and Stephen V. Tracy, *Greek and Latin Inscriptions in the USA: A Checklist* (New York: American Academy in Rome, 1997), 139.

V. Frederick J. Woodbridge Architectural Records and Papers, in the Avery Architectural and Fine Arts Library, Columbia University, New York (http://www.columbia.edu/cu/lweb/archival/collections/ldpd_3460607/)

A. Box 3, folder 12. Contents: copies of drawings of monuments at Pisidian Antioch.

3.12.1. *Tholos* in Tiberia Platea, copy of elevation and plan, ca. 7" × 10". For original drawing, see Box 4, folder 11, item 2. Original drawing (as copied) showed the walls of a circular cella inside the colonnade; Woodbridge edited the copy with a pencil, superimposing a draped statue on a base in place of the cella wall, and later updated the original drawing. In plan, this cella is shown as a solid cylinder, not as a circular room.

3.12.2. Imperial cult temple, copy of rear elevation drawing (for original drawing, see Box 4, folder 11, item 11).

3.12.3. Copy of item 2 above, in negative.

3.12.4. Copy of section and plan of Arch of Augustus, in negative (reduced in scale; original in Kelsey Museum Archives, I.E.35 above). Ca. 10" × 14".

3.12.5. Copy of elevation of Arch of Augustus, in negative (reduced in scale; original in Kelsey Museum Archives, I.E.38 above). Ca. 10" × 14".

3.12.6. Copy of elevation of imperial cult temple, in negative (reduced in scale, original in Kelsey Museum Archives, I.E.20 above). Ca. 10" × 14".

B. Box 4, folder 11. Contents: drawings and copies of drawings of monuments at Pisidian Antioch.

4.11.1. Imperial cult temple, restored elevation of corner akroterion in two scales. In his restored elevation of the temple, this element is seen at the smaller of the two scales. Original drawing, pencil on transparency, ca. 8.5" × 10.5".

4.11.2. *Tholos* in Tiberia Platea, restored elevation and plan, original drawing, pencil on transparency, ca. 11" × 18". The elevation drawing has a statue inside the *tholos* (see comment in entry for copy of this drawing in Box 3, folder 12, item (1).

4.11.3. *Tholos*, measured drawings of details on a single sheet. These drawings are all present in one or other of the notebooks in the Kelsey Museum Archives. Has (a) elevation of cornice with the word "LETTERS" in place of the inscription, (b) plan of roof tile, (c) section of seat, (d) elevation of Ionic capital, (e) drawing of decorated soffit of cornice, (f) elevation of composite capital, (g) elevation of architrave with fragmentary bull's head frieze above.

4.11.4. Arch of Hadrian and Sabina, rough tracing of preliminary elevation of the monument as a single-bayed arch, after and at the same scale as the original in the Kelsey Museum Archvies (I.E.54 above). Pencil on transparency.

4.11.5. Imperial cult temple, partial rear elevation, original, pencil on transparency, ca. 7.5" × 10.5". Possible working drawing for number 4.11.11 below.

4.11.6. Imperial cult temple, rough tracing of details of pediment and sima.

4.11.7. Imperial cult temple, elevation details: (a) corner akroterion, (b) rinceaux block, (c) sketch of Nike statue with restored head and legs, (d) small diagram of uncertain element, perhaps the pedestals on the stairs of the Tiberia Platea.

4.11.8. Imperial cult sanctuary, working drawing for restored plan of porticoes, showing parts of the north, west, and south porticoes (the hemicycle is absent). Working drawing for large restored plan, of which several copies are in the Kelsey Museum Archives (I.E.1–4 above). Later excavation by Mehmet Taşlıalan proved these restorations to be incorrect.

4.11.9. Imperial cult temple, actual state plan in 1924, pencil on transparency, ca. 23" × 16". Scale listed at 1:50. Many measurements are included.

4.11.10.Multiple monuments on a single sheet of heavy paper, ca. 7" × 11". One side has perspective, shaded view of Arch of Hadrian and Sabina as a single-bayed arch. Second side has along the right edge a molding profile labeled "profile of blocks with 'DIV' inscrips," and at left a perspective, shaded view of one restored pier of the Arch of Hadrian and Sabina.

4.11.11. Imperial cult temple, restored rear elevation. Pencil on heavy paper, original drawing. Dated October 14, 1971.

4.11.12. Copy of Antonine *tholos* elevation and plan, with cella wall (cf. discussion under Box 3, folder 12, item 1).

4.11.13. Same as item 12.

4.11.14.Copy of *tholos* elevation and plan, with Wite-Out covering cella wall and a statue sketched over it (cf. description under Box 3, folder 12, item 1).

4.11.15. Copy of reconstructed elevation of the Arch of Hadrian and Sabina as a single-bayed arch. Original in Kelsey Museum Archives (I.E.54 above).

4.11.16.Copy of elevation of imperial cult temple (original in Kelsey Museum Archives, I.E.20 above). This copy shows corrections to an earlier version of the same drawing.

C. Box 5, folder 15. Contents: prints of 3 photographs from negatives in the Kelsey Museum Archives.

D. Box 5, folder 16. Contents: numerous photographs showing views of Pisidian Antioch, collected into 13 smaller (unnumbered) folders. These photographs belong to 2 separate series, taken during 2 different visits to Pisidian Antioch. The 2 series are intermingled among the 13 folders.

Series 1. The smaller series, containing ca. 20 photographs, is a sampling of snapshots taken during the excavations in 1924. Several of the photographs in this smaller series were taken by Enoch E. Peterson and are not preserved in the Kelsey Museum Archives.

Series 2. The larger series, containing ca. 100 photographs, shows views from a much later trip to Pisidian Antioch (exact date unknown), when the areas excavated in 1924 had become partly reburied. Woodbridge himself might have taken these photographs. This series contains individual snapshots printed 1, 2, or 3 to a sheet and sequences of snapshots that have been taped together to form panoramic views of the site. These are the only known copies of this series of photographs. See also Box 5, folder 17.

E. Box 5, folder 17. Contents: 6 small folders containing additional photographs that belong to Box 5, folder 16, series 2.

F. Box 5, folder 18. Contents: prints of photographs taken by G. R. Swain during 1924 excavations of Pisidian Antioch. Copies of these photographs are preserved in the Kelsey Museum Archives. Per the correspondence between Woodbridge and Louise A. Shier in Box 5, folder 19, of this archive, these photographs were sent to Woodbridge by Shier in 1971.

G. Box 5, folder 19. Contents: various correspondences concerning the architectural drawings of Pisidian Antioch, as well as drawings of two inscriptions with the words "Aug[usta] Pla[tea]" and

"Tiberia Platea" preserved. Correspondents are Louise A. Shier of the University of Michigan and Harald Ingholt.

VI. In the Ashmolean Library, Oxford
Epigraphical notebooks of Sir William Ramsay, including that for 1924. Ramsay was present from the start of the season until June 14, 1924. He revisited Yalvaç in 1925 and 1926.

VII. At the Public Library, Belediye or Museum (first opened in 1965) of Yalvaç
In the Kelsey correspondence (II.A) there is evidence that photographs relating to the social life of Yalvaç were sent to the mayor for deposition in the public library. Their whereabouts and survival have not yet been investigated.

VIII. At the British Institute of Archaeology at Ankara
A collection of squeezes of 143 inscriptions of Pisidian Antioch made in 1977 from the collection in Yalvaç Museum and from stones now located in the town of Yalvaç.

IX. At the Institute of Advanced Study Princeton
Epigraphic squeezes made by D. M. Robinson and deposited at the Institute for Advanced Study.

Glossary

aedile. A Roman magistrate who represented the *plebs* of the city and who was also in charge of urban infrastructure, games, and grain allotments.

agonothete. The person who oversaw the organization and events of a festival in Greek cities of the Roman period. The *agonothete* was often selected or appointed at the establishment of a festival.

ambo. A raised platform in the nave of a church from which clergy could address the congregation.

bema. The area of the church that contained the altar, usually located in front of the apse; the sanctuary.

bucranium. A depiction of a bull's head or skull draped with garlands; thought to refer to the sacrifice of bulls whose heads were then displayed on temple walls.

Capitolium. Any temple dedicated to Jupiter Optimus Maximus. The name derives from the location of the first temple ever dedicated to Jupiter Optimus Maximus, which stood on the Capitoline hill in Rome.

cardo. A north-south oriented road in a Roman city with a grid plan. The main north-south road of a city was called the *cardo maximus.*

cavea. The auditorium or tiered seating section of a theater.

chancel. The space around the altar; the holiest part of a church, often set off from the nave by a barrier.

chora. The surrounding territory controlled by a Greek city. This territory normally contained numerous small villages and towns.

crepidoma. The upper level of the foundation of a Greek temple, which had three steps. It was located above the *euthynteria* and below the *stylobate.*

cuneus. Wedge-shaped seating section of the theater divided by staircases.

decumanus. An east-west oriented road in Roman cities with a grid plan. The main east-west road of a city was called the *decumanus maximus*; it intersected the *cardo maximus.*

diazoma. Horizontal walkways separating the seating sections of the theater. Also referred to as *praecinctio* in Latin.

dolium. A large ceramic or stone vessel used to store wine, olive oil, and other liquid perishables.

duoviri. The two chief magistrates of a Roman *municipium* or *colonia*.

euergetism. Literally, "good deeds." Public benefaction or patronage for the benefit of the community.

euergetist. Literally, someone who does good works—much like a modern philanthropist. In the Greek cities of Asia Minor, *euergetists* were wealthy citizens who funded the construction of buildings, festivals, and sacrifices in order to win prestige for themselves and their communities. In many cases imperial officials such as governors also acted as *euergetists*.

euthynteria. The uppermost layer of the underground foundation of a Greek temple (the *stereobate*).

gallery. An open space that runs along the upper level of a colonnaded side aisle of a basilica.

genius. The personified spirit of a person, place, or thing, which was eligible to be worshipped as a divinity. The concept is akin to the Sumerian *me*, Egyptian *ka*, and Persian *fravashi*.

gnomon. An object, such as the needle of a sundial, that projects a shadow used as an indicator.

hierodouloi. Slaves or freedmen who belonged to or were attached to a god or temple.

lesche. A council chamber or club room used as a place of meeting.

loggia. An open-sided, roofed or vaulted gallery, either freestanding or along the front or side of a building, often at an upper level.

ludi. Public games held in honor of particular deities. Various types of *ludi* included *ludi circenses* (chariot races) and *ludi scaenici* (theatrical performances).

neokoros and neokorate. In the Augustan period, each of the Roman provinces in Asia Minor had one city designated as *Neokoros*, which translates loosely as "temple warden." The *Neokoros* city was granted the honor of overseeing the imperial cult at a provincial level. This entailed, among other things, holding annual festivals, which were attended by delegates from cities throughout the province.

naiskos. A small temple or shrine, often used as a visual motif in funerary and religious contexts.

narthex. An entrance hall or porch preceding the nave of a church.

nymphaeum. A fountain house.

odeion. Small, usually roofed, theater, generally used for musical performances, poetry competitions, debates, and lectures.

oikos. A Greek house. The term can also refer to the household or family.

orchestra. The area in a theater between the *cavea* (seating section) and the stage building. During the classical and Hellenistic periods, chorus singers and dancers performed in the orchestra, and in the Roman imperial period the area often was adapted as an arena for public spectacles.

parados. The primary side entrance and exit into a Greek theater. The main theater entrances and exits of a Roman theater were referred to as the *aditus maximi*, which were on either side of the orchestra between the seating section and the stage building.

platea. An open urban space for public use, similar to the modern plaza.

propylon (*pl.* propyla). A monumental gate or entranceway to a sanctuary or other form of architectural complex.

prosphora. Loaves of leavened bread used in the celebration of the Eucharist and given to pilgrims.

scaena. Stage building of a theater.

scaenae frons. Front of the stage building of a theater, which became increasingly adorned with decoration such as niches, columns, and statues throughout the Roman imperial period.

Sebasteion. A temple or shrine dedicated to one or more members of the imperial family.

solea. The pathway between the nave and the *ambo* along which clergy walked.

Solomon's knot. A decorative motif featuring interlocking circles or ovals, which can form a latticelike pattern.

stoa. A long, rectangular building or covered walkway (portico), commonly found in agoras (marketplaces) and in sanctuaries.

temenos. The holy area around a temple, altar, or shrine. Traditionally, a masonry wall or an inscribed set of boundary stones demarcated the *temenos* of a Graeco-Roman temple.

tetrastoön. A columned porch or colonnade that encloses a courtyard on all four sides. Also refers to a public square or forum.

tholos. A circular building.

vomatorium. A vaulted passageway leading to the seating sections of a theater or amphitheater.

Bibliography

Note: Abbreviations used in this volume can be found in the style sheet of the American Journal of Archaeology *(accessible at http://www.ajaonline.org/index.php?ptype=page&pid=2#9).*

Abbasoğlu, H. 2001. "The Founding of Perge and Its Development in the Hellenistic and Roman Periods." In *Urbanism in Western Asia Minor: New Studies on Aphrodisias, Ephesos, Hierapolis, Pergamon, Perge and Xanthos*, ed. D. Parrish, 173–199. JRA Supplement 45.

Akurgal, E. 1969. *Ancient Civilizations and Ruins of Turkey: From Prehistoric Times until the End of the Roman Empire*. Trans. J. Whybrow and M. Emre. Istanbul: Mobil Oil Türk A. S.

Akurgal, E., and U. B. Alkim, eds. 1974. *Mansel'e Armağan: Mélanges Mansel*. Ankara: Türk Tarih Kurumu Basimevi.

Alcock, S. 2005. "Roman Colonies in the Eastern Empire." In *The Archaeology of Colonial Encounters*, ed. G. Stein, 297–329. Santa Fe: School of American Research.

Alzinger, W. 1974. *Augusteische Architektur in Ephesos*. Vienna: Österreichisches Archäologisches Institut im Selbstverl.

Anderson, J. G. C. 1913. "Festivals of Men Askaenos in the Roman Colonia at Antioch of Pisidia." *JRS* 3:267–300.

Arundell, F. V. J. 1834. *Discoveries in Asia Minor*, 2 vols. London: R. Bentley.

Ashby, T. 1935. *The Aqueducts of Ancient Rome*. Ed. I. A. Richmond. Oxford: Clarendon Press.

Ashmole, B. 1972. *Architect and Sculptor in Ancient Greece*. New York: New York University Press.

Aulock, H. von. 1977. *Münzen und Städte Pisidiens*, vol. 2. Tübingen: E. Wasmuth.

Aurenhammer, M. 1995. "Sculptures of Gods and Heroes from Ephesos." In *Ephesos, Metropolis of Asia*, ed. H. Koester, 251–280. Valley Forge, PA: Trinity Press International.

Avi-Yonah, M. 1963. "La mosaïque juive dans ses relations avec la mosaïque classique." In *La mosaïque gréco-romaine, Paris, 20 août–3 septembre 1963*, 325–334. Paris: Éditions du Centre national de la recherche scientifique.

Bacon, F., J. Clarke, and R. Koldewey. 1902. *Investigations at Assos: Drawings and Photographs of the Buildings and Objects Discovered during the Excavations of 1881–1882–1883*. Cambridge, MA: Archaeological Institute of America.

Balsdon, J. P. V. D. 1969. *Life and Leisure in Ancient Rome*. New York: McGraw-Hill.

Barnes, T. D. 1996. "Christians and the Theater." In *Roman Theater and Society*, ed. W. J. Slater, 161–180. Ann Arbor: University of Michigan Press.

Barton, I. M., ed. 1989. *Roman Public Buildings*. Exeter: University of Exeter.

Barton, T. 1995. "Augustus and Capricorn: Astrological Polyvalency and Imperial Rhetoric." *JRS* 85:33–51.

Bayhan, S. 2005. *Priene. Miletus. Didyma*. Trans. A. Gillett. Istanbul: Keskin Color.

Beacham, R. C. 1992. *The Roman Theatre and Its Audience*. Cambridge, MA: Harvard University Press.

Bean, G. E. 1968. *Turkey's Southern Shore: An Archaeological Guide*. New York: Praeger.

———. 1980. *Turkey beyond the Meander*. London: E. Benn.

Beard, M., J. North, and S. Price. 2002. *Religions of Rome*, vol. 1: *A History*. Cambridge: Cambridge University Press.

Bearzot, C., F. L. Gattinoni, and G. Zecchini, eds. 2003. *Gli stati territoriali nel mondo antico*. Milan: V&P Università.

Belayche, N. 2008. "*LUNA/MHN AΣKAHNOΣ*: un dieu romain à Antioche (Pisidie)." In *Ritual Dynamics and Religious Change in the Roman Empire*, ed. O. Hekster, S. Schmidt-Hofner, and C. Witschel, 327–348. Leiden: Brill.

Berndt, D. 2002. *Midasstadt in Phrygien. Eine sagenumwobene Stätte im anatolischen Hochland*. Mainz: P. von Zabern.

Bekker-Nielsen, T. 2008. *Urban Life and Local Politics in Roman Bithynia: The Small World of Dion Chrysostomos*. Aarhus: Aarhus University Press.

Bieber, M. 1939. *The History of the Greek and Roman Theater*. Princeton: Princeton University Press.

———. 1961. *The History of the Greek and Roman Theater*, rev. 2nd ed. Princeton: Princeton University Press.

Bingöl, O. 1998. *Magnesia ad Meandrum [Menderes Magnesiası]*. Ankara: Aydın Valiliği.

Birley, A. R. 1997. *Hadrian: The Restless Emperor*. London and New York: Routledge.

Blackman, D. R., and T. A. Hodge. 2001. *Frontinus' Legacy*. Ann Arbor: University of Michigan Press.

Blue, B. 1994. "Acts and the House Church." In *The Book of Acts in Its Graeco-Roman Setting*, ed. D. Gill and C. Gempf, 119–122. Grand Rapids, MI: Eerdmans.

Boatwright, M. T. 1987. *Hadrian and the City of Rome*. Princeton: Princeton University Press.

———. 1991. "Plancia Magna of Perge: Women's Roles and Status in Roman Asia Minor." In *Women's History and Ancient History*, ed. S. Pomeroy, 249–272. Chapel Hill: University of North Carolina Press.

———. 2000. *Hadrian and the Cities of the Roman Empire*. Princeton: Princeton University Press.

Boffo, L. 1985. *I re ellenistici e i centri religiosi dell'Asia Minore*. Florence: La Nuova Italia.

———. 2003. "Centri religiosi e territori nell'Anatolia ellenistica." In *Gli stati territoriali nel mondo antico*, ed. C. Bearzot, F. Landucci Gattinoni, and G. Zecchini, 253–269. Milan: Vita e Pensiero.

Bohtz, C. 1981. *Das Demeter-Heiligtum*. Berlin: W. de Gruyter.

Bookidis, N., and R. S. Stroud. 1997. *The Sanctuary of Demeter and Kore. Topography and Architecture*. Princeton: The American School of Classical Studies at Athens. Corinth 18.3.

Borchhardt, J. 1976. *Die Bauskulpter des Heroons von Limyra. Das Grabmal des lykischen Königs Perikles*. Berlin: Gebr. Mann.

Borchhardt, J., and G. Stanzl. 1990. "Ein hellenistischer Bau des Herrscherkultes: Das Ptolemaion in Limyra." In *Götter, Heroen, Herrscher in Lykien*, ed. J. Borchhardt, 79–87. Vienna: A. Schroll.

Bowersock, G. 1982. "The Imperial Cult: Perceptions and Persistence." In *Jewish and Christian Self-Definition*, ed. B. Meyer and E. P. Sanders, 171–182. London: SCM Press.

Bradley, G. J., and J. P. Wilson, eds. 2006. *Greek and Roman Colonization: Origins, Ideologies, and Interactions*. Swansea: Classical Press of Wales.

Brixhe, C., and T. Drew-Bear. 1978. "Un noveau document néo-phrygien." *Kadmos* 17.1:50–54.

Brixhe, C., and E. Gibson. 1982. "Monuments from Pisidia in the Rahmi Koç Collection." *Kadmos* 22.2:130–169.

Brothers, A. J. 1989. "Buildings for Entertainment." In *Roman Public Buildings*, ed. I. M. Barton, 97–125. Exeter: University of Exeter.

Broughton, T. R. S. 1938. "Roman Asia." In *An Economic Survey of Ancient Rome*, ed. T. Frank and A. C. Johnson, 499–916. Baltimore: Johns Hopkins University Press.

Brown, P. 1992. *Power and Persuasion in Late Antiquity: Towards a Christian Empire*. Madison: University of Wisconsin Press.

Bru, H. 2002. "Un arc de triomphe à Antioche." In *Actes du Ier Congres International sur Antioche de Pisidie*, ed. T. Drew-Bear, M. Taşlıalan, and C. Thomas, 359–368. Lyon and Paris: Université Lumière.

———. 2009. "L'origine des colons romains d'Antioche de Pisidie." In *L'Asie Mineure dans l'Antiquité: échanges, populations et territoires: regards actuels sur une peninsula*, ed. H. Bru, F. Kirbihler, and S. Lebreton, 263–287. Rennes: University of Rennes Press.

Bru, H., and Ü. Demirer. 2006. "Dionysisme, culte impérial et vie civique à Antioch de Pisidie (première partie)." *RÉA* 108:581–611.

Bru, H., F. Kirbihler, and S. Lebreton, eds. 2009. *L'Asie Mineure dans l'Antiquité: échanges, populations et territoires: regards actuels sur une peninsula*. Rennes: University of Rennes Press.

Brunt, P. A., and J. M. Moore. 1967. *Res Gestae Divi Augusti. The Achievements of the Divine Augustus*. Oxford: Oxford University Press.

Buckler, W. H., W. M. Calder, and C. W. M. Cox. 1924. "Asia Minor, 1924. I.—Monuments from Iconium, Lycaonia and Isauria." *JRS* 14:24–84.

Buckler, W. H., W. M. Calder, and W. K. C. Guthrie, eds. 1933. *Monumenta Asiae Minoris Antiqua*, vol. 4. Manchester, NH: Publications of the American Society for Archaeological Research in Asia Minor.

Burdy, J., and M. Taşlıalan. 1997. "L'aqueduc d'Antioch de Pisidie." *Anatolia Antiqua (Eski Anadolu)* 5:133–166.

Burdy, J., M. Taşlıalan, M. Waelkens, and S. Mitchell. 1998. "The Aqueduct, Nymphaeum, and Bath House." In *Pisidian Antioch: The Site and Its Monuments*, ed. S. Mitchell and M. Waelkens, 175–200. London: Duckworth Press.

Burdy, J., and M. Taşlıalan. 2002. "L'aqueduc d'Antioche." In *Actes du Ier Congres International sur Antioche de Pisidie*, ed. T. Drew-Bear, M. Taslialan, and C. Thomas, 323–336. Lyon and Paris: Université Lumière.

Burrell, B. 2004. *Neokoroi: Greek Cities and Roman Emperors*. Leiden: Brill.

Byrne, M. 2002. "The Date of the City Gate of Antioch." In *Actes du Ier Congres International sur Antioche de Pisidie*, ed. T. Drew-Bear, M. Taşlıalan, and C. Thomas, 193–200. Lyon and Paris: Université Lumière.

Calder, W. M. 1912. "Colonia Caesarea Antiocheia." *JRS* 2:78–109.

———. 1920. "Studies in Early Christian Epigraphy." *JRS* 10:42–59.

Calza, G. 1926. *Ostia: Historical Guide to the Monuments*. Milan: Bestetti e Tumminelli.

Camp, J. M. 2001. *The Archaeology of Athens*. New Haven: Yale University Press.

Carter, J. C. 1983. *The Sculpture of the Sanctuary of Athena Polias at Priene*. London: Thames and Hudson.

Cavalier, L. 2005. *Architecture romaine d'Asie Mineure: les monuments de Xanthos et leur ornementation*. Paris: De Boccard. Scripta Antiqua 13.

Chaniotis, A. 2007. "Theatre Rituals." In *The Greek Theatre and Festivals*, ed. P. Wilson, 48–66. Oxford: Oxford University Press.

Chastagnol, A., M. Leglay, and P. Le Roux, eds. 1984. *L'Année épigraphique*. Paris: Presses Universitaire de France.

Cheesman, G. L. 1913. "The Family of the Caristanii at Antioch of Pisidia." *JRS* 3:253–266.

Chi, J. 2002. "Studies in the Programmatic Statuary of Roman Asia Minor." PhD dissertation, New York University, New York, NY.

Christol, M., and T. Drew-Bear. 1999. "Antioche de Piside capitale provinciale et l'oeuvre de M. Valerius Diogenes." *Antiquité tardive* 7:39–71.

Christol, M., T. Drew-Bear, and M. Taşlıalan. 2001. "L'Empereur Claude, le Chevalier C. Caristanius Fronto Caesianus Iullus et le Culte Impérial à Antioche de Pisidie." *Tyche* 16:1–20.

Clauss, M. 2001. *Kaiser und Gott. Herrscherkult im römischen Reich.* Munich: K. G. Saur.

Cooley, A. 2009. *Res Gestae Divi Augusti. Text, Translation, and Commentary.* Cambridge: Cambridge University Press.

Cooper, K. 1996. *The Virgin and the Bride.* Cambridge, MA: Harvard University Press.

Cormack, R. 1990. "The Temple as the Cathedral." In *Aphrodisias Papers: Recent Work on Architecture and Sculpture*, ed. C. Roueché and K. Erim, 75–88. Ann Arbor, MI. JRA Supplement 1.

Corpus Inscriptionum Latinarum (CIL). 1863–1936. 16 vols. Berlin: G. Reimerum.

Coulton, J. J. 1976. *The Development of the Greek Stoa.* Oxford: Clarendon Press.

———. 1987. "Roman Aqueducts in Asia Minor." In *Roman Architecture in the Greek World*, ed. S. Macready and F. H. Thompson, 72–84. London: Thames and Hudson.

Crouch, D. P. 1993. *Water Management in Ancient Greek Cities.* Oxford: Oxford University Press.

D'Andria, F. 2001. "Hierapolis of Phrygia. Its Evolution in Hellenistic and Roman Times." In *Urbanism in Western Asia Minor. New Studies on Aphrodisias, Ephesos, Hierapolis, Pergamon, Perge and Xanthos*, ed. D. Parrish, 96–115. Portsmouth. JRA Supplement 45.

D'Andria, F., and T. Ritti. 1985. *Hierapolis, vol. 2: le sculture del teatro.* Rome: G. Bretschneider.

Davies, A. M., and B. Levick. 1971. "Κοπτοπωλησ." *CR* 21:162–166.

Davies, P. J. E. 2000. *Death and the Emperor: Roman Imperial Funerary Monuments, from Augustus to Marcus Aurelius.* Cambridge: Cambridge University Press.

Davis, L. 1983. *The First Seven Ecumenical Councils (325–787): Their History and Theology.* Wilmington: M. Glazier.

Debord, P. 1982. *Aspects sociaux et économiques de la vie religieuse dans l'Anatolie gréco-romaine.* Leiden: Brill.

Deichmann, F. W. 1939. "Frühchristliche Kirchen in antiken Heiligtümern." *JdI* 54:105–136.

de Laborde, L. 1861. *Voyage de l'Asie Mineure.* Paris: Firmin Didot Frères.

Demirer, Ü. 2002. *Pisidian Antioch: St. Paul, Sanctuary of Men, Yalvaç Museum.* Ankara: Dönmez Offset.

———. 2003. "Pisidia Antiochiasi 2003 Yili Çalişmalari." Unpublished.

———. 2004. "Pisidia Antiochiasi 2004 Yili Çalişmalari." Unpublished.

des Courtils, J., and L. Cavalier. 2001. "The City of Xanthos from Archaic to Byzantine Times." In *Urbanism in Western Asia Minor: New Studies on Aphrodisias, Ephesos, Hierapolis, Pergamon, Perge, and Xanthos*, ed. D. Parrish, 149–171. Portsmouth. JRA Supplement 45.

Dessau, H., ed. 1954. *Inscriptiones Latinae Selectae (ILS).* Berlin: Weidmann.

Dignas, B. 2002. *Economy of the Sacred in Hellenistic and Roman Asia Minor.* Oxford: Oxford University Press.

Dodge, H. 1999. "Amusing the Masses: Buildings for Entertainment and Leisure in the Roman World." In *Life, Death, and Entertainment in the Roman Empire*, ed. D. S. Potter and D. J. Mattingly, 205–255. Ann Arbor: University of Michigan Press.

Doni, C. 2009. "The Pisidians: From Their Origin to Their Western Expansion." In *L'Asie Mineure dans l'Antiquité: échanges, populations et territoires: regards actuels sur une peninsula*, ed. H. Bru, F. Kirbihler, and S. Lebreton, 213–223. Rennes: University of Rennes Press.

Dorl-Klingenschmid, C. 2001. *Prunkbrunnen in kleinasiatischen Städten. Funktion im Kontext.* Munich: Fritz Pfeil. Studien zur antiken Stadt 7.

Drees, L. 1968. *Olympia: Gods, Artists, and Athletes.* New York: Frederick A. Praeger.

Drew-Bear, T. 2000. "Pisidia Antiokheia Tiyatrosunun Yazıtları." *Araştırma Sonuçları Toplantısı* 17.1: 209–211.

———. 2005. "La copie des *Res Gestae* d'Antioche de Piside." *ZPE* 154:217–260.

Drew-Bear, T., M. Taşlıalan, and C. Thomas, eds. 2002. *Actes du Ier Congres International sur Antioche de Pisidie.* Lyon and Paris: Université Lumière.

Dunbabin, K. 1978. *The Mosaics of Roman North Africa: Studies in Iconography and Patronage.* Oxford: Clarendon Press.

———. 2003. *The Roman Banquet: Images of Conviviality.* Cambridge: Cambridge University Press.

Dunn, J. D. G., ed. 2003. *The Cambridge Companion to St. Paul.* Cambridge: Cambridge University Press.

Edmondson, J. C. 1996. "Dynamic Arenas: Gladiatorial Presentations in the City of Rome and the Construction of Roman Society during the Early Empire." In *Roman Theater and Society*, ed. W. J. Slater, 69–112. Ann Arbor: University of Michigan Press.

———. 2007. "The Cult of Mars Augustus and Roman Imperial Power at Augusta Emerita (Lusitania) in the Third Century AD: A New Votive Dedication." In *Culto imperial: política y poder*, ed. T. Nogales and J. Gonzáles, 541–575. Rome: L'Erma di Bretschneider.

Ehrenberg, V., and A. H. M. Jones. 1955. *Documents Illustrating the Reigns of Augustus and Tiberius.* Oxford: Clarendon Press.

Eilers, C. 2002. *Roman Patrons of Greek Cities.* Oxford: Oxford University Press.

Elsner, J. 1991. "Cult and Sculpture: The *Ara Pacis Augustae*." *JRS* 81:50–61.

Erdemgil, S. 1991. *Ephesus.* Istanbul: NET Turistik Yayinlari.

Erim, K. T. 1986. *Aphrodisias: City of Venus Aphrodite.* London: Miller, Blond & White.

Evans, H. B. 1993. "*In Tiburtium Usum*: Special Arrangements in the Roman Water Systems (Frontinus, Aq. 6.5)." *AJA* 97:447–455.

———. 1994. *Water Distribution in Ancient Rome: The Evidence of Frontinus.* Ann Arbor: University of Michigan Press.

Eyice, S. 2002. "Thekla at Antioch." In *Actes du Ier Congres International sur Antioche de Pisidie*, ed. T. Drew-Bear, M. Taşlıalan, and C. Thomas, 111–122. Lyon and Paris: Université Lumière.

Favro, D. 1996. *The Urban Image of Augustan Rome.* Cambridge and New York: Cambridge University Press.

Fayer, C. 1976. *Il culto della Dea Roma.* Pescara: Trimestre.

Fears, J. R. 1981. "The Cult of Jupiter and Roman Imperial Ideology." *ANRW* 2.17.2:3–141.

Fishwick, D. 1970. "On C.I.L., II, 473." *AJP* 91:79–82.

———. 1991. *The Imperial Cult in the Latin West: Studies in the Ruler Cult of the Western Provinces of the Roman Empire*, vol. 2, part 1. Leiden: Brill.

———. 2002. *The Imperial Cult in the Latin West: Studies in the Ruler Cult of the Western Provinces of the Roman Empire*, vol. 3, part 1. Leiden: Brill.

Frank, T., and A. C. Johnson, eds. 1938. *An Economic Survey of Ancient Rome.* Baltimore: Johns Hopkins University Press.

Fraser, P. M., and E. Matthews, eds. 1987. *A Lexicon of Greek Personal Names*, vol. 1: *The Aegean Islands, Cyprus and Cyrenaica.* Oxford: Clarendon Press.

———. 1997. *A Lexicon of Greek Personal Names*, vol. 3A: *The Peloponnese, Western Greece, Sicily and Magna Graecia.* Oxford: Clarendon Press.

———. 2005. *A Lexicon of Greek Personal Names*, vol. 4: *Macedonia, Thrace and the Northern Regions of the Black Sea*. Oxford: Clarendon Press.

French, D. H., G. H. Brown, S. A. Jameson, G. Dunbar, and E. Rosenbaum. 1963. "Report of the Council of Management and of the Director for 1962." *AnatSt* 13:3–17.

Gaertringen, H. von. 1906. *Inschriften von Priene*. Berlin: G. Reimer.

Gauthier, P. 1985. *Les cités grecques et leurs bienfaiteurs*. Athens: École française d'Athènes.

Gazda, E., ed. 2002. *The Ancient Art of Emulation: Studies in Artistic Originality and Tradition from the Present to the Classical*. Ann Arbor: University of Michigan Press.

Gebhard, E. R. 1996. "The Theater and the City." In *Roman Theater and Society*, ed. W. J. Slater, 113–127. Ann Arbor: University of Michigan Press.

Gill, D., and C. Gempf, eds. 1994. *The Book of Acts in Its Graeco-Roman Setting*. Grand Rapids, MI: Eerdmans.

González, J. 1988. "The First Oath Pro Salute Augusti Found in Baetica." *ZPE* 72:113–127.

Goodchild, R. G., J. M. Reynolds, and C. T. Herington. 1958. "The Temple of Zeus at Cyrene." *PBSR* 26:30–62.

Gradel, I. 2002. *Emperor Worship and Roman Religion*. Oxford: Clarendon Press.

Granfield, P., and J. Jungmann, eds. 1970. *Kyriakon: Festschrift Johannes Quasten*. Münster: Aschendorff.

Grant, M. 1952. "A Capricorn on Hadrian's Coinage." *Emerita* 20:1–7.

Grech, P. 2002. "The Background of Romans X.5–13 and Paul's Discourse at Antioch." In *Actes du Ier Congres International sur Antioche de Pisidie*, ed. T. Drew-Bear, M. Taşlıalan, and C. Thomas, 53–60. Lyon and Paris: Université Lumière.

Green, J. R. 1994. *Theatre in Ancient Greek Society*. London and New York: Routledge.

Gregory, T. E., and H. Mills. 1984. "The Roman Arch at Isthmia." *Hesperia* 53.4:407–445.

Grether, G. 1946. "Livia and the Roman Imperial Cult." *AJP* 67.3:222–252.

Gros, P. 1990. "Théâtre et culte impérial en Gaule Narbonnaise et dans la pénisule ibérique." In *Stadtbild und Ideologie: die Monumentalisierung hispanischer Städte zwischen Republik und Kaiserzeit*, ed. W. Trillmich and P. Zanker. Munich: C. H. Beck.

Güven, S. N. 1983. "Aspects of Roman Arches in Asia Minor." PhD dissertation, Cornell University, Ithaca, NY.

———. 1998. "Displaying the Res Gestae of Augustus: A Monument of Imperial Image for All." *JSAH* 57.1:30–45.

Hall, A. 1986. "R.E.C.A.M. Notes and Studies No. 9: The Milyadeis and Their Territory." *AS* 36:136–157.

Hamilton, W. J. 1842. *Researches in Asia Minor, Pontus and Armenia, with some account of their antiquities and geology*. London: J. Murray.

Hanfmann, G. 1983. *Sardis from Prehistoric to Roman Times: Results of the Archaeological Exploration of Sardis 1958–1975*. Cambridge, MA: Harvard University Press.

Hänlein-Schäfer, H. 1985. *Veneratio Augusti: eine Studie zu den Tempeln des ersten römischen Kaisers*. Rome: G. Bretschneider.

Hanson, J. A. 1959. *Roman Theater-Temples*. Princeton: Princeton University Press.

Hardie, M. 1912. "The Shrine of Mên Askaênos at Pisidian Antioch." *JHS* 32:111–150.

Harmankaya, A., and Ş. Gümüş. 2006. "Pisidia Antiokheiası 2005 Yılı Çalışmaları." ANMED: Anadolu Akdenizi Arkeoloji Haberleri 4:147–151.

Hauck, G. F. 1988. "Water Flow in the *Castellum* at Nîmes." *AJA* 92:393–407.

Hellenkemper, H. 1994. "Early Church Architecture in Southern Asia Minor." In *"Churches Built in Ancient Times": Recent Studies in Early Christian Archaeology*, ed. K. Painter, 213–238. London: University of London.

Hellström, P. 1996. "The Andrones at Labraynda. Dining Halls for Protohellenistic Kings." In *Basileia, die Paläste der hellenistischen Könige: internationales Symposion in Berlin vom 16.12.1992 bis 20.12.1992*, ed. W. Hoepfner and G. Brands, 164–169. Mainz: P. von Zabern.

Hellström, P., and T. Thieme. 1982. *Labraunda. Swedish Excavations and Researches 1.3: The Temple of Zeus.* Stockholm: Svenska forskningsinstitutet i Istanbul.

Hill, S. 1996. *The Early Byzantine Churches of Cilicia and Isauria.* Aldershot and Brookfield: Variorum Reprints.

Hinson, E. G. 1996. *The Early Church: Origins to the Dawn of the Middle Ages.* Nashville: Abingdon Press.

Hodge, A. T. 1989. "Aqueducts." In *Roman Public Buildings*, ed. I. M. Barton, 127–150. Exeter: University of Exeter.

———. 1991. *Future Currents in Aqueduct Studies.* London: Redwood Press.

———. 1992. *Roman Aqueducts and Water Supply.* London: Duckworth Press.

———. 1996. "*In vitruvium pompeianum*: Urban Water Distribution Reappraised." *AJA* 100:261–276.

Hoepfner, W. 1990. "Bauten und Bedeutung des Hermogenes." In *Hermogenes und die hochhellistische Architektur*, ed. W. Hoepfner and E. L. Schwandner, 1–34. Mainz: P. von Zabern.

Hoepfner, W., and G. Brands, eds. 1996. *Basileia, die Paläste der hellenistischen Könige: internationales Symposion in Berlin vom 16.12.1992 bis 20.12.1992.* Mainz: P. von Zabern.

Højte, J. M. 2005. *Roman Imperial Statue Bases from Augustus to Commodus.* Aarhus: Aarhus University Press.

Holmberg, E. 1979. *Delphi and Olympia.* Gothenburg: P. Åström.

Horsley, G. H. R., and S. Mitchell. 2000. *The Inscriptions of Central Pisidia.* Bonn: Rudolf Habelt.

Howgego, C., V. Heuchert, and A. Burnett, eds. 2005. *Coinage and Identity in the Roman Empire.* Oxford: Oxford University Press.

Huskinsons, J., ed. 2000. *Experiencing Rome: Culture, Identity, and Power in the Roman Empire.* London and New York: Routledge.

Inan, J. 1989. Der Demetrios- und Apolloniosbogen in Perge. *IstMitt* 39:237–244.

———. 1993. "Neue Forschungen zum Sebasteion von Boubon und seinen Statuen." In *Akten des II. Internationalen Lykien-Sumposions, Wien, 6.–12. Mai 1990*, ed. J. Borchardt and G. Dobesch, 213–239. Vienna: Österreichischen Akademie der Wissenschaften.

Inan, J., and E. Rosenbaum. 1966. *Roman and Early Byzantine Portrait Sculpture in Asia Minor.* London: Oxford University Press.

Ingholt, H. 1954. *Parthian Sculptures from Hatra: Orient and Hellas in Art and Religion.* New Haven: The Academy. Memoirs of the Connecticut Academy of Arts and Sciences 12.

Inscriptiones Graecae (IG). 1981–1998. 3rd ed. Berlin: Gualterus de Gruytea.

Işik, F., and H. Yilmaz. 1989. "Patara 1988." *Kazi sonuçlari toplantisi* 11.2:1–21.

Isler, H. P. 1994. "Ancient Theatre Architecture." In *Teatri greci e romani*, ed. P. C. Rossetto and G. P Sartorio, 1:86–125. Rome: Edizioni SEAT.

Johnson, S. F. 2006. *The Life and Miracles of Thekla: A Literary Study.* Washington, DC: Center for Hellenic Studies, Trustees for Harvard University.

Jones, A. H. M. 1937. *The Cities of the Eastern Roman Provinces.* Oxford: Clarendon Press.

———. 1986. *The Later Roman Empire, 284–602: A Social, Economic, and Administrative Survey*, vol. 2. Baltimore: Johns Hopkins University Press.

Jory, E. J. 1996. "The Drama of the Dance: Prolegomena to an Iconography of Imperial Pantomime." In *Roman Theater and Society*, ed. W. J. Slater, 1–27. Ann Arbor: University of Michigan Press.

Journal of Excavations. See Robinson and Peterson 1924. See also appendix 2.C, p. 189, this volume.

Kalinowski, A. 2002. "The Vedii Antonini: Aspects of Patronage and Benefaction in Second-Century Ephesos." *Phoenix* 56:109–149.

Karamut, I. 1989. "Pisidia Antiocheia'st yakminda bulunan Men kutsak alani." *Turk Arkeoloji Dergisi* 28:171–187.

Kern, O. ed. 1900. *Die Inschriften von Magnesia am Maeander*. Berlin: W. Spemann.

Kitzinger, E. 1970. "The Threshold of the Holy Shrine: Observations on Floor Mosaics at Antioch and Bethlehem." In *Kyriakon: Festschrift Johannes Quasten*, ed. P. Granfield and J. Jungmann 2:639–647. Münster: Aschendorff.

———. 1974. "A Fourth Century Mosaic Floor in Pisidian Antioch." In *Mansel'e Armağan: Mélanges Mansel*, ed. E. Akürgal and U. B. Alkim, 385–395. Ankara: Türk Tarih Kurumu Basimevi.

Kızıl, A. 2009. "Das Baltalı Kapı in Mylasa, die Labrys und die Augen des Zeus." *Anatolia Antiqua* 17:255–264.

Kleijn, G. de. 2001. *The Water Supply of Ancient Rome: City Area, Water, and Population*. Amsterdam: Gieben.

Koenigs, W., and W. Radt. 1979. "Ein kaiserlicher Rundbau (Monopteros) in Pergamon." *IstMitt.* 19:317–354.

Kondoleon, C. 1995. *Domestic and Divine: Roman Mosaics in the House of Dionysos*. Ithaca and London: Cornell University Press.

Krautheimer, R. 1983. *Three Christian Capitals: Topography and Politics*. Berkeley and Los Angeles: University of California Press.

———. 1986. *Early Christian and Byzantine Architecture*, 4th ed. revised by R. Krautheimer and S. Ćurčić. New York: Penguin Books.

Krzyzanowska, A. 1970. *Monnaies colonials d'Antioche de Pisdie*. Warsaw: Éditions scientifiques de Pologne.

Kuttner, A. 1995. *Dynasty and Empire in the Age of Augustus: The Case of the Boscoreale Cups*. Berkeley and Los Angeles: University of California Press.

Labarre, G. 2009. "Les origines et la diffusion du culte de Men." In *L'Asie Mineure dans l'Antiquité: échanges, populations et territoires: regards actuels sur une peninsula*, ed. H. Bru, F. Kirbihler, and S. Lebreton, 389–414. Rennes: University of Rennes Press.

Labarre, G., and M. Taşlıalan. 2002. "La dévotion au dieu Men: les reliefs rupestres de la Voie Sacrée." In *Actes du Ier Congres International sur Antioche de Pisidie*, ed. T. Drew-Bear, M. Taslialan, and C. M. Thomas, 257–312. Lyon and Paris: Université Lumière.

Landskron, A. 2005. *Parther und Sasaniden: das Bild der Orientalen in der römischen Kaiserzeit*. Vienna: Phoibos.

Lanckoroński, K. 1890. *Die Städte Pamphyliens und Pisidiens*, vol. 1. Vienna: F. Tempsky.

Lane, E. 1964. "A Re-Study of the God Men." *Berytus* 15:5–58.

———. 1967–1968. "A Re-Study of the God Men, Part II: The Numismatic and Allied Evidence." *Berytus* 17:13–47.

———. 1971. *Corpus Monumentorum Religionis Dei Menis*, vol. 1: *The Monuments and Inscriptions*. Leiden: Brill.

———. 1975a. *Corpus Monumentorum Religionis Dei Menis*, vol. 2: *The Coins and Gems*. Leiden: Brill.

———. 1975b. "The Italian Connection: An Aspect of the Cult of Men." *Numen* 22:235–239.

———. 1976. *Corpus Monumentorum Religionis Dei Menis*, vol. 3: *Interpretations and Testimonia*. Leiden: Brill.

———. 1978. *Corpus Monumentorum Religionis Dei Menis*, vol. 4: *Supplementary Men-Inscriptions from Pisidia*. Leiden: Brill.

———. 1990. "Men: A Neglected Cult of Roman Asia Minor." *ANRW* 18:2161–2174.

Lane Fox, R. 1987. *Pagans and Christians*. New York: Knopf.

Lazzarini, M. L. 1976. *Le formule delle dediche votive nella Grecia arcaica*. Rome: Accademia nazionale dei Lincei.

Le Glay, M. 1976. "Hadrien et l'Asklépieion de Pergame." *BCH* 100.1:347–372.

Lequien, M. 1740. *Oriens christianus, in quatour patriarchatus digestus*. Paris: Ex Typographia regia.

Lehmann, P. 1954. "The Setting of Hellenistic Temples." *JSAH* 13:15–20.

Levick, B. 1958a. "Two Pisidian Colonial Families." *JRS* 48:74–78.

———. 1958b. "An Honorific Inscription from Pisidian Antioch." *AS* 8:219–222.

———. 1965. "Two Inscriptions from Pisidian Antioch." *AS* 15:53–62.

———. 1966. "The Coinage of Pisidian Antioch in the Third Century AD." *NC* 6:47–59.

———. 1967a. *Roman Colonies in Southern Asia Minor*. Oxford: Clarendon Press.

———. 1967b. "Unpublished Inscriptions from Pisidian Antioch." *AnatSt* 17:101–121.

———. 1968. "Antiocheia 15." *RE Supplement* 11:49–61.

———. 1970. "Dedications to Mên Askaênos." *AnatSt* 20:37–50.

———. 1971. "The Table of Mên." *JHS* 91:80–84.

Levick, B., and S. Jameson. 1964. "C. Crepereius Gallus and His Gens." *JRS* 54:98–106.

Lewis, N., and M. Reinhold, eds. 1951. *Roman Civilization. Selected Readings*. New York: Columbia University Press.

L'Huillier, P. 1996. *The Church of the Ancient Councils: The Disciplinary Work of the First Four Ecumenical Councils*. Crestwood, NJ: St. Vladimir's Seminary Press.

Lolos, Y. A. 1997. "The Hadrianic Aqueduct of Corinth (with an Appendix on the Roman Aqueducts in Greece)." *Hesperia* 66.2:271–314.

Longfellow, B. 2005. "Imperial Patronage and Urban Display of Roman Monumental Fountains and Nymphaea." PhD dissertation, University of Michigan, Ann Arbor, MI.

———. 2010. *Roman Imperialism and Civic Patronage: Form, Meaning and Ideology in Monumental Fountain Complexes*. Cambridge: Cambridge University Press.

L'Orange, H. P. 1953. *The Iconography of Cosmic Kingship*. Oslo: Aschehoug.

MacDonald, W. L. 1982. *The Architecture of the Roman Empire*, vol. 2: *An Urban Appraisal*. New Haven: Yale University Press.

Macready, S., and F. H. Thompson, eds. 1987. *Roman Architecture in the Greek World*. London: Thames and Hudson.

Mägele, S., J. Richard, and M. Waelkens. 2007. "A Late-Hadrianic Nymphaeum at Sagalassos (Pisidia, Turkey): A Preliminary Report." *IstMitt* 57:469–504.

Magie, D. 1950. *Roman Rule in Asia Minor: To the End of the Third Century after Christ*. Princeton: Princeton University Press.

Maguire, H. 1994. "Magic and Geometry in Early Christian Floor Mosaics." *JÖBG* 44:265–274.

Mahoney, A. 2001. *Roman Sports and Spectacles: A Sourcebook*. Newburyport, MA: Focus Publishing/R. Pullins Co.

Malissard, A. 1994. *Les Romains et l'eau: fontaines, salles de bains, thermes, egouts, aqueducs*. Paris: Les Belles Lettres.

Mansel, A. 1956. "Bericht über Ausgrabungen und Untersuchungen in Pamphylien in den Jahren 1946–1955." *AA* 71:34–120.

———. 1975. "Die Nymphaeen von Perge." *IstMitt* 25:367–372.

Marin, E. 2001. "The Temple of the Imperial Cult (Augusteum) at Narona and Its Statues: Interim Report." *JRA* 14:81–112.

Marin, E., and M. Vickers, eds. 2004. *The Rise and Fall of an Imperial Shrine. Roman Sculpture from the Augusteum at Narona*. Split: Arheoloski muzej.

Marksteiner, T. and M. Wörrle. 2002. "Ein Altar für Claudius auf dem Bonda tepesi zwischen Myra and Limyra." *Chiron* 32:545–569.

Mathews, T. 1971. *The Early Churches of Constantinople: Architecture and Liturgy*. University Park and London: Pennsylvania State University Press.

McLean, B. H. 2002. *An Introduction to Greek Epigraphy of the Hellenistic and Roman Periods from Alexander the Great down to the Reign of Constantine (323 BC–AD 337)*. Ann Arbor: University of Michigan Press.

Mellor, R. 1975. *ΘΕΑ ῬΩΜΗ: The Worship of the Goddess Roma in the Greek World*. Göttingen: Vandenhoeck & Ruprecht.

———. 1981. "The Goddess Roma." *ANRW* 2.17.2:952–1030.

Mendel, G. 1912–1914. *Catalogue des sculptures grecques, romaines et byzantines*. Constantinople: En vent au.

Miller, S. G., ed. 1990. *Nemea. A Guide to the Site and Museum*. Berkeley and Los Angeles: University of California Press.

Mitchell, S. 1976. "Legio VII and the Garrison of Augustan Galatia." *CQ* 26.2:298–308.

———. 1987. "Imperial Building in the Eastern Roman Provinces." *HSCP* 91:333–365.

———. 1988. "Maximinus and the Christians in AD 312: A New Latin Inscription." *JRS* 78:105–124.

———. 1990. "Festivals, Games, and Civic Life in Roman Asia Minor." *JRS* 80:183–193.

———. 1991. "Ariassos 1990." *AnatSt* 41:159–172.

———. 1993. *Anatolia: Land, Men, and Gods in Asia Minor*. Oxford: Clarendon Press.

———. 1995. *Cremna in Pisidia: An Ancient City in Peace and War*. London: Duckworth.

———. 2002. "The Temple of Men Askaenos at Antioch." In *Actes du Ier Congres International sur Antioche de Pisidie*, ed. T. Drew-Bear, M. Taşlıalan, and C. Thomas, 313–336. Lyon and Paris: Université Lumière.

Mitchell, S., and M. Waelkens. 1998. *Pisidian Antioch: The Site and Its Monuments*. London: Duckworth Press with The Classical Press of Wales.

Monaco, G. 1994. "In the Open Air." In *Teatri greci e romani*, ed. P. C. Rossetto and G. P. Sartorio, 1:38–43. Rome: Edizioni SEAT.

Moore, G. 1965. "Cramming More Components onto Integrated Circuits." *Electronics* 38.8:114–117.

Moretti, A. 1985. "Statue e ritratti onorari da Lucus Feroniae." *RendPontAcc* 55–56:71–109.

———. 1993. "Des masques et des théâtres en Grèce et en Asia Mineure." *RÉA* 95:207–223.

Morgan, C. 1990. *Athletes and Oracles. The Transformation of Olympia and Delphi in the Eighth Century BC*. Cambridge: Cambridge University Press.

Murphy-O'Connor, J. 1996. *Paul: A Critical Life*. Oxford: Clarendon Press.

Newby, Z. 2003. "Art and Identity in Asia Minor." In *Roman Imperialism and Provincial Art*, ed. S. Scott and J. Webster, 192–213. Cambridge: Cambridge University Press.

New York University. 1993. *Aphrodisias: Results of the Excavations at Aphrodisias in Caria Conducted by New York University*. Mainz: P. von Zabern.

Ng, D. 2007. "Manipulation of Memory: Public Buildings and Decorative Programs in Roman Cities of Asia Minor." PhD dissertation, University of Michigan, Ann Arbor, MI.

Nielsen, I. 1990. *Thermae et Balnea: The Architecture and Cultural History of Roman Public Baths*. Aarhus: University of Aarhus Press.

Nollé, J., and F. Schindler. 1991. *Die Inschriften von Selge*. Bonn: Habelt.

Norris, F. W. 2007. "Greek Christianities." In *The Cambridge History of Christianity*, vol. 2: *Constantine to c. 600*, ed. A. Casiday and F. W. Norris, 70–117. Cambridge: Cambridge University Press.

O'Connor, C. 1993. *Roman Bridges*. Cambridge: Cambridge University Press.

Oliver, J. H. 1941. *The Sacred Gerusia*. Baltimore: American School of Classical Studies at Athens. Hesperia Supplements 6.

Ortaç, M. 2002. "Zur Veränderung der kleinasiatischen Propyla in der frühen Kaiserzeit in Bauform und Bedeutung." In *Patris und Imperium: kulturelle und politische Identität in den Städten der römischen Provinzen Kleinasiens in der frühen Kaiserzeit*, ed. C. Berns et al., 175–185. Leuven: Peeters.

Ossi, A. 2005/2006. "Architectural Reconstruction Drawings of Pisidian Antioch by Frederick J. Woodbridge." *The Bulletin of the University of Michigan Museums of Art and Archaeology* 16:5–30.

———. 2009. "The Roman Honorific Arches of Pisidian Antioch: Reconstruction and Contextualization." PhD dissertation, University of Michigan, Ann Arbor, MI.

Ossi, A., and B. Rubin. 2007. "Pisidian Antioch Revisited: An Archival Excavation." *Minerva* 19.4:20–23.

Owens, E. J. 1991. "The Kremna Aqueduct and Water Supply in Roman Cities." *GaR* 38:41–58.

———. 2002 "The Water Supply of Antioch." In *Actes du Ier Congres International sur Antioche de Pisidie*, ed. T. Drew-Bear, M. Taşlıalan, and C. Thomas, 337–348. Lyon and Paris: Université Lumière.

Owens, E. J., and M. Taşlıalan. 2008. "The Fountain-house at Pisidian Antioch and the Water Supply of the Roman Colony: Changes in Water Management and Use." In *Cura aquarum in Jordanien: Proceedings of the 13th International Conference on the History of Water Management and Hydraulic Engineering in the Mediterranean Region, Petra/Amman 31 March 2007–09 April 2007*, ed. C. Ohlig, 301–312. Siegburg: Deutschen Wasserhistorischen Gesellschaft.

———. 2009. "'Beautiful and Useful': The Water Supply of Pisidian Antioch and the Development of the Roman Colony." In *The Nature and Function of Water, Baths, Bathing, and Hygiene from Antiquity through the Renaissance*, ed. C. Kosso and A. Scott, 301–317. Leiden: Brill.

Özhanlı, M. 2009a. "Pisidia Antiokheiası 2008 Kazısı." *Kazı Sonuçları Toplantısı* 31:75–84.

———. 2009b. "Pisidia Antiokheiası Kazıları 2008." ANMED: Anadolu Akdenizi Arkeoloji Haberleri 7:70–74.

Özgür, M. E. 1990. *Aspendos: A Travel Guide*. Istanbul: NET Turistik Yayinlar.

Pagels, E. 2003. *Beyond Belief: The Secret Gospel of Thomas*. New York: Random House.

Painter, K, ed. 1994. *"Churches Built in Ancient Times": Recent Studies in Early Christian Archaeology*. London: University of London.

Papalexandrou, A. 2003. "Memory Tattered and Torn: *Spolia* in the Heartland of Byzantine Hellenism." In *Archaeologies of Memory*, ed. R. van Dyke and S. Alcock, 56–80. Malden: Blackwell.

Parrish, D. 2001. "The Urban Plan and Its Constituent Elements." In *Urbanism in Western Asia Minor: New Studies on Aphrodisias, Ephesos, Hierapolis, Pergamon, Perge, and Xanthos*, ed. D. Parrish, 9–41. Portsmouth. JRA Supplement 45.

Parrish, D., ed. 2001. *Urbanism in Western Asia Minor: New Studies on Aphrodisias, Ephesos, Hierapolis, Pergamon, Perge and Xanthos*. Portsmouth. JRA Supplement 45.

Pearce, J., M. Millett, and M. Struck, eds. 2001. *Burial, Society and Context in the Roman World*. Oxford: Oxbow Press.

Pedley, J. 2005. *Sanctuaries and the Sacred in the Ancient Greek World*. Cambridge: Cambridge University Press.

Petrakos, B. 1977. *Delphi*. Athens: Ekdoseis Klio.

Pfrommer, M. 1990. "Wurzeln hermogeneischer Bauornamentik." In *Hermogenes und die hochhellenistische Architektur*, ed. W. Hoepfner and E. L. Schwandner, 69–83. Mainz: P. von Zabern.

Philpott, R. 1991. *Burial Practices in Roman Britain: A Survey of Grave Treatment and Furnishing, AD 43–410*. Oxford: Tempus Reparatum.

Pleket, H. W. 1965. "An Aspect of the Emperor Cult: Imperial Mysteries." *The Harvard Theological Review* 58.4:331–347.

Plommer, H. 1954. *History of Architectural Development*, 2 vols. London: Longmans.

Pollitt, J. J. 1986. *Art in the Hellenistic Age*. Cambridge: Cambridge University Press.

Pomeroy, S., ed. 1991. *Women's History and Ancient History*. Chapel Hill: University of North Carolina Press.

Potter, D. S. 1999. "Entertainers in the Roman Empire." In *Life, Death, and Entertainment in the Roman Empire*, ed. D. S. Potter and D. J. Mattingly, 256–325. Ann Arbor: University of Michigan Press.

———. 2004. *The Roman Empire at Bay AD 180–395* (London and New York).

Potter, D. S., and D. J. Mattingly, eds. 1999. *Life, Death, and Entertainment in the Roman Empire*. Ann Arbor: University of Michigan Press.

Poulter, A. 1994. "Churches in Space: The Early Byzantine City of Nicopolis." In *"Churches Built in Ancient Times": Recent Studies in Early Christian Archaeology*, ed. K. Painter, 249–268. London: University of London.

Price, S. R. F. 1984. *Rituals and Power: The Roman Imperial Cult in Asia Minor*. Cambridge: Cambridge University Press.

———. 2005. "Local Mythologies in the Greek East." In *Coinage and Identity in the Roman Empire*, ed. C. Howgego, V. Heuchert, and A. Burnett, 115–134. Oxford: Oxford University Press.

Radt, W. 1999. *Pergamon. Geschichte und Bauten einer antiken Metropole*. Darmstadt: Primus.

Ramsay, W. M. 1883. "The Graeco-Roman Civilisation in Pisidia." *JHS* 4:23–45.

———. 1906. "The Tekmoreian Guest-Friends: An Anti-Christian Society on the Imperial Estates at Pisidian Antioch." In *Studies in the History and Art of the Eastern Provinces of the Roman Empire*, ed. W. Ramsay, 305–377. Aberdeen: Aberdeen University Press.

———. 1911. "The Sanctuary of Mên Askaênos at Pisidian Antioch." *The Athenaeum* 4372 (August): 192–193.

———. 1911–1912. "Sketches in the Religious Antiquities of Asia Minor." *BSA* 18:37–79.

———. 1912. "The Tekmoreian Guest-Friends." *JHS* 32:151–170.

———. 1916. "Colonia Caesarea (Pisidian Antioch) in the Augustan Age." *JRS* 6:83–134.

———. 1918. "Studies in the Roman Province Galatia II: Dedications of the Sanctuary of Colonia Caesarea." *JRS* 8:107–145.

———. 1922. "Studies in the Roman Province Galatia." *JRS* 12:147–186.

———. 1924. "Studies in the Roman Province Galatia VI: Some Inscriptions of Colonia Caesarea Antiochaea." *JRS* 14:172–205.

———. 1926. "Studies in the Roman Province of Galatia VII: Pisidia; VIII: Map of Yalowadj; IX: Inscriptions of Antioch of Phrygia towards Pisidia (Colonia Caesarea)." *JRS* 16:102–119.

———. 1928. "Anatolica Quaedam." *JHS* 48:46–53.

———. 1930. "Anatolica Quaedam." *JHS* 50.2:263–287.

———. 1939. "Early History of Province Galatia." In *Anatolian Studies Presented to William Hepburn Buckler*, ed. W. M. Calder and J. Keil, 201–225. Manchester: Manchester University Press.

Ramsay, W. M., ed. 1906. *Studies in the History and Art of the Eastern Provinces of the Roman Empire.* Aberdeen: Aberdeen University Press.

Ramsay W. M., and A. von Premerstein. 1927. *Monumentum Antiochenum.* Leipzig: Dieterich. Klio 19.

Ratté, C. 2001. "New Research on the Urban Development of Aphrodisias in Late Antiquity." In *Urbanism in Western Asia Minor: New Studies on Aphrodisias, Ephesos, Hierapolis, Pergamon, Perge, and Xanthos*, ed. D. Parrish, 117–148. Portsmouth. JRA Supplement 45.

———. 2002. "The Urban Development of Aphrodisias in the Late Hellenistic and Early Imperial Periods." In *Patris und Imperium: kulturelle und politische Identität in den Städten der römischen Provinzen Kleinasiens in der frühen Kaiserzeit*, 5–32. Leuven: Peeters.

Rawson, E. 1987. "*Discimina Ordinum*: The *Lex Julia Theatralis*." *PBSR* 55:83–114.

Reynolds, J. 1980. "The Origins and Beginnings of the Imperial Cult." *PCPS* 26:70–84.

———. 1986. "Further Information on Imperial Cult at Aphrodisias." *StClas* 24:109–117.

———. 1995. "Ruler-cult at Aphrodisias in the Late Republic and under the Julio-Claudian Emperors." In *Subject and Ruler: The Cult of Ruling Power in Classical Antiquity*, ed. A. Small, 41–50. Ann Arbor, MI. JRA Supplement 17.

———. 2000. "New Letters of Hadrian to Aphrodisias: Trials, Taxes, Gladiators and an Aqueduct." *JRA* 13:5–20.

Revell, L. 2009. *Roman Imperialism and Local Identities.* Cambridge: Cambridge University Press.

Ritti, T. 1979. "Due iscrizioni di età augustea da Hierapolis." *Epigraphica* 41:183–187.

———. 1983. "Epigrafi dedicatorie imperiali di Hierapolis di Frigia." *RendLinc* 38:171–182.

———. 1985. *Hierapolis*, vol. 1: *fonti letterarie ed epigrafiche*. Rome: G. Bretschneider.

Robert, L. 1940. *Les gladiateurs dans l'Orient grec.* Paris: E. Champion.

Robinson, D. M. 1924a. "A Preliminary Report on the Excavations at Pisidian Antioch and at Sizma." *AJA* 28:435–444.

———. 1924b. "A Latin Economic Edict from Pisidian Antioch." *TAPA* 55:5–20.

———. 1925. "Note on Inscriptions from Antioch in Pisidia." *JRS* 15:253–262.

———. 1926a. "Roman Sculptures from Colonia Caesarea (Pisidian Antioch)." *ArtB* 9:4–69.

———. 1926b. "Greek and Latin Inscriptions from Asia Minor." *TAPA* 57:195–237.

———. 1926c. "Two New Heads of Augustus." *AJA* 30:125–136.

———. 1926d. "Note on Inscriptions from Antioch in Pisidia." *JRS* 15:253–262.

———. 1926e. "The Res Gestae Divi Augusti as Recorded on the Monumentum Antiochenum." *AJP* 47.1:1–54.

———. 1928. "Eine Nike aus Antiochia in Pisidien." In *Antike Plastik. Walther Amelung zum 65. Geburtstag*, 200–205. Berlin: W. de Gruyter.

Robinson, D. M., and E. E. Peterson. 1924. Journal of Excavations, Antioch of Pisidia. Unpublished journal, Kelsey Museum collection at the Bentley Historical Library, University of Michigan, Ann Arbor.

Roehmer, M. 1997. *Der Bogen als Staatsmonument. Zur politischen Bedeutung der römischen Ehren-bögen des 1. Jhs. n. Chr.* Munich: Tuduv-Verlagsgesellschaft.

Rogers, G. M. 1991a. "Demosthenes of Oenoanda and Models of Euergetism." *JRS* 81:91–100.

———. 1991b. *The Sacred Identity of Ephesos: Foundation Myths of a Roman City.* London and New York: Routledge.

Romeo, I. 2002. "Panhellenion and Ethnic Identity in Hadrianic Greece." *CP* 97:21–40.

Rose, C. B. 1997. *Dynastic Commemoration and Imperial Portraiture in the Julio-Claudian Period.* Cambridge: Cambridge University Press.

———. 2005. "The Parthians in Augustan Rome." *AJA* 109:21–75.

Rossetto, P. C., and G. P. Sartorio, eds. 1994. *Teatri greci e romani: alle origini del linguaggio rappre-sentato: censimento analitico,* 3 vols. Rome: Edizioni SEAT.

Roueché, C. 1991. "Inscriptions and the Later History of the Theatre." In *Aphrodisias Papers 2, The Theatre, a Sculptor's Workshop, Philosophers, and Coin-Types,* ed. C. Roueché and K. T. Erim, 99–108. Ann Arbor: University of Michigan Press.

Roueché, C., and K. T. Erim, eds. 1991. *Aphrodisias Papers 2, The Theatre, a Sculptor's Workshop, Philosophers, and Coin-Types.* Ann Arbor: University of Michigan Press.

Rubin, B. B. 2008. "(Re)Presenting Empire: the Roman Imperial Cult in Asia Minor, 31 BC–AD 68." PhD dissertation, University of Michigan, Ann Arbor, MI.

Ruddock, T., ed. 2000. *Masonry Bridges, Viaducts, and Aqueducts.* Burlington: Ashgate.

Ruggieri, V. 2004. "La scultura bizantina nel museo archeologico di Antiochia di Pisidia (Yalvaç): rapporto preliminare: parte I." *Orientalia Christiana Periodica* 70:259–288.

———. 2005. "La scultura bizantina nel museo archeologico di Antiochia di Pisidia (Yalvaç): rapporto preliminare: parte II." *Orientalia Christiana Periodica* 71:59–96.

———. 2006. "La scultura bizantina nel territorio di Antiochia di Pisidia." *JÖBG* 56:267–296.

Şahin, S. 1999. *Die Inschriften von Perge,* vol. 1. Bonn: R. Habelt. Inschriften griechischer Städte aus Kleinasien 54.

Sandys, J. E. 1927. *Latin Epigraphy: An Introduction to the Study of Latin Inscriptions.* Cambridge: Cambridge University Press.

Scheer, T. 1993. *Mythische Vorvater: zur Bedeutung griechischer Heroenmythen im Selbstverstandnis kleinasiatischer Stadte.* Munich: Maris.

Schmid, S. 2001. "Worshipping the Emperor(s): A New Temple of the Imperial Cult at Eretria and the Ancient Destruction of Its Statues." *JRA* 14:113–142.

Schorndorfer, S. 1997. *Öffentliche Bauten hadrianischer Zeit in Kleinasien: Archäologisch-historische Unterschungen.* Münster: Lit.

Scott, S., and J. Webster, eds. 2003. *Roman Imperialism and Provincial Art.* Cambridge: Cambridge University Press.

Sear, F. 2006. *Roman Theatres: An Architectural Study.* Oxford: Oxford University Press.

Seval, M. 1980. *Step by Step Ephesus.* Istanbul : Minyatür Publications.

Shanks, H. 1979. *Judaism in Stone: The Archaeology of Ancient Synagogues.* New York: Harper and Row.

Sherk, R. K. 1988. *The Roman Empire: Augustus to Hadrian.* Cambridge: Cambridge University Press.

Slater, W. J., ed. 1996. *Roman Theater and Society.* Ann Arbor: University of Michigan Press.

Small, D. B. 1987. "Social Correlations to the Greek Cavea in the Roman Period." In *Roman Architecture in the Greek World,* ed. S. Macready and F. H. Thompson, 85–93. London: Thames and Hudson.

Smekalova, T. N., and S. L. Smekalov. 2001. Magnetic Survey on the Acropolis of Pisidian Antioch. Unpublished report prepared for Roger Bagnall.

Smith, R. R. R. 1987. "The Imperial Reliefs from the Sebasteion at Aphrodisias." *JRS* 77:88–138.

———. 1988. "Simulacra Gentium: The Ethne from the Sebasteion at Aphrodisias." *JRS* 78:50–77.

Snyder, G. F. 2002. "The God-Fearers in Paul's Speech at Pisidian Antioch." In *Actes du Ier Congres International sur Antioche de Pisidie*, ed. T. Drew-Bear, M. Taşlıalan, and C. Thomas, 45–52. Lyon and Paris: Université Lumière.

Solmsen, F. 1903. *Inscriptiones graecae ad inlustrandas dialectos selectae*. Leipzig: B. G. Teubner.

Spanu, M. 2002. "Considerazioni sulle *plateae* di Antiochia." In *Actes du Ier Congres International sur Antioche de Pisidie*, ed. T. Drew-Bear, M. Taşlıalan, and C. Thomas, 353–358. Lyon and Paris: Université Lumière.

Spawforth, A. 1985. "The World of the Panhellenion I: Athens and Eleusis." *JRS* 75:78–104.

———. 1986. "The World of the Panhellenion II: Three Dorian Cities." *JRS* 76:88–105.

Standing, G. 2003. "The Claudian Invasion of Britain and the Cult of Victoria Britannica." *Britannia* 34:281–288.

Stein, G. 2005. *The Archaeology of Colonial Encounters*. Santa Fe: School of American Research Press.

Stewart, S. 2003. *Columbarium*. Chicago: University of Chicago Press.

Stierlin, H. 1986. *Klienasiatisches Griechenland. Klassische Kunst und Kultur von Pergamon bis Nimrud Dagh*. Stuttgart: Belser.

Strocka, V. M. 1981. *Das Markttor von Milet*. Berlin: W. de Gruyter.

Studies in Attic Epigraphy, History, and Topography Presented to Eugene Vanderpool. 1982. Princeton: American School of Classical Studies at Athens. Hesperia Supplement 19.

Sturgeon, M. 2004. *Corinth, Sculpture: The Assemblage from the Theater*. Princeton: Princeton University Press.

Susini, G. C. 1973. *The Roman Stonecutter: An Introduction to Latin Epigraphy*. Trans. A. M. Dabrowski. Oxford: Blackwell Press.

Swain, G. R. 1924. Archaeological Results of First Importance Attained by the Near East Research of the University of Michigan during Its First Campaign. Unpublished report, Francis W. Kelsey papers, Kelsey Museum collection at the Bentley Historical Library, University of Michigan, Ann Arbor.

Swetnam-Burland, M. 2010. "*Aegyptus Redacta*: The Egyptian Obelisk in the Augustan Campus Martius." *ArtB* 92.3:135–153.

Syme, R. 1995. *Anatolica: Studies in Strabo*. Oxford: Oxford University Press.

Tabbernee, W. 1997. *Montanist Inscriptions and Testimonia: Epigraphic Sources Illustrating the History of Montanism*. Macon: Mercer University Press.

Taft, R. 1998. "*Quaestiones disputatae*: The Skeuophylakion of Hagia Sophia and the Entrances of the Liturgy Revisited." *OC* 82:53–87.

Talloen, P., and M. Waelkens. 2004. "Apollo and the Emperors (I). The Material Evidence from the Imperial Cult at Sagalassos." *Ancient Society* 34:171–216.

———. 2005. "Apollo and the Emperors (II). The Evolution of the Imperial Cult at Sagalassos. " *Ancient Society* 35:217–249.

Taşlıalan, M. 1990. *The Journeys of St. Paul at Antioch of Pisidia*. Ankara: no publisher.

———. 1991. *Pisidian Antioch: The Journeys of St. Paul to Antioch*. Istanbul: Cem Ofset Matbaacılık Sanayı A. Ş.

———. 1993. "Pisidia Antiocheia'sı 1991 Yılı Çalışmaları." *Müze Kurtarma Kazıları Semineri* 3:263–290.

———. 1994. "Pisidia Antiocheia'sı 1992 Yılı Çalışmaları." *Müze Kurtarma Kazıları Semineri, 26–29 Nisan 1993*, 4:245–284.

———. 1995. "Pisidia Antioacheia'sı 1993 Yılı Çalışmaları." *Müze Kurtarma Kazıları Semineri, 25–28 Nisan 1994,* 5:287–309.

———. 1997. "Pisidia Antioacheia'sı 1995 Yılı Çalışmaları." *Müze Kurtarma Kazıları Semineri, 8–10 Nisan 1996,* 7:221–251.

———. 1998. "Pisidia Antioacheia'si 1996 Yılı Çalışmaları." *Müse Kurtarma Kazilari Semineri, 7–9 Nisan 1997,* 8:323–356.

———. 2000. "Pisidia Antioacheia'sı 1998 Yılı Çalışmaları." *Müze Kurtarma Kazıları Semineri, 26–28 Nisan 1999,* 10:7–18.

———. 2001. "Pisidia Antioacheia'sı 1999 Yılı Çalışmaları." *Müze Kurtarma Kazıları Semineri, 24–26 Nisan 2000,* 11:133–148.

———. 2002. "Excavations at the Church of St. Paul." In *Actes du Ier Congres International sur Antioche de Pisidie,* ed. T. Drew-Bear, M. Taşlıalan, and C. Thomas, 9–32. Lyon and Paris: Université Lumière.

Taşlıalan, M., R. T. Bagnall, T. Smekalova, and S. Smekalov. 2003. "Magnetic Survey on the Acropolis of Pisidian Antioch." *Archaeologia Polona* 41:278–280.

Taylor, L. R. 1931. *The Divinity of the Roman Emperor.* Middletown, CT: American Philological Association.

Taylor, R. 1997. "Torrent or Trickle? The *Aqua Alsietina,* the *Naumachia Augusti,* and the *Transtiberim.*" *AJA* 101:465–492.

———. 2003. *Roman Builders: A Study in Architectural Process.* Cambridge: Cambridge University Press.

Thomas, E. 2008. *Monumentality and the Roman Empire: Architecture in the Antonine Age.* Oxford: Oxford University Press.

Tiradritti, F., ed. 2000. *Egyptian Treasures from the Egyptian Museum in Cairo.* Vercelli, Italy: White Star.

Tölle-Kastenbein, R. 1994. *Das archaische Wasserleitungsnetz für Athen und seine späteren Bauphasen.* Mainz: P. von Zabern.

Toller, H. 1977. *Roman Lead Coffins and Ossuaria in Britain.* Oxford: BAR.

Tomlinson, R. A. 1976. *Greek Sanctuaries.* New York: St. Martin's Press.

Toynbee, J. M. C. 1934. *The Hadrianic School: A Chapter in the History of Greek Art.* Cambridge: Cambridge University Press.

———. 1971. *Death and Burial in the Roman World.* Ithaca: Cornell University Press.

Trebilco, P. 1991. *Jewish Communities in Asia Minor.* Cambridge: Cambridge University Press.

Trimble, J. 1999. "The Aesthetics of Sameness: A Contextual Analysis of the Large and Small Herculaneum Woman Statue Types in the Roman Empire." PhD dissertation, University of Michigan, Ann Arbor, MI.

Tuchelt, K. 1983. "Bermerkugen zum Tempelbezirk von Antiochia ad Pisidiam." In *Beiträge zur Altertumskunde Kleinasiens. Festschrift für Kurt Bittel,* ed. R. M. Boehmer and H. Hauptmann, 501–522. Mainz: P. von Zabern.

Turcan, R. 1983. *Numismatique romaine du culte métroaque.* Leiden: Brill.

Ulrich, R. B. 1993. "Julius Caesar and the Creation of the Forum Iulium." *AJA* 97:49–80.

Uz, D. M. 1990. "The Temple of Dionysos at Teos." In *Hermogenes und die hochhellenistische Architektur,* ed. W. Hoepfner and E. L. Schwandner, 51–61. Mainz: P. von Zabern.

Van Dam, R. 2002. *Kingdom of Snow: Roman Rule and Greek Culture in Cappadocia.* Philadelphia: University of Pennsylvania Press.

Van Dyke, R., and S. Alcock, eds. 2003. *Archaeologies of Memory*. Malden: Blackwell.

Vermeule, C. 1968. *Roman Imperial Art in Greece and Asia Minor*. Cambridge, MA: Belknap Press.

Veyne, P. 1990. *Bread and Circuses: Historical Sociology and Political Pluralism*. Trans. B. Pearce. London: Penguin.

Virgilio, B. 1981. *Il "tempio stato" di Pessinunte fra Pergamo e Roma nel II–I secolo a.C. (C.B. Welles, Royal corr., 55–61)*. Pisa: Giardini.

Waelkens, M. 1986. "The Imperial Sanctuary at Pessinus: Archaeological, Epigraphical and Numismatic Evidence for Its Date and Identification." *EpigAnat* 7:37–73.

———. 1993a. "Sagalassos: History and Archaeology." In *Sagalassos*, vol. 1: *First General Report on the Survey (1986–1989) and Excavations (1990–1991)*, ed. M. Waelkens, 37–82. Leuven: Leuven University Press.

———. 1993b. "The 1992 Excavation Season. A Preliminary Report." In *Sagalassos*, vol. 2: *Report on the Third Excavation Campaign of 1992*, ed. M. Waelkens and J. Poblome, 9–42. Leuven : Leuven University Press.

———. 1999. "Sagalassos. Religious Life in a Pisidian Town during the Hellenistic and Early Imperial Period." In *Les syncrétismes religieux dans le monde méditerranéen antique*, ed. C. Bonnet and A. Motte, 191–226. Brussels: Institut historique belge de Rome.

———. 2002. "Romanization in the East. A Case Study: Sagalassos and Pisidia (SW Turkey)." *IstMitt* 52:311–368.

———. 2004a. *Interactive Dig Sagalassos: Hadrianic Nymphaeum Report 4*. http://www.archaeology.org/interactive/sagalassos/field04/nymphaeum4.html (24 July 2005).

———. 2004b. *Interactive Dig Sagalassos: Hadrianic Nymphaeum Report 5*. http://www.archaeology.org/interactive/sagalassos/field04/nymphaeum5.html (24 July 2005).

Waelkens, M., D. Pauwels, and J. Van Den Bergh. 1995. "The 1993 Excavations on the Upper and Lower Agora." In *Sagalassos*, vol. 3: *Report on the Third Excavation Campaign of 1993*, ed. M. Waelkens and J. Poblome, 23–32. Leuven: Leuven University Press.

Waelkens, M., L. Vandeput, C. Berns, B. Arikan, J. Poblome, and E. Torun. 2000. "The Northwest Heroon at Sagalassos." In *Sagalassos*, vol. 5: *Report on the Survey and Excavation Campaigns of 1996 and 1997*, ed. M. Waelkens and L. Loots, 553–593. Leuven: Leuven University Press.

Wankel, H., ed. 1979–1984. *Die Inschriften von Ephesos*. Bonn : Habelt.

Ward-Perkins, J. B. 1954. "Constantine and the Origins of the Christian Basilica." *PBSR* 22:69–90.

———. 1980. *Imperial Roman Architecture*. New York: Penguin Books.

Webb, P. A. 1996. *Hellenistic Architectural Sculpture: Figural Motifs in Western Anatolia and the Aegean Islands*. Madison: University of Wisconsin Press.

Weber, G. 1904. "Wasserleitungen in kleinasiatischen Städten." *JdI* 19:86–101.

Welch, K. 1998. "Greek Stadia and Roman Spectacles: Asia, Athens, and the Tomb of Herodes Atticus." *JRA* 11:117–145.

———. 1999. "Negotiating Roman Spectacle Architecture in the Greek World: Athens and Corinth." In *The Art of Ancient Spectacle*, ed. B. Bergmann and C. Kondoleon, 125–145. Washington, DC: National Gallery of Art.

Westholm, A. 1963. *Labraunda. Swedish Excavations and Researches* 1.2: *The Architecture of the Hieron*. Lund: CWK Gleerup.

White, L. M. 1990. *Building God's House in the Roman World: Architectural Adaptation among Pagans, Jews, and Christians*. Baltimore: Johns Hopkins University Press.

Wiegand, E. 1937. Review of D. Krencker and M. Schede, *Denkmäler Antiker Architektur*, vol. 3: *Der Tempel in Ankara. Gnomon* 13:414–422.

Williams, M. 2000. "Jews and Jewish Communities in the Roman Empire." In *Experiencing Rome: Culture, Identity, and Power in the Roman Empire*, ed. J. Huskinson, 305–333. London and New York: Routledge.

Wilson, A. N. 1997. *Paul: The Mind of the Apostle*. New York: Norton.

Winter, B. W. 2002. "The Imperial Cult and Early Christians in Roman Galatia (Acts XIII 13–50 and Galatians VI 11–18)." In *Actes du Ier Congres International sur Antioche de Pisidie*, ed. T. Drew-Bear, M. Taşlıalan, and C. Thomas, 67–76. Lyon and Paris: Université Lumière.

Witherington, B. 1998. *The Paul Quest: The Renewed Search for the Jew of Tarsus*. Downers Grove: InterVarsity Press.

Witulski, T. 2002. "Galatians IV 8–20 Addressed to Pisidian Antioch." In *Actes du Ier Congres International sur Antioche de Pisidie*, ed. T. Drew-Bear, M. Taşlıalan, and C. Thomas, 61–66. Lyon and Paris: Université Lumière.

Woolf, G. 1998. *Becoming Roman: The Origins of Provincial Civilization in Gaul*. Cambridge: Cambridge University Press.

Wörrle, M. 1988. *Stadt und Fest in kaiserzeitlichen Kleinasien. Studien zu einer agonistischen Stiftung aus Oenoanda*, Munich: Beck. Beiträge zur Alte Geschichte 39.

Yegül, F. 1992. *Baths and Bathing in Classical Antiquity*. Cambridge, MA: Harvard University Press.

———. 2000. "Memory, Metaphor, and Meaning in the Cities of Asia Minor." In *Romanization and the City: Creation, Transformations and Failures*, ed. E. Fentress, 133–153. Portsmouth. JRA Supplement 38.

Zanker, P. 1968. *Forum Augustum. Das Bildprogramm*. Tübingen: Wasmuth.

———. 1988. *The Power of Images in the Age of Augustus*. Trans. A. Shapiro. Ann Arbor: University of Michigan Press.

Zuckerman, C. 2002. "The Dedication of a Statue of Justinian at Antioch." In *Actes du Ier Congres International sur Antioche de Pisidie*, ed. T. Drew-Bear, M. Taşlıalan, and C. Thomas, 243–253. Lyon and Paris: Université Lumière.

Zuiderhoek, A. 2009. *The Politics of Munificence in the Roman Empire*. Cambridge: Cambridge University Press.

Index